REACHING OLYMPUS
TEACHING MYTHOLOGY THROUGH READER'S THEATER SCRIPT·STORIES

THE *REACHING OLYMPUS* SERIES PRESENTS
THE ROAD TO CAMELOT

LEGENDS OF KING ARTHUR AND THE KNIGHTS OF THE ROUND TABLE

WRITTEN AND ILLUSTRATED BY ZACHARY HAMBY
EDITED BY RACHEL HAMBY

DEDICATION

For Dad and Mom, who taught me how to live,

&

Dr. Tita Baumlin, who brought Camelot to life.

"It is not good just to live, but to live in a good way."

—Geoffroi de Charny, 14th-century knight—

ISBN-10: 0982704941
ISBN-13: 978-0-9827049-4-3
LCCN: 2015903223

The *Reaching Olympus* Series Presents, *The Road to Camelot:* Legends of King Arthur and the Knights of the Round Table

Written and Illustrated by Zachary Hamby

Edited by Rachel Hamby

Published by Hamby Publishing in the United States of America

Copyright © 2016 Hamby Publishing

All rights reserved. Portions of this book may be photocopied for classroom use only. No portion of this book may be reproduced in any form or by an electronic or mechanical means, including information storage and retrieval systems, without permission in writing from the publisher, except by a reviewer, who may quote brief passages in review. Special permissions are required for commercial or public performances of these scripts. Contact the author for more information about the fees associated with these types of performances.

TABLE OF CONTENTS

INTRODUCTORY MATERIALS

Introduction to the Series	7
Using This Book in the Classroom	11
The Road to Camelot	13
The Quest for Character	15

SCRIPT-STORIES: LEGENDS OF KING ARTHUR AND HIS KNIGHTS

The Begetting of Arthur	17
A Tale of Two Swords	31
Shadows of the Past	47
The Bride of the King	63
The White Hart	79
Gawain and the Green Knight	95
The Knight of the Lake	111
The Loves of Lancelot	125
The Knight of the Cart	141
The Tale of Beaumains	159

Return of the Misbegotten	177
The Quest of the Holy Grail	195
The Trial of Guinevere	213
The Fall of Camelot	231

GAMES, PUZZLES, EXTRA STORIES, AND OTHER FUN STUFF

So You Want To Be a Knight	249
The Quest for Character	251
Merlin the Boy Magician	253
The Knights of the Round Table	255
The Holy Grail	257
Castles and Catapults	259
Conspiracy in Camelot	261
Camelot Find-It Picture Puzzle	279
Camelot Find-It Picture Puzzle Key	281

APPENDICES

Glossary of Important Names	283
Pronunciation Guide	285
About the Author	287

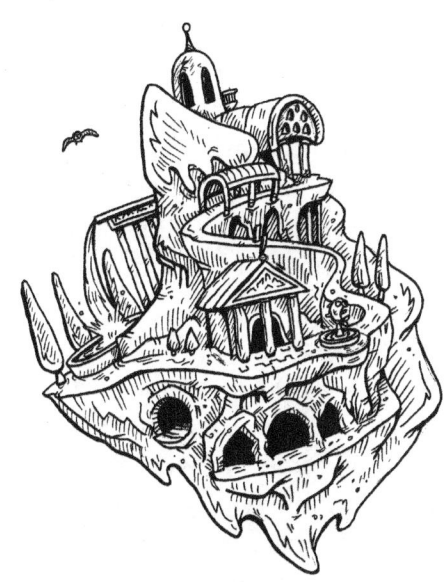

REACHING OLYMPUS:
AN INTRODUCTION TO THE SERIES

The faces of the souls of the Underworld could not have been more death-like. It was years ago, but I remember it well. In a matter of weeks I had gone from inexperienced student to full-time teacher. What was even more startling was that four long years of college had not prepared me for the subject matter I would be required to teach—a class called World Short Stories and (gulp) Mythology. I remembered a few short stories from my survey literature courses, but with mythology, I was drawing a blank. In my cobwebbed memory there stood a woman with snake-hair and a psychedelic image of a wingéd horse—but that was it. Not to worry though. I had two whole weeks to prepare. After that I needed to fill a whole semester with mythological learning.

As any competent educator would, I turned to my textbook for aid. At first things looked promising. The book had a classy cover—black with the aforementioned wingéd horse on it. Bold, gold letters tastefully titled it *Mythology*. Edith Hamilton—in the same lettering—was apparently the author. Yes, my judgment of the cover was encouraging, but what I found inside was anything but.

When I opened the text to read, I quickly realized I was doomed. Edith Hamilton had written her book in code. It was the same indecipherable language used by those who write literary criticism or owner manuals for electronic devices. Every sentence was a labyrinth, curving back in on itself, confusing the reader with many a subordinate clause and cutting him off completely from context with outdated aphorisms. If she wasn't randomly quoting Milton or Shakespeare, she was spending a paragraph differentiating between the poetic styles of Pindar and Ovid. It was as if Edith Hamilton was annoyed at having been born in the twentieth century and was using her writing style as some kind of literary time travel. Originally published in 1942, *Mythology* reflects the writing style of the day—a style that has grown increasingly more difficult for modern readers to comprehend. I knew if I could barely understand Hamilton's language, my students were going to be even more lost than I was.

Designed for average learners, Mythology was a junior-senior elective—the kind of class that was supposed to be entertaining and somewhat interesting. With Edith Hamilton tied around my neck, I was going down—and going down fast. It was at this point that the stupidly optimistic part of my brain cut in. "Maybe it won't be so bad," it said. "Don't underestimate your students." My ambitions renewed thanks to this still, small voice, and I laid Edith to the side, somehow sure that everything would turn out all right in the end. This was still more proof that I knew nothing about mythology.

Before I continue to tell how my tragic flaw of youthful optimism led to my ultimate downfall, I should take a minute to say a kind word about Edith Hamilton. In a time when interest in the classical writings of Greece and Rome was waning, Edith Hamilton revitalized this interest by writing several works that attempted to capture the creativity and majesty of Greco-Roman civilization. Hamilton's *Mythology* was one of the first books to take a comprehensive look at the Greco-Roman myths. The popularity of mythology today owes a great debt to this book and its author. Fifty years after its publication, it is still the most commonly used mythology textbook in high school classrooms. Ironically, *Mythology* is no longer on an average high-schooler's reading level. As I mentioned earlier, Hamilton's writing style, with its ponderous vocabulary and sphinx-worthy inscrutability, further alienates any but the most intrepid of readers.

My first semester of teaching Mythology was a disaster. If I hadn't been so idealistic and gung-ho, I probably would have given up. Instead the new teacher within me stood up and said, "No! I'm going to do this, and we're going to make it fun! After all, Mythology is filled with all kinds of teenage interests: family murder, bestiality, incest, etc. It'll be just like watching TV for them."

Utilizing every creative project idea under the sun, I threw myself into making the class work. We drew pictures, we read aloud, we watched related videos, wrote alternate endings to the stories—yet every time I kept coming up against the same brick wall: the text. It did not matter how enjoyable the activities were. Whenever we turned to the actual stories and cracked open that dreaded book, the life was sucked out of my students, and I was staring at their Underworld faces once again.

My last resort was boiling the stories down to outlines and writing these out on the whiteboard. Even that was better than actually reading them. At least the students would get the basic facts of the story. One student, possibly sensing I was seconds away from the breaking point, made the comment, "I didn't know this class would be a bunch of notes. I thought it would be fun."

Then I gave up.

When I look back on that semester, I realize that I failed a whole batch of students. They came and went thinking that studying mythology was a brainless exercise in rote memorization. Perhaps the failure of that first experience would not have been so stark if a success hadn't come along the next year.

The second time through the class, I was determined not to repeat the mistakes of the past. There must be some way of avoiding the text—somehow relating the stories without actually reading them. But then I thought, "Isn't this supposed to be an English class? If we don't actually read, can it be called English? What has this outdated text driven me to?"

When I looked into the stories, I could see excellent tales trapped behind stuffy prose. How could I get the students to see what I saw? How could I set those good stories free?

On a whim I decided to try my hand at rewriting one of the myths. I had dabbled in creative writing in college, so surely I could spin one of these tales better than Edith Hamilton had. The idea of dividing the story into parts struck me as a good one. Maybe that would foster more student involvement. A few hours later, I had created my first Reader's Theater script. (At the time I had no idea that there was an actual term for this type of thing or that there was sound educational research behind reading aloud.) Part of me was excited. The other part was skeptical.

"These kids are high-schoolers," I said to myself. "They'll never go for this." I looked at some of the elements I had included in my script: overly-dramatic dialogue, sound effects, cheesy jokes. What was I thinking? Since I had already spent the time and energy, I decided to give it a shot.

There are those grand moments in education when something clicks, and those moments are the reason that teachers teach. My script clicked. It clicked quite well, in fact. The students loved reading aloud. They were thrilled beyond belief to not be reading silently or taking notes or even watching a video. They performed better than I ever dreamed possible. They did funny voices. They laughed at the cheesy jokes. They inhabited the characters. They even did the sound effects.

As I looked around the room, I noticed something that was a rarity: My students were having fun. Not only that, but they were getting all the information that Edith Hamilton could have offered them. When the script was done, I encountered a barrage of questions: "Why did Zeus act like that to Hera? What is an *heir*? Why did Aphrodite choose to marry Hephaestus? Did the Greeks have *any* respect for marriage?" Did my ears deceive me? Intelligent questions—questions about character motivation, vocabulary, and even historical context? I couldn't believe it.

I was also struck by another startling fact: The students were asking about these characters as if they were real people. They were able to treat the characters as real people because real people had inhabited their roles. Zeus was not some dusty god from 3,000 years ago. He was Joe in the second row doing a funny voice. Something had come from the abstract world of mythology and become real. And as for the quiz scores, my students might not remember the difference between Perseus and Theseus, but they definitely remembered the difference between Josh and Eric, the two students who played those roles. On top of all this, the class had changed from a group of isolated learners to a team that experiences, laughs, and learns together.

After the success of that first script, I realized I had created some kind of teaching drug. It was an incredible teaching experience, one that I wanted to recreate over and over again. I wouldn't and couldn't go back to the old world of bland reading. So I didn't.

The great moments of Greek mythology flew from my keyboard, and I created play after play. Despite my overweening enthusiasm, I knew that too much of a good thing could definitely be bad, so I chose stories that would spread out the read-aloud experience. We would still use Edith Hamilton in moderation. After all, a few vegetables make you enjoy the sweet stuff all the more.

Over the course of that semester, I discovered a new enthusiasm in the students and myself. They enjoyed learning, and I enjoyed teaching. I had students arguing over who would read which parts—an unbelievable sight for juniors and seniors. Laughter was a constant in the classroom. As the Greeks would say, it was a golden age of learning.

Now I have the chance to share this technique with other teachers. With these plays, I hope my experiences will be recreated in other classrooms. Mythology should not be an old dead thing of the past, but a living, breathing, exciting experience.

USING THIS BOOK IN THE CLASSROOM

Script-stories (also known as Reader's Theater) are a highly motivational learning strategy that blends oral reading, literature, and drama. Unlike traditional theater, script-stories do not require costumes, make-up, props, stage sets, or memorization. Only the script and a healthy imagination are needed. As students read the script aloud, they interpret the emotions, beliefs, attitudes, and motives of the characters. A narrator conveys the story's setting and action and provides the commentary necessary for the transitions between scenes.

While Reader's Theater has been enormously successful with lower grade-levels, it is also a great fit for older learners as well. Students of any age enjoy and appreciate the chance to *experience* a story rather than having it read to them. For years now script-stories have been the tool that I use to teach mythology to high-schoolers. I wouldn't have it any other way. Below are the answers to some of the most frequently asked questions concerning the use of script-stories in the classroom.

How do you stage these stories in the classroom? Hand out photocopies of the particular script for that day. (Note: It is perfectly legal for you to photocopy pages from this book. That is what it was designed for!) Certain copies of the scripts should be highlighted for particular characters, so that whichever students you pick to read parts will have their lines readily available. (This is not necessary, but it does make things run more smoothly.) Some teachers who use Reader's Theater require their students to stand when reading their lines or even incorporate physical acting. As for the sound effects in the plays *(fanfare)*, noisemakers can be distributed to the students and used when prompted. Otherwise, students can make the noises with their own voices.

How do you structure a class around script-stories? How often do you use them? Too much of a good thing can be bad. In my own classroom I do employ the script-stories frequently—in some units we read a story every day of the week—but I do supplement with other notes, texts, activities, and self-created worksheets. Some of these activities are included in the back of the book. For other examples of these activities, check out my website *www.mythologyteacher.com*. Also available on the website are sample course outlines that show teachers how to structure a semester or year-long mythology course.

How do you assess script-stories? A quick reading quiz after the completion of a script is an easy way to assess comprehension. In my own classroom I ask five questions that hit the high-points of the story. I never make the questions overly specific (for example, asking a student to remember a character's name like Agamemnon or Polydectes). Each script in this book comes with five recall questions for this purpose.

Another form of assessment is by trying to foster as much discussion as possible. How well students discuss will tell you how well they have comprehended the story. The discussion questions included in this book have seen success in my own classroom.

    I hope you find this book to be a great resource. It was designed with the intent of helping a much wider audience experience the timeless tales of world mythology in a new manner. Below I have listed some further notes concerning the script-stories. Thanks for purchasing this book. Please feel free to contact me if you have any questions.

Sincerely,

Zachary Hamby
mr.mythology@gmail.com
www.mythologyteacher.com

FURTHER NOTES FOR TEACHERS

UNIT PLAN The script-stories in this book are organized in the order in which they should be read. The stories range between 25-45 minutes in length. Teaching one a day and including some of the suggested activities (see individual teacher pages) should yield at least a 14-day unit. Supplemental activities from the back can be inserted as well. For even more information on setting up a unit using these scripts, visit *mythologyteacher.com*, where sample course outlines are available.

INTENDED AUDIENCE: 6th-12th grade

LENGTH: Script-stories range between 25-45 minutes in length

SCRIPT-STORY PROCESS

- Every student will need a copy of the script-story.
- Reading parts may be highlighted for greater reading ease.
- As the teacher, you are the casting director. Assign the parts as you deem best.
- Give your largest parts to your strongest readers but still try to draw out the reluctant participant.
- As the teacher, you should take the part of the narrator. Actively participating only makes it more fun for you and the students.
- Cut loose and have fun. Script-stories allow students to see their teacher in a whole new light.

POSSIBLE MODIFICATIONS

- Costumes, props, and even sets can be added to any script-story to make it more engaging.
- Requiring the students to stand while reading their parts creates a stronger dynamic between speaking roles.
- Encouraging students to write their own script-stories gets them thinking about the elements of storytelling and the use of dialogue.
- Assigning one student to be responsible for all the sound effects in a script can involve someone who is not a strong reader in the performance. Including certain tools that actually make the indicated sound effects (noise-makers, coconuts, etc.) is another excellent way to add interest.

THE ROAD TO CAMELOT

"And through the field the road runs by to many-towered Camelot"

~Alfred, Lord Tennyson~

There is a certain sense of wonder that comes from reading the tales of King Arthur and his Knights of the Round Table—an inkling that you are seeing into a world that is both part of our history and part of our dreams as well. It is a world filled with fantasy (wizards, sorceresses, and dragons), yet it still suffers from the harsh realities of life (unrequited love, the painful sacrifices of duty, and doomed romance.) It is a world that is medieval—yet not at the same time. Instead of the past as it was, it is the past as we wish it had been.

The legends of Arthur and his court have been the favorites of poets, painters, and politicians for centuries. Perhaps this is because they tap into our deepest ideals of justice, romance, and valor. Or perhaps because, although they are fantasy, they do not shy away from asking tough questions: Can love trump duty? Can lofty ideals change human nature? Can a person create a legacy that will endure past his own lifetime?

For Europeans the Arthurian legends are a part of their majestic past. The ideals of the Round Table inspired kings, who tried to form a link between their reign and that of Arthur. Victorian poets such as Tennyson used Arthurian tales of Britain's past to inspire his country toward a glorious future. Painter-poets such as Rossetti and other Pre-Raphaelites used the stories to feed their yearning for a simpler age.

The Arthurian legends are impactful for non-Europeans as well. In America, where the legends were re-interpreted with a more democratic slant, Arthur's humble beginnings and his notions of equality at the Round Table found a new audience. The presidency of John F. Kennedy was frequently compared to the splendors of Camelot. Author T.H. White re-spun Arthur's life into his novel, *The Once and Future King*, from which Broadway made Arthur the subject of a popular musical, *Camelot*.

There is no question that the Arthurian legends have impacted the world, and this led to the inevitable question: Was there a real King Arthur? Many scholars have attempted to identify the historical person who inspired the legends. Their theories culminate in this: If there was a real King Arthur, he lived in Britain during the years following the departure of the Roman Empire and fought against the invading hordes of Saxons. This Arthur, a warlord who fended off barbarian invasion, may have had his "Camelot" at a site now known as Cadbury Castle. (In fact, there are several different proposed locations for the historical Camelot.) As further proof of Arthur's existence, there is even a tomb at Glastonbury Abbey that claims to be Arthur and Guinevere's final resting place.

As exciting as these historical findings are, they are also bittersweet. No matter how many discoveries are made toward pinpointing this historical Arthur, he is not the Arthur of legends. No real-life person could encompass all that Arthur means. The legendary King Arthur exists outside time, outside reality, and outside possibility. Yet, rather than limiting his appeal, this merely increases it—especially for students of myth and legend. Arthur and his Camelot cannot be found in the real world because they are simply larger-than-life.

The process by which history and myth merged to create the unique feel of the Arthurian legend is too complex to detail here. At their most basic level, the stories are a man's life—a man who strove for more and achieved much, but maybe not as much as he hoped. We see Arthur's birth, his youth, his middle years, and finally his death. We see his youthful enthusiasm fade into complacence, and in the end, when he is faced with many enemies, we see that youthful fire reborn. Along the way, Arthur comes to embody something larger than himself. Arthur and Camelot become one, and when one falls, so falls the other.

Arthur's tale is ultimately a tragedy—a failed experiment—an attempt at something better in the midst of a dark age. Camelot may have ended in failure, but it still inspires us with its legacy. As the lyrics from the musical *Camelot* say:

> *Don't let it be forgot*
> *that once there was a spot*
> *for one brief shining moment*
> *that was known as Camelot.*

The script-stories contained in this book are retellings of the Arthurian legends. The source they follow most closely is Thomas Malory's *Le Morte D'Arthur*. As with the other books in this series, I have sometimes condensed multiple characters into one, rearranged events for continuity, and added some storytelling flourishes. That being said, the material is true to the spirit of the source, and all major plot points are in place. In other words, you could still pass a test on Arthurian legends by reading this version! If you want the full flavor of the original, you should seek out *Le Morte D'Arthur* or the romances of Chretien de Troyes. I hope you find this textbook useful and enjoy your time adventuring in the world of Arthur.

RECOMMENDED READING

- Bishop, Morris. *The Middle Ages.* New York: Houghton Mifflin Harcourt, 2001. Print.
- Malory, Thomas. *Le Morte D'Arthur Vol. I.* New York: Penguin Classics, 1970. Print.
- Malory, Thomas. *Le Morte D'Arthur Vol. II.* New York: Penguin Classics, 1970. Print.
- Troyes, Chretien de. *Arthurian Romances.* New York: Penguin Classics, 1991. Print.
- White, T.H. *The Once and Future King.* New York: Ace, 1987. Print.

The Quest for Character

THE QUEST FOR CHARACTER

"Herein may be seen noble chivalry, courtesy, humanity, friendliness, hardiness, love, friendship, cowardice, murder, hate, virtue, and sin. Do after the good and leave the evil."

~ Preface to *Le Morte D'Arthur* ~

A knight halts his horse in the midst of the forest. Ahead the road forks, and two different paths are presented to him. One path is wide and well-kept, free of brush. The other is narrow and nearly overgrown. The path that the knight chooses may determine the outcome of his quest or even his life. But he must act, he must choose, or the quest will be lost.

This is a common theme in tales of chivalry—knights presented with choices. In one story a knight named Sir Bors encounters a dilemma. He rides up on a scene where two victims are being simultaneously abducted by two different knights. The victims are a maiden and Bors's brother. Bors must now choose. He has sworn to aid all maidens in distress, but he also wants to help his brother. This dilemma affects his future, but also the future of the two in need.

There is no better message to give to young people than the importance of making good choices. Choices made today affect the rest of their lives. Now more than ever, young people are faced with perils and pitfalls that can divert their lives from the path to success and contentment. But how do they know which path to take? On what criteria should they base their decisions? This is where Character Education comes in.

The legends of King Arthur present a teaching tool like none other. These tales of chivalry have been used as instruction and inspiration for hundreds of years. On the surface is a great story. But beneath it is a guidebook to life. Characters in the story are striving for a high ideal. In the midst of the brutal chaos of the Middle Ages arises a kingdom based on the principles of justice, equality, and mercy. Camelot is a prototype utopia, and it embodies many of the morals we still cherish today.

But like any society, Arthur's kingdom is flawed. Equality among his knights does not mean equality for the servant classes. His knights, while striving for perfection, are still human. In an effort to do good, evil still creeps in. Cracks begin to form in Camelot. Poor choices are made, and one by one these bring about the destruction of the kingdom.

Although the physical Camelot passes away, its spirit remains. The Passing of Arthur, the most beautiful part of the tale, sees the noble king departing this earth. Yet the legend persists that one day Arthur will return. Camelot will stand as a symbol for generations to come. The final message of the story is this: The old ways can come back. Being noble, courageous, and true can become a priority once again.

Each of these script-stories comes with a section called "Character Quest." These sections feature positive character traits to discuss with students, using the story as a springboard for discussion. Literature is an excellent teaching tool, and the world of Arthur provides an entertaining way to approach it. Like the knights of Camelot, students can learn to prize character.

While Character Education is not often a prescribed part of a school's curriculum, it is important to teach, and it can be done in a way that is respectful and relevant to students of diverse backgrounds. Many aspects of Character Education are too lengthy to explore here. I highly recommend the book, *Character Matters* by Dr. Thomas Lickona, wherein the author shows the need for character education, success stories of implementation, and other ideas for helping young people make good choices.

RECOMMENDED READING

- Lickona, Thomas. *Character Matters*. New York: Touchstone, 2004. Print.

THE BEGETTING OF ARTHUR
TEACHER GUIDE

BACKGROUND

From 43 A.D. when Roman troops first conquered Britain until their occupation ended around 410 A.D., the Romans ruled the Britons—making sweeping changes to the land and culture of Britain. Three of these changes had the greatest impact. First, the Romans developed sturdy roads across the country. Secondly, they established important city sites, such as Londinium (London). And, thirdly, when the entire Roman Empire changed religions, the Romans converted Britain to Christianity as well.

Because of the Romans' lengthy occupation and influence on Britain, many British storytellers were eager to link their own legacy to that of the Greece and Rome. When these storytellers created new British legends, they linked them onto the familiar Greek and Roman myths. In Roman mythology Aeneas was a survivor of the Trojan War who traveled from Troy to Italy, searching for a new home for the Trojan people. In Italy Aeneas's descendants eventually founded Rome.

According to British legend, Aeneas had a great-grandson named Brutus, who was run out of Italy after killing his father in a hunting accident. Like Aeneas before him, Brutus went searching for a new home. He traveled the seas and finally discovered an island named Albion, which was inhabited by a race of savage giants. Brutus and his comrades slew the giants, and Brutus renamed his new island home *Britain* after himself. Then he founded a new city called Troia Nova or "New Troy."

SUMMARY

Uther Pendragon, the father of King Arthur, is the ruler of all England. But the Duke of Tintagel has rebelled against him. The two finally sign a peace treaty, and the duke comes to Uther's castle for a feast. When Uther catches sight of the duke's wife, Igraine, he is immediately smitten. He makes eyes at Igraine, and the duke grows angry. Knowing that Uther desires his wife, the duke leaves the feast in anger.

Fearing that Uther will try to steal his wife, the duke returns to his twin castles—fortifying one against attack and secretly placing his wife in the other. Uther attacks the duke, sending his armies against the thick walls of Castle Tintagel but to no avail. Finally, Ulfius, one of Uther's knights, pleads with his king, begging him to find another way of gaining Igraine. Uther decides to seek out Merlin, a magician who lives in the deep woods.

Merlin is brought before Uther and agrees to use magic to help him spend one night with Igraine. His price is that the child conceived upon that night will be given into Merlin's care. Uther agrees, and Merlin changes the king's appearance into that of the duke. Uther, disguised as the duke, rides to the castle where Igraine is being hidden and spends the night with her.

Meanwhile, the duke leads his army forth from his besieged castle and is slain by Uther's men. After visiting Igraine Uther rides away, his strange behavior leaving Igraine in confusion. Igraine then learns from a servant that her husband was slain. She wonders at the identity of the man who spent the night with her.

Arriving back at his camp, Uther learns that the duke was slain. He is overjoyed, for this means he can claim Igraine as his wife. A few weeks later Uther sends a proposal of

18   The Road to Camelot

marriage to Igraine, and she accepts. Once she is brought to the castle, Uther declares to her that it was he who spent the night with her in a disguise. Igraine is overjoyed at this news, for she is carrying Uther's son, and now the child will not be shamed. Uther also agrees to care for the three young daughters of the duke and Igraine.

When Uther and Igraine's son is born, Merlin arrives to claim him. The boy will be raised by a kindly knight, and he will be completely unaware that he is Uther's son. Later, Uther is overcome in battle by his enemies and he dies. With no heir to succeed Uther, England is left without a king.

ESSENTIAL QUESTIONS

- How do our actions affect others?
- What do our actions say about our character?

ANTICIPATORY QUESTIONS

- Who were the parents of King Arthur?
- Who was Merlin?
- What is a siege?

CHARACTER QUEST

Choices Throughout his life King Arthur will be affected by the actions of his selfish father, Uther. How do Uther's actions affect the other characters in the story? Which effects are positive, and which are negative? How could poor choices in our own lives affect others?

CONNECT

Coat of Arms In this activity you will create a coat of arms. Divide a sheet of paper evenly into six different sections. In each section do the following: 1. Draw an animal that you feel represents yourself. 2. Draw your greatest accomplishment. 3. Draw something great you see yourself accomplishing in life. 4. Draw your most prized possession. 5. Draw a symbol of your strength (not an animal). 6. Draw a person who is special in your life. Now your coat of arms is complete.

TEACHABLE TERMS

- **Idiom** This script features several idioms. "Make eyes at" on pg. 20 means "to flirt." "Come to blows" on pg. 20 means "to fight." "Gave up the ghost" on pg. 29 means "to die."
- **Jargon** The King Arthur legends contain many examples of jargon related to knights, lords, and ladies. Examples from this script include *steward* (pg. 26) a servant in charge of a household, *helm* (pg. 26) a helmet, *duke* (pg. 19) a wealthy noble, *duchess* (pg. 19) the wife of a duke, and *dame* (pg. 19) a married woman.
- **Simile** On pg. 28 the script says that Merlin emerged "like a ghost from the wood." This is an example of a simile.
- **Character Motivation** Analyze what motivates Merlin in this story. Why does he assist Uther in this affair with Igraine? What does he hope to gain from it?

RECALL QUESTIONS

1. Why do the duke and Uther fail to make a treaty?
2. Whose help does Uther get to help him trick Igraine?
3. How is Igraine tricked?
4. What must Uther do for his accomplice in return?
5. What is Igraine's reaction to learning that Uther is the father of her baby?

THE BEGETTING OF ARTHUR

CAST

UTHER	*Ruler of All England*
MERLIN	*Wise Enchanter*
IGRAINE	*Wife of the Duke*
DUKE	*Rebellious Duke*
ULFIUS	*One of Uther's Knights*
MESSENGER	*Servant of the Duke*

NARRATOR: It so happened when Uther Pendragon was king of all England, that there existed a rebellious duke, the Duke of Tintagel, and he made war with the king for many months.

After much bloodshed, the two agreed to call a truce and be peaceable once again. Uther invited the duke to call upon him in his castle, and the duke decided to bring his lovely wife along.

UTHER: Welcome, my lord! Come! Let's feast together, and we will forget all about this little conflict between us.

DUKE: I am glad that you have invited me here. I have brought the duchess along as well. Allow me to introduce my wife, Igraine.

NARRATOR: When Uther beheld the duke's wife, he was taken breathless. He had never seen such a beauty in his life.

UTHER: *(breathlessly)* Stunning! Never before have I seen such glory!

DUKE: She is the fairest dame in the land.

UTHER: *(slyly)* Yes, I should say so.

NARRATOR: As they feasted, Uther could not stop looking at Igraine. She was captivating—the way she held herself, the way her auburn hair fell about her shoulders, the way her eyes flirted about the room.

UTHER: *(to himself)* I must have this woman!

DUKE: So, Uther, what are your plans for the future?

UTHER: I propose a toast!

DUKE: Very well. A toast to what?

UTHER: A toast—a toast to the most beautiful maid in the land! The sun seems to shine from her eyes. She has bewitched me when so many other women leave me cold. *(pause)* It is she alone that I want.

DUKE: *(laughs)* If such a woman exists, I would love to see her. Who is this woman, Uther? Bring her before us.

UTHER: *(pointedly)* Oh, but she already is. To Igraine!

NARRATOR: Most of the court laughed, thinking it was a joke, but the duke saw the king's sincerity and did not raise his cup. Nor did he raise his eyes from Uther all evening. At every interval possible, the king was smiling and tipping his cup to Igraine. At last, the duke could stand it no longer.

DUKE: *(angrily)* Sir, I believe that you desire something that is mine!

UTHER: I do not know what you mean, sir.

DUKE: No? You make eyes at my wife in my very presence! Is this how Uther Pendragon treats his honored guests?

UTHER: *(laughs)* Come, old man! Sit! Eat! I mean no harm! If I see a pretty thing, I am distracted by it. I am a man after all!

DUKE: *(angrily)* You will *not* be distracted by what is mine! Or we shall come to blows once again!

UTHER: *(angrily)* How dare you speak to me in such a manner—and in my own hall!

DUKE: You may keep your hall and your food! I have no use for you! Come, Igraine, we are leaving.

UTHER: If you leave this place, you will break our truce.

DUKE: I truce only with gentlemen—and *you* are not a gentleman! We leave at once!

UTHER: Careful, duke, my reach is long. I will come and claim what I desire.

DUKE: If you try, you will fail.

NARRATOR: These spirited words only made Uther's desire greater—loving the thrill of the chase. He watched the fair Igraine turn and sweep from the room.

UTHER: *(breathlessly)* This woman must be mine!

ULFIUS: Sir, should we prevent the duke from leaving?

UTHER: No, let him go. We will deal with him tomorrow. Tonight we feast. *(dreamily)* Igraine! Sweet Igraine!

NARRATOR: Night fell upon the castle, and Uther dreamed of Igraine until the dawn.

By the morningtide, the duke and his men had returned to his twin castles, Tintagel and Terrabil.

IGRAINE: *(confused)* Why are we in such a hurry, husband?

DUKE: Uther is a ruthless man. He takes what he wants, and you'd be blind not to see that he wanted you.

IGRAINE: What will you do with me?

DUKE: I shall put you in the top of Tintagel. There you shall be safe and guarded. Uther will come, but he will think that you are with me in Terrabil. Then if I am to fall in battle, at least, you may escape.

IGRAINE: *(distressed)* Husband, don't speak such words! Without you, I would die!

DUKE: It may come to such extremes, but I pray not. Men, take the duchess to the castle. Protect her there until your dying breath. I shall ready the knights, and we shall meet our *king* with open blade. Ride!

NARRATOR: And so Igraine was placed in the lonely tower of Tintagel. And there she wept for many days.

It did not take Uther long to give pursuit. His desires had not been quenched. He was prepared to lose many men for such a woman.

UTHER: There, Ulfius, the twin castles! Have the men form a perimeter!

ULFIUS: Yes, sir. Tell me, my lord. Why have we come here?

UTHER: Glory, my friend!

ULFIUS: *(questioningly)* Is that all?

UTHER: Do not question the heart of the king! It is nobler than your own. Its needs cannot be easily satisfied.

ULFIUS: No, my lord, I see that they cannot.

NARRATOR: The duke had made use of his time well. Terrabil was heavily fortified. Day after day, Uther's men crashed upon its defenses—but to no avail. *(sounds of fighting)* Many brave knights met their deaths before its gates.

At last, Sir Ulfius had the courage to speak the words that everyone had been thinking.

ULFIUS: Sire, this is folly. We have lost many knights. Should we Britons fight among ourselves? Let us make truce with the duke, and you can forget his wife.

UTHER: *(determined)* Never! We will not stop until he has given us what we want.

ULFIUS: We? *We* want nothing, my lord. It is *you* that want—and with your wanting you bring about our deaths.

UTHER: *My* desires are *your* desires, Ulfius. Remember that.

NARRATOR: Ulfius turned to go—his head hung low—and then a sudden idea came to his mind.

ULFIUS: Sire, what if there were a way to have your lady—without this senseless bloodshed?

UTHER: That's impossible!

ULFIUS: Exactly. It could be done by magic.

UTHER: What do you mean?

ULFIUS: There is an old magician who wanders these hills. He is said to be the son of a devil, but he has great powers. Perhaps he could help you.

UTHER: I will have nothing to do with witchcraft.

ULFIUS: But if he could help you—

UTHER: I'll think about it.

ULFIUS: The walls of Terrabil are thick, my lord. To wait will only waste our resources.

UTHER: Very well. Find me this man—this…

ULFIUS: Merlin. I will find him, sire, and bring him before you.

NARRATOR: And as the knights of Uther continued to lay siege to the castle of Terrabil, Sir Ulfius rode out to find the conjurer, Merlin.

Finding such a man was no easy task to the brave knight. He inquired in many muddy villages and rain-drenched streets, but none knew where to find the man rumored to be the son of a devil. He could take any shape at any time. He could not be found lest he *wanted* to be found.

ULFIUS: *(distressed)* All this searching for nothing.

NARRATOR: As Ulfius was returning to the king defeated and empty-handed, he beheld an old beggar man by the side of the road hunched over a scraggly bush.

ULFIUS: Old man, can you tell me the way to the castle of Terrabil? I seem to have gotten lost.

MERLIN: Shhhh! Quiet! I am speaking and must not be interrupted.

ULFIUS: You do not shush me! I am a knight of—

MERLIN: *(forcefully)* I said be quiet!

ULFIUS: How dare you! I shall beat you for your insolence!

MERLIN: I'll tell you how to find whom you seek—if you only sit patiently and *quietly* for half a second.

ULFIUS: *(surprised)* You know whom I seek?

MERLIN: *(angrily)* Confound it! I'm trying to talk to this caterpillar! Do you have any idea how hard it is to listen to a caterpillar?

ULFIUS: *(confused)* No, I can't say that I do.

MERLIN: It's very, very hard! I can't hear myself think—let alone him—with all your shouting!

ULFIUS: *(quietly)* Poor old coot. He's out of his mind.

MERLIN: *(talking to the caterpillar)* Yes. Yes. You don't say? Oh really! My, my. Well, that will teach him. I should say so. Yes, you as well. Thank you very much.

NARRATOR: The old man rose up from his stooped position, smoothed out his beard, and peered unimpressed at the mounted knight.

MERLIN: You seek Merlin, right? I happen to be Merlin. Mission accomplished. Now back to the king we go!

ULFIUS: *(shocked) You* are Merlin?

MERLIN: Nincompoops! You are all nincompoops! The caterpillar was right! There's nothing worth coming out of your cocoon for anymore!

ULFIUS: I'm extremely confused.

MERLIN: And I can see why! I'm surprised you can function with that puny, under-developed mind of yours! Lead the way! Lead the way! Shoo! Shoo! I haven't got forever, you know!

NARRATOR: Though Sir Ulfius was befuddled, he was gladdened to have found Merlin the magician, and he began to lead the old man back toward where Uther had laid siege to the duke's castle.

MERLIN: (*griping*) Walking is nasty business! I have no use for it!

ULFIUS: Would you prefer to ride my steed?

MERLIN: (*shocked*) Good heavens, no! Are you insane? I can't ride a horse! How would you like it if someone put a saddle on you and rode you around the countryside?

ULFIUS: (*confused*) I don't guess I have ever thought about it, sir.

MERLIN: Of course, you haven't. That's what's wrong with this country!

ULFIUS: (*tired*) You seem to complain a lot for one so wise.

MERLIN: What do you expect? I'm 120 years old! The older I grow, the crankier I get. People half my age complain until they're blue in the face.

ULFIUS: True, sir, true.

MERLIN: And don't get me started on teenagers…

ULFIUS: Very good, sir.

NARRATOR: Much to his relief, Sir Ulfius saw the tall spire of Castle Terrabil appear above the approaching hillside.

ULFIUS: Hark! I see the castle! We are nearly there.

MERLIN: Yes, of course we are. Don't state the obvious.

NARRATOR: With a smirk, Ulfius turned and led the old man down the valley toward the tent of the king. Uther's battering rams and siege engines hammered at the walls of the duke's castle.

MERLIN: (*sarcastically*) This is just brilliant! Absolutely brilliant! If you can't get the woman of your dreams, tear down her castle! How barbaric!

ULFIUS: I will go ahead to the king and announce your presence.

MERLIN: Tell him I wait for no man!

NARRATOR: Sir Ulfius ducked inside the king's tent.

UTHER: Ulfius, you have returned! Did you bring Merlin with you?

ULFIUS: Yes, your majesty.

UTHER: Is he well? Does he have anything to say?

ULFIUS: (*sarcastically*) Plenty.

UTHER: (*shouting*) Merlin! Come in! Come in!

NARRATOR: Merlin hesitantly stepped into the tent—his mouth bent down into a grimace.

UTHER: Come and meet your king!

MERLIN: (*offended*) Do not presume, sir, that I am capable of having *a king*! I was here far before you, and I will be here long after you. I have seen king after king come and go. Your meager existence does not impress me!

UTHER: *(laughing)* Merlin, old man! I like your spirit! I meant no offense by my comment! Please, sit—or if you wish, you may stand! I make no commands!

MERLIN: I shall do neither. I am extremely fond of *stooping*.

NARRATOR: The old wizard assumed an absurd half-stand, half-sit in the middle of the tent.

UTHER: *(confused)* Whatever. You are a strange man, Merlin!

MERLIN: So they tell me.

NARRATOR: Still stooping, Merlin crossed his legs. He was now floating a foot above the ground.

UTHER: *(shocked)* Zounds!

MERLIN: The floating? That's nothing. You should see how I sleep. *(pause)* But humor me! I know why you have sent for me, but let's just pretend I don't know and get on with it.

UTHER: Ah, Merlin. I like that in a man! Straight to the point!

MERLIN: And what do you like in a woman? *(pause)* Oh wait. Don't tell me.

UTHER: *(lovey-dovey)* But this woman, Merlin! The sun shines from her face! The wind kisses her cheeks! She is all that I have ever wanted!

MERLIN: Yes, yes—too bad she's married and all. Ahem. Well, I must be going!

UTHER: Wait! You have to help me get her, Merlin!

MERLIN: *(angered)* Well, I never! What is the world coming to? Give me the good old days! If a man wanted to steal someone's wife, he did it himself! None of this begging other people to do it for him!

UTHER: *(panicked)* Please, Merlin! You must! You must help me!

MERLIN: *(suddenly calmed)* Oh, please. Calm down. I'm going to help you. I have to be a bit dramatic. I knew what you were going to ask me before I came here.

UTHER: You will help me then?

MERLIN: Yes—*but* you must give me something in return!

UTHER: *(gladly)* Anything! Anything you ask! I will at once!

MERLIN: Careful, king. You do not know what I will ask for!

UTHER: It does not matter! I will give it!

MERLIN: My price is a great one. If I allow you to lie by Igraine, you will beget a child upon her—

UTHER: *(mesmerized)* A child! Fantastic!

MERLIN: Fantastic for whom? Anyway, when this child is born, he must be given to me—

UTHER: Certainly! Certainly!

MERLIN: *(irritated)* Did you hear what I said? You must give me your child. Don't you want to know what I'm going to do with it?

UTHER: *(confused)* Please, Merlin. Tell me what you will do with it!

MERLIN: What do you care? I could put it in a stew for all you care. Dress it up like a Christmas Eve turkey! Put an apple in its mouth, and you wouldn't care—as long as you got your lady!

UTHER: *(weary)* My head is sore from this discussion! Will you help me or not?

MERLIN: Yes, I will help you to meet with this woman.

ULFIUS: What spell will you work, Merlin?

MERLIN: Does it really matter? If I say the king is going to get his lady, he will get his lady!

UTHER: He is right, Ulfius. We should not pester him.

MERLIN: A magician never reveals his tricks. *(pause)* Here's the trick—I will place a spell upon you, Uther Pendragon, one that will make you look as if you are the Duke of Tintagel.

ULFIUS: Marvelous!

MERLIN: Yes, it is a rather good idea, isn't it? Then you will ride into the castle Tintagel, which is where his wife is being kept, and she will not know you from her husband.

UTHER: *(cheering)* A wonderful plan!

MERLIN: When the child is born—

UTHER: *(remembering)* Oh, yes, the child!

MERLIN: *(sarcastically)* Oh, yes, remember him? He will be brought to me, and I shall do with him what I wish.

ULFIUS: What shall you do with the boy, Merlin?

MERLIN: *(enraged)* Train him! Train him *not* to be a mighty dunderhead like you!

ULFIUS: You certainly are a man of the strangest temper I have ever met.

MERLIN: Thank you. Now, I must go work my spell. When midnight has come, and the moon is directly overhead, you may ride out. Do not be troubled by the guards. They will hail you as their duke. Visit the woman and return.

UTHER: How will she be fooled?

MERLIN: Whatever you do—do not tarry! The disguise will not last long!

UTHER: Most excellent! I will, Merlin.

MERLIN: Of course, you will. *(sigh)* I'm off. Enjoy.

NARRATOR: And so the deal was struck. Uther waited until the moon floated right above and rode forth with a small group of men toward Tintagel. *(fanfare, hoofbeats)*

Watching from Terrabil, the duke saw Uther and his men departing their camp. His heart leapt. They were finally retreating!

DUKE: Men! The king and his cowards are running! At once, let's charge into their camp and destroy it!

NARRATOR: The duke raised the cry, and he and his lusty men rode to Uther's camp.

(*shouting and hoofbeats*) When they reached it, they were in for a surprise. What the duke had perceived to be a retreat was anything but. They were met with Uther's entire army—still entrenched.

DUKE: We have been tricked. There is devilry in this! Curses upon Uther!

NARRATOR: But curses could not save the duke, and there he fell, pierced by the arrows of Uther's men an hour before the unknowing king ever reached the duke's wife.

Uther, in his disguise, met no resistance at the gates of the castle Tintagel. The men only saw their lord coming home late—visiting his long-estranged wife.

UTHER: Take these horses, steward! I must be up to my wife's chambers!

NARRATOR: He made his way up to the very top of the tallest tower.

UTHER: Now, we will see how well Merlin's spell does.

NARRATOR: He found the door ajar—golden light pouring through a crack. He pushed upon it.

UTHER: (*breathless*) My lady!

NARRATOR: There was Igraine—her auburn hair shining in the firelight. She dropped what needlework she had in her hand and rose to greet her lord. Uther removed his helm and held his breath.

IGRAINE: (*surprised*) Husband? You have returned to me!

UTHER: Yes, my darling.

NARRATOR: And so Igraine was tricked by a man who was not her husband. Far away, under the same moon that wept for the tricking of Igraine, Merlin laughed a grim chuckle to himself.

MERLIN: Foolish Uther! You don't think about what your actions will bring! You don't care for that son who will come from Igraine's bed. You don't care for that sad duke that fell this night. The world shall know your sin—yet you will not be saddened. You are a strong but foolish king. From your misdeeds will come one greater than you. Yes, I will see to that.

NARRATOR: Back at Tintagel, Uther rode forth from the castle. Igraine was stunned by her husband's sudden leaving.

IGRAINE: Can this be the same man who shared my vows? He hasn't ever acted this way before.

NARRATOR: The hoofbeats of the men disappeared into the night. (*hoofbeats*) Igraine went to return to her chambers. But, suddenly from her high view, she beheld a man tearing into the courtyard—a man of her duke's. He called forth to his lady.

MESSENGER: Woe, my lady! Woe! Your husband has fallen!

IGRAINE: (*gasping*) No! It cannot be true! When?

MESSENGER: An hour ago! He fell before the tents of Uther!

IGRAINE: It cannot be! He was only just here. You must have passed him on the road.

MESSENGER: (*gravely*) I saw no such man. But I did see my lord die, and I weep for him. I have brought you his crest, so that you might remember him by it.

NARRATOR: Igraine fell upon the cold stones—weeping. Her husband was dead—an hour before—gone forever from her world. But then her thoughts shook with a new wonder.

IGRAINE: (*breathlessly*) Then who was this man who visited me tonight? A wizard? An evil spirit? I have been ruined—my honor tarnished! No one will have me! I am a harlot now. I am lost!

NARRATOR: And there Igraine wept in the cold night. Her three young daughters came to her but did not try to move her. They grieved as greatly as she did.

That night a child had been sired—a child unbeknownst by its mother and forgotten by its father.

UTHER: What now, Ulfius? I have known the woman of my dreams. Yet I am not satisfied. You tell me that you and your men have slain her husband?

ULFIUS: Yes, sir. He arrived advancing shortly after you left. He must have thought your departure was a retreat.

UTHER: He is a fool, and he has met a suitable end. (*thinking*) But Igraine—now, she is mine for the taking. (*happily*) Bless you, Merlin, wherever you are. You have worked your spell well.

NARRATOR: The troops of Uther Pendragon dismantled their tents and made their way back to his stronghold—rejoicing in their victory.

Uther bade his time, but after a fortnight, he sent his emissaries to Igraine—offering marriage. She answered his call in person.

IGRAINE: (*sadly*) Sire, mine has been no small loss. I mourn for my husband. I know that you fancy me, and I can do nothing but humbly accept your offer of marriage.

UTHER: (*happily*) This is a marvelous day! These words are music to my ears! (*concerned*) But, tell me, why are you so sad?

IGRAINE: I have lost a husband—but much more as well.

UTHER: Speak—for you will now be my wife, and you must keep nothing from me.

IGRAINE: (*quietly, slowly*) On the night of my husband's death, I was visited by a phantom—a form that appeared much like him.

UTHER: I see. Do you know who this man—or creature—is?

IGRAINE: No, sir. It was *not* my husband, for he was dead an hour before. Perhaps it was the working of an evil spirit. Whatever it was, it has gotten a child upon me, and my honor is dragged through the mud.

UTHER: (*not surprised*) Hmmmmm.

IGRAINE: (*sadly*) I felt that I must tell you this. I think that you will no longer want a disgraced creature such as me.

UTHER: On the contrary, this news is not surprising to me.

IGRAINE: (*confused*) Why?

UTHER: It was I—through a working of Merlin the conjurer—that visited your chamber that night, and it is my child you bear!

NARRATOR: There was a pause as the news sank in.

IGRAINE: *(overjoyed)* My lord, this is joyful news!

UTHER: Yes. Let's not talk about it anymore! We will feast and be married. You are my wife, and I'm your husband. What was once yours is mine. I will take up the care of your daughters—even though they are the daughters of the duke.

IGRAINE: Thank you, my lord. You are too good.

NARRATOR: And so it was done—Uther did as he said. He made Igraine his queen. But her daughters—while under his protection—also fell under his suspicion, and he deemed it best that they should be put away where he thought they could do the least harm.

With Margawse, the oldest, a marriage was arranged, and she was given to King Lot of Orkney to be the queen of his faraway realm. In the same manner, the second daughter was married off to another king of a distant land.

As for Morgan, the youngest of the three girls—raven-haired and cunning—she was put to school in a nunnery. It was not a wise deed of Uther, for there she nursed her hatred for him, and the murder of her father festered within her breast. She became a great worker of necromancy—vowing revenge upon Uther and her infant half-brother.

Soon, Igraine became great with child, and the day neared when the baby would be born. Like a ghost from the wood, Merlin appeared before the king on the day of the child's birth.

MERLIN: Uther! Uther, I say! I have returned to claim what you have promised me!

UTHER: Promised? What do you speak of, you old sorcerer?

MERLIN: *(outraged)* Our pact! Our bond! Do you remember nothing? Must I undo it all?

UTHER: Calm yourself, old friend. I remember now, and I will give you my son as I have promised. But, tell me, Merlin, what should be done with him?

MERLIN: I will do with him what I will. What do you care?

UTHER: I do care. He is my only son. My kingdom rests in his hands. In the wild forest with you is no place for a child.

MERLIN: Very true, very true. I have arranged for his raising by one of your knights, Sir Ector.

UTHER: Why?

MERLIN: The boy will know nothing of who his true parents are. He will be raised by Sir Ector as his own son! Nursed by his wife's own pap!

UTHER: I know of Ector. Is he a good man?

MERLIN: *(irritated)* Better than most! Better than most! If you were so concerned with the boy's well-being, perhaps you should not have made such a bargain!

UTHER: *(grimly)* I will not break my promise. My son is in my wife's arms. He has just entered this world. He has not even been christened. Do you want him now?

MERLIN: *(repelled)* Good Heavens, no! Wash him first! But this night, deliver him unchristened to an old man that you find by the gate at dusk.

UTHER: It shall be done.

MERLIN: Not to worry, Uther, old boy. He will be a great one. A real corker. *(under his breath)* Better than the lot around here by a long shot. *(loudly)* Now, I must be off.

UTHER: Farewell, Merlin—until our next dealing.

NARRATOR: The baby was delivered to an old man at dusk as promised—wrapped in a cloth of gold. It was Merlin in a disguise once again. He carried the baby through the woods—talking rapidly to the child, as if he were old enough to understand.

MERLIN: I will name you Arthur. Yes, that's a good name. Stop that fussing now! I've made all the arrangements. You will be raised in the household of Sir Ector until the time is right.

NARRATOR: Sir Ector did not know Arthur's true identity, but when Merlin appeared and told him to raise the child as his own, Ector agreed. All obeyed Merlin. And so the boy was delivered.

MERLIN: Now, to wait! If I have plenty of one thing, it is time!

NARRATOR: Uther soon forgot his son amid the warrings of the land.

In later days, his enemies became too much for him, and he fell in battle. Merlin was there to hear his final words. They were that his long-forgotten son should be king.

MERLIN: Leave that to me, sire.

UTHER: *(feebly)* Now, I die in peace.

NARRATOR: And so Uther gave up the ghost. Without a strong leader, all of England fell into darkness, and so it was for many years—until the son of Pendragon came of age and brought peace and justice back to the land of his father.

DISCUSSION QUESTIONS

1. Is Uther a good father? Explain.
2. Why is Igraine overjoyed to hear that Uther is actually the father of her child?
3. What does this tell us about her character? Explain.
4. Should Igraine have accepted Uther's proposal of marriage? Explain.
5. Why does Merlin agree to help Uther trick Igraine? What does this tell us about him?
6. Why does Merlin want Arthur to be raised away from his biological parents, ignorant of his true identity?
7. Do children always turn out to be like their parents? Explain.
8. How could the past deeds of Uther cause trouble for Arthur in the future?

A TALE OF TWO SWORDS
TEACHER GUIDE

BACKGROUND

When the occupying Roman forces pulled out of Britain in the 5th century A.D., their absence created a power vacuum. Britain was invaded by hordes of Anglo-Saxon warriors from the European mainland. The Britons, who had been living under Roman rule for hundreds of years, suddenly found themselves fighting to preserve their way of life. It is during this time of war and upheaval that the historical King Arthur would have lived. He would have been a Romanized Briton general leading his forces against the barbaric invaders. In fact, some pseudo-historical accounts say that Arthur defeated the Anglo-Saxons in a decisive battle at Badon Hill and ushered in a fifty-year period of peace for Britain.

Over time whatever historical details that existed about Arthur were mixed with myth. Storytellers adapted the story over and over—adding in anachronistic details and fantastical elements from a variety of sources. Pagan elements from Britain's Celtic, pre-Christian days include the goddess-like Lady of the Lake and the druid-like Merlin. Yet Arthur himself is presented as a Christian king, serving God and protecting the Church. To further confuse things, his knights seem to exist in the age of medieval chivalry—a time centuries after the historical Arthur. In the end King Arthur's tales belong to a "Once upon a time" imaginary setting, where the lines between history and myth are blurred.

SUMMARY

In the years after the death of Uther Pendragon, Britain becomes a dark and violent place. Merlin goes to consult with the Archbishop of Canterbury, the highest religious authority of the land, and tells him a miracle is needed. The archbishop prays, and a miracle occurs—a sword stuck through an anvil and stone appears in London. Upon the hilt letters of gold declare that whoever pulls the sword free from the stone is the true king of England. Many knights try to pull the sword free, but no one can. In an effort to draw more knights to London, the archbishop calls for all knights of England to attend a joust.

Sir Ector hears of the joust and brings his son, Kay, and Arthur, his adopted son, to London. Arthur, about sixteen years of age, is acting as Kay's squire. On the day of the joust Kay forgets his sword, and Arthur rushes back to their inn to retrieve it. Finding the door locked, Arthur spies a sword stuck in an anvil amid a churchyard. He easily pulls it free.

When Arthur presents the sword to Kay, Ector immediately recognizes it as the Sword in the Stone. Arthur explains how he retrieved it. Merlin appears, declares Arthur king, and agrees to mentor him in the duties of kingship.

Soon after Arthur is crowned king, King Lot of Orkney leads a rebellion of lesser kings against him. Through the help of Merlin, these rebellious kings are defeated. Arthur makes Camelot his capital city and summons all noble knights to join him there.

Years later, Arthur does battle with a rogue knight, and the knight is about to behead Arthur when Merlin intervenes by putting the knight to sleep. Merlin tells

32 The Road to Camelot

Arthur that they must visit an enchantress called the Lady of the Lake.

In the midst of a nearby lake is an arm holding a magnificent sword aloft, which is Excalibur. Arthur sees the Lady of the Lake, who tells Arthur that Excalibur shall be his. Arthur boards a boat and takes the sword and its scabbard. As they journey back to Camelot, Merlin tells Arthur that the scabbard is more valuable than Excalibur, as he who wears it will lose no blood—no matter how badly he is wounded.

ESSENTIAL QUESTIONS

- Why is it important to be humble?
- Can young people be effective leaders?

ANTICIPATORY QUESTIONS

- How does Arthur become king?
- What is jousting?
- What is Excalibur?

CHARACTER QUEST

Overcoming Circumstances We often cannot control our circumstances in life. What we can always control is our reactions to these circumstances. Will we accept them or overcome them? Howard Pyle, who wrote a famous children's version of the King Arthur legends, made this comment about life: "Any man...may draw forth the sword of success from out of the iron of circumstance." Although Arthur is born into a hard situation, he will rise to the challenge of being a better king than his father was. How will Arthur's humble childhood make him a better ruler? Why is it important for us to try to rise above the circumstances in which we are placed?

CONNECT

The Sword in the Stone **(1938) by T.H. White** First published as a stand-alone novel but now part of the larger work *The Once and Future King*, this classic tale puts a new twist on Arthur's boyhood. Merlin the wizard educates Arthur by turning him into a variety of animals. By observing the animal kingdom Arthur learns the best way to govern his own kingdom. *The Sword in the Stone* **(1963)** is a Disney animated film adaptation of the novel by T.H. White.

TEACHABLE TERMS

- **Alliteration** The line "it sang the same song he had heard the lady sing. Somehow, it soothed him" on pg. 45 contains frequent alliteration.
- **Symbol** Throughout Arthur's life Excalibur will be a symbol of his right to rule Britain. At the end of his life, he will return the sword to the Lady of the Lake signifying the end of his reign.
- **Foreshadowing** On pg. 45 comments from Merlin foreshadow events in Arthur's future.
- **Metaphor** On pgs. 45-46 Merlin compares Arthur to a sapling that will one day grow into a mighty oak.

RECALL QUESTIONS

1. What is written on the hilt of the Sword in the Stone?
2. Why does Kay need a sword?
3. Whom does Arthur make the overseer of all his lands?
4. Who gives Excalibur to Arthur?
5. Which is better, Excalibur or its scabbard, and why?

A TALE OF TWO SWORDS

CAST

ARTHUR	*Foster-Son of Sir Ector*
MERLIN	*The Good Enchanter*
ECTOR	*Arthur's Foster-Father*
KAY	*Ector's Son*
ARCHBISHOP	*Religious Leader*
LOT	*King of Orkney*
LADY	*Lady of the Lake*
SQUIRE	*Servant to a Knight*
THIEF	*Roadside Bandit*

NARRATOR: Times were dark in Britain during the years following the death of Uther Pendragon. His knights, becoming base and greedy, fought amongst themselves for the power to rule. Yet the throne remained empty. The land was broken and black, and many saw that something must be done soon, lest the land fall into ruin.

One day, quite unexpectedly, Merlin the good enchanter appeared from the deep wood and made his way to Londontown—there to speak with one as wise as he, the Archbishop of Canterbury.

ARCHBISHOP: *(questioningly)* Who's there?

MERLIN: Only an old man like you. One who wants to see this dark land healed.

ARCHBISHOP: *(amazed)* Merlin the wizard! The last time you were here, the people almost burned you at the stake for your sorcery. Luckily, I convinced them not to.

MERLIN: Ha! I would have liked to see them try! Archbishop, I come here on a most important errand. Our land is in turmoil without a king. You must pray for Heaven to give us a—a—what do you call those things?

ARCHBISHOP: Miracles?

MERLIN: Yes. That's it. One of those would do most nicely.

ARCHBISHOP: What should this miracle be?

MERLIN: *(irritably)* How should I know? Whatever it is, it should bring us a king. The land is dying.

ARCHBISHOP: Very well. I shall pray, and God will bless us with a miracle.

MERLIN: Pray it comes quickly! It's not even safe for old wizards to travel alone anymore! *(sigh)* I must be off.

ARCHBISHOP: Thank you for this news, but, Merlin, please do not return here. I'd hate to see you burned at the stake.

MERLIN: Ah. Don't worry. I'm not very fond of burning. It tickles.

NARRATOR: The old wizard left the churchman's chamber and slipped back into the night as easily as he had come. The archbishop prayed, and on Christmas Day a miracle came.

Many knights of England were gathered in Londontown for the Christ mass, and they packed the great cathedral. The archbishop was giving a joyous litany but then stopped in mid-chant, his lips trembling.

ARCHBISHOP: *(whispering)* It has happened.

NARRATOR: The knights and gentle men and women stared in shock as the archbishop ran from the church and into the courtyard shouting.

ARCHBISHOP: Heaven be praised!

NARRATOR: The people thronged after the archbishop, and they found him prostrate before a strange object in the churchyard—one that had not been there when they entered.

ARCHBISHOP: *(joyously)* It has happened! Heaven has sent us a miracle!

NARRATOR: They all gathered around closely and marveled at the shrine to which the archbishop bowed. A magnificent sword had been driven—almost to the hilt—into a coal-black anvil, which rested atop a large stone amid the courtyard.

ARCHBISHOP: A sword in a stone! A sword in a stone—driven there by the hand of God himself!

NARRATOR: The archbishop rose and moved closer. Upon the hilt, he could discern letters of gold.

ARCHBISHOP: *(reading)* Whoso pulleth out this sword from this stone and anvil is rightwise king born of all England.

NARRATOR: The people gasped and marveled at this. *(sounds of people gasping and marveling)*

ARCHBISHOP: We shall have a king again! And he shall be chosen by this miracle—this miracle of God!

NARRATOR: Soon a great murmur ran through the crowd, and many good knights stepped forward to try their hand—but none succeeded. The sword would not be moved. Man after man approached the task, but all left defeated. It would not budge an inch.

ARCHBISHOP: *(worried)* What can this mean? Heaven would not send this miracle for nothing! A king must be chosen!

NARRATOR: When all had tried and failed, the heart of the archbishop dropped.

ARCHBISHOP: Hope is extinguished.

NARRATOR: But he then remembered that while many knights were present in London for the feast, not *all* had been summoned. There were many country plantations that harbored noblemen as well. He needed a way to bring them all there.

ARCHBISHOP: *(shouting)* Attention! Attention! I decree that we must have a joust. Heaven has ordained it. All knights must attend, and whoever wins our tournament will be the bearer of the sword and king of all England.

NARRATOR: And so was the word sent out to every sword in the land. The word even reached the elderly Sir Ector, the guardian of Uther Pendragon's long-forgotten son. Under the care of the kindly Sir Ector, the baby Arthur had grown into a spry young lad of sixteen years. When the boy had questioned his guardian as to who his parents were, Ector could only say…

ECTOR: I do not know, my boy. An old man brought you from the woods. He told me to care for you—raise you as my own son. And I have. I can tell you no more.

NARRATOR: While Arthur had many questions about his past, he had accepted this and asked no more. In his youthful eagerness, he had grown up worshipping the ground his older foster-brother, Sir Kay, walked on. When the news came of the great joust in Londontown, Ector went at once to his sons.

ECTOR: *(yelling)* Kay! Prepare for a journey! We have been sent for! To joust!

KAY: *(eagerly)* Really? *(gruffly)* I mean, of course. I'm a knight now, and I must do these things.

ECTOR: Of course, my boy, of course. And the prize they joust for is the greatest prize—the crown!

KAY: *(doubtfully)* Father, do you think I could win it?

ARTHUR: *(happily)* Of course, you could, Kay! You're the greatest fighter I've ever seen.

KAY: *(hatefully)* What do you know?

ECTOR: Arthur! You shall come as well. You will keep Kay's sword and shield!

ARTHUR: *(excited)* Really?

KAY: Does he have to?

ECTOR: Now, boys, at once! Prepare! We leave tomorrow!

NARRATOR: Arthur had never been anywhere except the humble province of Sir Ector. This chance to go to London was undreamt of. He could not sleep the night before their departure.

It was snowing softly as the three rode into the crowded streets of the city on New Year's Day.

ECTOR: I can hear the joust!

KAY: I think that's just Arthur's knees knocking together.

ARTHUR: It's true. I'm a bit nervous. I've never been a squire before.

KAY: Hopefully, you won't be one for long.

NARRATOR: They deposited their things at the inn. Kay put on his armor and took his lance. Arthur made sure the horse was groomed and prepared for the tournament.

When all was ready, they rode toward the joust. The roar of the crowd echoed through the streets. *(cheering of a crowd)*

ARTHUR: *(eagerly)* Kay! This is going to be great! I can't wait to see you charging on your horse, swinging your sword, making—

KAY: *(shocked)* My sword! I left my sword at the inn! I've got to go back and get it!

ECTOR: There is no time! We are late enough! Your turn will be soon!

ARTHUR: Don't worry! I'll go back and get it!

KAY: Oh no, you don't. You should have reminded me in the first place.

ECTOR: He must, Kay. There is no time. Go, Arthur! Quickly!

ARTHUR: I'll get your sword, Kay! I promise!

NARRATOR: Arthur rushed quickly back through the deserted streets—back to the inn. He ran to its door but found it bolted.

ARTHUR: *(panicked)* Everyone is at the tournament!

NARRATOR: At that moment he remembered that when they had passed by the churchyard, he had seen a strange sight. There had been a great sword within, sticking halfway out of an anvil.

ARTHUR: That sword will have to do!

NARRATOR: He raced to the place where he had seen the sword, and dashing through the snow, he ran to the great stone. He never thought to doubt the fact that the sword would come loose once he pulled—and with the slightest of strength, the great weapon easily slid forth. *(metallic shing)*

ARTHUR: Now, I must get it back to Kay!

NARRATOR: Unaware of the miracle that had just occurred, Arthur jumped back onto his horse—sword in tow—and galloped back to the jousting field.

ARTHUR: *(shouting)* Kay! Kay! I have a sword!

KAY: Amazing. Maybe you are worth something. Give it to me! *(pause)* Wait a minute! This is not my sword!

ECTOR: Where did you get this sword, my boy?

ARTHUR: *(confused)* From a stone in a courtyard…

ECTOR: By Jove, this boy has pulled the sword from the stone!

KAY: *(surprised)* Arthur? Him?

ARTHUR: What does that mean?

ECTOR: *(overjoyed)* What does that mean? What does that mean? That is the whole point of this tournament! But you—you—have pulled the sword from the stone!

KAY: *(not happy)* Arthur? A king?

ECTOR: *(shouting)* Yes, Kay, yes! King of all England!

NARRATOR: Soon their shouting attracted the attention of those around them, and before they knew it, a great crowd was gathered—all staring in wonder. They asked to examine the sword. It *was* the Sword in the Stone. It even had the golden letters beneath the hilt. But a boy?

ARCHBISHOP: Silence, people, silence!

NARRATOR: The archbishop had pushed his way through the crowd.

ARCHBISHOP: Who has pulled out this sword?

KAY: *(still confused)* Arthur?

ECTOR: This boy!

ARCHBISHOP: Boy, what is your name?

ARTHUR: Arthur, sir.

ARCHBISHOP: I see.

KAY: *(angrily)* He can't be king! He's too young! He's an orphan! He can't be the king!

ARCHBISHOP: But he has pulled out the sword, young man.

KAY: Anyone can pull it out once it's been pulled! Someone else removed it, and Arthur found it! He's lying!

ECTOR: *(gruffly)* Silence, Kay!

ARCHBISHOP: Then—in front of all—let us test him. To the courtyard!

NARRATOR: A great crowd of people marched through the snowy streets—Arthur and the archbishop in the lead. To tell the truth, Arthur was a bit embarrassed by all this attention. Kay lagged sulkily behind. They reached the stone and the anvil, and the archbishop slid the sword back into its metallic grip. *(metallic shing)*

ARCHBISHOP: Now, let all look! If this boy pulls forth the sword, he is the king. God has sent us this miracle to show us our true ruler. Let none doubt and everyone swear their loyalty if this act is done.

NARRATOR: It was agreed. Arthur sheepishly walked toward the handle. It had seemed so easy before. Why, with everyone watching, was it so much harder now? Fear seized him. It had worked the first time, but what if it did not work again?

ECTOR: Go on, son.

NARRATOR: Arthur reached up and grasped the cold handle and slowly applied the pressure of his arm. The sword rose up from the stone—just as it had before—only this time, it sang. *(angelic choir)*

Light broke forth from the gray clouds, and a single ray fell upon the boy Arthur. Many swore that they heard angels singing that day, and all present agreed that it was the greatest sight that their eyes were to ever see.

ARCHBISHOP: Hail to Arthur! King of the Britons! Sovereign of all England!

ECTOR: Bow to your king, son.

KAY: Arthur?

NARRATOR: As all bowed, Kay scowled—but bent his knee as well.

ARCHBISHOP: Sir Ector, is this boy your son?

ECTOR: No, he is an orphan. He was brought to me on a cold winter night by Merlin the good enchanter. I have raised him as my own son.

MERLIN: He is the son of Uther Pendragon!

NARRATOR: An old man in a snow-covered traveling cloak stepped forward. It was Merlin.

MERLIN: He was begat long ago and forgotten. I have seen to it that he returned this day to claim his birthright.

NARRATOR: The people stared at the boy in further amazement.

MERLIN: Well, what are you waiting for? Praise! Grovel! This is your king!

NARRATOR: All of this terribly embarrassed Arthur. He stood there—a scrawny teenager who was now the object of so much scrutiny. Grown men began to kneel at his feet. Arthur didn't know what to do. He saw his foster-brother bowing, and he walked to him and put his hand on his shoulder.

ARTHUR: If I am to be king, Kay, I want you to be there with me. You're my brother. I'll make you the overseer of all my lands.

NARRATOR: Kay looked up and smiled.

ECTOR: *(merrily)* Come, Archbishop, let us have a celebration! A king has been chosen!

ARCHBISHOP: You speak wise words! A feast! A feast!

(cheers of the people)

NARRATOR: Arthur felt his heart sink. What now? He turned to the old, strange man who had stood forth from the crowd.

ARTHUR: Excuse me, sir.

NARRATOR: Merlin slowly turned.

MERLIN: *(kindly)* Oh yes. You.

ARTHUR: I know you have said that God has picked me, but might you be wrong? I don't know anything about…anything. I can't fight wars. I can't govern kingdoms.

MERLIN: Rome wasn't built in a day, lad. I shall teach you—help you.

ARTHUR: Yes, that will perhaps not be so bad.

MERLIN: Bad? Heavens, no! It will be the best thing that ever happens to you.

NARRATOR: Merlin made good on his word. He helped the boy-king set up his court at the castle of Camelot. The call went out to all the lesser kings and lords of Britain for them to come to Camelot and pledge their loyalty to the boy-king. It was about that time that Lot the King of Orkney and Lothian began to grumble against Arthur's right to reign.

LOT: Why should an illegitimate brat be our king? So what if he was Uther Pendragon's son? How can a boy lead men? I am married to Uther's adopted daughter. I have more of a right to be king than he does! The Sword in the Stone was just a cheap trick devised by that old warlock Merlin. I say we take Britain back! Who's with me?

(shouts of agreement)

NARRATOR: Lot found allies among the other kings of Britain, and together they began to muster their forces. News of Lot's amassing army reached Merlin.

MERLIN: Arthur, we must prepare for war. An army of hostile knights is heading toward Camelot. It is led by King Lot of Orkney.

ARTHUR: I don't understand.

MERLIN: Orkney. It's a miserable chain of islands off the northern coast of Britain.

ARTHUR: No, I mean, why is he leading an army against me?

MERLIN: Oh, that's easy. He wants your head. Or, more specifically, what rests upon it. He's perfectly willing to remove the former in order to receive the latter.

ARTHUR: I can't believe he'd kill me just to get my crown. He doesn't even know me.

MERLIN: Don't you know anything about politics? Lot has convinced ten other kings to rally to his cause. He says that you're too young, you have no experience—plus, it's a known fact that teenagers have no common sense. All of his claims are true, of course…

ARTHUR: Hey!

MERLIN: Yet he is missing one key point—you are meant to be the king, and he is not. He will just have to learn that the hard way.

ARTHUR: That's right! *I* pulled the sword out of the stone! Doesn't that mean anything to these lords?

MERLIN: The Sword in the Stone only showed your right to rule. It did not prove your *ability* to rule. Besides you could walk on water, and it would not change the way your foes feel about you. Lot and his allies have been your sworn enemies even before you were born. Two of the kings who oppose you are married to your half-sisters, who hate you with a fiery passion.

ARTHUR: I have half-sisters? And even *they* want me dead?

MERLIN: Welcome to the Middle Ages! But as much fun as this look at your family tree is, we have to prepare for war!

ARTHUR: I guess I was naïve. I thought by becoming king I would bring an end to war in Britain.

MERLIN: Only the dead have seen the end of war. But don't despair. There are still many lords who believe in you.

ARTHUR: Maybe Lot's right. I'm just a sixteen-year-old! What do I know about being king? Why would anyone want to follow me?

MERLIN: For the kingdom that they hope you will build. True, you are young, but you have a good heart, Arthur. Many lords have faith that you will be a different type of king. They have seen plenty of kings like Lot, but *you* give them hope.

NARRATOR: The boy-king smiled.

ARTHUR: Then, when all of this is over, I won't let them down!

MERLIN: Spoken wisely, my boy! Now let's muster an army.

NARRATOR: When Lot and his army arrived at Camelot, he found Arthur's own army of loyal knights arrayed upon the battle plain.

LOT: This milk-fed brat may have more guts than we thought! Tell the knights that the battle will begin tomorrow at daybreak. Then Britain will be mine! *(evil laugh)*

NARRATOR: That night, from the ramparts of Camelot, Arthur and Merlin viewed the thousand campfires of King Lot's army.

ARTHUR: There are so many. They have us easily outnumbered.

MERLIN: Don't fret. With this battle you will prove that you are worthy to be king. Now command your men to prepare for battle.

ARTHUR: But it is evening time.

MERLIN: *(sarcastically)* Really? I was wondering why it was so dark. Of course, it is evening time. That's the best time to launch a sneak attack, wouldn't you say? Lot's knights have just tucked themselves into bed.

NARRATOR: Arthur's army was quickly roused, and the boy-king sat astride his steed at the head of his knights. Merlin rode forward on his white donkey.

MERLIN: Now to give you a slight advantage.

NARRATOR: The old wizard uttered some strange words, and across the valley the many tents of the enemy army simultaneously collapsed. *(whooshing sound)* Lot's men—trapped beneath the fallen tents—shouted in confusion. *(confused shouting)*

MERLIN: I just couldn't help myself! Now shout, "Charge!" already!

ARTHUR: *(shouting)* Charge!

(battlecries, hoofbeats, sounds of battle)

NARRATOR: Thanks to the bravery of Arthur and his knights, the army of Lot and his allies was routed. Arthur's rule was legitimized—once and for all.

MERLIN: Bravo! You captured almost a thousand enemy knights. King Lot and his allies have fled to their castles. Now the question remains, your majesty—what will you do with these eleven traitorous kings? They have already sent envoys to beg you for mercy.

ARTHUR: What would my father have done?

MERLIN: He would have executed them and not thought twice about it.

ARTHUR: What shall I do?

MERLIN: Think twice.

ARTHUR: Hmmm. I will spare them. If they will pledge themselves to me, I will forget the past.

NARRATOR: The old wizard smiled.

MERLIN: The boy may make a good king after all.

NARRATOR: Soon the rebellion of the eleven kings became a distant memory. Under Merlin's tutelage Arthur grew into his position as High King of Britain.

MERLIN: A king must be fair! So many men gain power and then abuse it to keep others down. Your kingdom must be different!

ARTHUR: My kingdom will be based on justice.

MERLIN: Good, but remember justice doesn't mean getting *your* way all the time. Just because you are the king doesn't mean you are above the law. Justice means that the laws apply to everyone—even you.

ARTHUR: Of course! And what about mercy? I read in the Holy Scriptures about the importance of mercy. But so many kings are ruthless and cruel. Shouldn't my kingdom be based on mercy?

MERLIN: Naturally. And service to others. The only way to tame the beastly nature of man is through serving others.

ARTHUR: Perhaps I should give my knights the task of protecting those who are weaker than they are. Through this they will promote these ideas that we believe in—truth, justice, equality, mercy.

MERLIN: Ha-ha! Perfect, boy. Perfect!

NARRATOR: So Arthur ruled like no other monarch ever had—showing justice, mercy, and fairness in all that he did. As the next years passed, many knights rallied to Arthur's banner and pledged themselves to his cause.

Merlin often traveled afar for months at a time—carrying news of Camelot to the far reaches of Britain and returning with honorable knights to boost Arthur's growing army of justice.

Once while Merlin was gone on one of his missions, a terrified squire brought news to the young king.

SQUIRE: Sire! A rogue knight has set up a tent along the roadside. He's challenging any virtuous knight who passes to combat. He's crushed my master's body, and I only escaped with my life to bring you this news!

ARTHUR: Who does this man think he is? I'll have no rogue knights in *my* kingdom! Ready my horse!

NARRATOR: Arthur donned his armor and rode forth. *(hoofbeats)*

As Arthur galloped through the forest, a scruffy, old beggar man shot out of a thicket—running for all he was worth.

ARTHUR: Halt! What is the meaning of this?

MERLIN: *(frantic, old man voice)* No time! No time!

NARRATOR: A band of thieves burst out of the underbrush—following hot on the beggar's heels.

THIEF: Give us your purse, you old coot, or we'll cut your throat!

ARTHUR: Halt, dogs! I am Arthur! Leave that old man alone!

NARRATOR: The bandits stopped short and for the first time noticed Arthur.

THIEF: Ah! A knight! Run!

NARRATOR: King Arthur did not pursue them but turned to the old man to see if he was all right. The beggar looked up, and beneath his scraggly beard was an all-too-familiar face.

ARTHUR: *(amazed)* Merlin? What are you doing here?

MERLIN: *(huffing, puffing)* Running for my life. What does it look like?

ARTHUR: It thought you were away on one of your missions.

MERLIN: I was, but when I arrived in Camelot, they told me that you had ridden out to challenge a rogue knight yourself! You know, most kings just send their knights to do this kind of thing for them!

ARTHUR: I know. But I'm a different kind of king, remember? I believe in equality. Besides, why should my knights get to have all the fun?

MERLIN: Yes, but if *you* are killed in battle, all of this land will be lost. The hope of a thousand people will be extinguished.

ARTHUR: Don't be so full of gloom and doom. I think I can handle a simple battle.

MERLIN: Ha! Don't grow too confident that you lose sight of your own human weaknesses.

ARTHUR: You are one to talk. You were just being chased by that band of ruffians. Even with all your magic, they would have cut your throat if I hadn't stopped them.

MERLIN: Exactly, you dunce! I was trying to prove a point to you. Even I—an all-powerful wizard—am mortal, and I should be careful what situations I put myself in.

ARTHUR: Merlin, thank you for the lesson. But I am off to challenge this rogue knight.

MERLIN: This challenger is a mighty foe named King Pellinore, and he will cut your head off if you are not careful.

ARTHUR: We shall see, Merlin. We shall see.

MERLIN: Fine! Don't say I didn't warn you! You young people think you know everything! Why listen to Merlin? He can only see the future—nothing much!

NARRATOR: Arthur had been on the receiving end of Merlin's tantrums time enough, so he quietly rode on while the magician continued to rant.

MERLIN: I'm just like Cassandra of Troy! Nobody listened to her either, and then guess what happened?

NARRATOR: The old wizard suddenly realized the king was gone.

MERLIN: Oh thank goodness. I thought he'd never leave. I'll let him try it on his own for a while and see how it goes.

NARRATOR: Much satisfied, Merlin laid down beneath a tree and fell asleep to the sounds of swords crashing far away. Now, it should be noted that wizards do not actually sleep when it seems that they are doing so. In actuality, they're doing deeds miles away. Because of this, they never oversleep or miss important events—unless they mean to. Merlin awoke, we shall say, precisely when he meant to, and at once, rushed off through the forest to find Arthur.

MERLIN: *(happily)* He will have himself in a fine pickle by now, I assume.

(distant clanging of shield and sword)

NARRATOR: And, sure enough, he came into a clearing where an enormous knight stood with his sword raised over the weaponless Arthur.

MERLIN: *(booming)* King Pellinore! Stay your hand!

NARRATOR: Merlin's cry caused the huge knight's descending blade to stop in midair. Indeed Pellinore had almost brought Arthur to the point of death.

MERLIN: Do not slay this man! Do you not know who he is? He is King Arthur, and if you slay him, this kingdom will fall into utter darkness.

ARTHUR: *(angrily)* Merlin! I have this completely under control.

MERLIN: *(parent-like)* Shush!

NARRATOR: Merlin flailed his arms about in the air, babbled some strange words, and the massive form of Pellinore fell backward into the grass. *(crashing sound)*

ARTHUR: You killed him!

MERLIN: Relax. It is only a sleep-spell.

NARRATOR: Loud snoring escaped the visor of Pellinore's helm. *(snoring)*

MERLIN: That should hold him for several hours. He will catch up on his beauty rest, and you will get safely on your way.

ARTHUR: *(furious)* I can't believe this! I had him right where I wanted him.

MERLIN: Really? Standing over you ready to slay you was right where you wanted him? Interesting.

ARTHUR: Well, I would rather die than be called a coward.

MERLIN: So said Caesar—and he did.

ARTHUR: I can't be saved by my court magician every time I get into a scrape!

MERLIN: *(angrily)* Who are you calling a "court magician"? Would you like to find out what it's like to be a horse's behind?

ARTHUR: I'm sure you would know plenty about that!

MERLIN: Hmph! You young people are simply infuriating!

NARRATOR: Merlin stuck the end of his beard in his mouth and chewed it angrily. A slow smile spread across Arthur's face.

ARTHUR: I am sorry, Merlin. Forgive me. I just wanted to prove that I am capable of keeping my kingdom safe.

MERLIN: Well, try to see reason! *(softly)* Arthur, you are destined to lead. But you cannot put yourself in dangerous situations. And you must be willing to take help whenever you can get it!

ARTHUR: I am willing and thankful for your help. But, just for the record, I had this knight mostly beaten. You just came in at the last minute and finished him off.

MERLIN: Keep telling yourself that.

NARRATOR: Merlin motioned to the sleeping form of Pellinore.

MERLIN: You may not believe it, but one day he will be one of your greatest allies. You will give many aimless knights like him a cause to fight for. But for now let's leave him to his dreams of dragons and damsels. We have adventuring to do.

ARTHUR: I can't. I have broken my sword in battle. It just shattered in my hand!

MERLIN: I expected as much. That sword has outlived its usefulness. Let's go.

ARTHUR: But where?

NARRATOR: Merlin was already walking briskly away through the trees. Arthur dashed to catch up.

ARTHUR: Hey! Wait up!

MERLIN: There is a sword that was crafted by the magic of the faeries—on Avalon, the isle of magic.

ARTHUR: Is it a sword for me?

MERLIN: No, it's for Henry the stable boy. Of course, it's for you! The sword is Excalibur, and none may stand against it.

ARTHUR: It sounds like a mighty weapon.

MERLIN: It is. You will require only the finest of swords to protect you. With Excalibur you will bring freedom and peace to Britain for many years. But a sword is only as good as the man who uses it. So you must guard it—and yourself—very carefully. Now, watch your step.

NARRATOR: They descended down a slippery pile of rocks. Merlin almost fell several times and grumbled loudly. Finally, they reached the bottom, and through a small stand of trees, Arthur saw a great lake spread out before them.

ARTHUR: (in awe) Heaven preserve us!

MERLIN: Nice, isn't it?

NARRATOR: The water was of the clearest blue Arthur had ever seen. Mists covered what lay in the distance.

MERLIN: Beyond the mist lies the isle of Avalon and further on the plain of Camlann, where the last battle shall be fought—where you shall be killed by an evil knight.

ARTHUR: (determined) I shall face that day bravely.

MERLIN: And that is what will get you killed! But I have said too much. Behold! In the middle of the lake, what do you see?

ARTHUR: (looking, slowly) I can barely see …a hand! A hand coming up from the water! It's clad in a shining material decorated with sparkling jewels.

MERLIN: That is pure samite, my boy!

ARTHUR: And it's holding something out of the depths…a sword! The finest I have ever seen.

MERLIN: As it should be. It is Excalibur!

ARTHUR: How shall I reach it, Merlin?

MERLIN: Don't ask me! Ask her!

NARRATOR: Then Arthur beheld her, the glowing image of a woman, walking across the misty lake. Where her feet touched the water's surface, no ripples appeared, and as she came, Arthur heard a faraway music. (heavenly music) He was entranced.

ARTHUR: (stunned) Who is she?

MERLIN: The Lady of the Lake. Don't just stand there like a stump! Go out to her!

NARRATOR: There was a tiny boat on the shore of the lake. Arthur heard that in the lady's song she was beckoning to him. He got into the boat, and it began to move across the waters of its own accord.

LADY: *(musically)* Arthur. Arthur. I am the Lady of the Lake. Do you desire the sword in the midst of this lake?

ARTHUR: I do, my lady.

LADY: Then bring your craft forward and take it. For many years, I have guarded this sword. Now, I give it freely to you, if you will give it back when the time comes.

ARTHUR: I will, my lady.

NARRATOR: Arthur was in the center of the lake now. The samite-clad hand was within his reach—dutifully holding the sword aloft. He noticed draped across the arm was also a shimmering scabbard of gold.

LADY: Take the sword. It is Excalibur. It shall serve you well.

NARRATOR: The music grew louder in his ears, and he reached out. His fingers brushed upon the sword-hilt, and he felt its power go through him. He gripped it strongly. The mystical hand let go and sank beneath the waves. Excalibur and its scabbard were his own now.

ARTHUR: *(breathlessly)* Thank you! This is the greatest gift I have ever received!

NARRATOR: Arthur looked up to thank the Lady of the Lake, but she was not there, and, indeed, the mist had risen. All magic had left the place.

ARTHUR: *(shouting)* Merlin! Look! The sword is mine!

MERLIN: *(shouting back)* Of course, it is! Now row back here quickly!

NARRATOR: Arthur found the oars within the boat and grudgingly put down his new sword to take them up. As the sword moved through the air, it sang the same song he had heard the lady sing. Somehow, it soothed him. Arthur's boat once again reached the shore.

MERLIN: Did you get the scabbard as well?

ARTHUR: Yes. I have them both.

MERLIN: *(calmly)* Come. Let us go. Tell me, which do you like better? The sword or the scabbard?

ARTHUR: The sword, of course! With it, I may cut down any enemy with a single stroke.

NARRATOR: Arthur gleefully swished the sword through the air.

MERLIN: But the scabbard is the true prize. It is worth ten swords.

ARTHUR: How?

MERLIN: Well, when the scabbard is worn, no matter how badly you are wounded, you will not bleed. Keep it close. One day, a woman will steal it from you if you are not careful.

ARTHUR: *(laughs)* A woman? Come on, Merlin. Surely, you do not think me weak enough to be tricked by a woman.

MERLIN: We shall see. Now, my young king, let us return to Camelot. You are still very green—a sapling—and you have many things to learn before you become a mighty oak. Now you have Excalibur, and like the sword that you pulled from the stone, it will help guide you to your destiny.

NARRATOR: And so the two left that place, and far away, the Lady of the Lake, in her invisible kingdom, began to sing once again. Excalibur was in the hands of a good man, and there would be peace in Britain— for a time.

DISCUSSION QUESTIONS

1. Even though Merlin has magical powers, why does he tell the archbishop to pray for a miracle?
2. How did Arthur's childhood with Sir Ector make him a better person than if he had been raised as a prince?
3. How do the two swords in the story resemble and differ from each other? What purpose does each one serve?
4. The sins of Uther, Arthur's father, will follow him all the way through his life. Some decisions parents make affect their children positively, and others affect them negatively. What are some examples of both from real life?
5. What role does Merlin fill in Arthur's life? Explain.
6. What qualities will make Arthur a good king? Explain.
7. If you were made the ruler of the country at age sixteen, do you think anyone would oppose *your* rule? Explain.
8. How would the world be different if young people ruled it?

SHADOWS OF THE PAST
TEACHER GUIDE

BACKGROUND

Probably the most famous version of the King Arthur legends is Sir Thomas Malory's *Le Morte D'Arthur*, first published in 1485. In his work Malory fused the many previous versions of the Arthurian legends into a complex and sprawling narrative. *Le Morte D'Arthur* (French for "the death of Arthur") was a title added by the work's publisher. This title is an odd choice and a bit misleading because Malory's work tells about the entire story of King Arthur's life.

What about the author, Thomas Malory, himself? Not much is known about his life. Malory makes many comments in *Le Morte D'Arthur* alluding to the fact that he is writing his work while in prison. Records from the time period show that charges such as burglary, rape (abduction of a female), sheep-stealing, and ambushing a duke were leveled against him. It is a still a subject of debate whether or not these charges were legitimate. Malory had powerful enemies who could have easily framed him. In his writing Malory seems so devoted to the ideals of chivalry that it's hard to believe that he was in reality a criminal. In a postscript to his work, Malory, calling himself a "knight-prisoner," asks all the gentle men and women who read his work to pray for his speedy release.

SUMMARY

Bored by the day-to-day rituals of courtly life, Arthur longs for his bygone days of battle. While Merlin is away, Arthur receives a visitor at court, Queen Margawse, the wife of King Lot of Orkney—one of Arthur's former enemies. Arthur invites the beautiful Margawse to feast with him and loses himself in drink. When Arthur awakes the next morning, Merlin returns and delivers some troubling news. Arthur has spent the night with Margawse. Her mission had been to learn what information she could, and with her mission accomplished she has returned to Orkney. Even worse, Merlin tells him that she is his half-sister, the daughter of the Duke of Tintagel and the Lady Igraine. From their union Margawse will bear a child that will one day destroy Arthur's kingdom. Merlin leaves Camelot again, this time to consult with his master, Blaise.

Meanwhile, Arthur learns that Igraine, his mother, still lives, and he sends for her to be brought to Camelot. With her Igraine brings Arthur's youngest half-sister, Morgan. Morgan spends her time studying ancient manuscripts in Camelot's library. Soon afterward, Arthur receives a prophecy from Merlin: Arthur's son will be born on May Day.

Morgan spends her days studying books of necromancy, but Arthur believes her to be his ally. She asks him what is troubling him, and he tells the dilemma of the child who will be his doom. Since Arthur does not know how to find the child, Morgan suggests that he murder all the newborn babies in Britain. This will make sure the threat of his illegitimate son is neutralized. Arthur follows her suggestion. All the newborn babies of the kingdom (including Arthur's son) are gathered, loaded onto a boat, and pushed out to sea.

Outraged by this act, several kings of Britain lead a rebellion against Arthur, but they are defeated. When Merlin returns, he finds Arthur upon the field of battle—victorious but wounded. He chides Arthur for allowing Morgan to lead him into such folly and suggests that he remove her from Camelot at once. Arthur arranges a marriage for Morgan with King Uriens of Gore and sends her away. As Morgan is riding away, she receives a vision. Arthur's child has survived the wreck of the ship and will be raised by a king who will find him upon the beach. Morgan begins to plot her revenge against Arthur.

ESSENTIAL QUESTIONS

- How do you know someone is trustworthy?
- Why are evil deeds still evil—even though they are done for a good cause?

ANTICIPATORY QUESTIONS

- What is necromancy?
- How do you know someone is trustworthy?
- Why are evil deeds still evil—even though they are done for a good cause?

CHARACTER QUEST

- **Evil Deeds for a Good Cause** Morgan tells Arthur that he must do something evil to bring about good. How is this flawed reasoning? How does his evil act only bring about more evil? How can we apply this to our own lives?
- **Trustworthiness** Arthur is fooled by two of his half-sisters, Margawse and Morgan. What were some clues that they were not trustworthy? Should Arthur have been more perceptive? In your own life how do you know when someone is trustworthy or not?

CONNECT

Merlin (1998) This television miniseries retells the legends of Arthur from Merlin's point-of-view. Merlin aids Arthur in establishing his kingdom, but Camelot begins to crumble through the schemes of a supernatural being called Queen Mab and her henchwoman, Morgan le Fay.

TEACHABLE TERMS

- **May Day** First mentioned on pg. 55, this ancient springtime festival is celebrated on the first day of May in many cultures.
- **Imagery** The description of Morgan in the library "her fingers clenching and unclenching mechanically as her bright eyes scanned the book before her" on pg. 55 is an example of imagery. "Her eyes shining cat-like in the darkness" on pg. 57 is another example.
- **Personification** "The keel growled as the young men pushed the barge out to sea" on pg. 59 is an example of personification. The *keel* is the beam which runs lengthwise along the underbelly of a ship.
- **Infer** As the story progresses, the reader is given clues that Morgan harbors hostility toward Arthur and his kingdom. What details help the reader infer that Morgan is up to something?

RECALL QUESTIONS

1. How is Queen Margawse connected to King Arthur?
2. Who is Blaise?
3. On what day will King Arthur's child be born?
4. How does King Arthur try to make sure his child does not survive?
5. Who talks Arthur into this plan?

SHADOWS OF THE PAST

CAST

ARTHUR	*King of Britain*
MERLIN	*The Good Enchanter*
KAY	*Arthur's Seneschal*
ULFIUS	*Trusted Knight*
MARGAWSE	*Queen of Orkney*
IGRAINE	*Mother of Arthur*
MORGAN	*Half-sister of Arthur*
GAWAIN	*Son of Margawse*
LOT	*King of Orkney*
URIENS	*King of Gore*

NARRATOR: For the first time in years Britain was at peace, united under Arthur the High King. While Arthur dispensed justice from his court at Camelot, his valiant knights kept the country safe from villains, rogues, and bandits. Although Arthur felt a great deal of personal satisfaction in seeing his kingdom flourish, he felt an emptiness inside that he could not describe. Finally, he confided in his old mentor and friend, Merlin the wizard.

ARTHUR: Merlin, are you ever lonely?

MERLIN: If by lonely, you mean alone—then, yes. Eternally. Ever since I was a little boy, I have been...

ARTHUR: Different. Strange. Odd.

MERLIN: I'll supply my own adjectives, thank you. But that's the general idea. Although being...special made me lonely, it also gave me the power to change things. So I learned to live with my loneliness and committed myself to changing this country. And through you, I believe I have.

ARTHUR: I know. I wouldn't trade anything for Camelot or all the good it's done.

MERLIN: And this is just the beginning. Camelot will become mightier yet. I can't help feeling great pride in this. You, Arthur, are my legacy. But I fear I have passed my loneliness onto you. It's an unfortunate side effect of being a leader.

ARTHUR: At least other rulers have a family to give them comfort.

MERLIN: What am I? Chopped liver?

ARTHUR: You know what I mean. Blood relatives. Parents, brothers, sisters.

MERLIN: Ha! Family is a horrible burden for a king. His relatives are like a brood of vipers—all waiting for him to falter so they can sink their fangs into him.

ARTHUR: So a king cannot even trust his own family?

MERLIN: Especially not his family.

ARTHUR: Sometimes I think you're too cynical, Merlin.

MERLIN: No. Just realistic. *(pause)* Cheer up, my boy! I hate to see you like this. You've accomplished too much in your short life to feel distraught.

ARTHUR: Perhaps you are right.

MERLIN: That's the spirit. Now, tomorrow I must be off again. More business abroad. But I will return soon. Make sure Camelot is still standing when I return. *(chuckle)* Ha!

NARRATOR: The following day, as Arthur sat upon his throne receiving guests and petitions from his people, a fanfare of trumpets announced a special visitor. *(fanfare)* An elegant lady wearing a striking green gown paraded into the presence of the king. Walking stately at her heels were her four sons. Sir Kay, Arthur's foster-brother and seneschal, stood forward with a smirk to greet the lady.

KAY: *(snottily)* Well, well, well. If it isn't Queen Margawse of Orkney—the wife of the traitor, King Lot! You have a lot of nerve to show yourself in this court!

ARTHUR: Kay! Regardless of what has passed between me and Lot, we must greet this lady graciously.

MARGAWSE: Noble king, I have come from our distant kingdom to present myself and my sons at court.

KAY: Where is your husband? At home plotting another rebellion?

ARTHUR: Kay! The past is the past.

KAY: *(grumbling)* Once a rebel—always a rebel, I say.

MARGAWSE: *(ignoring Kay)* My lord, you are most gracious! As a sign of our goodwill, I have brought our oldest son, Gawain, to leave here at your court as a squire.

NARRATOR: The tallest boy, a strong-looking lad around the age of twelve, stepped forward.

GAWAIN: My king, I will do my best to serve you.

KAY: Perhaps *he* will be more loyal than his father was!

ARTHUR: Ignore him, Gawain. I accept your service. Queen Margawse, tonight we will feast! I am sorry that your husband could not visit Camelot himself.

KAY: *(sarcastically)* Yes. We'd especially like to give him a tour of our dungeons!

NARRATOR: A banquet was held that evening in Camelot. The king seated the elegant queen next to him and feasted happily. Partially to drown his loneliness, Arthur overindulged in the royal wine.

ARTHUR: *(drunkenly)* My lady, it is a shame that you cannot visit my hall more often. You are a charming creature! The isolated isles of Orkney must be a lonely place for you.

MARGAWSE: It's true, my lord. I am very lonely. My husband has little time for me. Your compliments are the first I have received in a long time.

ARTHUR: A shame! You are truly a stunning woman!

NARRATOR: The queen laid her hand gently on the king's arm.

MARGAWSE: You, too, my lord, are most handsome. Whoever will be your queen is a lucky woman.

NARRATOR: The king smiled.

ARTHUR: Steward, more wine!

NARRATOR: For Arthur the rest of the evening was lost in a haze.

The next thing Arthur knew, he was in his royal chambers with the morning light shining through the window. He shielded his eyes from the enemy sun. Then he noticed the dark form of Merlin seated upon the edge of his bed.

ARTHUR: Merlin? What are you doing here? Has something happened?

MERLIN: You tell me! Your—ahem—visitor showed herself out hours ago. It's nearly noon now.

ARTHUR: Visitor?

MERLIN: Queen Margawse of Orkney.

ARTHUR: What? You mean—last night? Oh no! Tell me I did not!

MERLIN: Don't sound so shocked! This seems to run in your family—going after other men's wives. Your father was Uther Pendragon, but your mother was married to another.

ARTHUR: Please don't lecture me, Merlin. I feel bad enough as it is.

MERLIN: You will feel much worse after this next bit of information. When Lady Igraine—that is your mother—married your father, she already had three daughters by her first husband. *(pointedly)* And Lady Margawse was one of those daughters. I know you wanted to be closer to your family, but this is ridiculous.

NARRATOR: Arthur's face went pale, and his stomach turned.

ARTHUR: *(breathlessly)* Queen Margawse is my half-sister? What have I done?

MERLIN: I think what you have done is obvious. What you have said is another matter. There's no telling what secrets you let slip last night.

ARTHUR: Can she not be trusted?

MERLIN: Of course, not! She is as devious as a cat. Her mission was obvious—to get information out of you any way she could. Now she is taking that information back to her husband. She left for Orkney this morning with her sons. Well, three of them anyway.

ARTHUR: Why just three?

MERLIN: Her oldest, Gawain, is to be trained as a knight, so he will remain here.

ARTHUR: *(angrily)* Send him back to his parents! We won't have the son of two traitors here in Camelot!

MERLIN: Do not judge the child by the parents. How would you fare if we judged you by your parents?

ARTHUR: Oh, Merlin! She has tricked me completely! How could I be so blind?

MERLIN: I have not told you the worst of it.

ARTHUR: What? There's more?

MERLIN: Margawse will conceive a child.

ARTHUR: Impossible!

MERLIN: Possible! Maybe I should have spent more time on your education! This child was probably not part of her original plan, but it will become a pawn for her and King Lot to use against you. She now carries the only heir to the throne—*your* throne.

ARTHUR: (*thoughtfully*) I will have a son.

MERLIN: A son—a monster. If you don't intervene, she will bear the child that will destroy your kingdom.

ARTHUR: What must I do?

MERLIN: I do not know yet. There are evil forces vying against your kingdom—forces that are not of this world. You do not only struggle against flesh and blood, but also against the unseen powers of the air! I must go to consult my old master, Blaise. He lives in the deep woods of Northumberland.

ARTHUR: (*in shock*) *Your* old master is still alive? He must be old indeed!

MERLIN: Keep your wisecracks to yourself! He is ancient—but wiser by far than you will ever be. Maybe he can give me guidance about the future.

ARTHUR: How long will you be gone?

MERLIN: Until I have answers.

ARTHUR: Merlin, what shall I do in the meantime? I am filled with dread!

MERLIN: Camelot must continue. Life must go on.

ARTHUR: I hate myself for making this mistake. What if I fail again?

MERLIN: We all fail, Arthur. But we must learn from our mistakes and press on.

NARRATOR: Arthur saw the old man no more that day, and on the morrow his servants reported that Merlin had ridden from Camelot in the early morning.

Arthur sat brooding in his throne room, mulling Merlin's words over in his mind. He called in Sir Kay and Sir Ulfius, an elderly knight of the court, to counsel him.

ARTHUR: A child threatens our kingdom. What must I do?

KAY: A child? How can a child threaten a kingdom?

ARTHUR: The Queen of Orkney carries my illegitimate child.

NARRATOR: The knights raised their eyebrows in shock.

KAY: Well, brother. You're telling us that your heir will be living in the court of one of our greatest enemies?

ARTHUR: Yes.

KAY: Then the child must be killed.

ARTHUR: Kill a child?

KAY: It's a security threat. It must be destroyed.

ULFIUS: Sire, if I may interject.

ARTHUR: Yes, Ulfius. What say you?

ULFIUS: Lot will never give you access to this child or his wife. If you try to do away with it, you risk yet another war with him.

KAY: Who cares? Lot deserves to be destroyed for what he has tried in the past!

ULFIUS: My king, I counseled your father when he warred against the Duke of Tintagel. I told him that no man would give up his wife without a fight.

ARTHUR: My mother. You're speaking of my mother, aren't you?

ULFIUS: Yes, the lady Igraine.

ARTHUR: Merlin told me of her only recently.

ULFIUS: She is a fine woman.

ARTHUR: Is? Does she still live?

ULFIUS: Of course, sire. Didn't you know?

ARTHUR: I did not! Where does she reside?

ULFIUS: After the death of your father, she took up residence at a nunnery, but I know her whereabouts.

ARTHUR: Go at once! She must be brought to Camelot!

ULFIUS: I will, sire!

NARRATOR: As the old knight was dispatched, Kay sneered.

KAY: My father, Ector, raised you, and my mother nourished you. Why do you want to mess with this Igraine person?

ARTHUR: She is my true mother, and I have never met her! Can you imagine how that feels?

KAY: No, I was a *legitimate* child. Speaking of that, what will you do about the Orkney child?

ARTHUR: I will just have to delay judgment on that for now.

NARRATOR: Several days later, Sir Ulfius returned to Camelot with two female guests in tow. One was an elderly woman—her gown simple and her hair white. She was Igraine, who had once been Uther Pendragon's queen, but now was little more than a forgotten widow. The second was a wise-looking girl with raven-black hair. Arthur greeted them joyfully.

ARTHUR: Igraine, welcome to Camelot!

NARRATOR: At the sight of her long-lost son, the old woman's eyes welled up with tears.

IGRAINE: My child, I thought I would never see you again! The last time I saw you, you were but a day old—wrapped in a cloth of gold.

NARRATOR: Arthur embraced the old woman. He had been hoping for an instant connection when they touched, but for some reason, her embrace left him strangely cold.

ARTHUR: When you heard that they made me king, why did you not come to me?

IGRAINE: Fear. I feared that you would not want a mother who gave you up like I did.

ARTHUR: It has all worked out for the best—as you can see.

IGRAINE: Yes! You remind me so much of your father—my darling Uther. *(sigh)* First I lost you. Then I lost him. I have not seen my older two daughters since their wedding days many years ago. All I have left is my little Morgan.

NARRATOR: She indicated the dark-haired girl who stood submissively behind her.

IGRAINE: I know I deserve nothing from you, Arthur, but please, grant me one request. Morgan is your half-sister, and these many years she has buried herself in books. She has no suitors because our position is now so lowly. Find her a royal match. Then my heart can rest easily.

NARRATOR: Arthur gazed on Morgan. In her he saw much of the same beauty he had seen in Margawse. Yet there also seemed to be innocence there, too. In response to his gaze, Morgan curtsied low to the ground.

ARTHUR: No need to bow! You are my sister, and you are most welcome at Camelot!

MORGAN: I thank you, noble King Arthur. I've heard many stories about Camelot and your court here, but I have only desired to see one thing.

ARTHUR: And what is that?

MORGAN: The library. Is it true that you have your very own?

ARTHUR: Of course! The holy monks prepared one for me in honor of my kingship!

NARRATOR: A wave of excitement passed over Morgan's face.

MORGAN: I went to school in a nunnery, and I must have read every parchment they owned there ten times.

IGRAINE: No wonder you never caught yourself a man! You were hidden away, reading!

MORGAN: Mother, what man would go to a nunnery looking for a wife?

ARTHUR: Ha! She is a clever girl! We will find her an excellent match!

IGRAINE: Oh, I hope you do! She is so hungry for knowledge. I wish she was as hungry for a husband.

NARRATOR: Igraine was given the position of Royal Mother. Morgan became a lady of the court as well—although she spent most of her time combing the dusty shelves of Camelot's library for its most ancient texts. Arthur took an active part in the knightly training of his nephew, Gawain. For the first time it was if the young king had a true family, and his loneliness left him.

Spring came, and Merlin had still not returned. One day a crow alighted on the walls of Camelot. A tiny scroll was attached to its leg. The men-at-arms removed the message and brought it to the king.

ARTHUR: It must be from Merlin!

NARRATOR: Arthur quickly deciphered the old man's scrawled handwriting.

MERLIN: (*voiceover*) Dear Arthur, Blaise has shown me much about the future. I will tell you all when I return, but I must get you this one message: I have discovered that the child of Margawse will be born upon May Day. Use this information as you will. Cordially, M.

ARTHUR: (*to himself*) May Day! That is fast approaching! But what can be done?

NARRATOR: Arthur's thoughts were interrupted by his royal mother.

IGRAINE: Arthur, I need your help.

ARTHUR: Yes, my lady.

IGRAINE: Perhaps you can speak to Morgan for me. Camelot is the perfect place to meet men, but ever since we arrived, she spends all her time in the library, poring over old documents! How will she ever catch the eye of a lord or knight if she always has her nose stuck in a book?

ARTHUR: (*distractedly*) Of course, my lady. I will speak to her.

NARRATOR: The library of Camelot was situated deep within the castle. Piles of scrolls, papers, and books covered the small room, which was lit only by a single flickering lamp. Morgan was seated there, her fingers clenching and unclenching mechanically as her bright eyes scanned a book before her. She did not see her kingly brother enter the room.

ARTHUR: Interesting reading?

MORGAN: (*gasping*) Ah!

NARRATOR: Morgan quickly slammed the thick book shut—throwing a dervish of dust into the air.

MORGAN: You startled me!

NARRATOR: Arthur drew nearer and glanced at the Latin inscription upon the book's cover.

ARTHUR: A strange choice of reading for a young lady. Have you been interested in necromancy long?

MORGAN: (*laughing*) Of course, not! I admit I am fascinated by the dark arts, but it's just a morbid curiosity I have!

ARTHUR: Your mother—I mean, *our* mother wanted me to talk to you about this. She says that you read too much.

MORGAN: (*laugh*) I'm afraid that Mother is still trying to make a lady out of me. But I cannot rest when I know there is more knowledge to be had.

ARTHUR: I am not much for reading. Merlin reads these books often. He is always telling me about the great men of the past—their rise and fall. I think you would like him a lot.

MORGAN: What is he like, brother?

ARTHUR: Oh, he is cantankerous. But his heart is good, and his powers are miraculous.

NARRATOR: Morgan's eyes shone at the mention of Merlin's powers.

MORGAN: You look on him like a father, don't you?

NARRATOR: Arthur was taken aback by this comment.

ARTHUR: I guess I do. Why do you say that?

MORGAN: I can see it in your eyes. Not that I know much about fathers. You see, mine died when I was just a little girl. I just remember fragments of him—wisps and bits here and there really.

ARTHUR: That must be terrible for you.

MORGAN: Not really. Time heals all wounds and rights all wrongs.

ARTHUR: At least you had a chance to know your father. You are lucky in that respect.

MORGAN: (*sudden anger*) Lucky? I would not say it was luck to have him murdered and taken away from me!

ARTHUR: Oh. I didn't mean anything by that. You see, I never knew my true father—Uther Pendragon.

NARRATOR: It may have been the flickering of the lamp, but Arthur thought he saw Morgan's lips quiver at the mention of his father's name.

MORGAN: You wish you could know more about him—about your family. That's why you summoned Mother and me here.

ARTHUR: Well, yes. How did—?

MORGAN: I can see things. Mother calls it my intuition.

ARTHUR: What else can you tell about me, Morgan?

MORGAN: Let me see your hand.

NARRATOR: The girl took her brother's hand into her own.

MORGAN: I can see you are troubled. A thought is always gnawing at your mind.

ARTHUR: It is.

MORGAN: You have a dilemma that you need solved, but you do not know how to solve it.

ARTHUR: (*eagerly*) Morgan, can you see? Can you see how to solve the problem?

MORGAN: (*slyly*) Arthur! Such powers are of the devil. What makes you think I possess such powers?

ARTHUR: Merlin uses magic, but his magic is not of the devil.

MORGAN: Hmmm. (*pause*) I cannot tell you the solution if I do not know what the problem is. What is troubling you?

NARRATOR: There in the darkness of the Camelot library, Arthur unfolded his heart to his half-sister. He told her of his affair with Margawse, who was just as much a stranger to Morgan as she had been to him. Morgan listened to all this intently.

ARTHUR: So you see, all of this—all of Camelot—is in danger of being destroyed.

MORGAN: *(strangely)* A shame.

ARTHUR: Unless I devise a way to avoid this catastrophe.

MORGAN: It is true that if you try to remove the child by force, Lot will have a cause against you. He will declare himself wronged. He will claim that the child was his own, and you murdered his son. It will be war.

ARTHUR: Then what can be done?

MORGAN: *(suddenly forceful)* You must collect all the newborn babies in the kingdom—and dispose of them.

ARTHUR: *(in shock)* What?

MORGAN: It is the only way. If all the babies die then it will be fair. Tell them there is a prophecy concerning a child born upon May Day—that it threatens the kingdom.

ARTHUR: They will never agree.

MORGAN: They must or they are not your subjects.

ARTHUR: I can't kill innocent children!

MORGAN: Then Camelot must fall, brother.

ARTHUR: It is evil—cruel!

MORGAN: You have brought so much good into this land. Think of all the good that will be lost if this act is *not* committed. How many children will die if your knights are not there to protect them? So I ask you, which is the greater evil? A small sacrifice—or losing Camelot forever.

NARRATOR: Arthur quickly departed, leaving Morgan alone in the library once again. Her eyes shone cat-like in the darkness, as her fingers traced ancient words, and her lips pronounced them.

That night horrific images haunted Arthur's dreams—flames of war raging across Britain, the towers of Camelot crumbling, children crying out in the darkness. The next morning Arthur, haggard and worn, went again to see Morgan.

ARTHUR: If I do what you say must be done, how can I explain it to my people?

MORGAN: Tell them it was a prophecy of Merlin. This will convince them.

ARTHUR: I can't blame this act on him!

MORGAN: You're not *blaming* it on him. You're telling the truth. He is the one who told you about the birth of the child, right?

ARTHUR: Yes, but—

MORGAN: Then there is no lie in your words.

ARTHUR: What if the lords rebel?

MORGAN: They have rebelled once and failed. Arthur, you are the most powerful king this land has ever seen. They will comply and will see no evil in your actions. You are acting under Merlin's orders.

ARTHUR: And this will be successful?

MORGAN: Yes. This act will achieve its goal. I have seen it. *(pause)* Trust me, Arthur. I am your sister, and I want what is best for you.

ARTHUR: I must think on this.

NARRATOR: Over the following nights Arthur knew no sleep—his nightmares growing more vivid.

ARTHUR: It is a heinous act, yet it will save many lives! I have done something horrible by siring this child. But I'll have to do something worse to undo it.

NARRATOR: When May Day was only a few days away, Arthur summoned Sir Ulfius to him. The knight noticed dark rings under the king's eyes.

ARTHUR: Ulfius, I am to give a strange decree. All my knights must ride forth—through all of Britain—and collect all the newborn babies in the land.

ULFIUS: Sire? Collecting babies?

ARTHUR: *(angrily)* Do you question your king?

ULFIUS: No, sire. But might I ask what should be done with them?

ARTHUR: Place them all upon a barge and push it out to sea. Then, think on it no longer.

ULFIUS: But so many innocent children! Sire, I don't think—

ARTHUR: I didn't ask you to think. Just follow my orders.

ULFIUS: You asked for my advice before—

ARTHUR: And I do not need it now.

NARRATOR: The old knight was shocked by Arthur's sharp words but recovered his composure.

ULFIUS: *(coldly)* I will do as you command.

NARRATOR: The decree went out. Any newborn child must be given up to the knights of the king—or be taken by force. The knights rode forth into every castle and simple shanty of the land. All newborn babes were ripped from their mother's pleading arms.

When the king's decree reached Lot's castle in Orkney, Margawse's labor pains had already begun.

MARGAWSE: No! He won't have this child! This son of mine will sit on his throne!

LOT: Hide her on the mainland. Take her to a peasant's hut. They will not search there. Deliver the child and return it here.

MARGAWSE: *(cry of pain)* Ah!

LOT: Hurry!

NARRATOR: But the knights of Arthur were thorough. They entered the hiding place of Margawse, just after her baby boy had been delivered. She sat in a peasant's hut nursing the newborn heir to Britain.

When the knights burst in, Margawse knew at once that her plans had failed. She fell upon her child and screeched.

MARGAWSE: *(crazy)* You shall not have him! He is mine! He is mine!

NARRATOR: But the knights threw her roughly aside and took the screaming baby. *(wailing child)*

Meanwhile, Sir Ulfius waited by the seashore for all the knights to return. This grisly business had taken days—even with their great speed. A weather-worn barge sat in the shallows. Squires were loading the crying newborns into the bottom of the boat. Many of the squires wept and averted their eyes in shame.

ULFIUS: *(emotionless)* Have all the knights reported in?

NARRATOR: The squires nodded their heads.

ULFIUS: I saw many dark days under Uther, but I never saw a deed as foul as this. Today is Britain's darkest day. Now push the vessel out to sea.

NARRATOR: The keel growled as the young men pushed the barge out to sea. The wailing of the babies grew fainter and fainter as the ship wandered adrift out over the waves. Soon, all their cries were lost in the gathering mist.

In his court for weeks afterward, Arthur had many troubles. The plan had not worked as flawlessly as Morgan had predicted. The lords and knights of Britain were infuriated. King Lot himself was there to lead the host of angry noblemen. How dare Arthur take their children from them? Even those who did not lose their own child brought the outrages of their people to Arthur's feet and cried them furiously.

ARTHUR: *(yelling)* People! People! I am sorry for your losses, but this thing had to be done! I received a prophecy from Merlin—

URIENS: There is the evil in this! It was a plan of Merlin, that son of a devil!

ARTHUR: No! No! It was for the good of the kingdom!

LOT: Where is that old warlock anyway? I bet he wanted our children as a sacrifice!

ARTHUR: That's ridiculous! A child was born on May Day—a child that would destroy this kingdom. I have taken care of the problem.

NARRATOR: King Lot, snarling, pointed an accusing finger at Arthur.

LOT: A likely story! You just wanted to kill our heirs! You wanted to wipe out our lines! Just because *you* have no son does not mean you have a right to take ours!

ARTHUR: Are you threatening your king, Lot?

LOT: And what if I am? How can we live under such a tyrant?

ARTHUR: Once already you have rebelled against me! And yet I spared you and allowed you to live! Do you challenge me again?

LOT: I do! You were a coward not to kill me the first time! All who defy this unjust king must rally to *my* banner!

(shouts of agreement)

NARRATOR: Many of the lords left in anger that day and began to muster their armies. War threatened Camelot once again.

Making his way down through the castle, Arthur found his half-sister in the library and angrily confronted her.

ARTHUR: *(angrily)* You did not tell me that this course of action would lead to more warfare!

MORGAN: *(calmly)* Arthur, you carry Excalibur. These wicked kings cannot stand against you. They will fall, and then you will have wiped out even more of your enemies.

ARTHUR: But it was not as you said.

MORGAN: I cannot see *all* of the future. At least now you can rest easy knowing that your illegitimate child is no more. Isn't that what you wanted?

ARTHUR: I wanted what was best for my people!

NARRATOR: As Arthur prepared for battle, he did not know that his struggles had all been for nothing. The ship of babes broke up on the churning waves and sank as it was meant to—but one child survived. Borne upon a piece of wreckage, a swaddled child was carried by the currents to a seaside castle, where he was found by the kind lord who lived there. Unbeknownst to the rest of the world, the child, Arthur's son, had lived.

A week later Merlin finally returned to Camelot. The battlefield before the castle was littered with slain warriors. The wizard noted this calmly, guiding his white donkey through the charred remains of barricades until at last he found Arthur himself—the blood of battle still upon his armor.

MERLIN: You have been busy while I was away.

ARTHUR: Lot and his allies brought a great army against me. Camelot has survived. Barely.

MERLIN: Tell me how this came to be.

NARRATOR: Arthur told Merlin all that had befallen. The old enchanter listened silently.

ARTHUR: I was so eager to erase my first mistake that I made an even bigger one. I took so many innocent lives. *(pause)* I am not fit to be king.

MERLIN: And yet your kingdom needs you now more than ever.

ARTHUR: How can I ever face them again after what I have done?

MERLIN: If you repent, Heaven will forgive you—and I suspect your people will, too. This is an important lesson. The mistakes of lesser men affect only themselves. Your mistakes affect the lives of thousands.

ARTHUR: *(thoughtfully)* I have been a fool. But I will spend the rest of my life making it up to them.

MERLIN: While there is no excuse for your actions, I fear you have been led astray. Didn't I tell you that your half-sisters hate you?

ARTHUR: Well, yes, but I thought Morgan was different. She seemed to be a true sister.

MERLIN: *(sarcastically)* Let's see. She convinced you to murder a boat-load of babies, started a civil war, and blamed the entire thing on me. She sounds lovely.

ARTHUR: I don't understand why she would want to harm me and my kingdom.

MERLIN: Your father killed her father, and she has never forgotten it. It's textbook revenge. You can spare her life if you want to. But, please, send her away from Camelot.

ARTHUR: I guess I was so enamored with the idea of having a family that it blinded me.

MERLIN: Family is what you make it, Arthur. Choose those who are loyal to you to be your family. Do not let blood decide that for you.

ARTHUR: You are right, Merlin. *(sigh)* At least one good thing has come of all this. King Lot has been slain. I'll never see his smug face again!

MERLIN: Neither will his family. And now his half-orphaned son is a squire in your court.

ARTHUR: Must I send Gawain away, too? He has been training so diligently!

MERLIN: Do not send him away. You have taken his father from him. The least you can do is train him up to be a good man. There is still hope for him.

ARTHUR: Did your master show you all this?

MERLIN: No. But Blaise has shown me much of the future. I have seen that my own time is short.

NARRATOR: Merlin surveyed the battlefield once again.

MERLIN: I saw another battle much like this one.

ARTHUR: In the future? Was it a battle that I will win? I must know what lies ahead.

MERLIN: Simply knowing what calamities lie in the future does not prevent them from happening. Fate does not change. A higher power governs us all.

ARTHUR: Then there is no hope?

MERLIN: There is always hope!

NARRATOR: The old wizard motioned for Arthur to follow.

MERLIN: Now, come. Let us fix this mess.

NARRATOR: When Arthur returned to Camelot, he did as Merlin had instructed him and found a way to dispose of Morgan. He arranged a marriage with King Uriens of Gore and then summoned Morgan and Igraine to him.

MORGAN: Brother! I am so thankful that you survived the battle.

ARTHUR: Is that so? I have made a decision. It is time you were married.

IGRAINE: Oh! At last! At last!

MORGAN: Married? But, Arthur, my place is here—by your side!

ARTHUR: I have already spoken with King Uriens of Gore. He desires a wife, and you shall be his.

MORGAN: *(forcefully)* I have no desire to marry some old buffoon!

ARTHUR: *(coldly)* Your desires no longer matter. I am the king, and I command it.

You shall go to the land of Gore—faraway and forgotten.

MORGAN: But I do not wish to go.

ARTHUR: I have spoken.

MORGAN: (*coldly*) I see.

IGRAINE: (*happily*) Oh, my dears! This is the happiest day of my life! What a wedding we will have!

MORGAN: Grrrr.

NARRATOR: Morgan turned and stormed from the throne room. Soon after she was wedded to King Uriens of Gore. Following the celebrations, the kingly groom rode away with his grimacing bride.

As Arthur watched their departure, it seemed as if a cloud of gloom was lifted from his mind.

ARTHUR: Farewell, sister. Enjoy your new life.

NARRATOR: Morgan saw her brother watching her departure from the battlements.

MORGAN: (*to herself*) You have not seen the last of me, brother. My first attempt to ruin your kingdom may have failed, but I will try again. You can make me a prisoner-bride to this old fool—thinking that will get rid of me. But I will use this to my advantage. I will return when you least expect it. And I will have my revenge!

URIENS: (*happily*) My beautiful bride! I know this arrangement is still new to you, but Gore is a beautiful place. You will grow to love it!

MORGAN: (*grumbling*) I doubt that.

NARRATOR: Suddenly, a vision passed before Morgan's eyes.

MORGAN: (*gasp*) Wait a minute!

NARRATOR: A screaming child was lying amid a pile of wreckage on a rocky beach. An old man bent over the child and carried him back to a nearby castle.

MORGAN: He lives! The child lives! (*loud laughter*)

NARRATOR: Morgan's laughter caused Uriens to grin.

URIENS: See? You are feeling better already!

NARRATOR: Morgan continued to laugh as she and her husband disappeared down the road.

DISCUSSION QUESTIONS

1. What mistakes does Arthur make in this story? Explain.
2. Why does Arthur have "issues" with his identity in relationship to his parents?
3. Many episodes in the King Arthur legends have similarities to biblical stories. What biblical story does the episode involving the newborn babies parallel?
4. Do Arthur's actions make him a bad person? Explain.
5. Why does Morgan want to destroy Arthur and his kingdom?
6. What makes Morgan a formidable adversary?
7. How do you think Morgan will take her revenge?

THE BRIDE OF THE KING
TEACHER GUIDE

BACKGROUND

Marriage during the Middle Ages seldom involved love. The parents of the bride and groom almost always arranged their children's marriages. Instead of being romanticized, these unions were practical. The wealthy class married off their children to obtain a dowry (land and goods associated with the bride) or to link their household with a title such as duke or lord. Only the poor were free to consider love in their marriage arrangements, but even impoverished fathers still held power over whom their daughters married.

This story about the meeting of Arthur and Guinevere puts a romantic spin on their union and unsurprisingly was not part of the original King Arthur legends. It was created by Howard Pyle, an American author who re-told the legends for younger readers. Perhaps Pyle felt a need to explain Arthur's deep love for Guinevere. In spite of the episode's absence in the original stories, it helps develop Arthur and Guinevere's characters.

SUMMARY

Guinevere becomes the object of Arthur's affections after the king is wounded in a joust and she tends his wounds—not knowing that she is nursing the king. Afterward, Arthur tells Merlin about his love of Guinevere. Merlin suggests if Arthur really loves her, Arthur should learn her true nature by disguising himself as a servant in her court. To accomplish this, the wizard gives Arthur a magical cap that will change his appearance into that of a peasant.

Arthur enters the service of King Leodegrance, Guinevere's father, as a garden servant and secretly observes the damsel that he loves. Soon distressing news reaches the court. Duke Rience of the neighboring kingdom has threatened war if Leodegrance does not give him Guinevere. The duke has a grisly habit of removing his enemies' beards and using them to line his cloak. Terrified by the duke's threat, Leodegrance is powerless to resist him and promises to deliver up Guinevere. The disguised Arthur hears this and vows to prevent Guinevere's marriage to this villain.

In secret Arthur purchases armor from Ralph, a local merchant, and disguises himself as an anonymous white knight. When Duke Rience arrives to claim Guinevere, the White Knight appears and challenges him to a duel. In the battle Duke Rience is killed. But before Guinevere can discover the true identity of her liberator, Arthur rides away and secretly returns to his life as a servant.

Soon after this event Guinevere is gazing down from her chamber window when she spies the same handsome knight cleaning his face in the castle fountain. She runs down to meet him, but when she arrives, it is only the garden-boy seated by the fountain. (Arthur had transformed by accident when he removed his hat to wipe the sweat from his brow.)

As Guinevere questions the garden-boy about the knight who was just there, she sees a golden medallion lying beside his foot. Piecing the clues together, Guinevere realizes that the garden-boy is secretly the White Knight and demands that he remove his hat. When he protests, she snatches the hat from his head, and he transforms into his true form.

The Road to Camelot

Arthur asks Leodegrance for Guinevere's hand in marriage, and he agrees and, as a wedding present, promises to give Arthur a round table that once belonged to Arthur's father. Merlin arrives and questions Arthur about Guinevere's intentions, but the young king tells Merlin the marriage has already been arranged.

ESSENTIAL QUESTIONS

- How well should you know someone before marriage?
- Is there such a thing as love at first sight?
- Should you tell a friend the truth, even when you doubt he or she will listen?

ANTICIPATORY QUESTIONS

- Who was the wife of King Arthur?
- How were marriages arranged in medieval times?
- Where did King Arthur get the Round Table?
- If you were a king, would you willingly live life as a peasant? Explain.

CHARACTER QUEST

- **True Nature** In this story Arthur wants to learn Guinevere's true nature. Why did Merlin think it was important for Arthur to get to know Guinevere before he married her? Why is it a good practice to learn everything you can about a person before you commit to him or her?

CONNECT

- *King Arthur* (2004) This action film attempts to show what a "real-life" Arthur would have been like in the Anglo-Saxon time period. Arthur is a former Roman general, who repels the advance of the Saxon invaders. The film makes many changes to the Arthurian characters, but Guinevere, appearing as a warrior-woman instead of a damsel-in-distress, is a stark contrast to the traditional version of her character.

TEACHABLE TERMS

- **Meet cute** This Hollywood screenwriter term is defined as a standard plot device in which a couple meets in a way that's charming, ironic, or just generally amusing. Is the meeting between Arthur and Guinevere a meet cute?
- **Imagery** "Flames of greed sprang up in the merchant's eyes" on pg. 70 is an example of imagery.
- **Social class** In this tale Arthur transforms from a king into a peasant—experiencing a drastic change in social class. What does this tell us about Arthur that he is willing to spend time as a peasant? For the most part characters in the King Arthur legends are noblemen and ladies, but think about the nameless servants and peasants working behind the scenes. What are their stories?
- **Foreshadowing** Merlin's comments concerning Guinevere on pgs. 77-78 seem to indicate that her marriage to Arthur is not a good idea.

RECALL QUESTIONS

1. What item causes Arthur to transform into a peasant?
2. Why does Merlin suggest that Arthur spend time in the court of King Leodegrance?
3. Who is the White Knight?
4. What does Ralph the merchant sell?
5. What wedding present does Leodegrance give to Arthur?

THE BRIDE OF THE KING

CAST

ARTHUR	*Young King of Britain*
MERLIN	*Good Enchanter*
LEODEGRANCE	*King of Cameliard*
GUINEVERE	*Leodegrance's Daughter*
RIENCE	*Evil Duke*
MILLICENE	*Guinevere's Lady*
RALPH	*Armor Merchant*

NARRATOR: Arthur's kingdom flourished for many years. Yet as his reign continued, many noted that the kingdom was missing one vital element—an heir. Arthur had not yet taken a queen and produced a child.

One day, Arthur and Merlin stood upon the high ramparts of Camelot, where they were buffeted by the chill wind. Merlin grumbled and clamped his hand tightly down on his skull cap to keep it from blowing away.

MERLIN: *(irritated)* Must we tarry here?

ARTHUR: Just for a moment, Merlin. I wanted to show you this high spot. I come here whenever I am troubled. From up here I can see far into my kingdom. Isn't it glorious?

MERLIN: *(sarcastically)* Oh yes. Dazzling. It's so rainy and miserable in this country that I'm surprised the whole place isn't covered in mildew.

ARTHUR: *(thoughtfully)* Merlin, do you think I should take a wife?

MERLIN: That's an abrupt transition. Hmmm. What a question! When you say *take* a wife, do you mean taking someone else's?

ARTHUR: *(shocked)* Of course not!

MERLIN: Oh good! I had a flashback to your father there for a minute. *(pause)* A wife, eh? Well, I can tell you this much—women are the greatest mystery of life. They can be the source of infinite happiness and infinite misery.

ARTHUR: So you're in favor of marriage!

MERLIN: Did I say that? What has put this thought of marriage in your head?

ARTHUR: My knights and lords. They say a king should have a wife.

MERLIN: That's because they have wives! And they hate them more than the devil himself. But misery loves company.

ARTHUR: They say I must have an heir.

MERLIN: Often the best heir a king can have is one *not* born of his own bloodline.

ARTHUR: (*disappointedly*) I guess you are right, old friend.

NARRATOR: Merlin could tell that there was something in the young king's voice—something different.

MERLIN: But, tell me—what maiden holds your heart? You seem to speak with one in mind.

NARRATOR: Arthur smiled.

ARTHUR: Well, now that you mention it, there is one. Her name is Guinevere, the daughter of Leodegrance of Cameliard. I thought if I married anyone, I would choose her.

MERLIN: Oh, Heaven help us! You're smitten! And how did this attraction begin?

ARTHUR: Do you remember six months ago when I dueled with that evil knight near Cameliard?

MERLIN: (*angrily*) Do I? You almost got yourself killed! Imagine losing the only hope Britain has ever had in a silly joust!

ARTHUR: I was injured *a bit*, and I was carried to the dwelling of a holy hermit.

MERLIN: If you ask me, there's something a bit odd about old men living alone in the wilderness.

ARTHUR: You mean like you?

MERLIN: Exactly. Bizarre behavior!

NARRATOR: Merlin touched his finger to his nose and winked.

ARTHUR: Anyway, as I was saying...I was in and out of consciousness with a fever when I saw an angel bending over me.

MERLIN: Ha. Let me guess. It was Guinefar.

ARTHUR: Guinevere! Anyway, when I came to, I asked the hermit whom I had seen. He said it was a damsel visiting his cell on a holy pilgrimage. And then he told me her name. Ever since then, she has been in my mind. She, of course, did not give me a second thought. Probably because she thought I was just a humble knight.

MERLIN: So if she had known you were a king, she would have been interested then? Clever girl.

ARTHUR: No. She didn't seem like that at all. She did not seem greedy or selfish.

MERLIN: It is providential that she did not find out your love for her or your true identity. The opportunity for power can corrupt any man—or woman in this case. Hmmm. I can see this damsel has captured your mind. But marriage is tricky business. It takes more than an ordinary woman to be a queen.

ARTHUR: Would she make a good queen, Merlin?

MERLIN: I cannot say.

ARTHUR: You can see the future, can't you?

MERLIN: Of course, I can, but I can't turn it on and off like a faucet.

ARTHUR: *(confused)* What is a faucet?

MERLIN: Nevermind. You must discover the answer to your own question by determining Guinevere's worth. And you must do this by spending time in her presence.

ARTHUR: That would be improper! Being in a damsel's presence without a formal proposition of marriage would be a scandal! It would bring shame on her and her family.

MERLIN: Oh, you medieval types and your prudish ways! You can bash a man's head in with a mace, but you get a weak stomach at the sight of a woman. Don't worry. I have a plan.

NARRATOR: From a fold in his robes Merlin pulled forth a ratty, wide-brimmed hat.

MERLIN: Here is the solution to your problem!

ARTHUR: What is? Something inside the hat?

MERLIN: It *is* the hat.

ARTHUR: What? I'm not going anywhere near Guinevere wearing that! It looks like something a stable-boy would wear.

MERLIN: Exactly. When you place this hat upon your head, it will change your appearance. Instead of looking like a noble king, you will look like a lowly peasant.

NARRATOR: Arthur stared blankly at the old wizard.

ARTHUR: Merlin, are you trying to develop a sense of humor? How is Guinevere going to be interested in me if I'm disguised as a peasant?

MERLIN: She's not going to be interested! This is a mission to discover her true nature. You don't want an air-headed wisp to be your queen, do you? You want someone who is pure of heart, someone who is trustworthy, someone who is kind to all—even lowly servants!

ARTHUR: So I'm going to lie about my identity and spy on her to see if *she's* trustworthy?

MERLIN: Exaaaactly. And here I thought you were dense.

ARTHUR: It will take time to keep up such a disguise. How can I afford to be away from Camelot so long?

MERLIN: There is trouble brewing in North Wales, the kingdom of Duke Rience. That evil duke has been stealing the land of his neighbors. His next victim will be Leodegrance, Guinevere's father.

ARTHUR: I have heard nothing of this! It's an outrage!

MERLIN: Then perhaps it is time you investigate. In the court of Cameliard is the best place for you to be—to keep an eye on the situation.

NARRATOR: Arthur paused in thought.

ARTHUR: All right. Give me the hat.

NARRATOR: He placed the tattered hat upon his head and was immediately transformed. Even though he retained his stature and build, his well-trimmed hair grew scruffy, dirt appeared beneath his fingernails, and his skin reddened as if from the constant sight of the sun. In wonder Arthur brought his hands up and felt his face.

ARTHUR: This is miraculous!

MERLIN: Yes, yes. Now go to Cameliard and offer your services as a gardener. There among the hedges and flowers you will daily see your lady. Watch her closely. Determine her worth. Meanwhile, I will consult the Powers That Be and find what the future holds. I'll see if I can get the faucet flowing.

ARTHUR: A wondrous plan, Merlin! I will.

NARRATOR: Arthur did as Merlin commanded. In his new disguise Arthur traveled to Cameliard castle and presented himself to the king for service. King Leodegrance took one look at the tall frame and firm build of the humble garden-boy and put him to work at once.

LEODEGRANCE: You look like a strong lad! My daughter is terribly fond of our garden. Tend it well, for I love to see her smile!

ARTHUR: I will, my lord.

NARRATOR: And so Arthur, the king of all England, began to work as a humble gardener. The physical labor was good for him. It was a welcome relief from life at Camelot, and the days slipped by. Earning his food and board by the sweat of his brow reminded him of his childhood in the country plantation of Sir Ector.

Plus, there was the presence of Guinevere. The damsel came to the garden every morning with her ladies-in-waiting. She was even more radiant than Arthur had remembered, and his resolve became even more firm: This was the woman for him. She was honest and kind in all her dealings with the servants—even the scruffy garden-boy. She was clever, too. In her father's old age she practically managed the day-to-day business of the castle.

One foggy morning Guinevere's father met her in the garden with a look of sorrow on his face. The new garden-boy just so happened to be tending the nearby bushes and overheard their conversation.

LEODEGRANCE: (hurriedly) My daughter, I have frightful news!

GUINEVERE: What is it, Father?

LEODEGRANCE: Our enemy, Duke Rience of North Wales, has sent me this.

NARRATOR: The king held up a parchment with the spider-like seal of Rience upon it.

LEODEGRANCE: He lays claim to our lands.

GUINEVERE: I can't believe it!

LEODEGRANCE: That is not all. He lays claim to you, too. He demands your hand in marriage, or he will raze Cameliard to the ground.

GUINEVERE: He cannot do that. Arthur, the High King, would never stand for it! No lord can take another lord's land by force. That is the law!

LEODEGRANCE: Laws only work if they are enforced, dear. Duke Rience has stolen all of our neighbor's lands, and Arthur has done nothing. There is no hope for us either.

We are too weak to stand up to him on our own. We have to agree to his terms.

GUINEVERE: We must fight this!

LEODEGRANCE: I'm sorry, my dear. I'm a weak old man. I cannot protect you.

NARRATOR: Arthur listened to all this intently. After her father departed, Guinevere wept angry tears.

GUINEVERE: *(weeping)* I am lost!

NARRATOR: When darkness fell, the garden-boy made his way out of Cameliard castle, down into the village that lay at the foot of the hill.

ARTHUR: No foul lord is going to be a tyrant in my kingdom.

NARRATOR: Arthur paused on the step of a merchant's shop.

ARTHUR: *(reading)* Ralph of Cardiff, Professional Armorer. Perfect!

NARRATOR: Making sure no one was watching, Arthur pulled the magical hat from his head. He felt his body and his clothes transform. Then he knocked upon the door.

RALPH: *(irritated)* Coming! Coming! We're closed, you know!

NARRATOR: A wrinkled face with a hawk-like nose answered the door.

RALPH: We're closed!

ARTHUR: Please, I am in need of armor.

RALPH: Armor, eh? I doubt *you* could afford the armor I have for sale. My armor is high quality stuff—fit for a king. Why don't you try the second-hand shop down the street? They're probably more your style.

ARTHUR: Please! I am a knight, and I have come to challenge Duke Rience, who threatens this kingdom.

RALPH: Well, you're a fool—soon to be a dead fool. Don't even try to buy anything on credit!

NARRATOR: Arthur produced a sack of gold coins and thrust it into the merchant's face.

ARTHUR: Will this change your mind?

RALPH: Great Caesar's ghost!

NARRATOR: At once the door flew open, and the merchant whisked Arthur inside.

RALPH: A thousand apologies, my lord! I had no idea you were *that* kind of customer. I thought you were just some of the local riff-raff. I am honest Ralph of Cardiff! I deal in only the finest of armors. Ralph's shields and suits have never been pierced—satisfaction guaranteed!

ARTHUR: So if your armor fails me and I die in battle, I can come back for a refund?

RALPH: Heh heh. You are a wise man! But I have never lost a customer yet—at least not because of a faulty product. Now what can I do for you?

ARTHUR: Show me your finest armor.

NARRATOR: The merchant led Arthur through room after room of impressive suits of armor, all grandly forged.

RALPH: These are the latest fashions from France. Note the fine lines of the design.

ARTHUR: None of these will do! I desire only the best!

RALPH: You know your armor, I see. You are a true connoisseur!

NARRATOR: At last Arthur spotted a suit of armor, gleaming white in the candlelight.

ARTHUR: Here. This is the armor that I wish to buy.

RALPH: Oh, a fine choice. This is from our Righteous Justice Collection for those special quests of purity. It's flashy, but I think you could pull it off. I can have it engraved with your crest, and it will be ready for pick-up in a fortnight.

ARTHUR: I must have it tonight, and I desire no crest upon it.

NARRATOR: The merchant paused.

RALPH: No crest, eh?

ARTHUR: No. I wish to remain anonymous.

NARRATOR: Arthur placed the bag of gold into the merchant's hand. Ralph, eying his customer suspiciously, took a piece of gold from the bag and bit its edge.

ARTHUR: It is true gold, I assure you.

RALPH: Men who wish to remain anonymous are often untrustworthy.

ARTHUR: Some are, but you must trust me. The money I gave you will cover this fabulous suit of armor and your finest weapons, yet I am also in need of a steed.

RALPH: On credit? No deal!

ARTHUR: If you do what I ask, I will make sure you have ten bags of gold—all twice as heavy as this one.

NARRATOR: Flames of greed sprang up in the merchant's eyes.

RALPH: But you have no hope of beating Duke Rience. Men say he is a giant, who collects the beards of his victims. He rips them right off their faces! Can you imagine?

ARTHUR: Then I will write a document so that you will get your payment—whether or not I survive the battle.

RALPH: *Now* you have a deal!

NARRATOR: A week hence on a drizzly morning the monstrous Duke Rience rode with his knights and men-at-arms into the realm of Leodegrance. He was coming to claim his bride, and his ebony armor was specially polished for the occasion. To keep up romantic appearances, he also carried an untidy bouquet of dried-up flowers in his grip.

Upon the ramparts of Cameliard Guinevere and her father gloomily watched the evil duke's approach.

GUINEVERE: Father, isn't there anyone who can fight for my honor?

LEODEGRANCE: Not me! Just look at the size of that villain! And he's wearing all black. That's a very bad sign. I'm sorry, my dear. I will miss you. Perhaps you can come visit me from time to time—but only if your new husband allows it!

GUINEVERE: I wish Heaven had given me a father with a spine!

NARRATOR: Staggering before Rience was a gray procession of chained peasants, tiredly slinging flowers left and right. Men-at-arms prodded them with spears from behind.

GUINEVERE: (*sarcastically*) This Rience certainly is a romantic. Those poor peasants!

NARRATOR: Rience stopped his procession before the drawbridge of the castle, puffed out his chest, and addressed Guinevere upon the castle walls.

RIENCE: Lady Guinevere, I have ridden this morning to claim you as my wife! Before me, I bring the tokens of my love—beautiful flowers gathered from my kingdom—the kingdom that will be your new home. What say you? May I claim your hand?

GUINEVERE: (*loudly*) Duke Rience, I must say I am relieved! If you only desire my hand, I shall have it removed and sent along with you. The rest of me may stay here.

(*giggles from the ladies-in-waiting*)

RIENCE: What? I don't get that.

NARRATOR: Rience frowned in confusion. One of his knights rode to his side and whispered in his ear.

RIENCE: (*angrily*) Argh! Apparently, Cameliard gives me nothing but insults!

LEODEGRANCE: Guinevere! Are you out of your mind?

GUINEVERE: Father! I will not go to be this man's wife! I don't love him.

LEODEGRANCE: What does love have to with it? We're talking about certain death here!

GUINEVERE: Then I would rather die!

LEODEGRANCE: Well, that's very noble of you, but what about the rest of us? We're just fine with the arrangement.

RIENCE: (*angrily*) You have one more chance, Leodegrance! Send your daughter forward or suffer the consequences! See the lining of my cloak here?

NARRATOR: The duke lifted his fur-trimmed cape.

RIENCE: It is trimmed with the beards of ten kings that I have defeated. I personally cut the beards from their faces. Nice, isn't it?

NARRATOR: Leodegrance clutched his own beard protectively.

GUINEVERE: Well, that's just disgusting.

RIENCE: Now give me your daughter, or my knights and I will tear down your castle piece by piece, burn your cropland, and take your women as—

ARTHUR: (*shouting*) Halt right there! That's quite enough, you pompous swine!

(*gasping from everyone*)

NARRATOR: Everyone searched the field below for the source of the brave voice.

RIENCE: *(enraged)* What? All right! Who said that? Who said that?

ARTHUR: I did!

NARRATOR: A white mounted knight galloped from behind the turrets of the castle. Cheers went up from the walls. *(cheering)* Guinevere felt her heart beating fast within her chest.

GUINEVERE: Who is this noble knight?

RIENCE: Is this some kind of joke? He does not even wear a crest!

ARTHUR: That is because it will be even more dishonorable for you to be beaten by a knight with no name!

RIENCE: How dare you! Your beard will be the eleventh to decorate my robe! Knights! Unhorse him at once!

NARRATOR: The black knights of Rience spurred themselves into action, the turf flying up from the furious hooves of their steeds. The White Knight readied his lance and positioned his own horse to face the five knights bearing down upon him. *(clanging noises and hoofbeats)*

There was a series of flashes as each of the five black knights impacted upon the White Knight's shield. Five riders hit the ground in succession, their steeds galloping away unmanned.

ARTHUR: You, sir, are a recreant knight. How cowardly to send your henchman after me! Now face me yourself—unless you lack the courage.

RIENCE: Such insolence! Your hacked-off head will hang as a decoration in my hall!

NARRATOR: Rience furiously pulled his helm onto his head and readied his jagged-tipped lance. The White Knight raised his spear toward Guinevere.

ARTHUR: My lady, I fight this duel for you. I seek to free you from the will of this evil duke.

GUINEVERE: I thank you, noble knight!

RIENCE: Silence! Yah! Yah!

NARRATOR: Rience spurred his horse forward. Arthur lowered his lance and did the same. *(hoofbeats)* The ground shook as the two powerful knights bore down on one another, their bodies thrown forward in the saddle, their lances braced beneath their arms for the impact that came in spray of splinters. *(crashing sound)* Both knights recoiled from the other's blow.

For a second it seemed neither knight had lost their mount. But slowly the body of Rience began to sway in the saddle and, with a clumsy fumble, fell to the ground. He was dead. The White Knight's lance had pierced his helm.

The men-at-arms of Duke Rience turned and fled, and the chained flower-bearers applauded. All those gathered on the ramparts of the castle cheered as well—Guinevere most of all. *(loud cheering)*

GUINEVERE: My liberator! Come inside our walls so that I can bestow a kiss upon you!

NARRATOR: The White Knight looked up and nodded toward his lady. Guinevere caught a faraway glimpse of deep brown eyes. They somehow looked familiar.

ARTHUR: Nothing would please me more, but I must go.

LEODEGRANCE: What? He's leaving?

GUINEVERE: No! Please, stay. You have just saved me!

ARTHUR: My mission is complete—and so I depart.

GUINEVERE: Wait! Will you not even give me your name? Your lineage?

ARTHUR: I am the White Knight, and that is all that you must know.

NARRATOR: Without another word, Arthur turned his horse and galloped away, leaving the spectators standing stunned.

In the following days it became the mission of Lady Guinevere to determine the identity of her mysterious champion.

GUINEVERE: Could it have been King Hengist?

MILLICENE: No, my lady. He is far too fat. This knight was built exactly as a knight should be.

GUINEVERE: Prince Octa from the West?

MILLICENE: No, not him. Remember, your father said the prince was hosting his own joust when the White Knight fought his battle.

GUINEVERE: There has to be an answer to this riddle. His eyes looked so familiar.

NARRATOR: Guinevere's lady-in-waiting moved near the chamber window and glanced down into the garden.

MILLICENE: Hmmm. My lady, there is a strange man by the fountain in the courtyard—washing his face in the waters there!

GUINEVERE: Probably one of Father's guests.

MILLICENE: He's very tall and regal. His clothes look expensive. I wonder what he's doing here.

NARRATOR: Guinevere glanced out the window and beheld the man herself. Her face lit up!

GUINEVERE: Millicene! It must be he! The White Knight!

NARRATOR: Guinevere tore from her chamber, down the winding staircase into the bright courtyard.

GUINEVERE: *(shouting)* Sir! Sir! Stay a minute!

NARRATOR: There was the fountain before her, gurgling softly, but instead of a regal gentleman sitting on its edge, as she had expected, there was only the scruffy garden-boy.

ARTHUR: Beg your pardon, miss?

GUINEVERE: Where did he go? The knight who was just here?

NARRATOR: The garden-boy stared at her blankly from beneath his wide-brimmed hat.

ARTHUR: It has been only me, miss.

GUINEVERE: You must be mistaken. I saw a man here with my very own eyes!

ARTHUR: No one is here but me, miss.

NARRATOR: Arthur fought to control his smile of amusement. He had not intended for Guinevere to spy him from above. He had only taken off the hat for a second to mop his brow in the heat of the day. But now he thought Guinevere's frustration made her all the more beautiful.

ARTHUR: Maybe if you describe him to me.

GUINEVERE: All right. He was very tall and well-framed—the best-looking man I have ever seen.

ARTHUR: Really? I must confess, I haven't seen anyone around here like that. Maybe you saw me and thought I was this man.

GUINEVERE: No, I think not. He had dark eyes and a handsome beard. If I have let him get away, I shall never forgive myself.

ARTHUR: Sounds like a daydream to me, miss. If I see your gorgeous knight, I'll tell him you're looking for him. *(laugh)*

NARRATOR: Just then Guinevere noticed something golden lying upon the ground near the garden-boy's foot.

GUINEVERE: Wait a minute. What is that?

ARTHUR: Nothing.

NARRATOR: She snatched the object up from the grass. It was a medallion.

ARTHUR: Oh. That's mine. I must have dropped it.

GUINEVERE: Yours? What would a peasant be doing with a golden medallion? That doesn't make any—*(gasp)*

NARRATOR: Guinevere's eyes grew wide.

GUINEVERE: I knew it! The White Knight *was* here!

NARRATOR: Arthur prepared to throw the hat from his head, reveal his true identity, and claim the kiss that was rightfully his.

GUINEVERE: And *you* stole his medallion!

ARTHUR: What? *(laugh)*

GUINEVERE: Don't laugh at me! How dare you steal from a noble knight like my champion!

NARRATOR: As the garden-boy continued to laugh behind her, Guinevere stalked away. She met her father at the garden entrance.

GUINEVERE: Father, I am getting rid that rude garden-boy at once! He is a thief!

LEODEGRANCE: Oh my! He *is* a saucy fellow! Why just the other day it was reported that he was neglecting his duties.

GUINEVERE: What do you mean?

LEODEGRANCE: He has been missing for many days. While the entire castle was preoccupied with the duel of Duke Rience and the White Knight, the peasant was off somewhere ignoring his responsibilities. He only showed up again yesterday, blaming his absence on a toothache.

NARRATOR: Suddenly, all the pieces added up in Guinevere's mind.

GUINEVERE: Ah-ha! That's it! No wonder he laughed at me! I could laugh at myself for not seeing it sooner.

LEODEGRANCE: Sounds like an old-fashioned case of avoiding work to me! These lazy peasants. That's what's wrong with Britain if you ask me—lazy peasants!

NARRATOR: Not only had Guinevere realized the true identity of the garden-boy, she also realized the game he had been playing with her.

GUINEVERE: Hmmm. Two can play at that game. Father! Call the garden-boy in at once.

LEODEGRANCE: Good idea! He has really angered me now! We'll give him a sound flogging.

NARRATOR: The garden-boy was sent for, and he humbly entered their presence.

LEODEGRANCE: So, peasant, I hear you've been stealing and shirking your duties!

GUINEVERE: (*clearing her throat*) Ahem.

LEODEGRANCE: Yes, dear?

GUINEVERE: It is customary for servants to remove their hats in the presence of a lady.

LEODEGRANCE: We don't need to stand on formalities. It will only take a second for us to punish this peasant, and he'll be out the door for good!

GUINEVERE: I want to see his face.

LEODEGRANCE: Are you sure? It's bound to be hideous. You know how these peasants look. Oh well. Fine. Garden-boy! Remove your hat at once.

ARTHUR: I cannot.

LEODEGRANCE: What? Bring me a whip! This brute must be flogged!

GUINEVERE: Why can you not remove your hat? Is it stitched to your head?

ARTHUR: No, my lady, it covers an ugly sore that your royal eyes should never behold.

LEODEGRANCE: Oooh. That's a good reason. Nevermind. Leave the hat in place. I have a weak stomach.

GUINEVERE: Father! Make him remove his hat!

LEODEGRANCE: I would, dear, but you know how I feel about open sores.

NARRATOR: Guinevere clasped her hands and strode slyly behind the garden-boy.

GUINEVERE: Very well. Since you have this hideous, pus-oozing sore, keep your hat. See if we care.

ARTHUR: It is most gracious of your ladyship—

NARRATOR: In a flash, Guinevere whisked the hat from the garden-boy's head. The transformation was instantaneous, and the gallant lord she had seen in the garden stood before her.

GUINEVERE: *(excitedly)* Magic! I knew it! Father, look! It is the White Knight. *(to Arthur)* What do you have to say for yourself? How dare you trick a noble lady!

LEODEGRANCE: No, Guinevere!

GUINEVERE: Oh, he needs a good lecture for concealing his identity from us!

LEODEGRANCE: Shhh! Dear! Shhhh!

NARRATOR: Guinevere noticed her father's face was locked into a look of fright.

GUINEVERE: Father, what is it?

LEODEGRANCE: *(to Arthur)* Your—your—your majesty. Forgive me! Forgive her!

NARRATOR: Leodegrance fell upon his knees before the transformed garden-boy.

GUINEVERE: *(confused)* Your majesty? What does he mean?

NARRATOR: Arthur beamed at his love.

ARTHUR: I am Arthur—the king of all England.

NARRATOR: Guinevere stared in new wonder.

LEODEGRANCE: Forgive me for my ignorance! I wasn't actually going to flog you! Forgive me for revealing your sore! It's really quite a lovely sore! The finest I've ever seen! Oh woe is me!

ARTHUR: Rise, Leodegrance. You have always been a faithful follower of mine. But if you wish to make amends with me, I will ask you one boon.

LEODEGRANCE: Yes! Just ask it, and the answer will be, "Yes!"

ARTHUR: You have the cleverest of women living with you here—one savvy enough to see through my disguise. I hid myself in your court to observe her true nature, and I must say I liked what I saw. She was always kind and compassionate to her servants—except those she suspected of thievery and insolence. *(laugh)*

NARRATOR: Guinevere blushed.

ARTHUR: King, I say honestly that I desire nothing more than the beautiful hand of your daughter, Guinevere. And the rest of her as well. That is, if she accepts.

NARRATOR: Arthur took Guinevere's hand, bowed, and kissed her trembling fingers. Guinevere smiled radiantly.

GUINEVERE: Of course! You saved me and my kingdom from a horrible fate! How could I not love you in return?

LEODEGRANCE: This is joyous news! My daughter will be the queen! And I have the perfect wedding present. It is a table that your father, Uther Pendragon, gave to me many years ago. He said he had no use for it himself. "Who needs a round table?" he said. But it is yours to have now!

ARTHUR: A round table. Intriguing.

NARRATOR: Arthur and Guinevere spent many more days together—strolling through the very garden where Arthur had admired her from afar. He was free to openly admire her now, and she gladly returned his looks of love.

Finally, with great reluctance, Arthur bade his love farewell.

ARTHUR: All the arrangements have been made. Three weeks from now we will become man and wife.

GUINEVERE: No matter how many years we share together, Arthur, you will always be my champion.

NARRATOR: Merlin himself came to escort Arthur back to Camelot—arriving on a white donkey. The young king greeted him happily.

ARTHUR: Greetings, Merlin!

MERLIN: Yes, yes. It is I. I guess you have enjoyed your time as a peasant.

ARTHUR: These months have been grand! It is such a relief to be removed from the pressures of court and the politics of ruling a kingdom.

MERLIN: Tell me about it. It's been a nightmare while you were gone.

ARTHUR: Merlin, I slew Duke Rience, and I have won the love of my heart.

MERLIN: Have you now?

ARTHUR: You don't seem excited for me.

MERLIN: I have consulted the Powers That Be about your love for Guinevere.

ARTHUR: Have you seen what a fine queen she will be?

NARRATOR: The wizard raised his eyebrows.

MERLIN: So...the arrangements have already been made?

ARTHUR: Yes, we are to marry in three weeks' time!

MERLIN: So soon? Does she love you?

ARTHUR: She has professed to.

MERLIN: Love is a strange thing. For some it is as solid as a rock. For others it shifts like sand.

ARTHUR: And you were right to suggest the disguise. It was the perfect way to see her true nature. Of course, she saw right through my masquerade—eventually. She is the cleverest girl, Merlin.

MERLIN: Did she love you *before* she saw through the disguise?

ARTHUR: Well, no. But how could she?

MERLIN: Indeed. *(pause)* Marriage for you is not like marriage for normal men. It is an affair of state. The fate of your kingdom may rest upon your marriage. Keep her close, Arthur.

ARTHUR: I feel as if the sunlight has never been as fresh as it is today. Camelot will be greater than ever before with Guinevere at my side. Her father is even giving us a round table that once belonged to my father. Isn't that intriguing? A round table!

NARRATOR: The young king stopped, suddenly remembering, and turned to his old friend.

ARTHUR: But wait. Merlin, you said something about the future. What did you see?

NARRATOR: The magician smiled sadly.

78   The Road to Camelot

MERLIN: I see nothing that can be changed, my boy. Nothing at all.

NARRATOR: Arthur beamed, and so king and mentor rode on—down the road to Camelot.

DISCUSSION QUESTIONS

1. Why does Merlin suggest that Arthur try to determine Guinevere's true nature before he marries her?
2. Does Arthur actually discover Guinevere's true nature? Explain.
3. Does Guinevere agree to marry Arthur too quickly? Explain.
4. What do Merlin's subtle warnings foreshadow for Arthur and Guinevere?
5. Why is Arthur's marriage more important than any other man's in his kingdom?
6. Why should Arthur have waited to receive Merlin's advice before pledging himself to Guinevere?

THE WHITE HART
TEACHER GUIDE

BACKGROUND

When pagan lands such as Britain were converted to Christianity, the medieval church gave many pagan symbols new religious significance. For instance, pagan fertility symbols such as eggs, rabbits, and evergreen trees were incorporated into Christian religious celebrations. Previously established pagan festivals became holy days (or holidays) such as Easter and Christmas.

In the Celtic, pre-Christian days of Britain, albino stags (or "white harts" as they were also called) were considered otherworldly creatures, whose appearance signaled the beginning of adventures. The creature's color symbolized its purity and connection to the supernatural world.

When Christianity came to Britain, because of the White Hart's purity and spiritualism, it became a symbol of Christ. In the Arthurian legends it is also a symbol for Arthur and his kingdom, a bright spot of purity in a dark world. Interestingly, the attributes of the White Hart are similar to those of the unicorn, a horned horse that also symbolized purity and Christ. Some have thought that the White Hart is the basis for the legend of the unicorn.

SUMMARY

Arthur installs the Round Table in Camelot castle, and Merlin explains that it once belonged to Arthur's father, Uther Pendragon. He also explains its symbolism—the idea that all who sit at it are equal. Arthur knights his teenaged nephew, Gawain, as the Round Table's first inductee. During the ensuing feast a white stag pursued by hounds bursts into the castle hall. After the stag retreats, Arthur declares that he will go after the creature. King Uriens of Gore and his knight Accolon agree to accompany Arthur on this quest.

The three companions set out in pursuit of the stag. When they near the border of Uriens's kingdom of Gore, they sight the stag and begin to chase it. It leads them for many miles, and their horses grow so exhausted that they stumble and die. Their riders are thrown and lose consciousness.

When Arthur awakens, he is in the ruins of a castle, and a strange damsel there tells him that his companions have been taken captive by an evil knight. She gives him a sword and armor to fight the evil knight. The damsel is actually Morgan, Arthur's half-sister, in disguise, and she has given Arthur a fake Excalibur in place of the real one.

Meanwhile, Accolon awakens nearby, and a dwarf, who is Morgan's servant, commands him to put on a different set of armor to fight a knight who is coming to challenge him. Accolon obeys because he is actually the secret lover of Morgan. Arthur and Accolon, both unaware of each other's identity, meet in battle. Accolon has been given the true Excalibur, and Arthur's blade shatters from the knight's assault. Accolon brings the king to the point of death and removes his opponent's helmet. When Accolon beholds Arthur's face, he is shocked and stays his hand. Morgan appears and explains to Arthur how she has gained new magical powers. She commands Accolon to kill the king. Just then a strange maiden rises from the nearby lake. She is Nimue the enchantress. Morgan commands Accolon to strike the king, but when he does, the power of Excalibur brings about his own death. The sword cannot kill its own master. Morgan commands her dwarf to kill Uriens, her unconscious husband who is lying nearby. Arthur ends the dwarf's life before he can do so. Morgan reveals that she still has Excalibur's magical scabbard and gallops away on her steed. Nimue conjures a horse and tells Arthur to catch Morgan.

Arthur chases Morgan all the way to the sea, where she flings his scabbard into the watery depths then vanishes. Arthur returns to Camelot with Nimue. Merlin forms an attachment to the young enchantress and tells Arthur that soon he will be going away. He will teach all his magic to Nimue, and then she will seal him up in a magical cave forever. With a few parting pieces of advice, Merlin leaves Camelot with Nimue.

ESSENTIAL QUESTIONS

- Should you ever seek revenge?
- Why is it wrong to punish others for the wrongs that have been done to you?
- How can too much assistance actually be a bad thing?

ANTICIPATORY QUESTIONS

- What is special about the scabbard of Excalibur?
- Who is Morgan?
- Do you think Merlin will always be a part of Camelot?

CHARACTER QUEST

Forgiveness/Revenge Morgan le Fay is obsessed with getting revenge on her half-brother, Arthur. How has revenge polluted her mind and made her into a monster? If she actually gets her revenge, will it make her as happy as she believes it will? Explain.

CONNECT

Medieval Bestiary While creatures such as the White Hart attained mystical significance, it was not the only animal that had special meaning or powers. People in the Middle Ages attributed many supernatural abilities to common animals. Locate a medieval bestiary in print or online, such as the one found at http://www.bestiary.ca and research the many interesting beliefs medieval people had about regular animals.

TEACHABLE TERMS

- **Symbol** The White Hart is a symbol of many things. First, as Merlin explains, it is the symbol of Arthur's kingdom. Secondly, it is a symbol of purity. Thirdly, it is a symbol for the unknown—embodying a spirit of adventure.
- **Mentor** The mentor (a role Merlin has served for Arthur) is a common archetype in hero stories. At some point the mentor must depart in order for the hero to achieve full potential. Analyze Merlin's role as Arthur's mentor.

RECALL QUESTIONS

1. Who is knighted as the first inductee to the Knights of the Round Table?
2. What does the stag chased by dogs symbolize?
3. How does Morgan le Fay attempt to kill Arthur?
4. What does Morgan steal from Arthur?
5. What will Nimue do to Merlin?

THE WHITE HART

CAST

ARTHUR	*King of Britain*
GUINEVERE	*Wife of Arthur*
MERLIN	*The Good Enchanter*
GAWAIN	*Nephew of Arthur*
URIENS	*King of Gore*
ACCOLON	*Knight of Arthur*
MAIDEN/MORGAN	*Evil Enchantress*
NIMUE	*Lake Maiden*
DWARF	*Servant to Morgan*

NARRATOR: Many changes had come to the castle of Camelot. First, King Arthur had taken a queen—the lovely Lady Guinevere. She was kind and compassionate and proved to be a just monarch. Secondly, an enormous, skillfully-carved round table now filled Camelot's feasting chamber. It had been a wedding present from Leodegrance, the father of Guinevere. In its sieges one-hundred-and-fifty knights could be seated side-by-side.

MERLIN: What do you think of your new table?

ARTHUR: I love it—although many of my knights say that it is a strange shape.

MERLIN: Strange shape? It's a circle. Don't they know geometry? I designed it as a circle on purpose.

ARTHUR: *You* designed it? I thought it once belonged to my father, Uther Pendragon.

MERLIN: Where did you think *he* got it? A caveman like him never could have thought of a round table! When I presented it to him, there was a whooshing sound as the symbolism went completely over his head.

ARTHUR: I see the symbolism, of course. Every other king has a rectangular table, and he sits at the head of the table because he is the person with all the power. Now the Round Table is a table with no head, so all the seats at it are equal. It's designed for the perfect kingdom, where no man will be above any other.

MERLIN: Hmmm. Maybe you *have* learned something. *(grumbling)* I had a whole lecture planned and everything.

ARTHUR: I guess I'm getting a bit old for your lessons.

MERLIN: Maybe so. *(pause)* When the student is ready, the master must depart.

ARTHUR: What do you mean, Merlin?

MERLIN: Nothing, nothing. Just that my time is growing thin.

NARRATOR: For a moment the wizard looked far older than he had ever looked before.

MERLIN: Well, enough talk! If I am correct—and I usually am—tonight is Michaelmas, the feast of Michael the Archangel.

ARTHUR: Yes. There will be quite a celebration. Guinvere has helped me make all the arrangments.

MERLIN: Is your marriage bringing you the joy that you hoped it would?

ARTHUR: I have never been happier!

MERLIN: That is good for me to hear. It will make things easier.

NARRATOR: Darkness fell, the torches were lit, and the hall was filled with feasting knights. (*shouts of celebration*) Amid the merriment, Arthur stood, drew Excalibur, and pointed to the Round Table.

ARTHUR: Your attention please! Since I have been king, I have had many knights, but tonight these knights become something new—something special. They are to become the Knights of the Round Table!

NARRATOR: All the noble lords and ladies cheered. (*sounds of loud cheering*)

ARTHUR: Now, where is my nephew? Where is Gawain?

NARRATOR: A teenaged boy stood and bowed to the king.

ARTHUR: Ah! There he is! All you damsels, look! Here is a young man worth your affection. Handsome and strong—just like his uncle. Ha! Wouldn't you say so, my queen?

GUINEVERE: (*playfully*) Hmmm. He *is* a handsome lad! But he looks nothing like you!

(*laughter from everyone*)

ARTHUR: (*laughing*) Treason! I am mortally wounded by these words. Gawain, today you become a knight. Did you spend last night in prayer?

GAWAIN: I did, uncle! I mean, *sire*. I have washed and put on the white robes of purity. I'm ready to join your service. But I ask one boon, sir.

ARTHUR: Ask, and it shall be yours!

GAWAIN: I wish for my younger brother, Gaheris, to be my squire.

ARTHUR: Of course! Now kneel.

NARRATOR: Gawain knelt before Arthur, and Excalibur was laid on both his shoulders.

ARTHUR: Now, rise, Sir Gawain!

(*cheers from the spectators*)

NARRATOR: Yet as quickly as it began, the cheering of the court gave way to a new commotion. (*clattering sound*) A sudden clattering resounded down the castle hallways.

MERLIN: Something approaches!

(howling of hounds)

ARTHUR: Hounds? Hunting in the castle?

(collective gasp)

NARRATOR: A pristinely white stag, powerful in horn and limb, bolted into the chamber, leapt nimbly up onto the Round Table, and galloped across it. *(cries of guests)* Behind it came a pack of black hounds, their jowls white with froth, howling and pursuing the stag for all they were worth.

ARTHUR: Merlin! What is the meaning of this?

MERLIN: Silence! Watch!

NARRATOR: The stag came to a stop before the king's seat and turned upon its pursuers, lowering its shining horns. The hides of the dogs bristled, and they lunged forward. The stag leapt over their snapping jaws and, skipping across the table once again, disappeared back down the hallway. The dogs took quick pursuit. *(murmuring from everyone)*

ARTHUR: A wonder! Surely we have seen a wonder today!

MERLIN: Aye, king. You have. A sign. A mighty portent.

NARRATOR: Everyone turned to Merlin.

ARTHUR: And—

MERLIN: And what?

ARTHUR: And what is the portent?

MERLIN: *(happily)* Oh, I get to explain something. Finally! *(clears throat)* Obviously, the White Hart symbolizes your kingdom—a symbol of purity in the barbaric forest of the world. The hounds symbolize your enemies, those who will always be at your heels—snapping and biting to destroy you.

ARTHUR: That is all?

MERLIN: The White Hart also presents you with a quest. It is the sacred duty of kings and knights to pursue this magical beast. It leads to adventure—and through that—truth.

ARTHUR: So you're saying that we should pursue and catch this stag?

MERLIN: Since the beast is otherworldly, it can never be caught, yet it should be pursued all the same.

GUINEVERE: But what is the purpose if there is no way to catch it?

MERLIN: It's symbolism, my dear.

NARRATOR: King Uriens of Gore, one of Arthur's guests, stood and addressed the king.

URIENS: For many months we have spotted this very same stag in my own kingdom of Gore. No matter how much we have pursued it with horse and hound, it cannot be caught. It must be a creature from the Otherworld!

ARTHUR: Amazing news!

URIENS: If you wish it, I shall guide your lordship to where we last spotted the hart. It would be an honor. I have searched for a way to repay you for giving me the greatest gift of my life—the hand of your beautiful sister.

ARTHUR: *(unenthusiastically)* Morgan. Of course. How is she these days?

URIENS: After our wedding, my beloved Morgan seemed to fall into a depression. She would have nothing to do with me. She threw the worst tantrums and cursed me with the blackest threats. But of late, she has never been happier. Just ask Sir Accolon here. He will tell you!

NARRATOR: Uriens motioned to a young knight seated at his side.

URIENS: Accolon has stayed at our castle for a twelve-month now. My wife and he are always in each other's presence. She is happy now, isn't she, Accolon?

NARRATOR: At these words Accolon fidgeted awkwardly.

ACCOLON: *(awkwardly)* Uh, yes. It's true. She is very happy these days.

ARTHUR: Then it is decided. I will go.

NARRATOR: Guinevere reached over and grasped her husband's hand.

GUINEVERE: Arthur, must you go? We have only just been married. All of this is so new to me—my new home, my new queenship. Tarry here a bit longer.

ARTHUR: I'm sorry, my love. You heard, Merlin. It is the duty of kings to hunt this beast, and my duty comes first.

GUINEVERE: *(sadly)* Oh. Very well then.

ARTHUR: I will return soon though. And then we shall be together.

NARRATOR: The king prepared to quest. On the morningtide Arthur, Uriens, and Accolon rode out from Camelot and journeyed for days toward the land of Gore.

URIENS: Sire, I sent a messenger ahead to let my wife know about our trip. It will thrill her to know that her beloved brother is coming for a visit!

ARTHUR: I doubt I am a welcome sight to my sister. I will quest for the stag and then return home.

URIENS: Nonsense! Oh, in her dark days, she used to go into the vilest rage when I mentioned your name. But since her change she is always desiring a meeting with you. "Send for Arthur," she says. "I want to pay him back for all he's done for me!"

ARTHUR: Hmmmm.

URIENS: It was last year when she finally came to her senses. It was as if something had given her a new love of life. Did you notice that change in her, Accolon?

ACCOLON: Uh…no, sir. No.

URIENS: Oh, that's right! I remember. It was right after Accolon came to our castle. *(pause)* Wait a minute.

ACCOLON: *(nervous coughing)* Oh, I remember now. I think it was the birth of your son that brought her new joy.

URIENS: No, I remember distinctly it was after *your* arrival, Accolon. I wonder why that would be?

ARTHUR: Ahem. Gentlemen, we are nearing the borders of Gore. Uriens, where have you seen the White Hart?

URIENS: *(thinking)* Now why would it be that her happiness was brought about by Accolon?

NARRATOR: Accolon was sweating profusely, but a sudden white flash within the forest caused Arthur to cry out.

ARTHUR: There! The hart!

URIENS: *(shouting)* After it!

ACCOLON: *(sigh of relief)* Whew.

NARRATOR: The riders spurred their horses into the dense forest. *(hoofbeats, horses whinnying)*

URIENS: *(screaming)* Sound the horn, Accolon! We are on the hunt!

(hunting horn)

NARRATOR: The horses raged beneath the knights, who drew their swords to slash at the limbs and vines that threatened to drag them from their mounts. If they lost sight of the white hindquarters before them, it was only for a second. They followed the hart steadily through all kinds of country. The horses soon grew tired, but their riders pushed them on.

URIENS: *(yelling)* We are almost upon it! Yah! Yah!

NARRATOR: Half an hour into the chase, their horses began to gasp for breath. These were not nimble steeds made for galloping—instead they were made thick to carry the weight of a fully-armored knight.

URIENS: *(yelling)* Press on! Press on! Yah, there! Yah!

NARRATOR: They burst from the forest—still on the stag's heels—and spread out before them they saw a large lake and the ruins of a castle on its banks. It was then that the first horse fell.

Uriens's horse snorted strangely, staggered, and fell beneath him. *(crashing sound)* Accolon's steed tripped over the tangled mass and threw the knight. *(crashing sound)* As for Arthur, the last thing he remembered was the sensation of being airborne, and then all was blackness. So it was for a time.

MAIDEN: *(sweet voice)* Sir! Sir! Are you all right?

NARRATOR: Arthur could hear a sweet voice. His eyes tried to focus in. He was in a dark place, but a white blur hovered above him. The blur solidified into the face of a beautiful, golden-haired maiden. Her expression was a mixture of panic and relief.

ARTHUR: What happened? Where am I?

MAIDEN: *(frantically)* I am so happy to see that you live, sir knight. But I'm afraid there is little time to explain. You are in the dungeon of a ruined castle. You and your friends have been captured.

ARTHUR: Captured? By whom?

MAIDEN: An evil knight. He found you where you fell by the lakeside and dragged you here—to make you his prisoner. He uses this abandoned castle as his lair.

ARTHUR: Where are the others?

MAIDEN: He has them chained in the chambers above. *(whimper of fright)* Heaven only knows what he's planning to do to them. I am also his prisoner. I was able to escape, but I could not rouse your friends. I came here to free you, so that you could fight the evil knight and free your comrades.

ARTHUR: Where is my sword? Did he take my sword?

MAIDEN: He did, but I was able to retrieve it for you.

NARRATOR: The damsel pulled a sword and scabbard from beneath her cloak.

MAIDEN: I have never seen a sword as wondrous as this one. Are you—?

ARTHUR: (*hurriedly*) Yes, I am King Arthur, and this is Excalibur.

MAIDEN: (*excitedly*) Oh, I thought so! I was so afraid you would not wake, and all would be lost. That villain must have stripped you of your armor, but I found some here in the dungeon. I know it has rusted, but put it on, and it will protect you well enough.

NARRATOR: Arthur's head was still swimming from the fall, but he stood and buckled on the new armor.

MAIDEN: Come. Follow me up this passageway.

NARRATOR: Arthur followed the maiden up through the ruins of the castle.

Meanwhile, Accolon was coming to his senses amid a thicket on the edge of the nearby woods.

DWARF: Wakey, wakey, loverboy!

NARRATOR: A plump dwarf had just finished dumping a bucket of water over him.

ACCOLON: Ah! What has happened? Where is the king?

DWARF: He is safe—for now.

ACCOLON: Are you one of my lady's dwarves?

DWARF: I am. My mistress bade me tell you that it's time to prove your love to her.

ACCOLON: She knows I will do anything she asks. What does she wish?

DWARF: A rogue knight has challenged her honor, and he is prepared to meet you on the field of battle. Are you prepared to defend your lady's honor?

ACCOLON: I have no armor!

DWARF: Here! I have brought you what you need.

NARRATOR: Accolon noticed a pile of armor nearby. Atop it sat a sword and jeweled scabbard that glittered in the night air.

ACCOLON: Such a sword! I have never seen a sword like it—except Excalibur!

DWARF: Take it! Take it! Do as the mistress commands you! Slay this foolish knight at any cost—even if it means your life!

NARRATOR: Accolon stared at the dwarf irritably.

ACCOLON: She certainly is bossy, isn't she?

NARRATOR: From across the clearing Accolon spied a fully-armed knight exiting the ruins of a lakeside castle.

DWARF: See! See! He comes already!

ACCOLON: Calm yourself, dwarf. I am a knight of King Arthur. I fear no one.

NARRATOR: Accolon pulled his helm into place, took up the mighty sword and scabbard, and marched into the clearing.

DWARF: If you only knew the truth! *(evil laugh)* You go to kill your king, loverboy!

NARRATOR: Laughing maniacally, the dwarf disappeared into the forest.
Watching from the castle ruins, the fair maiden called out to Arthur.

MAIDEN: Oh, dear me! There is the blackhearted knight fast approaching! Oh, be careful, beloved king! Methinks I might faint from nervousness.

NARRATOR: Arthur walked boldly toward his opponent.

ARTHUR: Damsel, I have nothing to fear with Excalibur and its scabbard by my side.

NARRATOR: As Arthur departed, the features of the damsel seemed to shift—reforming themselves into those of a raven-haired beauty.

MAIDEN: *(to herself, evil voice)* No. You *would* have nothing to fear *if* that were really Excalibur or its scabbard that you carry. *(evil laugh)*

DWARF: Psst! Lady Morgan!

NARRATOR: The dwarf appeared at the maiden's side.

MAIDEN: *(whispering)* Dwarf! Have you done as I told you?

DWARF: Yes, I gave him the king's sword and told him all that you said!

MAIDEN: Good! Now, let's see what that love-struck fool Accolon is good for. How fitting! The King of the Britons is going to meet his death at the hand of his own knight! *(evil laugh)*

DWARF: Unless King Arthur wins.

NARRATOR: She snarled at the dwarf.

MAIDEN: The sword I gave him is made of glass, and that armor is an even more fragile material! Plus, Accolon carries Excalibur itself! Even *you* could beat Arthur under conditions like that!

NARRATOR: In the midst of the tall grass, the two knights faced off. Neither had recognized the foreign armor of the other.

ARTHUR: *(yelling)* Hold, recreant knight! I have come to vanquish you!

ACCOLON: Indeed! I have come to do the same! Have at you! Ahhh! *(battlecry)*

NARRATOR: The two armored bodies crashed together. *(crashing sound)*

ARTHUR: *(yelling)* Taste the sting of my sword, coward!

NARRATOR: Arthur raised his sword into the air. Accolon did the same, and the two met in a shower of sparks. *(Clang!)* Much to Arthur's surprise, his blade shattered in his hand. He stared at its hilt dumbstruck.

ARTHUR: *(shocked)* What? This can't be! My sword has been broken!

ACCOLON: You villain! You can't stand against a mighty knight like me!

NARRATOR: Accolon swung the true Excalibur once again, and the king felt it cut through his armor and graze his flesh. Blood streamed down his side.

ARTHUR: What?

NARRATOR: Arthur grabbed at the scabbard that hung upon his belt—the one that was supposed to protect him.

ARTHUR: *(even more shocked)* Has the power of the Lady of the Lake abandoned me?

ACCOLON: *(yelling)* Ahhhhhh!

NARRATOR: Accolon leveled his sword and charged. Arthur sprang to the side, missing the charge, but fell backward to the ground. Accolon was upon him in a second.

ACCOLON: Now, I have you! And I will look on your face—before I end your life.

NARRATOR: Quickly removing his own helmet, Accolon yanked loose Arthur's helm. Then he stopped short.

ACCOLON: *(shocked)* My king?

ARTHUR: *(shocked)* Accolon! Is that you?

ACCOLON: *(shocked)* My king! Forgive me! I had no idea—

MAIDEN: Accolon! Finish the job!

NARRATOR: Accolon looked up in fright. The maiden stood nearby, but her disguise had faded completely.

ARTHUR: *(in shock)* Morgan!

ACCOLON: There has been a mistake, my love. This is Arthur—your own brother.

MORGAN: It is no mistake.

NARRATOR: The knight moved to release the king from his grip.

MORGAN: Stay!

ACCOLON: What?

MORGAN: I said, stay!

NARRATOR: The knight complied.

MORGAN: Accolon, I told you that in order for us to be together, sacrifices had to be made—blood had to be shed.

ACCOLON: But I thought you meant the blood of King Uriens. This is King Arthur!

MORGAN: Details. Details. Now be silent.

ARTHUR: I see you have made Accolon your slave. What will you do with me now, Morgan?

NARRATOR: Morgan smiled sweetly at Arthur.

MORGAN: I'm going to thank you.

ARTHUR: Thank me?

MORGAN: Yes. When you sent me away here to Gore—far away from Camelot—you thought I would waste away in exile. But here I have had a chance to grow deeper in my powers. So I must thank you. Your attempt to weaken me has made my magic mightier than ever.

ARTHUR: Then it is true! Merlin always told me you were a witch, but I refused to believe it!

MORGAN: Witch? *(laugh)* Witches are nothing compared to me. I am a goddess reborn. I am now Morgan le Fay.

NARRATOR: Arthur stared at his half-sister in shock.

MORGAN: Your small mind cannot comprehend it, but there are ancient forces that reside in this land—forgotten powers that have slumbered for years. The new religion drove them underground. But they found me. They called to me from the ancient places, the standing stones, the faerie mounds. They have chosen me as their vessel, and I now am more powerful than ever.

ARTHUR: I did not send you here to weaken your powers. I sent you here, so that you might have a normal life—a husband, a son.

NARRATOR: Morgan's eyes flashed.

MORGAN: *(psychotically)* A normal life? Do not taunt me! It is because of you that I will never have a normal life! You took away my father! You desecrated my mother! You destroyed my life!

ARTHUR: It was not me! Yes, my father did all that to you. But it was not me!

MORGAN: Oh, if I could find a way to punish him beyond the grave, I would. Believe me, I have tried. So, in his stead, I will punish you.

ARTHUR: Morgan, you have been wronged most grievously. But there is still hope.

MORGAN: Hope? *(laughs)* The man at the point of death speaks of hope.

ARTHUR: What about Uriens? What have you done with him?

MORGAN: Why do you care about that old toad? I do not. He is sleeping soundly nearby. Accolon is going to end his life—right after he ends yours.

ACCOLON: But, my love, I don't want to—

MORGAN: Silence! You will do what I command! I am ready to pass sentence on this so-called king.

NARRATOR: She knelt next to Arthur and playfully ruffled his hair.

MORGAN: *(fake kindness)* Arthur. Brother. You really should have killed me when you had the chance. Now *I* won't make the same mistake you did!

ARTHUR: Morgan, don't do this! I beg you. It's not my life I plead for. It's hope for all of Britain. Finally, mankind has a chance for something more—something better!

MORGAN: Merlin has made you into a fool. There is no hope for mankind. There is no nobility in man. Man was made to be oppressed, and that is what I will do—once you are out of the picture. They will worship me just like in the days of old. Now, Accolon, put this *king* to death.

NARRATOR: The knight paused, his face filled with anguish.

MORGAN: Do it, Accolon! Do you want to be the greatest knight in the land? I promised you that, and I can take it away just as easily! Now, Accolon!

NARRATOR: Accolon brought Excalibur close to Arthur's neck. A smile spread across Morgan's face.

MORGAN: Britain's great king—killed by his very own blade.

NIMUE: *(shouting)* Halt!

NARRATOR: The voice came from across the dark lake waters. A column of spray rose from the depths. *(tinkling of water)*

MORGAN: *(shouting)* No! Leave us! This does not concern you!

NARRATOR: A mysterious woman clothed all in white now stood in the midst of the lake.

MORGAN: *(hissing)* Nimue! How dare you interfere with my sacrifice!

NIMUE: The magic of the Lake created Excalibur, Morgan le Fay. No matter what dark powers you might have attained, that blade cannot be used to kill the one it was forged to protect.

MORGAN: We'll see about that! *(cry of rage)* Strike, Accolon!

NARRATOR: Accolon struck. There was a flash of flame in the air. *(Shazam!)* Arthur felt the weight of Accolon fall backwards from his body.

Arthur jumped up and found Excalibur—the true Excalibur—clenched in his hands. The charred body of Accolon lay on the ground below him—bleeding out the last of his life.

ACCOLON: *(dying)* Forgive me, my king.

NARRATOR: Morgan's wild eyes flicked from the knight's body to the sword now clutched in Arthur's hands.

NIMUE: Now, the sword's true owner wields it once again.

MORGAN: You may have cheated me out of one sacrifice, but I have another. Strike, dwarf!

NARRATOR: Arthur followed Morgan's gaze. Lying nearby was the unconscious body of Uriens. Morgan's dwarf stood over him, a twisted dagger clenched in his tiny fist.

ARTHUR: No!

NARRATOR: Arthur hurled Excalibur, and it cut through the air and caught the assassin-dwarf in mid-strike.

DWARF: *(cry of death)* Argh!

NARRATOR: Arthur rolled the lifeless dwarf from the body of Uriens and felt the king breathing.

ARTHUR: He lives!

MORGAN: For now! His life still will be mine to claim!

NIMUE: All your schemes have failed, Morgan.

MORGAN: Not all.

NARRATOR: The sorceress raised her arms, and a black cloud rose from the ground below her. *(whoosh)* It solidified into a steed, and Morgan sat astride it.

MORGAN: *(crazy)* Arthur, you might have regained your precious sword and saved the life of my detested husband—but I still hold this!

NARRATOR: She held up the scabbard of Excalibur.

MORGAN: I am no fool. I know what this scabbard is worth. Now come and take it—if you can.

NARRATOR: Morgan's steed reared, and she disappeared into the darkness. *(hoofbeats)*

NIMUE: Arthur, quickly! If she reaches the sea with the scabbard, all will be lost! Go!

NARRATOR: The lake maiden waved her arms, and a second horse surged from the waters of the lake. As it thundered past, Arthur hoisted himself onto its back and took up quick pursuit of Morgan. He chased her shadowy form through the countryside for many miles.

Finally, Arthur saw Morgan stop atop a high cliff—silhouetted against the moon. As he drew near, he could hear the sea crashing below. Morgan held out the scabbard she still carried.

MORGAN: Behold! The source of all your security—the tool that could one day save you from death! In my hand, Arthur, I hold your very life.

NARRATOR: Morgan turned to fling it over the edge of the cliff.

ARTHUR: Wait, Morgan! Do not do this to me! You were once my sister!

MORGAN: Never! You have been my enemy from the very day you were born. Your father destroyed my world, and I will destroy yours—piece by piece.

NARRATOR: Without another word she flung the scabbard far out into the black sea.

MORGAN: There it will lie forever—in the depths. Not even Merlin can bring it back now.

NARRATOR: Arthur drew Excalibur and pointed it at the sorceress.

ARTHUR: This night you have made war between us. If you wish me to be your enemy, I will be. You *are* a witch, and I will not suffer a witch to live.

MORGAN: *(laugh)* You speak to me of life and death? I am beyond them both! Yah! Yah!

NARRATOR: Morgan spurred her steed toward a nearby hill—one topped by a column of ancient standing stones. Arthur galloped after her, swinging his sword madly and snatching at her trailing cape.

MORGAN: *(laugh)* Ha! When will you learn? I am no longer of this world.

NARRATOR: There was a flash, and Arthur's steed reared up. *(horse whinny)* Arthur was now in the midst of the circle of standing stones—alone. Morgan le Fay had vanished completely.

ARTHUR: (*cry of anger*) Argh!

NARRATOR: Arthur struck at the stones with all his might but drew only feeble sparks. (*clashing sounds*)

MORGAN: (*faraway laughter*)

NARRATOR: Arthur helplessly lowered his sword to his side.

ARTHUR: (*weakly*) She is gone.

NIMUE: She will be back soon enough, I fear.

NARRATOR: The white lake-maiden now stood within the circle of stones.

ARTHUR: I thank you for your help, damsel. You saved my life. My sister has become more evil than I thought possible.

NIMUE: We, who are of this world and the next, have many parts to play. Some for good. Some for evil.

ARTHUR: Are you the Lady of the Lake?

NIMUE: I am *a* lady of the lake, yes. My name is Nimue.

ARTHUR: You must help me take King Uriens safely back to his castle and warn him about his treacherous wife.

NIMUE: He will discover her treachery soon enough.

NARRATOR: Arthur, bewildered by the day's events, brought a weary hand to his forehead.

ARTHUR: (*sigh*) I should never have come on this quest. I should never have followed the White Hart. I have lost so much.

NIMUE: What we lose in possessions, we gain in experience and knowledge.

ARTHUR: You sound like Merlin. I must return to him. I must return to Camelot.

NIMUE: Yes. You must. And I must go with you.

NARRATOR: Arthur was not for sure, but he thought, just for a second, he saw Nimue's form flicker, into that of a creature—a white stag.

Arthur and the lake-maiden returned to Camelot. When Merlin beheld the beauty of Nimue, he smiled a sad smile.

MERLIN: (*to himself*) So the time has come.

NARRATOR: Merlin took the maiden's silver hand into his own wrinkled palm. She curtsied before him.

MERLIN: I have been expecting you, Nimue.

NARRATOR: Over the next few weeks Arthur mourned the loss of his scabbard and the treachery of his half-sister. Guinevere was at a loss as to how to comfort her grieving husband.

GUINEVERE: I wish I could ease your suffering. You have been so gloomy these past weeks.

ARTHUR: Forgive me. I am troubled for Camelot. We have a powerful new enemy, and I must somehow keep my knights safe from her evil schemes.

GUINEVERE: I understand. The kingdom must come first.

NARRATOR: Meanwhile, Nimue the lake-maiden and Merlin spent all their days together. Arthur began to suspect that the old wizard had formed an attachment.

ARTHUR: Merlin, I never see you out of Nimue's presence. Have you fallen prey to your all-too-human urges? Those feelings that you often condemn others for? I guess even wizards are still men.

MERLIN: Hmph. You can think whatever you want! Nimue is my student, and I am teaching her my craft. That girl is like the sea—always drinking, but never full.

ARTHUR: Teaching her? Why?

MERLIN: I can tell you, but you won't understand. *(sigh)* My time has come. I'm going away soon. I am going on a journey.

ARTHUR: A journey to where?

MERLIN: Oh…oblivion. Nimue is going to learn all my knowledge and then use it to imprison me.

ARTHUR: *(angrily)* Then she intends to betray you!

MERLIN: Betray me? How is it betrayal if I know full well her intentions? My powers must pass on to her. Fate has said so. It is what it is.

ARTHUR: What will she do to you?

MERLIN: She is going to use my magic to seal me up in a cave—or maybe under a rock—or maybe in a tree. It's all a bit vague. Either way, you will be on your own, and I will never be able to help you again. In fact, we are leaving today.

ARTHUR: Today? Why did you not tell me sooner?

MERLIN: Because I knew you would try to stop me.

ARTHUR: Please, Merlin. I have already lost so much! Don't go!

MERLIN: Nonsense. How else can I retire unless I go where no one can reach me? Plus, Nimue has this plan all worked out in her pretty little head. I would hate to disappoint her.

NARRATOR: The wizard grinned.

MERLIN: She *is* quite fetching, isn't she?

ARTHUR: I will miss you!

NARRATOR: The king embraced his long-time mentor and friend.

MERLIN: Now. Now. I shall miss you as well. But do not fret. Perhaps we will see each other again, in a different time—a distant time.

ARTHUR: I don't know how I will rule Camelot without you.

MERLIN: All that Camelot has become is because of you. I have only been a teacher and a guide. But when the lessons are learned, the teacher fades away. Continue to do what is right until your dying breath, and you can never truly fail.

NIMUE: *(sweetly)* Merlin.

NARRATOR: The white lake-maiden came into their presence and wrapped her slender arm around Merlin's.

NIMUE: Are you ready to depart?

MERLIN: I am, my dear.

NIMUE: I have discovered the most beautiful cave in Cornwall, and I want to show it to you.

MERLIN: Of course. I cannot wait to see it.

NIMUE: Arthur, I will help guard Camelot. Tell your knights to watch for the tricks of Morgan le Fay. She will be seeking revenge more now than ever.

MERLIN: Well, goodbye, Arthur. I will not get too sentimental—but after all, I was there on the day of your birth, and you are the closest thing to a family I shall ever have. I tried to teach you as best I could. You have always striven to be a good man and do good to others. Because of that, you have changed this land, and I am proud of that.

NARRATOR: Merlin climbed atop his white donkey.

MERLIN: Well, I leave Britain in your capable hands. Reign well, my boy. And remember—a good king rules not by force but by example! Farewell!

NARRATOR: Kicking their mounts into motion, Merlin and the lake-maiden rode away into the dim twilight.

DISCUSSION QUESTIONS

1. Is Merlin right—does adventure lead us to truth? What truths can adventure teach us about ourselves or the world around us?
2. Arthur catches a brief glimpse of Nimue as the White Hart. Was the White Hart that led Arthur on a quest actually Nimue in disguise? If so, what was her motive for luring Arthur on an adventure?
3. For Arthur's development why is it necessary that Merlin leaves? How can too much reliance on others have a negative impact on someone's life?
4. Is Nimue good or evil? Explain.
5. Some have wondered how Merlin, who can see the future at times, would allow himself to be sealed up in a magical cave. Some think it is because he was in love with Nimue and blind to her plans. Others think Merlin *wanted* to be imprisoned. What theory do you agree with? Explain.
6. What role has Merlin played in Arthur's reign? Is Merlin speaking the truth when he says that he has only been a guide and helper in the making of Camelot? Explain.
7. How has Morgan become an even more formidable enemy than before?
8. How do the White Hart itself and the pursuit of the White Hart symbolize Arthur and his kingdom?

GAWAIN AND THE GREEN KNIGHT TEACHER GUIDE

BACKGROUND

Quests are where knights utilize the virtues and skills that they have been taught. A quest is typically about helping others, doing good deeds, or bringing greater truth into the world. But the quest is also about the knight's own personal growth. Quests help knights develop physically and mentally.

Gawain's quest with the Green Knight is the subject of the 14th-century poem *Sir Gawain and the Green Knight*, a favorite of British literature. This story puts Gawain in a precarious position. When a lord's wife desires Gawain's love, he is torn between two duties. It is the duty of knights to serve women, but it is also their obligation to maintain their virtue. If Gawain refuses the woman, he is denying his duty. If he gives in, he loses his honor.

Although this version of the story has changed some of the original details and lost some of the bawdy humor, it is faithful to the spirit of the original poem. Gawain goes questing, suffers defeat, but returns a wiser knight.

SUMMARY

Arthur's court is in the midst of its Christmas celebration when a mysterious visitor arrives—an enormous knight dressed all in green. The knight displays a sprig of holly, showing that he comes in peace. He proposes a challenge to Arthur and his knights. At first only Arthur will take the knight's challenge, but when everyone fears that the king will be killed, Gawain bravely volunteers to take the giant knight's challenge in Arthur's place. The knight issues his challenge: Gawain must take an axe and strike the Green Knight's neck. If this stroke does not kill him, the Green Knight gains the right to issue his own blow. Gawain bravely faces the challenge, severing the Green Knight's head. To everyone's shock, the knight continues to live, although beheaded. He picks up his still-living head, which declares that Gawain must meet the Green Knight in a year's time at a place called the Green Chapel. Then the knight departs.

Months later, Gawain embarks upon his quest, searching for the Green Chapel. He wanders for many months and finally cries out to heaven to assist him. Immediately he spies a strange castle. Inside he meets a lord, who invites him to stay with him and his lady. The lord tells Gawain that the Green Chapel is near, but he cannot show him the way for three days, for he is going on a hunt. While the lord hunts, Gawain will stay behind with the lord's wife and a strange old woman who lives in the castle.

The next morning the lord rides off to hunt. Gawain awakens to find the lady of the castle sitting on his bed. He protests that this is improper, but she declares love for him and wishes to receive a kiss. Gawain denies her, even though she appeals to his sense of chivalry, and the lady departs.

The second morning the same events are repeated. The lord departs, and the lady appears in Gawain's room. This time she tricks him into giving her a kiss by claiming that there can be no sin in a chaste kiss. The lady desires more, but Gawain refuses her.

The third morning the lord departs, and the lady comes to Gawain asking him to give her a love-token. He refuses, so she instead offers him one—her ring. Gawain turns down this gift, but then the lady offers her girdle—a magical scarf that protects anyone who wears it. Gawain accepts this gift since it will help him on his quest.

The following morning the lord has one of his servants lead Gawain to the Green Chapel. The Green Knight is there and tells Gawain it is time to receive his axe-blow. The Green Knight strikes twice but pulls away at the last minute. The third time the axe cuts Gawain's neck but rebounds before removing his head. Gawain declares he has won, thanks to the magical scarf. The Green Knight laughs and reveals his true identity—the lord who hosted Gawain. He identifies himself as a servant of Morgan le Fay, the old woman who appeared in the castle. He declares that Gawain has been tricked and failed on his quest because he accepted the lady's scarf—choosing safety over bravery. In actuality the scarf is not magical at all. Gawain returns to Camelot defeated but wiser.

ESSENTIAL QUESTIONS

- What should you do when your virtues and your duty conflict?
- Do you learn more by winning or losing?

ANTICIPATORY QUESTIONS

- Would you risk your life just to answer a dare?
- What is more important—bravery or safety?

CHARACTER QUEST

Duty and Virtue in Conflict In this story Gawain's sense of duty conflicts with his virtues. He has sworn to serve noble women, but the lady of the castle is trying to ruin his honor. Gawain chooses virtue over duty and escapes her temptation. The easy road would have been to give into her advances. How can we apply this to our own lives?

CONNECT

***Sir Gawain and the Green Knight* (Trans. Burton Raffel)** This 14th-century poem, originally written in Middle English, is a staple of English literature. The poem presents the conflict between two medieval traditions—a knight's duty to serve and his vow to be virtuous.

TEACHABLE TERMS

- **Manners/customs** The chivalric knight was expected to obey all requests given to him by a noble lady—except where these requests conflicted with his sworn oath of knighthood. This dilemma forms the central conflict of this story.
- **Allusions** On pg. 108 Gawain makes allusion to male characters from the Bible who found women to be a weakness—David, Solomon, and Samson.
- **Motif** The color green, symbolic of life and rebirth, is used as a motif in this story. Locate how many times the color green is mentioned throughout the story.

RECALL QUESTIONS

1. What does the Green Knight carry in his hand to show that he is peaceful?
2. What is the Green Knight's challenge?
3. What item does the lady of the castle attempt to give to Gawain?
4. What item does he accept from the lady?
5. What is the true identity of the Green Knight?

GAWAIN AND THE GREEN KNIGHT

CAST

GAWAIN	*Valiant Knight*
ARTHUR	*King of Britain*
KAY	*Arthur's Seneschal*
BEDIVERE	*Knight of Arthur*
GREEN KNIGHT	*Mysterious Opponent*
BERTILAK	*Country Lord*
LADY	*Wife of Bertilak*
BOY	*Servant to Bertilak*

NARRATOR: In the years following the departure of Merlin from Camelot, Arthur felt the pressures of ruling his kingdom more deeply than ever before. Yet in his old mentor's absence, the king learned to rely instead on the strength and wise counsel of his valiant knights.

Among the members of the Round Table, Gawain, Arthur's nephew, had earned distinction. Yet it was one quest in particular that solidified Gawain's reputation as one of Arthur's greatest knights—a magical quest that tested him most grievously and brought him dangerously close to destruction.

It all began at Christmastime in Camelot. While snow blanketed the world outside, the noble lords and ladies of Arthur's court gathered in the castle's great hall for fifteen days of singing, dancing, and feasting.

ARTHUR: We are assembled here today to celebrate the birth of our Holy Lord. Raise your goblets with me and—

(tremendous crash)

NARRATOR: A tremendous crash interrupted Arthur's words. Every head in the hall turned to the entryway where hurried shouts and the sound of clattering hoofbeats were ringing out. *(shouting and hoofbeats)*

KAY: What is that racket? Who dares disturb our feast?

NARRATOR: A colossal figure on horseback barreled into the room—knocking aside the men-at-arms who tried to bar his way. *(collective gasp)*

It was a knight full as big as a giant, and every bit of him was green—his enormous hands, his snarling face, his ratty beard, and his glittering shirt.

Even his massive steed was green, and at its rider's spurring, it bounded up onto the Round Table and galloped toward the king's seat. *(hoofbeats and crashing)* Platters flew to the sides as guests fell back from their seats in surprise, inches from the tearing hooves of the mount.

BEDIVERE: *(shouting)* Protect the king!

NARRATOR: King Arthur rose and drew Excalibur.

ARTHUR: (shouting) Halt, knight! I order you to stop!

NARRATOR: The Green Knight reined up—only feet from the king—and let out an earth-shattering laugh.

GREEN KNIGHT: (booming laugh) Ha! Greetings of the season, small knights!

KAY: (angrily) If you've come to fight, we will readily oblige you, sirrah!

NARRATOR: The emerald eyes of the giant shone gleefully.

GREEN KNIGHT: Nonsense! This is Christmas! I would not fight on this holy occasion. As you can see, I wear no armor, and I bear the holly of peace.

NARRATOR: He held out a sprig of holly clutched in his fist.

GREEN KNIGHT: Instead I bring a game—a challenge for anyone brave enough to take it. Who will step forward?

NARRATOR: There was a pause. The knights looked at one another out of the corner of their eyes.

ARTHUR: This man—or whatever he is—has issued a challenge. Will no one take it?

BEDIVERE: Well…I would, sire, but his entrance was kind of intimidating. There's no telling what kind of wicked challenge he might propose!

KAY: You know I would volunteer if I could, but I have a bad back.

GREEN KNIGHT: Ha! I have heard tales of the *brave* Knights of the Round Table! But all I find here is a bunch of cowering maids!

NARRATOR: Arthur could stand it no longer.

ARTHUR: Fine! I accept your challenge—since no one else will.

NARRATOR: The Green Knight spurred his horse to jump from the Round Table. (*clattering of dishes*) He dismounted and strode toward the king, holding aloft a massive axe for all to see.

GREEN KNIGHT: Here is my game. Take this axe and strike me upon the neck!

KAY: He calls that a game?

ARTHUR: I would be glad to! Maybe it would teach you some manners!

GREEN KNIGHT: But know this—once you have dealt your blow, I have the right to return it.

BEDIVERE: What good will that do you? Your head will be lying at your feet!

GREEN KNIGHT: This is my challenge. Do you accept it, Arthur?

NARRATOR: Arthur opened his mouth to reply.

GAWAIN: Wait!

NARRATOR: Gawain rose from his seat.

GAWAIN: Uncle, let me take your place! There is some trick in this challenge. My life is no matter, but if you were lost, Britain would be lost as well.

GREEN KNIGHT: The puny knight has a good point.

ARTHUR: I am not afraid.

GAWAIN: I know, but it is our duty to protect you. How could we live with ourselves if you lost your life?

ARTHUR: Gawain, your bravery puts the bravery of all others to shame.

NARRATOR: The other knights looked at one another sheepishly.

ARTHUR: You may play the Green Knight's game in my place.

NARRATOR: Gawain came forward and faced the grinning giant.

GREEN KNIGHT: Kind of runty, aren't you? Ha! Just remember—if I am not slain, I will surely slay you.

GAWAIN: Bring it forth! I will feed your head to the dogs!

NARRATOR: The Green Knight offered up the humongous axe and kneeled as Gawain took up the weapon.

GREEN KNIGHT: Take the axe. Strike hard and fast. Make you sure you do it with great skill, or your death will be sure.

NARRATOR: Gawain strained to raise the weapon above his head. The Green Knight bared his neck, toying absentmindedly with his beard, unconcerned about the coming death blow.

ARTHUR: *(breathlessly)* This knight is insane.

NARRATOR: Producing a victorious cry, Gawain brought the blade down with all his might.

GAWAIN: *(loud battlecry)* Ah!

NARRATOR: His stroke sliced neatly—severing flesh, meat, and bone. *(snickersnack)* Green blood sprayed in all directions, and the knight's head dropped heavily to the floor. There was a pause.

GREEN KNIGHT: *(crazed laughter)* Hee hee!

NARRATOR: The severed head of the knight started to howl with laughter—its eyes rolling gleefully in its head. Flopping up on its chin, the head gnashed and lunged toward those nearby.

GREEN KNIGHT: Rar!

(screaming of women, shouting of the crowd)

NARRATOR: The ladies swooned at the sight of the demon face, and their lords rushed forward to protect them.

ARTHUR: *(in shock)* Zounds!

NARRATOR: Then a new wonder shook them all. The headless body of the Green Knight stood up. Gripping the severed head by the hair, the corpse lifted it up before the stunned face of Gawain.

GREEN KNIGHT: You have a year, knight. Seek the Green Chapel on New Year's Day. There I shall meet you and do to you as you have done to me. Only I doubt you will be able keep your head as well as I have. *(crazy laugh)* Hee hee!

NARRATOR: The ghoulish face winked.

GREEN KNIGHT: Until then, sweet dreams! *(maniacal laughter)*

NARRATOR: Cradling its head like a newborn babe, the knight remounted his steed and galloped from the hall. Green mist hung in the air where the specter had been. A stunned silence filled the room.

ARTHUR: *(in shock)* What was that? No man of flesh and blood could have survived such a thing!

GAWAIN: He must be some kind of ghost or ghoul. But I do not fear the grave.

ARTHUR: Ghoul or not, in a year you must face him. It will come quickly.

GAWAIN: Let it come. What do I care? I'll seek this knight out. A spirit cannot harm a man of flesh and blood.

ARTHUR: But witchcraft does not follow human laws.

NARRATOR: The event was mentioned no more, but the merriment of the feast refused to be revived. The green visitor had cast an impenetrable gloom on the festivities.

Lent came and went and with it, winter. Spring, summer, and the harvest time played host to many great deeds, but no mind forgot that Gawain would soon have to embark on his promised quest. When the cold once again threatened and the Feast of All-Saints was at hand, Gawain prepared to leave.

ARTHUR: Take care, nephew. Come home in one piece.

GAWAIN: Know this, my king. I will search this land until I find the Green Chapel and face the Green Knight once again. I will not rest until I have succeeded. And I shall return.

ARTHUR: Very well then. Farewell.

NARRATOR: The ladies of the court wept piteously as Gawain rode his noble steed, Gringolet, from Camelot. His symbol, the five pointed star, blazed out from his shield triumphantly, each point representing the five wounds of Christ. But as the banners and the ramparts of the city faded into the distance, Gawain began to feel a dread of the goal he had sworn to reach.

He met with many adventures on his way. He found dragons and wolves and forest trolls and bulls and bears and ogres, and though time and time again he vanquished them through the power of God, he had not yet found the Green Chapel.

The weather grew colder and colder—oppressing his body and compacting his will. At night he slept on the barren rock, inside his frigid armor. By day, he fought the perils of the lonely path.

One morning after weeks of fruitless search, he cried aloud…

GAWAIN: Heaven help me!

NARRATOR: As if in answer to his divine distress call, the gray storm clouds pulled back, and he spied a castle upon a faraway hill. A cover of snow lay upon the lawn, but green grass-tips were beginning to poke through. A sparkling emerald moat encircled the grounds.

GAWAIN: Thank you!

NARRATOR: Crowning the hill, the shimmering white walls looked as though their perfect lines had been cut from paper. Gawain spurred Gringolet forward and thundered across the lowered drawbridge.

As he rode into the courtyard, distant shouts announced his presence, and upon dismounting, he saw a burly man approaching him cautiously.

BERTILAK: *(inquisitively)* Who goes there?

GAWAIN: It is I, Gawain, knight of the Round Table.

BERTILAK: *(overjoyed)* A knight of the Round Table! Here in my castle! And on Christmas Eve!

NARRATOR: A large black beard almost covered the lord's ruddy cheeks. He nearly whisked Gawain off his feet as he pushed him inside the hallways of the elegant castle.

BERTILAK: Heaven bless me! What will the wife say? She'll probably faint dead on the spot—after seeing a knight of the Round Table here in our castle!

GAWAIN: May I have lodging here at your castle, sir?

BERTILAK: Goodness! Of course, man, of course. Stay as long as you like. You're a celebrity, you know.

GAWAIN: I am?

BERTILAK: *(booming laugh)* Heavens, yes! I suppose you have even seen *the* King Arthur with your very own eyes.

GAWAIN: Of course, I have. He's my uncle.

BERTILAK: This is too much! Too much! The missus will go nuts! We will have a feast—probably not as grand a one as you have in Camelot. By the way, you must tell me what it's like there! I'm sure it's marvelous! Absolutely marvelous! Oh, but I forget! You must be tired! The steward will show you to your room. Freshen up a bit, and we will feast until we can feast no more. Then off to mass. It is Christmas Eve, you know. But look who I'm telling? I have one of God's champions under my very own roof! Ha! See you soon!

NARRATOR: Because of this barrage of speech, Gawain felt a bit bewildered, but after changing out of his armor and relaxing in a warm bath, he made his way down to the banquet hall. Seated at a long table of sumptuous dishes were the jovial lord and a voluptuous woman whom the knight perceived to be his lady.

BERTILAK: *(through mouthfuls of food)* Gawain! Come! Sit! Here is my wife! She has been dying to meet you!

NARRATOR: The lady rose at Gawain's approach. She was most fair. Bowing to him, she extended a porcelain hand.

LADY: *(seductively)* Oooh. It is so nice to meet you! I am soooo delighted to have such a big, strong young man like you here. Are all the knights in Camelot as handsome as you? Tee hee.

GAWAIN: Uh—I—well... *(cough)*

BERTILAK: *(loud laugh)* Ha! I see you two will get along well!

NARRATOR: At the far end of the table—hunched in the shadows—Gawain could make out an old woman shrouded in black. A pair of bristling eyebrows stuck out over her hooked nose. She gave the knight an eerie feeling as she met his gaze.

LADY: Do not mind her, handsome knight. Come sit by me.

NARRATOR: Gawain did as she bade him, and the image of the old woman soon left his mind. The lord bellowed and laughed loudly, and his lady whispered melodiously into Gawain's ear—her hand ever upon his forearm. Soon the fires died down, and the lord began to yawn and stretch.

BERTILAK: (*yawn*) Well, sir knight! The evening is drawing to a close, and yet we have never discussed your quest—if it can be discussed.

GAWAIN: It can, and I offer it willingly. I have come to fight the Green Knight at the Green Chapel.

LADY: (*gasp*) Oh my!

BERTILAK: (*in shock*) Sir knight, his evil chapel is only a short distance from here, but surely you do not wish to go there!

GAWAIN: I do. I have made a promise.

BERTILAK: This is grievous news indeed!

GAWAIN: Will you show me the way?

BERTILAK: I am afraid I am not as brave as you, my friend. I will not go near the place. It gives me the creeps! But I will send my page-boy to show the way.

GAWAIN: Thank you. I am most appreciative.

BERTILAK: But I'm afraid you must wait. Three days of hunting lie ahead for me. It is a yearly ritual, and that page-boy must go along to tend my hunting hounds.

GAWAIN: But—I cannot wait—

BERTILAK: I'm afraid you must, my lord. Perhaps in that time, you will reconsider your quest.

GAWAIN: If I must, I must. Perhaps a hunt will get my mind off it for a while.

BERTILAK: (*strangely*) Unfortunately, I only hunt alone, my lord. I felt you might enjoy staying behind here—with the women. My wife has taken quite a fancy to you. She's dying to hear some of your tales from Camelot.

NARRATOR: The lord looked to his beautiful wife, who smiled happily with anticipation.

LADY: Oh, yes! I'd love to know you better, Sir Gawain.

GAWAIN: I—uh—

BERTILAK: Then—it's settled! (*loud laugh*) Now to bed! There is a hunt tomorrow!

NARRATOR: That night, Gawain's dreams were haunted by the image of the Green Knight—his emerald axe sparkling in the darkness. He was awakened in the morn by the sound of Lord Bertilak's steed thundering out of the courtyard. He sat up.

To his shock, Gawain saw the lady of the castle was seated upon the foot of his bed.

GAWAIN: (*shocked*) My lady! This is not decent! You should not be here in my private chamber!

LADY: (*playfully*) Oh, Sir Gawain. Don't be so uptight!

GAWAIN: (stammering) But—but—your—your—husband!

LADY: Oh, he's miles away by now. You've been such a sleepy-head. You didn't even notice when I came in.

GAWAIN: I—uh—I think you should leave.

LADY: Leave? Why would I leave when I have a captive audience?

NARRATOR: The woman scooted forward. Gawain shied away.

LADY: Oh, Gawain. I have heard so many stories about you that I decided I must be alone with you—to know you better—if you know what I mean...

GAWAIN: My lady! I am an honorable knight! If you are insinuating what I think you are—!

NARRATOR: The lady suddenly looked hurt.

LADY: (confused) What? How could you think that? No! I am a married lady, sir. I only came to hear stories.

GAWAIN: (apologizing) Oh, I am sorry. I just assumed that—

LADY: (indignantly) You should be sorry! But I am willing to overlook it. Now you will tell me a story. But we have a custom in this land that you must obey.

GAWAIN: I will do whatever your ladyship desires.

LADY: The custom is that whoever is to tell the story must first be kissed—by me!

GAWAIN: What? My lady!

NARRATOR: The lady moved close and puckered her lips.

LADY: Be my love, Gawain!

GAWAIN: No! I am an honorable knight! I will not!

LADY: (quietly) Very well. I will go.

NARRATOR: Then the lady departed.
Hours later, horns announced the return of the lord. (fanfare) Gawain was sent for and guiltily went down to meet his host.

BERTILAK: (loudly) Young knight! What have you and my wife been up to today?

GAWAIN: (nervously) Nothing! Why? Why do you ask?

BERTILAK: She seems most upset about something!

GAWAIN: She wanted me to...tell her stories.

BERTILAK: And you did not? I am offended! That doesn't seem courteous. You are a knight. Give her whatever she requests. If she wants a story, give her a story. Give her two for good measure!

GAWAIN: Well, I...

BERTILAK: Tomorrow, perhaps?

NARRATOR: When the lady of the castle presented herself to sup, she acted as if nothing had happened—calmly seating herself beside Gawain. Much to his terror, she placed her hand upon his forearm and smiled warmly to him all throughout the night. He barely managed to finish his meal.

As Gawain stumbled up to his chambers, he noticed the black eyes of the old hag watching him from the shadowed end of the table. He shuddered.

GAWAIN: Two more days...two more days.

NARRATOR: That night he dreamed of the old woman. Her wrinkled face was upon the pillow with his, and her cracked lips tried to kiss his own. He awoke with a start.

It was morning. The lady was once again sitting on the edge of his bed, but this time she wore a pout of dissatisfaction.

LADY: (*sheepishly*) I spoke to my husband about you, you know.

GAWAIN: (*shocked*) What?

LADY: Yes. He was most displeased that you refused to give me what I wanted.

GAWAIN: He obviously didn't know what that was!

LADY: He told me to tell you that if you did not grant me my request that you are not truly a noble knight.

GAWAIN: I am not a noble knight if I do.

LADY: Hmmmm. Then this is a puzzle. If I cannot get what I want, then I must tell him I was refused. Then he may not show you the way to the Green Knight.

GAWAIN: If I do what you want, it won't matter if I find the Green Knight or not. I'll be powerless! Goodness gives me my power.

LADY: One little kiss. That is all I desire. Nothing more. A chaste kiss. A pure kiss.

GAWAIN: Then you will stop tormenting me?

LADY: Upon my word.

GAWAIN: Very well.

NARRATOR: Gawain leaned forward, and their lips met. Something smoldered between them, something that begged the knight not to let go, to kiss her until the end of time. But then he remember his quest, he remembered his host, and he remember his oath of knighthood.

GAWAIN: (*shouting*) Enough!

LADY: (*sadly*) Very well, my knight. You have given me my token. I will take it—though I admit I desired more.

GAWAIN: That is all you shall have.

LADY: We shall see.

NARRATOR: When the lord arrived home from the hunt once again, he barged into the room of his guest.

BERTILAK: Did you give her what she wanted?

GAWAIN: I did.

BERTILAK: A-ha. Wonderful. When my wife is happy, I am happy. Remember—deny her nothing. I hunt again tomorrow, but the day after I shall have my boy lead you to where the Green Knight resides.

NARRATOR: That night Gawain refused to come down from his chamber and barred the door against all requests. His sleep brought him little comfort. Once again, the image of the Green Knight stood before him, asking for his neck, but this time the old hag was behind him, cackling.

He awoke. The lady's head was resting happily beside his own.

GAWAIN: *(cry of shock)* Ah! You swore to leave me alone!

LADY: I did, and I mean it. I have only come to ask you a favor.

GAWAIN: I will not give you what you want! I will not!

LADY: All knights must give a token to a lady when she asks it. If you will not give me your love, you must give me something else.

GAWAIN: Leave me! Please leave me!

LADY: You know, Sir Gawain, you are absolutely no fun. Very well. I will leave you, but first I must give you *my* present.

NARRATOR: She reached within the neck of her robe and pulled forth a shining ring.

LADY: *This* is a token of my love.

GAWAIN: I refuse it! You're tricking me! Your husband will find it, and my quest will be ruined!

LADY: This little thing? He would never find it! He's far too dumb to notice anyhow!

GAWAIN: No!

LADY: Well, you must take something. Fine. I hoped not to resort to this.

NARRATOR: She began to untie the green sash at her waist. Gawain averted his eyes.

GAWAIN: Please! My lady!

LADY: Oh, Gawain, relax. I can see that your heart is far too pure for temptation. That is why I am granting you this glorious gift—my girding sash.

NARRATOR: As she removed her sash, the jewels embedded within it glimmered.

LADY: It is a magical scarf. It will protect you from any blow.

GAWAIN: Any blow?

NARRATOR: Gawain took the airy object into his hands.

LADY: You have beaten me, Gawain. I am a sinful woman. Go and face your Green Knight. You shall remain pure and noble.

NARRATOR: She made her way to the chamber door but turned back one final time.

LADY: And if for some reason you do change your mind…you know where to find me.

NARRATOR: With the lady gone, Gawain stared at the sash in wonder. This was exactly the object with which he could defeat the Green Knight. He tied it about his waist at once.

When the braying of the hounds announced the return of his host, Gawain met him triumphantly in the courtyard.

GAWAIN: Three days have passed, my lord! Tomorrow, you must honor your bargain and provide me with a guide to the Green Chapel.

BERTILAK: And what about my wife?

GAWAIN: Uh, what about her, my lord?

BERTILAK: *(shrewdly)* What did you two do to pass the time? Anything I should know about?

GAWAIN: *(shocked)* No! Definitely not!

BERTILAK: Did she give you anything? Any gifts?

GAWAIN: Nothing. Nothing. Well, a kiss of brotherhood.

BERTILAK: Good! Then you are blessed. Tonight we shall feast to your honor, and though we hate to see you go, we will wish you the best!

NARRATOR: The two feasted as planned, but as the night progressed, the lady did not show herself. Gawain thought little of it, and when he retired to his chambers, the glittering eyes of the old hag did not stare forth from the darkness.

As the cock crowed the morning cry, a servant knocked upon Gawain's door. The knight was ready. No dreams had disturbed his sleep, for he had the magical sash about his waist. He ordered the servant to lead the way, and soon they were making their way through the frosty countryside.

GAWAIN: Faster, boy! My destiny awaits! Tell me, what stories have you heard of this Green Knight?

BOY: He is a demon! A ferocious killer!

GAWAIN: Bring him on, I say. Nothing can stop a knight of the Round Table.

NARRATOR: A gnarled wood soon overshadowed their path, and the page-boy cast nervous glances toward the unwavering knight. He pointed to a distant green hill with a cave in its side. A green mist hung in the air around it.

BOY: The Green Chapel is in there! It is an unholy place! I will go no further!

GAWAIN: No need, boy. You have done your duty. Run home to your master.

NARRATOR: As the youth dashed away, Gawain hoisted his shield and rode boldly toward the entrance of the cave. A sudden sound caused Gringolet to start. It was the grinding of an axe. *(sound of the grinding of an axe)*

GAWAIN: Heaven help me!

NARRATOR: At the base of the hill stood the Green Knight himself—his head reattached and examining the sharpness of his axe.

GREEN KNIGHT: Greetings, knight. I see you have come to fulfill our bargain.

GAWAIN: I have.

NARRATOR: Gawain silently dismounted and knelt on the ground in front of the giant. He heard the Green Knight's muscles creak ever-so-slightly as he raised the huge axe above his head.

GREEN KNIGHT: This blow is in retribution for the blow dealt myself one year past. Bear it well.

NARRATOR: Gawain felt his guts tighten inside of him and clenched his eyes shut in anticipation of the blow.

GREEN KNIGHT: *(battle cry)* Ahhhhh!

NARRATOR: The axe sang as it cut downward, and the air of its descent pushed upon the back of Gawain's neck. He flinched in spite of himself, but he felt no blow.

GREEN KNIGHT: *(loud laughing)* A-ha! A-ha! A knight of the Round Table afraid to die! You should have seen how you flinched! But that was only a test. Now here comes the real blow.

GAWAIN: Let it come! I will not flinch like a coward this time!

NARRATOR: The axe was raised again. Whoosh, it fell.

GREEN KNIGHT: *(battle cry)* Ahhhhhh!

NARRATOR: Gawain stayed firm, but with the axe's fall came no blow.

GREEN KNIGHT: Hmmm. Better. This time you did not flinch like a servingmaid. Perhaps you are not the woman I thought you to be. *(pause)* Not that it matters though, knight. This final blow shall be the true one. I shall strike and take your head.

GAWAIN: Swing your hardest. *(whispering)* Heaven protect me.

GREEN KNIGHT: *(battle cry)* Ahhhhh!

NARRATOR: Gawain felt the weapon pierce the skin of his neck, and his mind leapt toward oblivion. But no further advance did the axe head make. It instead seemed to rebound off an invisible barrier—leaving only a slight scratch upon the nape of his neck.

Gawain sprang up at once, drawing his sword and rounding on the giant.

GAWAIN: *(happily)* Ha! I have passed your test and survived your blow. Now, let us duel and end this trial!

NARRATOR: The Green Knight did not move to attack. He only leaned upon the handle of his weapon and grinned broadly.

GREEN KNIGHT: *(loud laughing)* Ha-ha! Passed my test? How do you figure?

GAWAIN: My bravery has saved me from your blade!

GREEN KNIGHT: *(snort)* Your bravery? That's a laugh. By the way, why are you wearing women's clothing?

GAWAIN: *(defensively)* I'm not!

GREEN KNIGHT: Really? Is there not a lady's sash around your waist?

GAWAIN: Errr. But how did you—?

NARRATOR: The giant reared back and laughed.

GREEN KNIGHT: *(laughing)* Perhaps you would recognize me better in another form.

NARRATOR: The giant's frame shrank down into the form of Gawain's former host, Lord Bertilak.

GAWAIN: You! You are the Green Knight?

BERTILAK: No fooling you! *This* was not the test. The real test happened back at my castle. Three times my lady came to you, trying to ruin your virtue. On the third day, she succeeded.

GAWAIN: No, she did not! I kept my honor.

BERTILAK: You might have refused her love, but when you took her sash, you sacrificed your bravery for safety—and then lied about it. Right then and there, you failed!

GAWAIN: The magical sash was the test?

BERTILAK: (laugh) Magical? That sash is not magical. It couldn't protect you from a stiff wind! It was a trick! The only reason you didn't lose your head is because I held back my stroke at the last second.

GAWAIN: But—I...

BERTILAK: Yes, you have failed, but who could have not fallen for such a clever trick? My lady and I are servants to Morgan le Fay, and it was she who devised this trap for you—to ruin your virtue. It was Lady le Fay that appeared each night in the form of the old crone.

GAWAIN: (in shock) You're right! I have lost my honor! I am not worthy to live!

NARRATOR: Gawain held out his sword in the palms of his hands.

GAWAIN: Take my sword and use it to put me to death.

BERTILAK: (laugh) Ha! That is perhaps what Lady le Fay would have me do, but I have decided rather to release you. You have admitted your error and learned a valuable lesson. Why chop off a head that has been filled with so much wisdom?

NARRATOR: Gawain reached back to his neck where warm blood trickled.

GAWAIN: This wound goes deeper than it appears. It has reached down to my pride.

BERTILAK: Assuredly! Go, good knight. But in the future, watch for the tricks of Lady Morgan. Next time you may not escape with your life.

NARRATOR: Gawain pulled forth the shining sash.

GAWAIN: I will wear this always about my arm to remind me of my own weakness. Like the great ones before me, David, Solomon, and Samson, I have been brought low by the charms of a woman.

BERTILAK: It happens to the best of us. I too have fallen under the spell of the Lady le Fay and will remain so until the end of my days. Farewell, good sir knight.

NARRATOR: Turning his back upon the Green Chapel, Gawain remounted Gringolet and rode reflectively from the enchanted wood. As he passed beneath the final branches, he looked back over his shoulder. The glow of the Green Knight could no longer be seen.

Gawain returned to Camelot in defeat. Everyone gathered there rejoiced at his return but noticed a change in the young knight. He had come back wiser, and they all rejoiced that God above had given such heavenly wisdom to one of the greatest among them.

DISCUSSION QUESTIONS

1. What lesson does Gawain learn on this quest?
2. Throughout the story what are some of the clues that hint at the story's ending and the Green Knight's real identity?
3. In myths and legends women are often presented as evil temptresses, like the lady of the castle in this story. Is this an accurate picture of women? Explain.
4. Can you learn just as much by losing as winning? Explain.
5. Is Gawain brave? Explain.
6. Was Gawain technically cheating by accepting the "magical" sash? Explain.
7. Should you ever cheat in order to win? Explain.
8. What should you do when your duty and your virtues come into conflict?
9. How does this happen in Gawain's story?
10. Even though he is not willing to "cheat" with the lord's wife, he is willing to cheat in the Green Knight's challenge by accepting the green sash. Are there different levels to cheating—some being acceptable and others not? Or all instances of cheating wrong? Explain.

THE KNIGHT OF THE LAKE
TEACHER GUIDE

BACKGROUND

Lancelot is not mentioned in the earliest King Arthur legends. He is a character that was added later by French poets, who adopted and adapted the original British legends. The French authors transformed the fragmented stories into the courtly epics we know today. In their version of the story Lancelot, a French knight, became the greatest knight in King Arthur's court.

Chretien de Troyes is the French author whose Arthurian romances introduce the Holy Grail, the character of Lancelot, and his affair with Arthur's queen, Guinevere. His 12th-century poem *Lancelot, the Knight of the Cart* makes Lancelot its hero—giving him the quest of rescuing Guinevere from an evil knight.

Since Malory, writing a few hundred years later, used Chretien and other French poems as sources when creating his *Le Morte D'Arthur*, Lancelot retained his central place in Arthur's story. In fact, Lancelot has such a prominent place in Malory's work, that some argue that he is the main character of *Le Morte D'Arthur* instead of Arthur himself.

SUMMARY

Lancelot grows up in the magical palace of the Lady of the Lake, unaware of his true identity. When Lancelot is of age, the Lady tells him that he is actually the son of King Ban of Benwick and his wife, who abandoned him on the lakeside. Now Lancelot is to journey to King Arthur's court and along the way prove himself worthy of knighthood. She tells the boy that he must have a heart of diamond and another of wax—a hard heart toward enemies and a kind heart toward ladies. Lancelot rides off toward Camelot.

Along the way Lancelot encounters a damsel who has lost her falcon up a tree. She asks him to retrieve the bird for her. In order to do so, he must remove his armor. When he is about half-way up the tree, a rogue knight appears, commanding the boy to come down. The whole thing has been a trap. Lancelot skillfully defeats the knight with a tree branch and avoids capture. The falcon-damsel declares that she was forced into the trick by the knight and thanks Lancelot for saving her. She asks Lancelot to free forty damsels from the evil sorceress, Morgan le Fay, who is her mistress. In order to sneak Lancelot into Morgan's castle, the damsel puts Lancelot to sleep and waits for her mistress to come along the road. When Morgan le Fay appears, the damsel convinces her to take Lancelot back to her dungeons as her paramour—or love.

Lancelot awakes in Morgan le Fay's dungeon, but the falcon-damsel frees and arms him. She sends him to rescue the forty damsels and warns him that two giants guard the castle grounds. Lancelot goes into the tall tower of the castle, where the damsels are held prisoner, and battles one of the giants, whom he defeats by knocking him from the top of the tower roof. Lady Elaine, one of the imprisoned damsels, has been sentenced to boil in a cauldron for eternity, unless the bravest knight in the world rescues her. Lancelot is able to free her. With the forty damsels in tow, Lancelot prepares to battle the second giant but finds that the falcon-damsel has already dispatched him, using sleeping herbs. The Lady of the Lake arrives and congratulates Lancelot on learning true knighthood. She

112   The Road to Camelot

agrees to lead Lancelot to Camelot where he will be knighted by King Arthur.

ESSENTIAL QUESTIONS

- How do our experiences shape us?
- How do you become a hero?

ANTICIPATORY QUESTIONS

- What is a giant? How tall is a giant?
- Who is the best knight of Camelot?
- What does it mean to have a heart of diamond?
- What does it mean to have a heart of wax?

CHARACTER QUEST

Experience In this story Lancelot is a young warrior trying to prove his worth. He goes upon his first quest, and although he has many failures, the experience he gains along the way helps prepare him for knighthood. How do our experiences—whether they are successes or failures—help shape us into the people we become? Can you think of an important lesson that you learned from a failure?

CONNECT

***Le Morte D'Arthur* by Thomas Malory** First published in 1485, this classic work fuses previous versions of the King Arthur legends into a complex and sprawling narrative. It is the ultimate version of the King Arthur legends. From the moment Lancelot is introduced into the epic, he almost becomes the main character of the story. His adventures and his eventual love for Queen Guinevere take center stage.

TEACHABLE TERMS

- **Metaphor** The Lady of the Lake's advice to Lancelot on pg. 114 that he must have two hearts—one of diamond and one of wax—is a metaphor for the two different ways a knight must act.
- **Idiom** Lancelot says, "No need to wake a sleeping giant" on pg. 121. This is wordplay off the common idiom. Usually the saying is used figuratively, but in this case it is used literally.
- **Third person** Gog the giant speaks in third person in order to make him seem less intelligent or more beast-like than the other characters.
- **Damsel-in-distress** This term applies to a female character in danger, one who is typically rescued by a knight or a prince. This story features forty damsels-in-distress. Examine how the falcon-damsel in the story is *not* a damsel-in-distress.

RECALL QUESTIONS

1. Who raised Lancelot?
2. Why does Lancelot have to take off his armor and climb a tree?
3. Who abducts Lancelot and traps him in a dungeon?
4. Two of what type of creature guard the castle of maidens?
5. A knight should have two types of hearts. What are they?

THE KNIGHT OF THE LAKE

CAST

LANCELOT	*Young, Prospective Knight*
LADY	*Enchantress of the Lake*
DAMSEL	*Young Maiden*
ROGUE	*Bandit Knight*
MORGAN	*Evil Enchantress*
MAIDEN	*Captive Maiden*
ELAINE	*Beautiful Princess*
GOG	*Giant*

NARRATOR: The young man, Lancelot, had been raised up by a lady whom he had always assumed was his mother. She certainly cared for him like a mother, calling him pet names like "white one" and giving him anything his heart desired. Yet the lady did not seem quite mortal. She never seemed to age, even as he aged. Her hair shifted and flowed like water, and her voice had the power to enchant whoever heard it. Even their castle-home and the servants who attended there seemed otherworldly. So one day, Lancelot asked.

LANCELOT: Do we live in an enchanted castle?

LADY: Why do you ask that, my white one?

LANCELOT: I look out from our castle windows, and I see a vast countryside all around us. Yet whenever we set foot outside the castle grounds, this world fades away. We appear standing on the shores of a great lake, and there is no sign of our castle anywhere.

LADY: The Lake is only an illusion that hides our true home.

NARRATOR: Then the boy asked a question he had never dared ask before.

LANCELOT: Are you my mother?

NARRATOR: The lady laughed a musical laugh.

LADY: *(musical laugh)* No, I am not. Though I would love to claim you, white one. You are the son of King Ban of Benwick and his queen.

LANCELOT: Then why was I not raised by them?

LADY: I am the Lady of the Lake. When you were just a baby, your mother left you on the shores of my watery home. She was searching frantically for your father on the nearby battlefield, and in her haste, she sat you down and left you.

LANCELOT: Did she not come back for me?

LADY: She did, but I already had you in my arms. Once I picked you up, I knew I never could let you go.

LANCELOT: Why didn't you return me to my mother?

LADY: She left you lying there all alone. A woman like that does not deserve a child like you, white one. Besides, does *she* live in an enchanted castle? Could *she* have loved you better than I could have? Could *she* have given you a better education?

LANCELOT: I guess not.

LADY: Your mother called you Galahad, but I gave you a new name—Lancelot.

LANCELOT: What does my name mean then?

LADY: What does it mean? It means nothing. But doesn't it sound lovely? I have loved you as my own for these past eighteen years, but today I am sad because it is time for you to leave me.

LANCELOT: Leave you? Why?

LADY: To become a knight, of course!

LANCELOT: You mean those warriors I have read about in books? They truly exist?

LADY: Of course, they do, and you will be a great name among them. Why do you think I have charged my servants to train you in horsemanship, swordsmanship, and every courtly grace?

LANCELOT: That means there is a King Arthur, too! I thought he was nothing but a fairy tale.

LADY: *(musical laugh)* Most people consider *us* to be a fairy tale. King Arthur is as real as anything.

LANCELOT: Then tell me, what must I do to be a knight?

LADY: A knight is a complex being, Lancelot. He must have two hearts. One heart must be made of diamond—as hard as a stone—for you will slay many evil knights and beasts without mercy. But your other heart must be soft and tender like wax, for you must always treat ladies and damsels with respect and always be gentlemanly in their presence. You must do any deed that they ask of you—as long as there be no dishonor in it. And if enemies ever beg for mercy, you must give it to them.

LANCELOT: Is that all?

LADY: All? That is a hefty task! I am sending you to Camelot. Along the way you will encounter adventures, and through them, you will prove yourself worthy to be a knight. By the time you reach Arthur's castle, he will have no choice but to knight you.

NARRATOR: At this the Lady of the Lake waved her hand, and a suit of shining white armor and a magnificent sword appeared before Lancelot. The boy looked up to the Lady happily.

LANCELOT: These are for me?

LADY: Yes. A steed will also be yours—its hide as white as the driven snow. You shall be my White Knight.

NARRATOR: After a tearful goodbye, Lancelot left the only home he had ever known. As the boy stepped off the castle drawbridge, the world shifted, and he stood upon the edge of a large lake. The shimmering image of the Lady hovered in the lake's midst, watching and weeping at the departure of her adopted son. Lancelot waved one final farewell and headed down the road toward Camelot.

Once upon the road, it did not take long for a quest to find Lancelot. A massive tree grew by the roadside, and a sullen-faced damsel hunched against its trunk, picking at the rocks at her feet with a stick. When the damsel saw Lancelot approaching, she called out to him—although oddly her voice was without emotion.

DAMSEL: *(monotonously)* Help me, sir. Oh please. Help.

LANCELOT: *(nobly)* What's the trouble, damsel? Has an evil knight kidnapped you? Has an evil sorceress imprisoned your one true love?

NARRATOR: The damsel wrinkled her nose.

DAMSEL: No. None of that. My pet falcon got away from me. He's perched in the top of this tree and won't come down.

NARRATOR: Lancelot looked up into the tree's highest limbs. Sure enough, a falcon was perched there. *(falcon cry)*

LANCELOT: Oh.

DAMSEL: Can you fetch Talon for me?

NARRATOR: This did not seem like the quests that Lancelot had read about in his books.

LANCELOT: And you're sure that an evil sorceress didn't have anything to do with this?

DAMSEL: Look! Do you want my quest or not? I can find some other chucklehead to climb this tree for me.

NARRATOR: Lancelot was about to refuse her, but then the commission of the Lady of the Lake came into his mind.

LANCELOT: Of course, I accept your quest, damsel! It is my duty. I shall bravely face the dangers you have presented me with!

DAMSEL: *(sarcastically)* Oh, yes. Climbing a tree is sooo dangerous.

LANCELOT: I shall retrieve your beloved bird and soothe your broken heart.

DAMSEL: Well, it's just a bird. It will probably come down on its own eventually.

LANCELOT: No! Although certain death threatens me, I, Lancelot, shall serve you.

DAMSEL: Please. Don't make me puke. Just get the bird already.

NARRATOR: Lancelot walked forward and began to hoist his leg up the trunk.

DAMSEL: Whoa there, Sir Stupid. You can't climb a tree in your *armor*! Do you want to fall and break your neck?

LANCELOT: *(grumbling)* Right about now, yes. *(to the maiden)* You are right! How foolish of me. Please, damsel, avert your maidenly eyes.

DAMSEL: Oh brother.

NARRATOR: Lancelot unbuckled his belt and pulled his mail-coat off over his head. Now wearing only his shirt and tights, he began to hoist himself up the tree.

DAMSEL: (*yawning*) Watch for splinters. I'll be here when you get done.

NARRATOR: As Lancelot shimmied up the high tree, he grumbled to himself.

LANCELOT: (*muttering*) I can't believe this. I'm climbing a tree in my underwear—just to capture some mangy bird. (*sigh*) But I guess a damsel asked me to do it, so I must have a heart of wax.

NARRATOR: Lancelot climbed higher and higher, until he had almost reached the perch of the falcon. (*falcon cry*)

LANCELOT: Shut up, you stupid bird! Come here! Come here!

DAMSEL: Any day now…

NARRATOR: He reached for the falcon, which only flew higher in the tree.

LANCELOT: Grrrr.

NARRATOR: Just then the sound of an approaching rider drew Lancelot's attention. (*hoofbeats*) A fully-armed knight, who bore no coat of arms, galloped into the clearing and saluted the damsel below.

ROGUE: Good work, wench!

DAMSEL: Okay, he fell for it. He's up the tree in his underwear. He shouldn't be much of a challenge now—not that he was much of a challenge to begin with. (*whistles*) Talon! Come!

NARRATOR: At the damsel's summons the falcon took flight—circling lightly back down to her awaiting arm. Lancelot watched all this in shock.

LANCELOT: (*angrily*) Sabotage!

DAMSEL: Can I go back to my castle now or what?

LANCELOT: Damsel! I cannot believe this! I risked my life for you! Was this all a ruse?

DAMSEL: Yep. Tough luck.

ROGUE: (*yelling*) Come down, knight! I already have your fine armor here—or maybe I should say *my* fine armor. But I also intend to slay you and add your head to my collection!

LANCELOT: You recreant knight, this trick of yours is totally dishonorable! I have no weapons, no armor, and I'm currently up a tree. Don't you believe in a fair fight?

ROGUE: Anyone stupid enough to fall for *this* trick does not deserve a fair fight! I mean, who hasn't heard of the old damsel-with-a-falcon-up-a-tree trick? Come down here so I can skewer you.

LANCELOT: Never! (*to himself*) Maybe I can just wait him out.

NARRATOR: The rogue knight produced an enormous battle-axe and began to sharpen it with a whetstone. (*scraping sound*)

LANCELOT: Or on the other hand, he could have an enormous axe… (*sigh*)

ROGUE: Come down, boy, or I'll chop you down!

NARRATOR: Lancelot eased down several branches lower in the tree.

LANCELOT: Ha! I may not have armor or a sword, but I will still find a way to vanquish you! I have honor, and in that way you are unarmed!

DAMSEL: *(to the knight)* Yeah, but you can't cut someone's head off with honor. Well, I would love to stick around and listen to you two males strut and grunt at each other some more, but my mistress will be missing me.

ROGUE: Silence, wench! You'll be done when I say you're done!

DAMSEL: You said you'd let me go as soon as you treed a knight—and this kid is about as close to a knight as you'll get in these parts.

ROGUE: We've gotten this one, yes, but killing knights is just like eating roasted lamb legs—you can't have just one.

DAMSEL: This is a violation of our agreement!

ROGUE: *(snicker)* Imagine that! A rogue knight going back on his word.

DAMSEL: Why you—!

NARRATOR: While the damsel and her captor continued to argue, Lancelot stealthily pulled a dead, but solid, branch loose from the tree. *(branch crack)*

LANCELOT: *(to himself)* Remember, Lancelot. This knight won't give you mercy, so don't give him any! Have a heart like a diamond!

NARRATOR: Lancelot leapt down the remaining distance to the ground and brandished his tree limb.

ROGUE: *(in shock)* What?

LANCELOT: Ha-ha! I am Lancelot, and I do not need a weapon to tear you *limb from limb*—

ROGUE: *(battlecry)* Ahhhh!

NARRATOR: The rogue knight slashed at Lancelot with his axe. Lancelot ducked, and the blow missed. The axe sank deep into the trunk of the tree. *(shunk)*

LANCELOT: Ha! A miss! This is certainly because of your deceitful trick—

DAMSEL: Stop talking, you stupid boy! Fight!

NARRATOR: As the rogue knight struggled to free his weapon, Lancelot wielded his branch and smote him hard against the helm. *(Clang!)*

ROGUE: *(cry of pain)* Ahhh!

NARRATOR: The force of the blow sent the rogue knight sprawling backwards—his helm flying loose from his head.

LANCELOT: Ha-ha! You are defeated! Surrender!

ROGUE: Never!

DAMSEL: Finish him! Use the axe! He's getting up!

NARRATOR: Lancelot yanked the knight's axe loose from the tree and, swinging it high over his head, brought it down fast toward his opponent's exposed neck. (*snickersnack*) The knight's head rolled loose, and the damsel let out a little cry of shock.

DAMSEL: Ah! (*kindly*) You did it!

LANCELOT: (*out of breath*) You sound surprised.

DAMSEL: There for a minute I thought you were going to talk him to death.

LANCELOT: This was my first battle.

DAMSEL: (*sarcastically*) You're kidding.

LANCELOT: You mocked my chivalry, but my chivalry has saved your life, you…you…deceitful maiden!

DAMSEL: (*sarcastically*) Oooh. Such harsh language. I'm not deceitful. This rogue knight captured me while I was out gathering herbs and forced me to trick you. Not that I didn't enjoy it—or find it incredibly easy.

NARRATOR: Lancelot began to buckle his armor back on.

LANCELOT: Well, it was a cruel trick. I'm a knight! It's my duty to serve ladies.

DAMSEL: Oh please. Do you really buy into all that chivalry stuff?

LANCELOT: Of course! But don't worry. I can see that you are no lady. I shall certainly remove your name from my list of damsels in distress. Now, if you will excuse me, I must find my steed and continue on to Camelot.

DAMSEL: No wait! I apologize, Lancelot. I appreciate your help in freeing me. (*pause*) In fact, I need your help again.

LANCELOT: Ha! Let me guess—your pet hedgehog has fallen down a well.

DAMSEL: No. I am a slave-girl in the castle of an evil sorceress.

LANCELOT: Evil sorceress? That's more like it!

DAMSEL: This sorceress has spent the last year abducting and imprisoning forty maidens whose beauty rivals her own. She has locked them all in the tall tower of her castle. One she has even condemned to boil in a large pot of water for eternity.

LANCELOT: Then we must rescue them!

DAMSEL: I had a feeling you would say that. These maidens are a bunch of conceited airheads, but they are worth saving…I guess.

LANCELOT: Why aren't *you* imprisoned with the beautiful maidens? Didn't make the cut?

DAMSEL: (*sarcastically*) I guess there are advantages to being a troll. Do you want my quest or not?

LANCELOT: Of course! We must rescue these maidens at once!

DAMSEL: Easy there. This sorceress is Morgan le Fay, and her castle is guarded by two giants. You can't just go barging in.

LANCELOT: You're right! We'll have to think of a plan to get inside the castle walls. Perhaps if I could fashion a battering ram…

DAMSEL: Way ahead of you.

NARRATOR: The damsel pulled a handful of dust from the pouch at her side and blew it into Lancelot's face.

LANCELOT: Ugh! What was that?

DAMSEL: Good night, sweet prince.

NARRATOR: Lancelot fell backward into the grass and soon snored softly.

DAMSEL: Now to clean up the scene a little bit.

NARRATOR: With much effort, the damsel dragged the dead body of the rogue knight into the underbrush.

DAMSEL: (grunting) This guy should have laid off the lamb legs every once in a while.

NARRATOR: Then the damsel sat down by the road, near the sleeping Lancelot. As luck would have it, Morgan le Fay soon came riding down the road, with a party of servants. When the damsel saw her mistress approaching, she jumped up and began to shout.

DAMSEL: Oh, my lady! Thank goodness! I am saved!

MORGAN: (angrily) There you are! I sent you out to gather herbs, and you never returned. I was planning to hunt you down like a dog!

DAMSEL: Oh, I am sorry. I was abducted by this knight here. Luckily, I was able to put him to sleep with a little bitterroot.

MORGAN: Hmmm. Clever girl. I knew I kept you around for a reason.

DAMSEL: I was about to remove his head. Care to watch? Although it is a shame to lose such a pretty face. At first I thought you might like him to be your new love. You've been so sad since the last one died tragically. But then I thought this one's probably a bit young for you.

NARRATOR: Morgan shot the damsel a withering look.

MORGAN: (angrily) What?

DAMSEL: I mean, no offense, my lady. You're no spring chicken. If you took this lad as your love, there would be talk among the other sorceresses.

MORGAN: (raging) Silence that tongue of yours before I rip it out! I shall have any love I want! Servants, tie this boy up and take him back to the dungeons of Castle Chariot.

NARRATOR: The servants rushed to comply, carrying the sleeping Lancelot between them.

MORGAN: This boy will be my love—or else. If he won't be mine willingly, I'll just have him stuffed. Then I can look at his beauty whenever I want.

DAMSEL: You have such a way with men.

MORGAN: I know.

DAMSEL: Lancelot will be a perfect match for you.

MORGAN: Lancelot, eh? What an interesting name. Beautiful—yet meaningless—just like him. (cruel laugh) I go to work some magic. When I return, I will make him an offer that he cannot refuse—

and I will see that *you* are whipped for your cheekiness.

DAMSEL: You are too kind.

NARRATOR: Morgan le Fay rode on, and the servants and the damsel returned to the sorceress's sinister castle, Castle Chariot.

Hours later, Lancelot awoke to find himself chained to a wall in a dark dungeon. Several ghostly skeletons hung from chains similar to his own. One even had a wreath of roses about its head.

LANCELOT: That damsel has betrayed me…again! How could I be so foolish as to trust her twice? Curse my heart of wax!

NARRATOR: Just then a door across the room opened, and the familiar form of the damsel appeared.

LANCELOT: You! I knew I shouldn't have trusted you!

DAMSEL: Shhh! This was all part of my trick to get you inside the castle. You are now in Morgan le Fay's dungeon!

LANCELOT: I have read of her! She is the sworn enemy of her half-brother, King Arthur.

DAMSEL: Exactly. She's a nasty customer. And she has brought you here to make you her paramour—her love.

LANCELOT: Impossible. I would never love her.

DAMSEL: But see. That's just the deal with evil sorceresses! They don't take *no* for an answer. See these thin fellows next to you? They were the last ones who refused her.

NARRATOR: Lancelot glanced again at the rose-wreathed skeleton next to him.

LANCELOT: Oh, I see. Nevertheless, death is preferable to being the love of one I don't love in return.

DAMSEL: Not the kind of death she has planned for. She's planning to turn you into her favorite piece of taxidermy!

LANCELOT: Help me out of these chains. We must escape.

DAMSEL: It's not that easy. This castle is guarded by two man-eating giants, Gog and Magog.

LANCELOT: There are no guards?

DAMSEL: When you have man-eating giants, guards are a bit overkill, don't you think?

LANCELOT: When you say *giants*, how big do you mean?

DAMSEL: Ever heard of Goliath?

LANCELOT: Yes.

DAMSEL: Bigger.

LANCELOT: *(excitedly)* Finally! A quest worthy of a knight!

DAMSEL: Only you would be excited by that news. Now, I'll release you. I have your armor here as well. The forty damsels are trapped in the high tower.

LANCELOT: I will rescue them. In spite of all your disparaging remarks, you have recognized that *I* am the man for this job. That is why you chose me.

DAMSEL: That and extremely limited options. Let's go.

NARRATOR: The falcon-damsel reunited Lancelot with his precious set of white armor and led him through the twisting passageways of the dungeon.

DAMSEL: Luckily for you, Lady Morgan is away from the castle, or you would have no chance of saving the damsels. I'll wait for you in the courtyard.

LANCELOT: I will not fail!

NARRATOR: When Lancelot neared the castle courtyard, he heard a distant rumbling. *(snoring of a giant)* Sprawled haphazardly across the castle entryway was an enormous, slumbering monster. It was a fifteen-foot-long giant, complete with a warty, bulging nose and massive limbs. For a necklace it wore a string of human skulls.

LANCELOT: No need to wake a sleeping giant—for now. But where is the second giant?

NARRATOR: Lancelot snuck past the sleeping giant and, spying the high tower, made for it. Within the tower was a staircase, which twisted upward at a perilous angle. Lancelot's armor clanked loudly as he rushed up the stairs. *(clanking sounds)*

LANCELOT: Well, so much for the element of surprise.

NARRATOR: The staircase ended at a doorway, and Lancelot burst through it. As he entered the chamber beyond, a spiked club whizzed over his head, striking the wall behind him. *(crash)* A snarling giant towered over him, and in the corner of the chamber huddled forty maidens. *(shrieking maidens)*

GOG: *(snarling)* Argh!

NARRATOR: The giant raised his spiked club for yet another swing. Lancelot boldly held up his hand.

LANCELOT: Halt, giant!

NARRATOR: Confused by this action, the giant paused.

LANCELOT: It is I, Lancelot of the Lake, and I demand that you release these damsels at once.

NARRATOR: The giant's club caught Lancelot in the chest and sent him flying across the room. *(Clang!)* There was a metallic crash as he rebounded off the stone wall. *(maidens shriek)*

GOG: Stupid knight! Begging Gog for mercy is futile! Now, Gog will squeeze out your brains and have your liver as a light afternoon snack.

NARRATOR: The giant grabbed Lancelot and hurled him upward with such force that the knight crashed through the chamber-roof. *(crashing sound, maidens shriek)*

Finding himself now lying on the slope of the tower roof, Lancelot gasped for breath. The giant's head, baring his blackened teeth, appeared through the newly formed hole in the roof.

GOG: Awww. Don't run. Come back, knighty-knight! Gog is ready to play some more!

NARRATOR: Lancelot scrambled higher toward the roof's peak as the giant crawled up through the hole. Gog stood, careful to keep his balance on the inclined roof.

GOG: Gog will crack you like a walnut and send you for a fall. Now come here!

NARRATOR: The hand of Gog shot out and latched onto Lancelot's ankle. Lancelot clung desperately to the tower steeple.

LANCELOT: (*grunting*) Ugh!

GOG: Turn loose, tricky knight!

NARRATOR: Lancelot released one of his hands and drew his sword. He hacked at the tough skin of the giant's wrist.

GOG: Ah! Stop that! Stop that! (*cry of pain*) You will make Gog angry! You will not like Gog when he is angry!

NARRATOR: Gog released Lancelot's leg, lost his balance, and tottered uneasily on the edge of the tower roof.

GOG: (*growling*) No! Gog will see you fall!

LANCELOT: You first!

NARRATOR: Lancelot let go of the tower steeple and slid down the slope of the roof. His body slammed into Gog—knocking the unsteady giant out over the edge.

GOG: Noooooooooo! (*fading away*)

NARRATOR: The giant fell. With a tremendous boom, he impacted on the cobblestones far below. (*boom*)

LANCELOT: (*breathlessly*) Nothing to it!

NARRATOR: Lancelot—clinging to the lip of the roof—eased his way back into the tower chamber. The forty maidens still cowered in the corner, but when they saw Lancelot victorious, they shrieked—with joy this time. (*shrieks of joy*)

MAIDEN: We thought that you were dead, good sir knight!

LANCELOT: No. I am victorious. The giant has fallen to his death. Now come with me! You are nearly free, but there is one more giant I must deal with!

MAIDEN: Wait, sir! We can't leave without Elaine.

LANCELOT: Who?

NARRATOR: The maidens pointed to a raised platform where a cauldron stood. In the midst of its boiling waters sat a beautiful maiden—her features frozen in a look of pain. Her beauty stunned Lancelot.

MAIDEN: This is Elaine of Corbenic. Lady Morgan has cursed her to forever boil in this pot. Only the bravest knight in the world is able to break the spell and free her.

NARRATOR: Lancelot stepped boldly forward.

LANCELOT: Then let her be free.

NARRATOR: He removed his glove and brushed his finger across the maiden's delicate cheek. Elaine's glittering eyes regained their sight, and the damsel rose dripping from the cauldron waters.

ELAINE: (*confused*) What has happened? Who are you, handsome knight?

LANCELOT: There is no time to explain. We must be gone from this place at once!

NARRATOR: Lancelot and the forty maidens made their way down the tower staircase.

LANCELOT: Take care! I go to slay the second giant.

NARRATOR: Lancelot rushed into the courtyard. Gog lay in its midst—his putrid blood filling the web of cracks that radiated out from his body. Magog, his giant-brother, lay where he had before, across the castle gate.

LANCELOT: Still asleep? That crash could have woken the dead!

DAMSEL: Apparently not.

NARRATOR: The falcon-damsel appeared from behind the reclining giant.

DAMSEL: This sleeping beauty *is* dead. I decided to deal with the oaf myself.

NARRATOR: She held up a bag of herbs.

DAMSEL: I overdosed him on bitterroot. You wouldn't believe how much of that stuff it takes to overdose a giant! Now help me move him out of the way.

NARRATOR: Working together, the damsels and Lancelot dragged the deceased giant away from the castle gates.

LANCELOT: Now let's get you damsels out of here before Morgan le Fay returns.

NARRATOR: He flung open the castle gates, but a hooded figure seated on horseback barred the way. *(collective gasp)*

DAMSEL: *(in shock)* It's Lady Morgan!

LADY: Hardly, my dear.

NARRATOR: The figure threw back her hood to reveal not the cruel face of Morgan le Fay but the beautiful countenance of the Lady of the Lake.

LANCELOT: *(in shock)* My Lady! What are you doing here?

LADY: My Lancelot! I have used my magic to watch your progress, and I have seen you prove yourself most wonderfully with this quest!

LANCELOT: Have I learned true knighthood?

LADY: Of course, you have. You faced your foes with a heart of diamond. Yet you dealt gently with these maidens using your heart of wax. Has he not, ladies?

(giggling from the damsels)

DAMSEL: Eh.

NARRATOR: Elaine, standing amid the damsels, beamed at Lancelot in adoration.

ELAINE: One touch from him saved me from Morgan le Fay's evil spell!

LADY: Of course, it did. Handsome bravery trumps hideous, old black magic any day. I only wish I could see Morgan le Fay's face when she returns and sees how all her plans have failed. *(laugh)* Lancelot, King Arthur will have no choice but to knight you at once when you arrive in Camelot with these forty-one rescued damsels!

DAMSEL: Uh. Just forty. Technically, I rescued myself.

LANCELOT: Damsel, you must admit that I have proved myself in the ways of chivalry.

NARRATOR: For the first time the falcon-damsel smiled.

DAMSEL: Yes. You've been all right…I guess. But don't let it go to your head!

LADY: Now, let us travel to Camelot! I will give my Lancelot an entrance that King Arthur will never forget!

LANCELOT: Thank you, my Lady—for everything.

NARRATOR: The Lady of the Lake held true to her word. Forty-one beautiful damsels arrived in Camelot, amid a sparkling cloud of dew droplets. They were all riding pristinely white palfreys, and the Lady of the Lake shimmered in their midst like a mirage. Lancelot brought up the rear of the procession, his armor shining with white star-light. Dragged in the dirt behind his steed followed the heads of two giants, Gog and Magog.

The Lady of the Lake was right. It was an entrance that Camelot would never forget.

DISCUSSION QUESTIONS

1. Do you agree with the Lady of the Lake that a good warrior should have two hearts, one of diamond and one of wax? Explain.
2. Is it important that Lancelot is raised by the Lady of the Lake instead of his true parents? Explain.
3. Is Lancelot a hero? Explain.
4. Is the falcon-damsel a hero as well? Explain.
5. What traits make Morgan le Fay an especially evil character? Explain.
6. What lessons does Lancelot learn about knighthood on this adventure?
7. What do you think will transpire between Lancelot and Elaine, the damsel he saved from the boiling pot?

THE LOVES OF LANCELOT
TEACHER GUIDE

BACKGROUND

Elaine of Corbenic and Elaine of Astolat are two different characters in *Le Morte D'Arthur*—both of whom fall in love with Lancelot. Elaine of Corbenic is the daughter of the Fisher King, who seduces Lancelot by taking the form of Guinevere and bears his son, Galahad. Elaine of Astolat is a maiden who dies because of her unrequited love for Lancelot. For the purposes of this version of the story, the two have been combined into one character.

Alfred, Lord Tennyson made Elaine of Astolat famous in his poem *The Lady of Shalott*. Secluded in a tower, his version of Elaine can only view the outside world through a magical mirror. When she spies Lancelot upon the road one day, her mirror cracks—along with her heart. Despondent that she will never have the love of Lancelot, she leaves her tower and boards a boat—sailing down toward Camelot. As she sails, she sings her last song. She sings until her blood freezes, her eyes darken, and she dies. When her boat sails silently into Camelot, all the nobles of Camelot emerge from their halls to behold the sight. Only Lancelot is bold enough to approach her boat. He comments, "She has a lovely face; God in his mercy lend her grace."

SUMMARY

Lancelot makes a grand entrance to Camelot, bringing with him many rescued damsels and the heads of two giants. The Lady of the Lake, his guardian, rides with him and presents him to Arthur for knighthood. Kay and Gawain contest Lancelot's worthiness for knighthood, but Arthur agrees to knight him. He also suggests a tournament where Lancelot can prove his abilities.

As Lancelot is introduced to the court, he meets Queen Guinevere. Since he has no lady to champion in the tournament the next day, Lancelot vows to champion the honor of the queen. In the tournament Lancelot easily defeats Gawain. Angry at his defeat, Gawain challenges Lancelot to sit in the Siege Perilous—a seat reserved at the Round Table for the world's greatest knight. Anyone unworthy who sits there will be destroyed by fire from heaven. Lancelot declines, claiming that the seat is not for him. Arthur, recognizing Lancelot as one of the greatest knights who has ever lived, is puzzled by this.

Years pass, and Lancelot becomes Arthur's best knight. He also begins to spend more and more time in the presence of the queen, and as her champion, they share a special relationship. In fact, they have developed feelings for one another.

Lancelot goes away on a quest, but as he journeys, he happens upon the castle of King Pelles, the Fisher King, and his daughter Elaine, a damsel whom Lancelot once rescued. When Elaine sees Lancelot, she is sure that he has come to offer her marriage, but the knight assures her that he has no feelings for her. Heartbroken, Elaine enlists the help of her maidservant, who is an enchantress, to win Lancelot's heart.

Meanwhile, King Pelles greets Lancelot warmly and displays the mighty relics that his family has protected for generations—the platter from the Last Supper, the spear that pierced the side of Christ, and the Holy Grail, Christ's cup. When Lancelot retires to his chambers for the evening, Elaine has her maidservant transform her so that she looks like Queen Guinevere. Then she sneaks into

Lancelot's room and declares her love. Lancelot, fooled by Elaine's disguise, is overcome with passion and spends the night with Elaine. But in the morning, when the magic has faded, he sees Elaine's true identity. At first he threatens to kill her for causing him to betray his queen, but then his maddening guilt takes over his mind, and he runs from the castle of King Pelles.

For months Lancelot lives in the wilderness as a mad hermit. His betrayal of Guinevere has driven him insane. The queen sends out knights to search for Lancelot. Elaine, too, is searching for him. Elaine finds Lancelot and prays that the Holy Grail will heal him. The Grail appears, and Lancelot's mind is healed. The knight returns to Camelot and his queen. Elaine—completely brokenhearted—prepares for death. Later, a ship floats down the river by Camelot and inside is the body of Elaine. No mark is found upon her, but a note declares that she died of love.

ESSENTIAL QUESTIONS

- What is love?
- Can you create love where there is none?
- Is love more important than duty?

ANTICIPATORY QUESTIONS

- What is the Holy Grail?
- Can you trick someone into loving you?
- Can someone truly die of a broken heart?

CHARACTER QUEST

Love Guinevere and Lancelot share an instant connection—a type of love-at-first-sight feeling. Do you believe in love at first sight? Elaine falls in love with Lancelot, but he does not return her love. Through trickery she tries to force Lancelot into loving her and ends up driving him temporarily insane. Why is love an emotion that cannot be forced? What is the best way to approach love?

CONNECT

"The Lady of Shalott" by Alfred, Lord Tennyson Adapting his source material from *Le Morte D'Arthur*, Tennyson presents the Lady of Shalott as a cursed damsel who must spend her life observing the outside world through a magical mirror. Compare Tennyson's version of Elaine to the one presented in "The Loves of Lancelot."

TEACHABLE TERMS

- **Inner conflict** Lancelot suffers from an inner conflict. On one hand he wants to serve his king, but on the other he does not want to deny his love to Guinevere, the king's wife. He is torn between his devotions.
- **Round character** Even though Elaine begins as a silly character, throughout the story she matures, recognizing her previous actions as foolish. This change in her character makes her a round character.
- **Love triangle** This story creates a love triangle among Lancelot, Guinevere, and Elaine.

RECALL QUESTIONS

1. What is the Siege Perilous?
2. King Pelles is the keeper of what object?
3. How does Elaine trick Lancelot?
4. What effect does this have on Lancelot?
5. What happens to Elaine?

THE LOVES OF LANCELOT

CAST

LANCELOT	*Knight of the Lake*
LADY	*Enchantress of the Lake*
GUINEVERE	*Queen of Britain*
ARTHUR	*King of Britain*
KAY	*Seneschal of Britain*
GAWAIN	*Knight of Arthur*
ELAINE	*Princess of Corbenic*
BRISEN	*Servant to Elaine*
PELLES	*Maimed King of Corbenic*

NARRATOR: When Lancelot of the Lake rode into the city of Camelot, he led a procession of forty-one damsels and bore the severed heads of two giants. His guardian, the Lady of the Lake, also rode with him. A crowd gathered around them, murmuring with amazement. King Arthur himself even came out into the courtyard to behold the spectacle firsthand.

ARTHUR: Welcome to Camelot, young man! You have made quite an entrance!

NARRATOR: Lancelot dismounted, knelt before the king, and displayed his sword before him.

LANCELOT: Lancelot of the Lake at your service, sire!

ARTHUR: You are a relation to the Lady of the Lake, I see. Why have you come to Camelot, my boy?

LANCELOT: To join the Round Table. For many years, I have heard stories of your brave knights!

LADY: It was I who raised this boy. I have trained him myself. Once you have knighted him, he will officially be the greatest knight in the world!

NARRATOR: Sir Kay and Sir Gawain, standing near the king, scoffed to one another.

KAY: Ha! He's just a boy! How can he be "the greatest knight"? He's not even old enough to shave!

LANCELOT: With all due respect, sir, I am eighteen—the proper age for knighthood.

GAWAIN: That just means you're barely old enough. Kay is right. The lad has not even been properly tested.

LADY: *(defensively)* Lancelot has rescued forty-one damsels and slain two giants. What other test could he need?

KAY: Ha! Giants? Lah-dee-dah.

GAWAIN: Slaying a clumsy giant is one thing, but how would he match up against trained knights? That's what I want to know!

LANCELOT: *(angrily)* Sir, I would be happy to show you my skill!

GAWAIN: Is that a challenge?

ARTHUR: My guests! Please excuse the rudeness of my knights. Of course, Lancelot shall be knighted. One cannot argue that he has earned the right. Afterward, he will also be given a chance to prove his abilities.

GAWAIN: Yes, a tournament! I leap at the chance to teach this little runt a thing or two about jousting!

LANCELOT: I think it is you, sir, who will learn a lesson.

GAWAIN: Why you—!

NARRATOR: Gawain moved angrily forward, but Arthur graciously intervened.

ARTHUR: Gentlemen, let's leave the fighting for tomorrow. Tonight, we feast. Now, come, Lancelot. I must introduce you to the ladies of the court. I am sure they will be happy to meet a handsome lad like you.

NARRATOR: Arthur led Lancelot and his companions into the great hall of Camelot where Queen Guinevere and her ladies-in-waiting were seated for a grand feast.

ARTHUR: Lancelot, allow me to introduce my queen, Guinevere.

NARRATOR: When Lancelot beheld the queen, he was immediately astounded by her beauty. For some reason he had expected her to be old, past her prime. Who was this vibrantly beautiful woman, barely out of her maidenhood?

GUINEVERE: Welcome to Camelot, young knight.

LANCELOT: *(in awe)* My lady, I have heard stories of your beauty—but they are all lies!

GUINEVERE: I beg your pardon.

LANCELOT: They are lies because they do not tell half the truth! You are far lovelier than words can express!

GUINEVERE: *(laugh)* You are too kind! You are most welcome here in Camelot.

NARRATOR: Lancelot smiled, as Arthur led him away.

In the feast that followed the chatty Lady Elaine, one of Lancelot's forty-one rescued damsels, was seated next to Queen Guinevere. She spent the evening bending the queen's ear.

ELAINE: *(lovey-dovey)* Oh, I think Lancelot is the most handsome man I have ever seen!

GUINEVERE: Hmm. Do you fancy him?

ELAINE: I do. He saved me from a magical boiling cauldron, you know. One touch from him broke the spell. It was love at first touch, I guess you could say. Just between you and me, my lady, I have already decided that I will marry him. That is, if he is willing. Tee hee. How romantic to be married to a knight—to be your champion! *(sigh)* My father was a king, you know, and my mother always told me, "Darling, never marry a king. His only love is his kingdom. Marry a knight, so that he will love you only."

NARRATOR: Guinevere furrowed her brow.

GUINEVERE: That is not *always* the case.

ELAINE: Oh, my lady! I didn't mean that was the way it was with you and King Arthur! I'm sure your passion is endless!

GUINEVERE: Well, I would not say that either. We are content—happy even.

ELAINE: Of course! *My* father is King Pelles, the Maimed King. Perhaps you have heard of him before? Our enchanted castle-home is one outsiders can never reach unless they stumble upon it accidentally. Because of that we never get visitors—not intentional ones anyway. Tee hee. Our castle lies in the middle of a wasteland of gnarled trees. Our kingdom has gone downhill since Father's wounding...

NARRATOR: As Elaine chattered on, Guinevere fell into deep thought. She glanced toward where Lancelot and Arthur conversed happily.

ELAINE: Our family has always been the protectors of a number of holy relics. The greatest is the Holy Grail. Perhaps you have heard of it? I'm sure Lancelot will want to align himself with an illustrious family like mine. Then he can be the protector of the Grail like my father has been. Only I hope Lancelot won't be wounded like my father was. *(whispering)* He was wounded through the thighs! Talk about a tender spot! That had to hurt! Tee hee.

GUINEVERE: I wish you happiness. Lancelot will make you a great match.

NARRATOR: The queen looked toward Lancelot again. This time, he was looking back. He smiled and respectfully bowed his head. Just then, Arthur rose and clapped a hand on Lancelot's shoulder.

ARTHUR: In the morning Lancelot will be knighted and assume his place at the Round Table. There will follow a grand tournament in honor of his knighthood!

NARRATOR: Gawain and Kay looked at one another and scowled.

GAWAIN: We'll see if he lives long enough to enjoy it. *(snicker)*

LADY: Well-spoken, Arthur. As you know, every knight fights for the honor of his lady-love.

NARRATOR: Gawain rose and lifted his goblet.

GAWAIN: Yes, it is true. I fight for my lady-love, whom I have seated here beside me.

NARRATOR: The damsel seated next to Gawain swelled in happiness.

GAWAIN: The lady Estelle—uh...I mean, Gertrude.

NARRATOR: The damsel shot Gawain an angry look as he quickly reseated himself. *(laughter from everyone)*

LADY: As I was saying...I have trained Lancelot in this courtly grace. Please let him choose a woman from your court to champion in battle.

NARRATOR: Elaine clasped the arm of the queen and whispered into her ear.

ELAINE: *(whispering)* Oh, my lady, what if he should pick me? He would fight for my honor! It would be too much joy for my heart to bear!

LANCELOT: In truth no maiden holds my heart. But if I were to choose a lady to honor based on sheer beauty…I could choose no other woman than Queen Guinevere. Arthur, I humbly ask to champion the honor of your queen.

NARRATOR: At this suggestion Arthur beamed, but Guinevere only blushed.

ARTHUR: An excellent idea! What do you say, my queen?

GUINEVERE: If this is what the young knight desires, he shall be my champion.

NARRATOR: The next morning Lancelot was knighted in a grand ceremony at the Camelot chapel.

Outside the city walls, colorful pavilions had been erected for the purpose of the tournament. The Knights of the Round Table appeared, decked out in their finest armor, and the entire court arrived at the testing field to watch the joust.

ARTHUR: *(shouting)* Competitors, come before your king!

NARRATOR: The knights removed their helms. Many of the faces of the knights were broken from years of battles, while Lancelot displayed his own flawless features.

ARTHUR: *(grandly)* We fight before God—for valor, for chivalry, for justice. Let no man show cowardice. Let every man show mercy! Lancelot and Gawain shall take the field first!

NARRATOR: Lancelot rode near to the queen's pavilion.

LANCELOT: My queen, since I am your champion, you must give me some token of your favor. That is the way it is done.

GUINEVERE: *(stately)* Very well, young knight. Here is a token.

NARRATOR: The queen drew a silken scarf forth from the folds of her garments and handed it to Lancelot, who reverently tied it about his arm.

LANCELOT: My lady, I thank you.

GUINEVERE: Fight well, brave knight, and my honor can be assured.

ARTHUR: Now, let's see some jousting!

NARRATOR: The match-up between Lancelot and Gawain ended quicker than anyone could have imagined. Lancelot stayed as solid as stone. In the first round Gawain's lance shattered, and, much to his own surprise, he was knocked from his steed. *(Clang!)*

GAWAIN: Gah!

NARRATOR: As Gawain cursed and picked himself up from the ground, the crowd began to chant for the young knight of the lake.

ALL: Lancelot! Lancelot! Lancelot!

NARRATOR: Gawain was only the first knight to fall beneath Lancelot's lance. No one had ever seen a knight with so much prowess. With each new victory, everyone's admiration for Lancelot grew greater and greater.

Following the joust, the knights limped back into the castle for the evening feast, nursing their bruised bodies.

GAWAIN: *(cry of pain)* Ouch! I can't believe that pretty-boy rookie bested us!

KAY: *(moaning)* I think my ribs are broken.

NARRATOR: As the knights gathered at the Round Table, Arthur drew Lancelot close to him.

ARTHUR: Merlin, my old master, enchanted each siege of the Round Table to spell out in golden letters the name of the man who occupies it. As you can see, there are still many open sieges.

NARRATOR: Lancelot pointed to a nearby siege covered by a rich cloth.

LANCELOT: What is this one?

GAWAIN: Ha! I knew he would want that one!

NARRATOR: Gawain jerked the cloth loose from the covered seat—revealing the glowing, golden letters upon it, which seemed to move like tongues of flame.

LANCELOT: Those words. What do they mean? They are in a strange language.

ARTHUR: It is the language of heaven. That is a special seat. Merlin warned us about it. Only the greatest knight who will ever live may sit there. Anyone else will be destroyed. It is the Siege Perilous.

GAWAIN: We've already had a demonstration of its power. Sir What's-his-name tried to sit there, and he was incinerated by a blast of fire that fell from heaven. *(pause)* Care to try it, Lancelot?

ARTHUR: Gawain!

GAWAIN: What? If Sir Lancelot is so wonderful, why shouldn't he sit there?

KAY: *(moaning)* Have him try it. Seeing him get fried by a bolt of lightning would sure make me feel better right about now.

ARTHUR: Kay!

NARRATOR: Ignoring the knights' jests, Lancelot stared intently at the siege's golden letters.

LANCELOT: I do not know how I know, but this seat is not for me.

GAWAIN: Then you admit it? You are *not* the greatest knight in the world!

LANCELOT: I never said I was!

GAWAIN: Then why did you prance in here with your maidens and your giant-heads like you owned the world?

ARTHUR: Gawain, enough! Lancelot has shown nothing but honor since he arrived. You must put away your jealousy and befriend him. There are many things that he can learn from you.

KAY: Yeah. Like how to fall off a horse in the first round of a tournament!

GAWAIN: Grrrr.

NARRATOR: The minstrels sang, and the pipers played long into the night. During the celebration, the queen called Lancelot to her.

GUINEVERE: You fought very bravely today. Even in a friendly tournament, a knight can be killed. Gawain was out for blood, I think.

LANCELOT: My queen, when I looked at you, all fear left me. I knew that I could do anything if you were my lady! I say truly if I am ever to marry, I would only marry one of your beauty.

GUINEVERE: Your words are sweet.

NARRATOR: Arthur watched his wife and the young knight happily converse, and a thought began to gnaw at his mind. If Lancelot of the Lake was not the knight to sit upon the Siege Perilous, who was?

ARTHUR: Hmmm. There is no more promising knight than Lancelot. Perhaps Merlin's prophecy was wrong.

NARRATOR: Over the following years, Lancelot became Arthur's greatest knight and one of his closest friends. Whenever there was a vital quest to be undertaken, Arthur declared…

ARTHUR: I'll send Lancelot! He is the best of my knights. Do not let me down, my friend!

LANCELOT: Not to worry, my king. I will win glory for both you and the queen.

NARRATOR: While Arthur spent all of his time with the day-to-day business of Camelot, the queen spent many happy hours in the presence of Lancelot. Guinevere gave Lancelot a beautiful woman to praise, and he gave her the attention that she had been missing from Arthur.

While their interaction began innocently enough, a mutual attraction began to grow up between them. One cold morning, the queen found the handsome knight waiting in the dark hallway near her chamber.

GUINEVERE: *(surprised)* Lancelot!

LANCELOT: I have grievous news, my lady.

GUINEVERE: *(sadly)* Don't tell me! Are you going on a quest again?

LANCELOT: I am afraid so.

GUINEVERE: I miss you when you are gone. I mean, all of us here in Camelot do.

LANCELOT: When I am away, you are ever in my mind—spurring me on to mighty deeds.

GUINEVERE: I know you think of me often, and I am flattered, but you should find some other lady to occupy your thoughts.

LANCELOT: I have tried, but I cannot. Rest assured that there is only one love in my heart, and there will be only one for all of eternity. I am your servant until I die.

GUINEVERE: Lancelot, you should not say such things.

LANCELOT: Have you ever wondered what would have happened if we had met at a different time—in a different place?

GUINEVERE: It's pointless to think of such things.

LANCELOT: I know. We both have our duty. But sometimes I dream about what could have been.

GUINEVERE: Dreams are beautiful things, but they are not for us. Goodbye, Lancelot.

LANCELOT: Farewell, my queen.

NARRATOR: Leaving Guinevere behind, Lancelot found his steed within the castle stables. He mounted and spurred his horse into the dawning day.

LANCELOT: *(to himself)* The queen is right. I must put her from my mind and focus on my quest.

NARRATOR: But try as he might, he could not, and with each mile he trekked, his heart grew more and more sick for the love of the fair Guinevere.

Three days out from Camelot Lancelot entered a strange wood—one where the trees were withered and sparse. The grass was brown and lifeless, and the air was stagnant. Yet as he plodded onward, he took little notice of this. At last when he looked up, he beheld a dark castle upon a high hill.

LANCELOT: Strange. I have traveled this road many times, but I have never seen this castle before. I'll find lodging there for the night.

NARRATOR: He made his way into the castle courtyard, and immediately a thin maiden and her servingmaid stood forth from the gloom.

ELAINE: *(excitedly)* Lancelot! I knew you'd come! What took you so long?

LANCELOT: Excuse me, my lady?

ELAINE: It is me—Elaine! I knew you'd come back for me!

LANCELOT: Come back for you?

ELAINE: Stop playing games, Lancelot! Years ago, you rescued me from Morgan le Fay's cauldron!

LANCELOT: Oh, I apologize. I had forgotten. How are you, Lady Elaine?

NARRATOR: The maiden's features sank.

ELAINE: You mean, you haven't come here for my hand in marriage?

LANCELOT: *(laugh)* Marriage? I didn't mean to come here at all. I just stumbled upon your castle.

ELAINE: Well, this is an enchanted castle. You *can't* find it when you want to. You have to discover it by accident. But I thought that's why it took you so long to come here. Have you not been searching for me all these years?

LANCELOT: I am sorry, my lady, no.

NARRATOR: Elaine suddenly burst into tears and fell into the arms of her servingmaid.

ELAINE: *(crying)* Dame Brisen, I can't believe it! All these years! All this waiting! And he hasn't even been looking for me!

BRISEN: Look what you've done now, you dishonorable knight!

LANCELOT: *(sigh)* Is the lord of this castle home? Hopefully, he will be less hysterical.

BRISEN: He'll be back from fishing soon.

LANCELOT: Why would a lord be fishing?

BRISEN: He's the Fisher King. It's all he can do these days with his wound the way it is. He can't even walk, sir. *(whispering)* He had a sword run through his…lower regions. Very painful.

LANCELOT: What a strange place!

BRISEN: I know. Usually they aim for the heart or the head—not down there.

LANCELOT: No. I mean, this castle is a strange place. Nevermind.

NARRATOR: The tearful Elaine turned to Lancelot again.

ELAINE: I can't believe that you don't love me!

LANCELOT: I can't believe that you think I would. I barely know you.

ELAINE: What is it about me that you don't love? It can't be my looks. Father says I am the most beautiful woman in all of Britain!

LANCELOT: Your father is severely mistaken. There is no woman in all of Britain whose beauty can rival Queen Guinevere's.

ELAINE: Oh! *(screaming and weeping)*

LANCELOT: This is ridiculous. I will await the king inside.

NARRATOR: Lancelot rode off toward the castle.

ELAINE: *(crying)* Dame Brisen, how could he be so cruel?

BRISEN: Oh, you foolish girl! Control yourself!

ELAINE: I love him! I love him!

BRISEN: He *obviously* does not love you! He said so just now!

ELAINE: *(angrily)* I love him! *(sudden idea)* I *must* have him! He shall be my husband! And you shall help me!

BRISEN: Oh, no—

ELAINE: I know that you are a magic-worker. My father has told me so!

BRISEN: I will work no magic for you!

ELAINE: *(child-like)* Yes! Yes! Yes! Or I shall tell Father, and he shall have your hair pulled out.

NARRATOR: The old dame pursed her lips and stared at the young girl coldly.

BRISEN: *(coldly)* Magic cannot create love!

ELAINE: *(thinking)* Lancelot seems to love Queen Guinevere!

BRISEN: But not in a lustful manner! He loves her as his queen!

ELAINE: *(excitedly)* He is at her command. She holds some power over him. Dame Brisen, that's it! You must make me appear as the queen! And I will visit him as he stays the night at our castle!

BRISEN: And what then? What if you trick this man? Do you think he will love you because of it?

ELAINE: No, but if there is a child, his honor will force him to marry me!

BRISEN: Madam! He is a man of honor. If he commits a sin with one he does not love, it might drive him mad!

ELAINE: Bah. What do you know? He should be meeting with Father soon. Now let's work out a plan.

BRISEN: *(grudgingly)* Yes…my lady.

NARRATOR: When the Fisher King arrived back to his castle, being borne on a litter by his servants, his daughter and her dame came to him at once.

ELAINE: Father, how was your fishing trip?

PELLES: *(sourly)* All the fish are dead, and the water is brown. This land is completely cursed. Ever since I was wounded, things have never been the same.

ELAINE: I have a request, Father. There is a knight here, and I want him to be my husband.

BRISEN: Sire, your foolish daughter has the notion that she will trick this knight into getting a child upon her!

PELLES: *(in shock)* What?

ELAINE: It is Lancelot! Remember, I told you about him.

PELLES: Lancelot! The name sounds familiar. Wait a minute. Dame Brisen, didn't you foresee that if Elaine had a son with a knight named Lancelot, he would be the one who could lift this curse from our land?

BRISEN: Yes, but at the time, I didn't know *how* she planned to get that son.

PELLES: Dame, you are at our command! Help my daughter get her knight. Only through this deception will our land be healed!

BRISEN: I can't believe this! *(pause)* Fine. I will do what you wish—but I don't like it one bit!

NARRATOR: Lancelot had been seated in the great hall of the Maimed King's castle. The king was carried in on his litter and greeted the young knight warmly.

PELLES: Lancelot, welcome! Welcome to Castle Corbenic! While you stay here, let me know if there is anything you desire. Everything I have is at your disposal.

LANCELOT: You are kind, King Pelles. All I desire is a good dinner and a warm bed to sleep in.

PELLES: I think that can be arranged. We will have a great feast, but, first, let me show you the treasures that my castle holds.

LANCELOT: Treasures?

PELLES: I come from a great lineage. My ancestor was Joseph of Arimathea, the man who lent his tomb to Christ.

LANCELOT: *(surprised)* That is a mighty line!

PELLES: Yes, and after his resurrection, the Christ appeared to Joseph and presented him with holy relics that we have guarded throughout the years.

NARRATOR: The king clapped his hands, and a procession of white-clad women began a solemn march into their midst. A sudden spirit of awe moved with them.

LANCELOT: Heaven above!

NARRATOR: A scent like the smell of Heaven wafted into the hall, and a dove flew forth with a censure of gold in its beak—spilling holy powder over the room.

PELLES: *(grandly)* Behold the wonders of Christ!

NARRATOR: Each pale woman carried a glittering object in her hands.

PELLES: Behold, Knight of the Round Table, the Cup of Christ! The same cup Our Savior's lips touched at the Last Supper and the same cup that caught His blood upon the cross.

NARRATOR: The first woman held a golden cup adorned with jewels above her head, and it sparkled there like an extension of heavenly glory.

LANCELOT: *(breathlessly)* The Holy Grail!

PELLES: Behold, Knight of the Round Table, the Longinus spear, the same that pierced the side of Christ.

NARRATOR: The second woman held the golden spear above her head. It too glittered with an otherworldly light.

PELLES: And, finally, the platter from which Christ supped at the last meeting of His disciples.

NARRATOR: The platter was raised in the same manner, and the grail procession turned and began its solemn march back down the hallway. The sweet smell left the air, and Lancelot sat breathlessly.

LANCELOT: *(breathlessly)* My lord, that is the greatest sight I have ever seen!

NARRATOR: The two men talked late into the night. Through all their dealings, the vision of the Grail never left the mind of Sir Lancelot. When the time came to retire, the king bade him goodnight.

PELLES: I hope you enjoy your stay with us, Sir Lancelot.

NARRATOR: Lancelot made his way to his chambers. After he had entered his door and shut it behind him, two dark forms appeared in the hallway outside.

ELAINE: He has gone in to sleep, Dame Brisen. Transform me now!

BRISEN: You don't know what you're doing!

ELAINE: Do it now!

BRISEN: Very well. *(chanting)* Seem as you are not—speak as you are not—know what is not yours to know.

NARRATOR: The darkness of the hallway hid the transformation, but Elaine felt her face. It had changed. She giggled to herself.

ELAINE: Tee hee. Now, let me do this deed. Thank you, dame.

BRISEN: Don't thank me. I wash my hands of this foolishness.

NARRATOR: Paying her maid no mind, the damsel unbolted the door-latch and made her way inside to the sleeping knight. Her footfalls awoke Lancelot, and he stirred in his bed.

LANCELOT: Who's there?

ELAINE: (*softly*) It is I, Queen Guinevere.

NARRATOR: Lancelot lit a candle, and the pale face of Guinevere appeared before him in the darkness.

LANCELOT: (*shocked*) My lady! But how did you get here?

ELAINE: I followed you, my champion. All the way from Camelot! You are right. We must be together!

LANCELOT: But what about Arthur?

ELAINE: He will never know.

LANCELOT: But there is no honor in this.

NARRATOR: The woman moved seductively forth.

ELAINE: No—but there is love. And that is the most important thing.

NARRATOR: She fell into Lancelot's arms, and his resistance failed.

LANCELOT: I have loved you from the first moment I saw you.

ELAINE: I, as well.

NARRATOR: The morning sun found the two lovers still in each other's arms. Lancelot slowly opened his sleep-burdened eyes and almost fell out of the bed!

LANCELOT: (*angrily*) You! What are you doing here?

ELAINE: What do you mean?

LANCELOT: What have you done with Guinevere?

NARRATOR: Lancelot hurriedly scanned the room, half-expecting to see Guinevere somewhere nearby. Surprised by his actions, Elaine raised her hand to her face.

ELAINE: The spell has faded! Lancelot, it was I that you laid by last night—not your queen. It was done through an enchantment.

LANCELOT: (*shocked*) This cannot be! I have shamed myself and my queen, and all for nothing!

ELAINE: Please, Lancelot, I love you. You must stay with me and make me your wife!

NARRATOR: The knight stared at her coldly.

LANCELOT: (*hatefully*) I will never give you my love. You have made me betray my honor and my queen. I can no longer be called a knight. But at least I will take *you* down with me!

NARRATOR: He grabbed up his sword and advanced toward the damsel.

ELAINE: Lancelot, no! Mercy! You must show me mercy!

NARRATOR: Elaine fell at Lancelot's feet, weeping.

ELAINE: (*crying*) Mercy, Lancelot, mercy.

LANCELOT: Argh!

NARRATOR: Lancelot threw down his sword.

LANCELOT: Why can't I kill her? What's stopping me? I've already lost all my virtue!

ELAINE: Lancelot, please!

LANCELOT: Don't call me that name! I'm no longer Lancelot! Now I can never return and face her again. I can't! And I won't! There's nothing for me! Nothing!

NARRATOR: A wild light came into his eyes.

LANCELOT: (*shouting*) No! (*crazed cries*)

NARRATOR: He tore from the room and bolted down the hallway. His crazed cries of grief were heard far away, disappearing into the night.

ELAINE: (*weeping*) No! Come back! Come back!

NARRATOR: Soon the grim form of King Pelles appeared in the doorway, borne by his servants. He stared at his frightened daughter sadly.

ELAINE: (*gasp*) Father!

PELLES: We have committed a horrible sin tonight. We have destroyed the mind of this knight. Because of this the Grail and its objects have disappeared. They have left us.

ELAINE: (*weeping*) I will make it right, Father.

PELLES: I'm afraid no one can do that now, my dear—no one.

NARRATOR: Lancelot ran through the dark, wasted forest. The knight insanely scratched at his face, screaming and crying to the moon like a beast. He had wronged his love, his king, and destroyed everything he stood for. He would forget himself and be lost to madness.

After a month with no word from Lancelot, the court of Camelot grew worried. No one bore his absence harder than the queen. She commissioned knights to go out and search for him. Despite all her efforts, no word of Lancelot came.

GUINEVERE: (*sadly*) Oh, Lancelot. Have you left Camelot forever?

NARRATOR: That winter in the coldness of her father's desolate castle, Elaine gave birth to a son, Galahad, and entrusting the child to nuns who lived in a convent nearby, she began to search for the knight she had ruined.

ELAINE: Please, sisters, take care of this child. I may not return. I go to right what I have wronged.

NARRATOR: Her old dame went with her as she journeyed.

ELAINE: Thank you, Dame Brisen. I have been a silly creature—a horrible beast. I don't know how you have put up with me all these years. I'm such a stupid thing.

BRISEN: Oh, my lady. You have grown. You have grown so much. Maybe there is a way to make it right.

ELAINE: That is my only hope.

NARRATOR: They searched through all of Britain for a year, calling for the lost knight, Sir Lancelot. In the meantime, Lancelot, living alone in the wilderness, had become a mad hermit. His beard had grown long and haggard. He lived on berries and sat all day in his own filth. It was in this state that Elaine, one evening, happened upon him.

BRISEN: Look out, my lady! It is a wild man!

ELAINE: No. Wait! Lancelot? Is that you? Give me your name, sir!

LANCELOT: (*crazy*) If a man has no name, he cannot give it! Shame is my name, and shame shall I ever be called!

ELAINE: Dame Brisen, it is he!

BRISEN: Be careful, my lady! He has gone wild!

NARRATOR: Elaine ran to Lancelot and cradled his dirty head. His crazed, confused eyes rolled from side to side.

ELAINE: (*screaming*) He is mad! What can we do?

BRISEN: He has been wounded in his heart and in his mind. Only a miracle can bring him back!

ELAINE: A miracle?

NARRATOR: Elaine, holding Lancelot in her arms, looked up into the pale sky above.

ELAINE: Please! The power of the Holy Grail once resided with my family—but it has left us. We do not deserve it, but please, let this vessel return one last time and heal this man I have wronged.

NARRATOR: Suddenly a dove, holding a golden censure in its mouth, flew above through the boughs of the trees, and a heavenly light filled the clearing. (*angels singing*)

ELAINE: It is happening! It is happening!

NARRATOR: The light blanketed Lancelot, and he shuddered. His lips moved in silent words, and scales seemed to fall from his eyes. He sat up and stared at Elaine in wonder.

LANCELOT: (*dreamlike*) I saw Him! I saw Him!

ELAINE: Who, Lancelot? Who?

LANCELOT: The Christ! He put the cup to my lips and let me drink. He has healed me.

ELAINE: (*tearfully*) Thank you! Thank you!

NARRATOR: The knight stood and stared at the weeping maiden in wonder.

LANCELOT: My lady, why do you weep? This is a cause for rejoicing! The Grail has brought me back.

ELAINE: Lancelot, I have so much love for you, but I know that you cannot ever return it.

LANCELOT: (*solemnly*) You have saved me, and I thank you for it. But you cannot ask me to create love where there is none.

ELAINE: I know.

BRISEN: Someone approaches!

NARRATOR: A knight was riding through the thicket. It was Sir Gawain. During his long search his beard had grown out coarsely. Burrs and brambles were stuck within it. His face looked weary.

GAWAIN: What goes on here? I saw a great light blazing in the sky!

BRISEN: This is Sir Lancelot. He had become mad, but now he is healed.

GAWAIN: Lancelot, we have been searching for you everywhere! The queen is most sick with grief!

ELAINE: (*quietly*) He is still weak. You must take him back to Camelot. The Grail has healed him. Take him back to his king – and his queen.

GAWAIN: I will.

NARRATOR: Gawain hoisted the grizzled Lancelot upon his horse.

LANCELOT: Thank you, Gawain. Thank you.

NARRATOR: Gawain mounted behind the drooping Lancelot, and the two rode away.

BRISEN: (*slowly*) My lady, are you all right?

ELAINE: (*sadly*) My life is spent.

NARRATOR: Not long after, when a nighttime mist shrouded the river that flowed near Camelot, a splendid barge floated silently from the fog. The watchmen hailed it and rowed out to it. They found it empty except for a golden-haired maiden, lying with her arms folded in death. No wound was upon her body, but her spirit had left her just the same. A note was clasped in her hand.

ELAINE: (*voiceover*) I died for love of him whom I ruined. I died of love for him whom I healed. I died for love of him who could not return my love.

NARRATOR: The watchmen carried the note back to Camelot, and Lady Elaine disappeared into the mists forever.

On the borders of the wasted realm of the Fisher King in a quiet nunnery, a forgotten child was housed—the son of Lancelot, who would become the holiest and greatest knight that Britain would ever know.

DISCUSSION QUESTIONS

1. What is Lancelot's inner conflict?
2. Why does Lancelot go temporarily insane?
3. Do you pity Lancelot and Guinevere? Explain.
4. Why does Guinevere feel herself drawn to Lancelot?
5. Does Guinevere love both Arthur and Lancelot? Explain.
6. Can you trick someone into loving you—as Elaine attempted to do? Explain.
7. Does King Pelles deserve to lose the Holy Grail? Explain.
8. Even though Elaine acts foolishly, does she redeem herself? Explain.
9. Do you feel sorry for Elaine? Explain.

THE KNIGHT OF THE CART
TEACHER GUIDE

BACKGROUND

Love and marriage had very little to do with one another in the Middle Ages. After all, marriages were often arranged by the parents of the couple, not the couple themselves. For this reason, many people considered the idea of romantic love to be extra-marital. Knights in troubadour poetry always had a lady fair—a noble woman of higher rank that they worshipped from afar. This woman and often the knight himself were already married to other people, but this did not stop them from loving. The knight's unrequited love tortured his soul, and he became willing to give up anything—even his knightly honor—in the name of love. This romantic concept is called "courtly love."

Within the Arthurian romances, the character of Lancelot, King Arthur's best knight and the secret lover of his queen, is the epitome of courtly love. Chretien de Troyes, a French poet, first introduced the character of Lancelot in *Lancelot, the Knight of the Cart*. As opposed to Arthur, who operates out of a sense of justice and duty, Lancelot is devoted to courtly love, giving himself over completely to his love for Guinevere. They are two men, two friends, serving opposing ideals.

SUMMARY

Returning to Camelot after a long absence, Lancelot learns that Guinevere has been abducted by a strange knight who rode into Camelot and demanded to be given the queen if he was able to defeat one of Arthur's best knights. Since Lancelot was away, Sir Kay begged Arthur to allow him to fight the strange knight. The knight, named Meleagant, bested Kay easily and rode away with the queen and Kay as his prisoners.

Lancelot and Sir Gawain decide to follow the knight's trail. Lancelot happens upon a dwarf driving a cart, but the dwarf will only give Lancelot information if he agrees to ride within the back of the cart. Since this is how criminals were transported in the Middle Ages, a knight doing this would be very dishonorable. Since the dwarf claims to know where Guinevere has been taken, Lancelot sacrifices his honor and rides in the cart. Gawain is scandalized by this, but Lancelot declares he is willing to do anything to retrieve the queen.

The dwarf drives Lancelot to his mistress, who turns out to be Morgan le Fay. The enchantress tells Lancelot that Guinevere has been taken into the magical kingdom of Gore by the strange knight. There are two ways to get into Gore—one is a razor-sharp sword bridge, and the other is an underwater bridge. Lancelot and Gawain split up—each attempting to gain entrance to Gore by a different bridge.

Lancelot attempts the Sword Bridge, which is as thin and sharp as a sword's blade. Crossing it, he loses his balance and falls, badly wounding his hands. He manages to cross the bridge but faints from the blood he has lost.

When Lancelot awakens, he is in Gore, and the elderly king of that land, Bagdemagus, tells him that his son, Meleagant, is the one who took Guinevere from Camelot. The knight will only give her back if Lancelot beats him in battle, but Lancelot's hands have been badly wounded. Lancelot declares that there is no time to waste, and he will fight the knight even though his hands are wounded.

Lancelot faces the knight, and in spite of his wounded hands, is about to beat him when he spies Guinevere watching their battle from the palace walls. Lancelot is so distracted by his love that he cannot battle. Meleagant, taking advantage of this, is about to shoot Lancelot in the back with an arrow when Bagdemagus intervenes—declaring the contest void.

That night Lancelot sneaks from his room in the palace and manages to locate Guinevere's cell, and the two of them spend the night together.

The next day Lancelot departs the castle after learning that Gawain has become trapped while crossing through the Underwater Bridge. Lancelot frees him with the help of a damsel, who claims to be Bagdemagus's banished daughter. Returning to the castle with the damsel and Gawain, Lancelot confronts Meleagant and defeats him in battle. Lancelot, Guinevere, Kay, and Gawain return to Camelot.

ESSENTIAL QUESTIONS

- What is more important—love or honor?
- Would you do something dishonorable in the name of love?

ANTICIPATORY QUESTIONS

- Would you risk your life for love?
- A constant dilemma for Lancelot is whether he should be loyal to his duty to Arthur or to his love for Guinevere. Which should he choose?

CHARACTER QUEST

Fidelity Lancelot feels that his highest duty is to his feelings, while others would say that his highest duty is to his king and his oath of knighthood. Guinevere undergoes a similar struggle between her marriage vows and her feelings for Lancelot. How do their feelings challenge their fidelity? By which should they choose to live?

CONNECT

Tristan + Isolde **(2006)** This is a film adaptation of the Tristan and Isolde legend, which closely parallels the Lancelot and Guinevere love story. A knight named Tristan falls in love with Isolde, the wife of King Mark. He is now torn between his knightly duty to Mark and his love for Isolde.

TEACHABLE TERMS

- **Idiom** Meleagant tells Lancelot, "You almost lost your head," on pg. 149 during their duel. This is wordplay on the idiom "lose your head."
- **Symbol** The cart in this story begins as a symbol of Lancelot's shame, but the by the end of the story, Guinevere uses it as a symbol of Lancelot's devotion to her pg. 156.

RECALL QUESTIONS

1. What dishonorable act does Lancelot do in order to locate Guinevere?
2. What bridge does Lancelot use to cross into Gore?
3. How is he wounded while crossing it?
4. Why do Kay's wounds never heal?
5. Lancelot rescues Gawain from what perilous place?

The Knight of the Cart

CAST

LANCELOT	*Britain's Best Knight*
GUINEVERE	*Queen of Britain*
KAY	*Seneschal of Camelot*
GAWAIN	*Knight of Camelot*
SQUIRE	*Kay's Squire*
MELEAGANT	*Evil Knight of Gore*
DWARF	*Cart Driver*
VILLAGER ONE	*Villager*
VILLAGER TWO	*Villager*
MORGAN	*Evil Enchantress*
BAGDEMAGUS	*Old King of Gore*
DAMSEL	*Princess of Gore*

NARRATOR: Lancelot had been long from Arthur's court. He had succumbed to a fit of madness, lived in the wilderness as a crazed hermit, and was saved only by the spiritual powers of the Holy Grail.

Now Lancelot was finally returning, riding down the road that led to Camelot with his fellow knight Gawain. Lancelot's greatest desire was to see his lady-love, Queen Guinevere, once again. After all that had transpired and the months of separation, proving his love to her had become the most important thing in his life.

Lancelot and Gawain rode into a clearing where broken lances and fragments of shields littered the ground. The turf had been torn up by the powerful hooves of chargers.

GAWAIN: A fight has occurred here.

LANCELOT: It's probably nothing that concerns us. Let's press on to Camelot.

SQUIRE: Sirs! Please help!

NARRATOR: A startled squire, his face flecked with blood, ran out of the forest.

GAWAIN: What has happened here, boy?

SQUIRE: A terrible fight between two knights! The queen was abducted!

LANCELOT: *(panicked)* The queen? Guinevere, you mean?

SQUIRE: Yes, sir! An evil knight defeated Sir Kay, who was protecting her.

LANCELOT: Kay? Why was she being protected by Kay? I should have been here!

GAWAIN: Easy, my friend. *(to the squire)* What was the knight's name, boy? Did he bear a symbol upon his armor?

LANCELOT: There's no time for that! Show me which way he went!

NARRATOR: The boy pointed a frightened finger westward, and Lancelot galloped away where he pointed. *(hoofbeats)*

GAWAIN: Lancelot, wait! *(sigh)* Nevermind. Now, boy, in great detail tell me what has happened.

SQUIRE: All the trouble began this morning when a strange knight rode into Camelot and challenged the Knights of the Round Table to battle! He did not give his name, but he was a giant man and his armor was covered in spikes.

GAWAIN: What does all this have to do with the queen?

SQUIRE: The evil knight said he had many prisoners held at his castle, but the only way he would release them was for Arthur to stake the life of Guinevere on a duel.

GAWAIN: The king agreed to such a thing?

SQUIRE: Not at first. But then Sir Kay swore he would leave Camelot forever if Arthur did not promise to grant him a request.

GAWAIN: That blustering fool! I bet I know what his request was! He wanted to fight the evil knight, didn't he?

SQUIRE: Yes, and the king was forced to send the queen out with Kay for the duel. I think even the king knew this was a horrible idea, but he did not stop it. The evil knight vanquished Kay very easily, and then he had his servants carry Kay and the queen away westward. I barely escaped with my life.

GAWAIN: Thank you for this information, boy! Return to Camelot and tell them that Lancelot and I will retrieve the queen!

NARRATOR: Gawain headed westward through the forest—searching for Lancelot's trail. Suddenly, he came upon a dead horse in the path—its hide covered with frothy sweat.

GAWAIN: This is Lancelot's steed. He has ridden his horse to death! He must now be on foot.

NARRATOR: As Gawain continued through the wilderness, a rocky road appeared, and he saw a dwarf driving a rickety cart toward him. *(rattling cart)*

GAWAIN: Dwarf! Dwarf! Halt, I say!

NARRATOR: The ugly dwarf snarled and pulled up the reins.

DWARF: What is it? I have to get this load to my mistress!

GAWAIN: Tell me, dwarf—have you seen an evil knight pass this way?

NARRATOR: The dwarf smiled a crafty smile.

DWARF: *(chuckle)* Hee hee. The only knight I've seen is the one that is riding in the back of my cart.

GAWAIN: *(laughing)* Ha! That joke is in poor taste, dwarf! No honorable knight would ever dare ride in the back of a—*(in shock)* What?

NARRATOR: The dwarf was right. A knight was in the back of the cart, his head hung in shame. Gawain suddenly realized who the knight was.

GAWAIN: Lancelot! What on earth are you doing? Get out of there at once!

DWARF: *(chuckle)* Hee hee hee.

GAWAIN: Don't you know that only criminals ride in the back of carts?

DWARF: Hee hee. Criminals on their way to be whipped in the public square.

GAWAIN: See? Even the dwarf knows it's a disgrace! Have you gone mad—again?

LANCELOT: I know what I'm doing, Gawain. Leave me be. I must find the queen—at any cost! This dwarf knows the way, and I must pay his price.

DWARF: As I told him, only my mistress can tell him where the evil knight has gone, and the only way I will take him to my mistress is if he rides in my cart.

GAWAIN: What a nasty offer! I would have flatly refused.

DWARF: Well, he hesitated for a moment, but then he jumped right aboard.

NARRATOR: Gawain was speechless.

LANCELOT: Leave me be, Gawain. You wouldn't understand. Drive on, dwarf. We're wasting daylight.

NARRATOR: The dwarf cracked his whip, and the cart continued to rattle violently down the road. Gawain rode angrily alongside it.

GAWAIN: Lancelot, what if rumor of this gets back to Camelot? What if everyone finds out you're a…*(whispering)* cart-knight?

LANCELOT: My honor is worth nothing if I don't rescue the queen.

NARRATOR: As Gawain huffily rode alongside the cart, the forest road led through a village. The dwarf slowed his cart to a crawl and rang a little bell. *(ringing of a bell)*

DWARF: Yoo-hoo, townspeople! See this dishonorable knight? He dares to ride within a cart like a common criminal!

VILLAGER ONE: He must have done something horrible!

VILLAGER TWO: That dwarf must be taking him to hang for his crimes!

VILLAGER ONE: Good! Any knight who rides in a cart like that deserves to die!

GAWAIN: *(whispering)* See? Even these peasants are looking down on you now!

NARRATOR: The townspeople's taunts turned violent as they began to hurl stones. Lancelot merely lowered his head and allowed these to pelt him.

DWARF: Hee hee!

NARRATOR: At the far side of the village the cart finally came to a crossroads, and the dwarf reined up the horse. There was a flash, and a raven-haired lady appeared before them.

DWARF: My lady!

MORGAN: Well, well, well. Do my eyes deceive me? Is this Lancelot, the best and most honorable knight in the world, riding in a cart? *(cruel laugh)*

GAWAIN: It's Morgan le Fay!

LANCELOT: I should have known she was behind this! What have you done with the queen?

MORGAN: Me? I am innocent—for once. You seek a knight named Meleagant. He's my great nephew, you know. I used to be his tutor when he was a boy. I taught him everything he knows. *(mock fear)* Oh dear. I hope he didn't get the idea of abducting the queen from me…

LANCELOT: *(angrily)* If he has harmed one hair on her head…

MORGAN: Relax. He has taken her into the land of Gore. That used to be *my* kingdom before Arthur turned my husband against me and banished me from it forever.

GAWAIN: You tried to murder your own husband, King Uriens, in cold blood!

MORGAN: Details. Details.

LANCELOT: Well, you've played your trick. I've ridden in your disgraceful cart. Now, tell me how to get into Gore. Which road must I take?

MORGAN: That's just the thing, Sir Cart-knight. Even though I'm banished from Gore, the kingdom still holds traces of my enchantment. No one can get into Gore if the ruler, currently my husband's nephew, does not wish it. It is sealed against you.

LANCELOT: If you tell me that the queen is lost forever, I will end your life.

NARRATOR: Lancelot drew his sword.

MORGAN: Do really think you can harm me with a sword?

LANCELOT: I'd like to try!

MORGAN: Relax. There are two pathways that remain open to you, two bridges into the land of Gore, but I'm afraid they're very perilous. I made them that way. To the left lies the Sword Bridge and to the right lies the Underwater Bridge.

GAWAIN: An underwater bridge? That doesn't make sense!

MORGAN: Obviously, pumpkin. That's why they're magical. These are the only paths upon which a person may enter Gore.

LANCELOT: Gawain, we each should try one of them. That way if one of us fails, the other might succeed. Which do you choose?

GAWAIN: I will choose the Underwater Bridge. It makes no sense, but I don't like the sound of the Sword Bridge.

MORGAN: Yes, one slip on the Sword Bridge will leave you half a man! Literally. Aren't I just full of good ideas? Do be careful, knights. Now, if you will excuse me, I have to go spread some juicy gossip. After all, I just saw Lancelot riding in a cart! *(evil laugh)*

NARRATOR: The lady, her dwarf, and the cart vanished in a flash.

GAWAIN: Well, then, I guess I will see you in Gore—if we both survive.

NARRATOR: The two knights separated. Lancelot headed down the left branch of the crossroads. The sound of torrential waters soon filled the forest, and a deep gorge appeared. At first, Lancelot saw no bridge across the gorge, but then a thin, glinting line appeared in the space between the two cliffs.

LANCELOT: *(in awe)* The Sword Bridge.

NARRATOR: The bridge was as thin as a sword blade—and appeared just as keen.

LANCELOT: It would be impossible to cross this bridge and live!

NARRATOR: From the bridge there was a thirty-foot drop to the black waters that rushed below. An armored knight would have no chance of swimming if he fell.

LANCELOT: Remember, Lancelot. This is for your love!

NARRATOR: Lancelot dismounted and walked toward the bridge. Arms stretched out to either side, he extended one foot out and placed it firmly on the thin sword-edge. Then balancing delicately, he brought his other foot forward and set it down. One more step, and then another. Two more steps, and he would be halfway across the bridge.

LANCELOT: Perhaps this will not be as hard as I thought.

NARRATOR: Just then a sudden gust of wind caught him by surprise. He flailed to the side.

LANCELOT: Ah! No! Ahhhh!

NARRATOR: Lancelot found himself dangling from the side of the bridge. The edge of the bridge was already slicing through the hard leather of his gloves. His weight was pulling him downward, and in a moment, the blade would reach the soft flesh of his palms and sever his hands in two.

Lancelot began to sway side to side, inching his grip along, shimmying forward. The bridge cut deeper into his gloves. Now he was only a couple of feet from the opposite cliff.

LANCELOT: Ahhh! *(cry of pain)*

NARRATOR: Lancelot lunged out for the cliff's edge and caught ahold of it. His arms were trembling, his hands gushing blood, but somehow he found the strength to lift himself and climb up onto the edge of the cliff.

LANCELOT: *(breathlessly)* I have made it. I have made it.

NARRATOR: He examined his hands. In the last instants of his crossing, the Sword Bridge had cut deeply into his palms. Blood was gushing from them. His head grew woozy, and he slumped forward into the grass. And he knew no more.

When Lancelot regained his senses, he was lying in a warm bed. An old, frail man was seated in a chair beside him.

BAGDEMAGUS: *(old man voice)* Oh! You're awake! Finally.

LANCELOT: Who are you?

BAGDEMAGUS: I am King Bagdemagus. This is my castle—the castle of Gore. My men found you by the Sword Bridge and brought you here.

LANCELOT: *(frantically)* Is Queen Guinevere here? Is she all right?

BAGDEMAGUS: Oh, yes. She is very well cared for. We are very hospitable here in Gore.

LANCELOT: Really? But she was brought here forcibly by a black-hearted knight!

BAGDEMAGUS: *(surprised)* Black-hearted knight? No, no, no. You must mean my son, Meleagant.

LANCELOT: I'm confused. You say that the evil knight is your son?

BAGDEMAGUS: Evil? *(laugh)* Meleagant is not evil. He's just a boy, and like all boys he's a little—rambunctious.

LANCELOT: He abducted the queen!

BAGDEMAGUS: And someone called Sir Kay, I think. But all's fair in love and war! And Meleagant *loves* his little games—capturing knights and maidens. It's his own little version of chess. His doctors say it's good for his mental stability.

LANCELOT: You allow him to do this?

BAGDEMAGUS: I can't come between my son and his happiness! And his collection makes him happy! But I'm not a monster. I make him feed and water his captives everyday. I tell him, "Meleagant, we must be humane!"

NARRATOR: Lancelot stared at the old man in confusion.

LANCELOT: I must fight your son.

BAGDEMAGUS: He is eager to fight you as well. But I'm afraid I don't understand all this battling business. He was rather angry when I put you up here. He threw a little tantrum, in fact. It was quite cute. I think he was hoping to add you to his collection. But for it to be a fair fight, you must heal first! Look at your hands! You are in no condition to fight.

NARRATOR: Blood-stained bandages had been tightly wrapped around Lancelot's palms.

BAGDEMAGUS: You're lucky that bridge didn't cut all the way through your hands. We found the remains of the last knight who tried to cross the Sword Bridge! We had to piece him back together like a puzzle. Nasty business!

LANCELOT: If I defeat your son in battle, will he release all his captives—including the queen?

BAGDEMAGUS: Of course. Of course. He always follows the rules of these little games of his.

LANCELOT: Then I'm afraid I cannot wait. I must free the queen at any cost.

BAGDEMAGUS: Oooh. Meleagant is quite spirited. Why not wait until your hands are better?

LANCELOT: It must be now. I will need a sword, a lance, and a charger.

BAGDEMAGUS: All right. But I hate to see you die. You seem like such a nice young man.

NARRATOR: The king left to make all the arrangements. Soon a squire came to

Lancelot's room with armor to ready him for battle. Lancelot tenderly slid the new gloves over his lacerated hands. He took up the provided sword and squeezed its pommel. He winced. There was pain—but not enough to stop him.

When the squire led Lancelot to the jousting field, the knight caught his first sight of Meleagant. The giant man stood, holding his spiked helm, beside his frail father. He had a baby-face that made an odd mismatch to his massive build.

MELEAGANT: Glad you could join us, dishonorable knight! I heard about your little cart ride! *(evil laughter)* Ha!

LANCELOT: *(sigh)* I guess the whole world has heard about that.

BAGDEMAGUS: Meleagant! Be polite! He is our guest. If he wants to ride in a cart like a worthless scumbag, that's *his* business. I mean, I wouldn't be caught dead doing that, but…

MELEAGANT: Are you ready to die, cart-knight?

BAGDEMAGUS: Die? Why do these contests need to be so brutal? How about a nice game of tag for once? That's what I say!

LANCELOT: *(coldly)* I am ready, evil knight.

BAGDEMAGUS: All right. You boys have a nice time. Let's make this good, clean fun. I'll be over here watching.

NARRATOR: Without any warning, Meleagant threw on his helm and charged forward—swinging an oversized mace above his head.

MELEAGANT: Ahhhh! *(battlecry)*

NARRATOR: Lancelot blocked the blow of the mace with his shield. *(Clang!)* But the weapon's spikes penetrated the shield. Meleagant jerked back his mace, ripping the shield from Lancelot's grip.

MELEAGANT: Whoops! Looks like you lost your shield!

BAGDEMAGUS: Very good, boys. Very good. After this, maybe we'll have some refreshments!

NARRATOR: Meleagant pried the battered shield from his mace and flung it to the ground. *(clanging noise)*

MELEAGANT: You'll make a perfect addition to my collection. I've never had a cart-knight before.

LANCELOT: Ha! This "cart-knight" will defeat you and free all those whom you have imprisoned!

NARRATOR: Just then Lancelot happened to glance up, and his heart almost stopped. In the distance, standing in the window of a tall tower of the castle, was a woman that had to be Guinevere.

LANCELOT: *(breathlessly)* There she is!

GUINEVERE: Lancelot!

NARRATOR: A whizzing sound filled Lancelot's ears, and he ducked just in time. Meleagant's mace passed closely by his head. *(whooshing sound)*

MELEAGANT: Bah! You almost lost your head there!

BAGDEMAGUS: Oooh. Good one, son. Nice banter.

NARRATOR: Lancelot made a clumsy slice at his opponent's shield and simultaneously craned his neck to get another glimpse of his love.

LANCELOT: (*overjoyed*) Look! She's all right! I don't believe it! (*yelling*) Guinevere!

MELEAGANT: Shut up and fight! Argh!

NARRATOR: The weapons of the knights crashed together, and the combatants struggled furiously against one another—each trying to gain an advantage. Lancelot used this opportunity to glance over his shoulder.

LANCELOT: (*shouting*) Guinevere!

NARRATOR: Watching from the heights of the tower, Guinevere gasped.

GUINEVERE: Why does he keep looking at me? (*shouting*) Fight, Lancelot, fight!

NARRATOR: Meleagant thrust Lancelot to the ground.

MELEAGANT: (*roaring*) I'll splatter your brains like jelly!

BAGDEMAGUS: Now, now. Play nice.

NARRATOR: Meleagant reared up and brought his mace down with all his might, intending his blow to crush Lancelot's skull, but it struck only grass. Lancelot was gone.

MELEAGANT: What? Grrrr. Where did he go?

NARRATOR: Meleagant spun around. Lancelot stood not far away, his back turned.

LANCELOT: Guinevere!

MELEAGANT: (*to the squire*) Squire, bring me my bow!

GUINEVERE: Oh no! Behind you! Behind you!

LANCELOT: Huh? I can't hear you, my sweet!

MELEAGANT: An arrow in the back of the neck. A perfect death.

BAGDEMAGUS: No, Meleagant! His back is turned! Meleagant! Bad boy!

NARRATOR: Ignoring his father, the foul knight took the bow into his hands and drew it tight.

BAGDEMAGUS: Meleagant! I said, "No!"

NARRATOR: Meleagant sneered and nocked an arrow into his bow.

BAGDEMAGUS: Enough!

NARRATOR: King Bagdemagus ran forward and slapped the bow from his son's hands.

MELEAGANT: (*whining*) Father, why did you do that? I was going to kill him!

BAGDEMAGUS: We do *not* shoot our guests in the back.

MELEAGANT: (*childlike*) Aww, Father. Just let me kill this one!

NARRATOR: They both glanced to where Lancelot was shouting messages of love up to his lofty queen.

BAGDEMAGUS: See? He's practically insane! Let's give his mind and body time to heal, and then we will continue this duel. Who knows? Between now and then, perhaps you two will become fast friends.

MELEAGANT: *(grudgingly)* Yes, Father.

NARRATOR: Reluctantly, Meleagant left the battlefield.

LANCELOT: *(frantically)* King! King! Can you tell me how one might climb this tall tower here? How can I reach the queen?

BAGDEMAGUS: Oh, I'm afraid you can't, young man. The queen is locked in her room—for her own protection. Her purity is my main concern. I see you're very fond of her, but it is best if you leave her be.

LANCELOT: *(desperately)* Don't you understand? I'll *die* if I don't see her soon!

BAGDEMAGUS: You young people are so dramatic! *(pause)* Oh my. Look at the blood dripping from your gloves. I fear the wounds in your hands have reopened. Heal up, and then you and Meleagant can continue your little game. If you win, you can see the queen.

NARRATOR: But Lancelot was not listening. He was soaking up his last glimpse of Guinevere and plotting a way to reach the high tower.

That night Lancelot snuck from his room. The corridors of the castle formed a complex web, and he made many wrong turns before he finally found the staircase to Guinevere's tower. As soon as he did, he saw Meleagant descending the staircase, and he ducked into the shadows. As soon as Meleagant had passed by into the darkness, Lancelot bounded up the stairs. The door to the high chamber was still ajar. Lancelot rushed into the darkened room and spied a form lying on the bed. He knelt and cradled it in his arms.

LANCELOT: My sweet! My sweet! Oh, how I have missed you these many years! I have come to prove my love to you! I'll never leave you again!

GUINEVERE: *(confused)* Lancelot?

NARRATOR: It was the voice of the queen, but it had not come from the body Lancelot now cradled. A candle was lit. Guinevere appeared across the room. Lancelot looked down to see the bruised face of Kay cuddled against his own.

KAY: *(weakly)* I—never—knew—you—cared…

LANCELOT: Ah!

NARRATOR: Kay's body dropped roughly to the floor. *(thud)*

KAY: *(groan)* Ughnnnn.

LANCELOT: Guinevere!

NARRATOR: Stepping over Kay's body, Lancelot neared Guinevere, but iron bars, dividing the chamber into two cells, stopped his progress. He placed his face against the cold metal.

LANCELOT: My queen! I am so relieved to see you again—safe and sound. All my trials are worth one glimpse of you!

NARRATOR: To Lancelot's surprise the face of Guinevere did not look happy.

LANCELOT: What is the matter?

GUINEVERE: Where have you been?

LANCELOT: It is a long story, my lady.

GUINEVERE: Please tell me. I think I deserve some answers. You went away and never returned! You left me without my champion. Then this evil knight showed up at Camelot, and Arthur just sat there and let him carry me off! He let *Kay* protect me! Where were you, Lancelot? If you had been there, I never would have been taken.

LANCELOT: I have been to the edge of insanity and back. I have faced trials you wouldn't believe and was saved only through the grace of God. But through it all I've realized something, Guinevere—my life is meaningless if I don't have your love.

GUINEVERE: Is that a fact? I thought the only thing I had left to rely upon was your love. But now I doubt even that. Meleagant told me about your little incident with—the cart.

LANCELOT: Oh, please forgive me for that disgrace! I only submitted myself to that shame because it was the only way I could find you again.

GUINEVERE: *(angrily)* I'm not mad that you did it. A knight should do such things for his lady! I'm angry because I heard that you *hesitated* a bit before you climbed into the cart!

LANCELOT: You can't be serious. I was giving up my honor for you! I only hesitated to think—

GUINEVERE: Oh. You had to think about it, huh? Was I not worth your honor?

LANCELOT: I crossed a bridge made of cut steel to reach you! How can you doubt my devotion? Look, Guinevere!

NARRATOR: Lancelot tore the bandages off his hand-wounds and held them up to the light for her to see.

LANCELOT: *Here* is the proof of my love!

GUINEVERE: Oh!

NARRATOR: At the sight of these wounds, Guinevere's anger cooled.

GUINEVERE: Oh, Lancelot. Forgive my harsh words. I have just been so angry. It took you leaving Camelot for me to realize how empty my life was without you. But by then you were gone—forever, it seemed.

LANCELOT: So…you love me, too? What about Arthur?

GUINEVERE: Arthur has proved that I mean nothing to him! He sat by and let me be taken to this place. You are my champion—and my love.

LANCELOT: *(happily)* How long I've waited to hear those words! Oh, how I long to embrace you!

GUINEVERE: Then do!

LANCELOT: These bars prevent me.

GUINEVERE: Bars? Bars cannot stand in the way of our love!

NARRATOR: Lancelot, looking at the bars in determination, gripped them in his bandaged hands and pulled with all his strength. Then, with a supernatural will, he forced them apart.

LANCELOT: (*grunting*) Grrrr! Ah!

NARRATOR: He rushed through the opening, sweeping Guinevere into his arms.

The two spent much time in each other's embrace. Soon the first traces of dawn began to show in the sky.

LANCELOT: We have almost spent the night! Hurry! We must escape this place before we are discovered.

GUINEVERE: Escape? What about Kay? He is too wounded to travel.

LANCELOT: Kay got you both into this mess. He can find his own way out.

GUINEVERE: If we leave him here, he will die. Every day he grows weaker. Meleagant comes every night and pours poison into his wounds, and they never heal. Meleagant is a deranged killer, but the old king thinks that he is some kindhearted child.

LANCELOT: We will just have to leave Kay to his fate.

GUINEVERE: How will we escape this land? Unless the king wills it, no one can enter or exit—unless it is by the Sword Bridge or the Underwater Bridge.

LANCELOT: The Underwater Bridge! I almost forgot. Gawain was going to try to enter Gore by that route before we were separated.

GUINEVERE: I have not seen him here.

LANCELOT: I must go there and see if our escape can be made through that route. Gawain must have fallen into peril. (*pause*) But I cannot stand to leave you again!

GUINEVERE: Then I command you to! And no knight can refuse the order of his lady.

LANCELOT: What about the bars? How will you explain them?

GUINEVERE: You let me worry about that. Now go, before the household awakes!

NARRATOR: After a few more tearful embraces, the lovers parted, and Lancelot fled the castle.

Lancelot commandeered a horse and rode through the forests of Gore, searching for the Underwater Bridge. A foul stench permeated the air, and he followed it to its source—a boggy, bubbling swamp. As he viewed it, a female voice called out.

DAMSEL: It's even worse than it smells.

NARRATOR: A damsel, bearing a falcon upon her arm and riding on a white palfrey, appeared from the thicket behind him.

LANCELOT: (*in shock*) You! I have not seen you since I rescued you from Morgan le Fay's castle many years ago! What are you doing here in Gore?

DAMSEL: Actually, I think I rescued myself. Gore is my home. I am the daughter of Bagdemagus, and Meleagant is my brother.

LANCELOT: I cannot believe that beast is your brother.

DAMSEL: His mind was poisoned long ago. Father thinks Meleagant keeps his captured knights and damsels in the castle dungeon, but in reality, Meleagant takes their heads. He has a grisly collection of them. I discovered it a month ago, and so Meleagant drove me away from our home—under penalty of death. Then he told our father that I had run away.

LANCELOT: I have come seeking for the Underwater Bridge.

DAMSEL: In that swamp is the Underwater Bridge, a tunnel that leads from the kingdom of Gore into your world. Your friend is trapped down there. I saw him attempt a crossing, but he lost his will half-way.

LANCELOT: Then there is no way he is still alive.

DAMSEL: He still lives. This swamp is no normal swamp. Its purpose is to trap—not to kill. Its waters slowly sap the will. Once your will leaves you, you are trapped within it forever. Many knights lie below.

LANCELOT: Then I must go. *(pause)* Wait a minute. The last time I met you, you tricked me up a tree to rescue your falcon. Is this another trick?

DAMSEL: I guess you will just have to trust me.

NARRATOR: Lancelot removed his armor and waded into the bog of the swamp, the mud sucking greedily at his legs. He dove in. The water was murky, but beneath the slime and sludge of the surface, he could see for a small distance. As he swam, figures started to loom out of the shadows—bodies of knights floating lifelessly in the murk, entangled by tentacle-like weeds. At last, the still form of Gawain appeared, snared by the same vegetation. Lancelot tore the tendrils loose from the knight, and gripping him in his arms, began to swim back toward the surface.

Ever since Lancelot had entered the swamp, he had noticed that his heart was growing colder and colder. His swim-strokes slowed and even stopped. He began to sink. Although he could not see the underwater vines, he felt them creeping closer—like veins of ice. His will began to leave him. It was then that he thought of Guinevere. His heart warmed, and he found his strength.

Lancelot and Gawain, covered in slime, broke the surface. *(splashing noises)*

LANCELOT: Damsel! Help us ashore!

NARRATOR: Gawain, now lying upon the swamp-bank, gasped back to life.

GAWAIN: *(coughing)* You saved me, Lancelot! You saved me!

LANCELOT: I must return to the castle and retrieve the queen.

DAMSEL: Wait!

NARRATOR: The damsel caught Lancelot's hands in her own.

DAMSEL: Your hands are wounded. Let me heal them for you. You will never defeat my brother if you fight with wounded hands. After you vanquish him, I will have my father allow you to return to your home.

NARRATOR: She rubbed an ointment on Lancelot's palms, and they suddenly tingled. The wounds magically closed—not even the sign of a scar remained.

LANCELOT: Most wondrous!

DAMSEL: Godspeed, knight of the cart. I will care for your friend. You must go to face my brother!

NARRATOR: Lancelot left the swamp and rode back to the castle of Bagdemagus. A commotion was arising from the courtyard, and Lancelot made toward it. Bagdemagus and Meleagant stood on a platform in the midst of a gathered crowd. Guinevere was tied to a chair there. The still-wounded Kay was tied to a seat beside her, his head slumped to the side. Behind the prisoners a huge executioner was sharpening an axe.

MELEAGANT: This woman is to be executed for harlotry! *(to Guinevere)* Admit it! Although you are married, you spent the night with this wounded knight!

NARRATOR: Meleagant pointed to Kay.

GUINEVERE: You can't be serious!

MELEAGANT: The bars that separated you were bent, and his blood was all over your bed. It looks like harlotry to me!

BAGDEMAGUS: This doesn't look good, my dear.

MELEAGANT: We already have the evidence! What does your knight-lover have to say for himself?

KAY: *(slurred mumbling)* Hmmmmmmm...

MELEAGANT: See! He admits it! Behead them both! Kill the tramp first!

LANCELOT: *(loudly)* Halt!

NARRATOR: All eyes turned toward Lancelot.

GUINEVERE: *(happily)* Lancelot!

LANCELOT: Foul knight, do you dare challenge the purity of the queen?

MELEAGANT: Purity! Ha! That's a laugh.

LANCELOT: I've come to defend her honor.

MELEAGANT: How fitting! A cart-knight is defending the honor of his harlot-queen. Let's end this once and for all!

BAGDEMAGUS: Now, now, boys. Let's not be hasty here. We don't want anyone to get hurt.

MELEAGANT: Butt out, Father! Too long have you pushed me around—treated me like a child! I'm going to massacre this knight and stick his head up on a pole. And there's *nothing* you can do about it, so there! Argh! *(cry of rage)*

NARRATOR: Meleagant grabbed the axe from the executioner's hands, jumped from the platform, and charged forward.

LANCELOT: Watch out, foul knight! I fight for the honor of my love!

MELEAGANT: Then I'll hack out your heart, and we'll see how well you love then!

BAGDEMAGUS: Hack out your heart? Where do kids get these things?

NARRATOR: As Meleagant cut the air with his menacing axe, Lancelot side-stepped and slashed at the knight's shoulder. It was a stroke dealt with such force that it severed Meleagant's arm. (snicker-snack)

BAGDEMAGUS: Oh my! See this is what happens! It's all fun and games until someone loses an arm!

MELEAGANT: Argh!

NARRATOR: With his remaining arm, Meleagant swung his axe. Lancelot blocked this blow. (Clang!)

LANCELOT: This time you are not fighting a wounded opponent. I am whole!

NARRATOR: Lancelot slashed Meleagant deeply across the abdomen with such a mighty stroke that it penetrated his armor. The evil knight fell to the ground—grabbing at the bleeding gash.

MELEAGANT: (childlike) No! No! I don't want to play anymore! I don't want to play anymore!

LANCELOT: Fair enough. Playtime's over.

NARRATOR: Lancelot ripped loose Meleagant's spiked helm.

LANCELOT: One last head for your collection!

NARRATOR: Lancelot neatly severed the evil knight's head. (snicker-snack)

BAGDEMAGUS: (in shock) What have you done? You've murdered my little boy!

DAMSEL: Father!

NARRATOR: Gawain and the falcon-damsel rode into the courtyard.

BAGDEMAGUS: Daughter? What are you doing back here?

DAMSEL: I've returned to show you the truth. You have been blinded to the evil actions of your son! He's been murdering innocent knights and damsels.

BAGDEMAGUS: Murder? No! They're just locked in the dungeon.

DAMSEL: No, Father. Come see for yourself. Come see what butchering your son has been up to.

NARRATOR: As the damsel led her bewildered father away to the dungeons, Lancelot ran to the platform and loosed the queen's bonds.

GUINEVERE: My champion! There is no knight for me but the knight of the cart.

NARRATOR: The two began to embrace, but the voice of Gawain interrupted them. He was examining the decapitated body of Meleagant.

GAWAIN: I came back to assist you, Lancelot, but I see you have handled things nicely. My queen, thank Heaven you are safe!

GUINEVERE: I praise you for your bravery in my rescue, Gawain.

GAWAIN: It was my duty. After you and Kay were taken away, Arthur wanted to come after you himself.

GUINEVERE: (surprised) He did?

GAWAIN: Of course, but I would not hear of it! It is a knight's duty to always think of his king first.

NARRATOR: This statement struck Lancelot with a wave of guilt.

GAWAIN: I know Arthur will be so relieved to see you safely home again in Camelot, my queen.

NARRATOR: Guinevere smiled sadly.

GUINEVERE: *(softly)* It is as if I had almost forgotten. Camelot and Arthur are waiting for us at home.

NARRATOR: Their conversation was interrupted. The damsel had returned from the dungeons with Bagdemagus, who held a handkerchief before his mouth.

BAGDEMAGUS: Such grisly sights—and so soon after lunch! *(gurgle)* Please accept my apologies, my friends! I had no idea that my son had grown so evil—and bloodthirsty. *(gurgle)* Thank Heaven for my daughter here who has shown me the truth. Do not worry about the path home. I will make it open to you.

NARRATOR: As the party readied for their departure, Gawain drew near to Lancelot and whispered to him.

GAWAIN: Lancelot, I know you have done a dishonorable deed on this quest. But, don't worry. I won't say anything to Arthur when we return to Camelot.

NARRATOR: Lancelot glanced nervously at the queen.

LANCELOT: What do you mean?

GAWAIN: The cart! How could you forget about riding in the cart?

LANCELOT: *(relieved)* Oh! Of course, the cart!

GAWAIN: What else would I have been talking about?

LANCELOT: Nothing! Nothing!

GAWAIN: Good. If you had done something worse than riding in a cart, I would doubt your honor.

NARRATOR: Bagdemagus and his daughter bade their visitors farewell.

BAGDEMAGUS: Farewell! I promise you will not have to use the Sword Bridge if you return! Our door will always be open! Come again!

GAWAIN: Fat chance. I say, the sooner we are out of this weird land, the better. It is like a bad dream.

NARRATOR: Lancelot glanced toward the queen.

LANCELOT: Yes, it *was* like a dream.

NARRATOR: Gawain and the wounded Kay rode ahead, leaving Lancelot and Guinevere riding side by side.

LANCELOT: It's strange. Part of me is saying, it's not too late. We *could* stay here—in Gore. Bagdemagus could make it so that no one would ever find us again. No one could ever condemn our love. We could be together—forever.

GUINEVERE: But then you think of Arthur and Camelot—and all that we have helped build.

LANCELOT: Yes. *(sigh)* Deep down, I think we both know that we cannot abandon it all—even for love.

GUINEVERE: We would never have peace.

LANCELOT: I guess it's back to loving in secret. A secret love is better than no love at all.

GUINEVERE: I know that I have your affection, and you know that you have mine. That is all that matters.

LANCELOT: You are my lady, and it is as you say.

NARRATOR: And so Lancelot and Guinevere crossed the mystical threshold back into the world of Britain—leaving behind the magical land of Gore forever.

DISCUSSION QUESTIONS

1. Arthur fails to defend Guinevere against Meleagant. Does she have a right to love Lancelot instead? Explain.
2. What is more important—love or duty? Explain.
3. How is Lancelot completely devoted to his love for Guinevere?
4. What are the supernatural elements of this story? Explain.
5. Now that Lancelot and Guinevere have officially begun an affair, what do you think will happen next? Explain.
6. What are the potential consequences of their affair? Explain.
7. Should Lancelot and Guinevere have stayed in the land of Gore? Would this have solved their problems or created more trouble for them? Explain.
8. Why did Lancelot and Guinevere feel the need to return home?

THE TALE OF BEAUMAINS
TEACHER GUIDE

BACKGROUND

Courtesy is a character trait that all knights were expected to exhibit. The word itself, closely related to other words like *court* and *courtesan*, originally referred to the type of manners expected from members of a royal court. Now it has been generalized to mean any type of behavior that shows respect for others.

Beaumains (the pseudonym of Gareth of Orkney) exemplifies the trait of courtesy. Although he is born of a wealthy family, he accepts a lowly position in Camelot's kitchen and politely bears the brunt of Sir Kay's taunts and scolding.

On top of being courteous to one another, knights were to be especially courteous to damsels and ladies—taking up their quests without question. When Beaumains takes up the quest of the rude damsel Lynette, he also refuses to respond to her jibes with his own insults. (Even though in this version of the story Beaumains does get his chance to put the damsel in her place, in the original story he never speaks a harsh word to her.) This type of courtesy extended toward females is why in modern times *chivalry* is sometimes equated with gentlemanly conduct—treating women with respect and deference.

SUMMARY

A mysterious young man comes to King Arthur's court. Although he is a strongly built lad, he is carried by two other boys. When Arthur questions him, the young man asks to make three requests of the king. The first is that he will be given food and drink at Camelot for a year. Arthur agrees, and the young man goes to work in Camelot's kitchens.

Sir Kay, Arthur's seneschal, picks on the boy—calling him "fair hands" and "Girl-hands" because of his small, white hands. Only Sir Lancelot is kind to the boy. For a year Girl-hands serves in the kitchen. Then one day a damsel named Lynette rides into Camelot, requesting that a knight be sent with her to free her sister from the Red Knight. Girl-hands, waiting on the royal table, asks the king for his second favor—that he be allowed to accompany the girl and free her sister. Kay scoffs at this idea, but Arthur allows it. Girl-hands asks for his third favor—he asks that Lancelot knight him. Since knights have to prove their worth, Girl-hands asks to joust with Sir Kay, whom he easily beats. As Lancelot knights him, the boy asks to be dubbed *Beaumains*, which means "fair hands."

Beaumains is sent out upon the quest, but Lynette is disgusted that the kitchen boy is to be her knight. She constantly ridicules Beaumains. When two rogue knights challenge Beaumains, he valiantly vanquishes them, but Lynette declares that this was just dumb luck.

At last they near the castle of the Red Knight, where Lynette's sister is being held. Finally, Lynette's constant rudeness gets the better of Beaumains. He tells her that he is not a commoner as she suspects. He is actually the younger brother of Sir Gawain, and his true name is Gareth of Orkney. He only took a lowly position at Camelot to teach himself humility and prove his worth on his merits alone. Lynette is stunned and apologizes.

The Red Knight's strength is derived from the sun, and during the morning hours he grows stronger and stronger with each passing hour. But after noon his

160 The Road to Camelot

strength fades by the same degrees. Because of this, Beaumains waits until after noon to battle the Red Knight. Beaumains defeats the Red Knight, who tells him that he began abducting damsels and murdering knights to get the attention of Sir Lancelot. He was bewitched by Morgan le Fay into hating Sir Lancelot and seeking for his death.

Beaumains returns Lynette and her rescued sister to Camelot. There he reveals his true identity as Gareth of Orkney. In a double ceremony, Beaumains marries Lynette's sister and his brother, Gaheris, marries Lynette.

ESSENTIAL QUESTIONS

- Should you be courteous to those who are not courteous to you?
- What can you learn from being humble?

ANTICIPATORY QUESTIONS

- If you had the choice between being a knight and working in Camelot's kitchen, which would you choose? Explain.
- Have you ever had someone be extremely rude to you? How did you respond?
- Why is it important to be courteous?

CHARACTER QUEST

Respect and Courtesy In medieval times respect was shown by addressing each other by formal titles, such as "my lady," "sir," and "your majesty." Bowing, curtseying, and kneeling were expected courteous acts that indicated respect. Knights were expected to be courteous toward each other and especially toward ladies and damsels. What are the some of the word or actions that indicate respect today? Why are courtesy and respect still important?

CONNECT

A Connecticut Yankee in King Arthur's Court **by Mark Twain** In this novel Camelot is turned upside down when "modern-day" man, Hank Morgan, is sent back into medieval times and attempts to bring the Arthur's court into the 19th century. By making fun of the formality and tradition that was a vital part of the King Arthur legends, Twain intended his novel to be a burlesque of European traditions.

TEACHABLE TERMS

- **Idiom** On pg. 168 Lynette says Sir Kay probably "had one foot in the grave." This is an idiom for being old and at the point of death.
- **Backstory** On pg. 174 after the Red Knight is defeated, he tells Beaumains his backstory—how he was tricked by Morgan le Fay into committing horrible crimes.
- **Theme** Beaumains's quest has many themes, and one is that people should not be judged by their status in society. Beaumains works hard to prove himself worthy of knighthood—instead of earning it simply because of his royal title.

RECALL QUESTIONS

1. What job is Beaumains given in the castle of Camelot?
2. Who is the only knight who is kind to Beaumains?
3. How does the Red Knight's strength increase and decrease?
4. Whose brother is Beaumains?
5. What does *Beaumains* literally mean?

THE TALE OF BEAUMAINS

CAST

ARTHUR	*King of Britain*
GAWAIN	*Knight of Arthur*
LANCELOT	*Arthur's Best Knight*
KAY	*Arthur's Seneschal*
GARETH	*Young Man*
LYNETTE	*Damsel in Distress*
KNIGHT ONE	*Evil Knight*
KNIGHT TWO	*Evil Knight*
RED KNIGHT	*Evil Knight*
LYONESSE	*Sister of Lynette*

NARRATOR: It was the feast of Pentecost, and the Knights of the Round Table sat in an uncomfortable silence. Although the table before them was laid with sumptuous dishes, no one was allowed to partake. King Arthur had previously declared…

ARTHUR: No one eats or drinks until a marvel has presented itself to us.

NARRATOR: The knights looked miserably at one another—their stomachs growling.

LANCELOT: Sire, I believe I saw a marvel this morning.

NARRATOR: The knights looked up hopefully, hungrily.

ARTHUR: Did you? What was it?

LANCELOT: I had the most painful wart on my foot, and it pained me for many months!

ARTHUR: *(questioningly)* And why is this wart a miracle? Did its shape resemble the Holy Grail? Did it speak to you?

LANCELOT: *(confused)* Nooo. This morning as I was bathing, it fell off! All by itself!

(grumbling from the knights)

ARTHUR: Not good enough. We'll just have to keep waiting.

LANCELOT: Well, I think it's a wonder. I thought it would be months before I was rid of that wart! I didn't have to scrape it off or anything.

GAWAIN: Please, Lancelot. If anything could make me lose my appetite at this point, it would be that!

NARRATOR: Gawain rose and made his way to the chamber window.

GAWAIN: Look! I see a strange sight—in the courtyard.

(murmuring of the knights)

ARTHUR: What is it? Please tell me it's something better than Lancelot's mystical wart!

GAWAIN: No a real marvel! A young man has arrived in court, and he's calling out for a meeting with you.

ARTHUR: *(hesitantly)* That's not exactly a marvel either.

GAWAIN: He is a sturdy lad, but he's being supported by two other men. He seems weak.

ARTHUR: Eh. Getting better.

GAWAIN: Did I mention there's a dwarf with them, too?

ARTHUR: A dwarf? Well, that's a different story. Very well! Let us eat. A marvel has presented itself!

(cheers from the knights)

NARRATOR: The knights dug greedily into the feast.

ARTHUR: *(through mouthfuls of food)* Make sure this feeble lad and his companions are brought before us.

NARRATOR: The stranger was brought into the hall of the Round Table. The knights saw he was a healthy young man, tall and broad-shouldered, but his hands were a bit small and white like a woman's. His ratty clothes and humble posture was a sign to them that he was not a nobleman.

ARTHUR: What brings you to Camelot on this joyful day, my boy?

GARETH: Sire, I am just a poor commoner, and I've come to appeal to your mercy.

ARTHUR: What is your name?

GARETH: I cannot say.

ARTHUR: Well, you *are* poor if you cannot even afford a name! Ha!

GARETH: I came to ask three favors of you. With this being Pentecost and all, I hoped you would grant them.

NARRATOR: Arthur waved a turkey leg benevolently at the lad.

ARTHUR: Ask whatever you wish, and I will grant it.

NARRATOR: Gawain, who had been eying the youth suspiciously, turned to the king in shock.

GAWAIN: *(hissing)* Sire, you do not know what he will ask.

ARTHUR: He seems like an honest lad.

GAWAIN: You can never trust the poor!

ARTHUR: Nonsense. I am happy to help all of my subjects.

GARETH: Your Majesty, I am weak from want of food. I walked almost all the way to Camelot, but I fainted from hunger.

LANCELOT: We were about to do the same before you arrived!

GARETH: Some passing travelers were kind enough to help me the rest of the way. I am nearly starved, and I will starve for sure if you do not take mercy on me.

ARTHUR: No one in Britain will go hungry while I am king.

GARETH: I am glad to hear you say so because I wish to ask my first boon. I wish to be fed here at your castle—for a full year.

GAWAIN: Never! We are not a charity, boy! We work for our meals here at Camelot!

ARTHUR: *(sarcastically)* Pardon me, Gawain. I forget. Am I king or are you?

GAWAIN: Well, sire. It's ridiculous for a man to ask to be fed and do no work for his meals. He should at least be put to a task.

GARETH: Sire, he is right. I will do whatever you ask—as long as I am given food and shelter for a twelve-month.

ARTHUR: It shall be done! Now let us all feast, and when we are finished, I will introduce you to Sir Kay, my seneschal. He is in charge of my household and will provide you with the work you require.

NARRATOR: When the boy was introduced to Sir Kay, the seneschal looked him over with disgust.

KAY: So you are the charity-project I heard so much about? You look strong enough, but they say that you are practically an invalid. I don't have much tolerance for weaklings.

NARRATOR: He noticed the boy's small, white hands.

KAY: Plus, you have the dainty hands of a maiden. Since men's work would probably be too much for you, I will put you in the kitchen. Yes, that's it. I'll make you a scullery maid. You and your dainty hands will not get too dirty there. *(cruel laugh)* Ha!

NARRATOR: So Kay put the mysterious boy to work in the kitchen, and there the seneschal daily taunted him.

KAY: Girl-hands! You missed a spot on this pot! Were you too busy tending your fingernails instead of making sure it was thoroughly scrubbed?

NARRATOR: Kay slapped the boy upside the head. *(slapping sound)*

KAY: Even the women here work harder than you do!

GARETH: I apologize, sir.

KAY: See that it doesn't happen again, or you will be beaten.

NARRATOR: A year passed in this manner, the boy performing each task before him and sleeping each night on the cold stones of the kitchen, huddled up among the castle dogs. All who encountered him treated him with disgust—except for one. Sir Lancelot showed the boy kindness and even dropped a coin for the boy when he happened to pass through the kitchen. The boy, in turn, grew to adore the knight.

By the time the feast of Pentecost came around again, Arthur had all but forgotten about the strange fair-handed boy who worked in the kitchen.

ARTHUR: No feasting yet, gentleman! We have yet to see a marvel!

(grumbling from the knights)

ARTHUR: What was the marvel last year? Was it the White Hart?

GAWAIN: No. Last year was the strong-looking peasant lad who went to work in the kitchen.

ARTHUR: Oh, yes. The one with the feminine hands.

GAWAIN: What was his name again? Limp-wrists or something like that?

KAY: Ha. You mean "Girl-hands"? Yes, he's still in the kitchen—stinking up the place! I think he has more fleas than the dogs do.

LANCELOT: *(angrily)* Kay, you are as cruel as you are stupid! You wrong that boy! He serves you without complaint.

NARRATOR: At this insult Kay's face grew red.

KAY: Ha! What kind of knight takes a peasant's cause against another knight? It's dishonorable!

ARTHUR: Quiet, gentlemen! Behold! It seems that our marvel has presented itself.

NARRATOR: Striding into the room came a maiden, wearing a hood and garment of all white.

ARTHUR: Fair damsel, welcome to Camelot. Why have you sought us out on this holy day?

GAWAIN: *(to himself)* Please say for a quest.

NARRATOR: The lily damsel bowed before them.

LYNETTE: I bring word from my sister, Lyonesse. She is captured and held against her will by the villainous Red Knight of the Red Lands.

KAY: How original. The Red Knight of the Red Lands. I bet he lives in the Red Castle, too.

GAWAIN: I have heard of this knight! He is a monster! I fought him once and barely escaped with my head intact. He is as strong as six men!

ARTHUR: Well, damsel. We have many knights here at your service. I will appoint one of them to your quest at once.

LYNETTE: Thank you, sire. You are very wise.

LANCELOT: I will gladly go on this quest, my liege. After all, if the knight truly has the strength of six men, it seems like a good match for my skills.

GAWAIN: Please, Lancelot. We all know that this type of quest requires brains over simple skill. I am the obvious choice.

LANCELOT: So, you admit that you have no skill?

ARTHUR: Gentlemen! Gentlemen! All of you are worthy candidates for such a quest!

NARRATOR: The king felt a tug at his royal sleeve. He turned. The kitchen boy was there at his side, looking at him eagerly.

KAY: Hey! What are you doing here, you urchin? I should whip you for being up here!

ARTHUR: Silence, Kay. What is it, boy?

GARETH: I wish to ask my second boon.

ARTHUR: Second boon? Oh yes. I promised you three, didn't I? What is it that you wish?

GARETH: I want to take up this maiden's quest.

KAY: (*roaring with laughter*) Ha!

ARTHUR: (*laugh*) Surely you must be joking!

GAWAIN: Boy, only knights can take up quests.

KAY: Ha! What will you use for armor? Will a pot be your helmet? Will a cauldron lid be your shield? And what about a sword? Oh wait! If someone attacks you, you can just fork them to death! Ha!

GARETH: The king made me a promise, and now I claim this promise.

ARTHUR: Well, I—

LANCELOT: The boy is right, Arthur. You promised.

KAY: I say we let Girl-hands go on this quest. When he challenges the Red Knight, he can cook his goose! Ha!

ARTHUR: Kay! Please! (*sigh*) I must keep my word.

LYNETTE: Excuse me.

NARRATOR: Everyone turned to face the pale damsel.

LYNETTE: Perhaps I am misunderstanding something. This boy works in your kitchen?

KAY: *Works* would be an exaggeration.

LYNETTE: I have come to you with the life of my sister at stake—a quest against a knight that almost took the life of the valiant Sir Gawain—and you're sending me away with a kitchen-boy to aid me?

ARTHUR: Err—well—it would seem so.

LYNETTE: (*cry of disgust*) Ugh! I don't believe this!

NARRATOR: The damsel stamped her foot, spun on her heels, and marched angrily from the room.

KAY: (*laughing*) Ha! Wait, maiden, wait! You haven't seen how Girl-hands can vanquish the dishes! He will give them all a sound scrubbing! Ha! Ha! (*loud laughing*) I can't breathe! I can't breathe!

ARTHUR: Be quiet, Kay. You're only making the situation worse.

GARETH: Sire, I would like to ask for my third boon.

GAWAIN: Haven't you caused enough trouble today, Girl-hands?

ARTHUR: (*sigh*) What else do you wish, boy?

GARETH: I wish for Sir Lancelot to knight me.

GAWAIN: Don't be foolish! Only those who prove their worth in tournament—in joust—can be knighted. That's nothing a peasant like you can do!

KAY: *(cracking up with laughter)* What knightly name should we give the boy? Sir Pot-licker? Sir Scrubs-a-lot? The Kitchen Avenger? Ha-ha!

GARETH: A joust, you say? And this challenge could be carried out against any knight here?

ARTHUR: Yes, but these are trained knights—

GARETH: Then I choose Sir Kay.

NARRATOR: The seneschal stopped laughing.

KAY: *(angrily)* What? A challenge, huh? It would be my pleasure to murder this little weasel! Very well, boy. I shall meet you on the field of battle!

NARRATOR: Kay swept from their presence to ready himself for the joust.

LANCELOT: Boy, do you have armor? A steed? I could loan you these things.

GARETH: You have been kind to me this past year—and for that I am very grateful. But I will have all that I require in order to joust with Kay.

LANCELOT: I don't see how—

GARETH: I will see you all at the challenge field in an hour's time.

NARRATOR: Many knights had gathered outside the city walls to see the kitchen-boy face off against Sir Kay. Even though they knew there was no way a penniless wretch could defeat a knight, they all wished somehow the boy could win. The infuriated damsel, Lynette, was in attendance there, too. When the boy arrived at the challenge field, he was accompanied by two strangers and a dwarf. Lancelot recognized these as the companions who had delivered the boy to the palace a year before. They now acted as his squires.

LANCELOT: This is a marvel!

NARRATOR: They carried a splendid suit of armor, which they fitted onto the boy. The dwarf came forth leading a beautiful stallion.

LANCELOT: This kitchen-boy is full of surprises!

NARRATOR: Sir Kay, on the other hand, was not impressed.

KAY: Where have you found the money to buy these things, Girl-hands? Have potato peelings somehow become currency? It wouldn't matter if you fought with Excalibur itself, I would still vanquish you.

NARRATOR: The kitchen-boy had completed his transformation into a fully armed knight.

GARETH: Sir Kay, if you are ready to joust, I am prepared.

KAY: Joust? This will be more like a massacre! Yah! Yah!

NARRATOR: Kay spurred his horse forward, letting his lance swing wildly, just for show. The kitchen-boy matched his pace and aimed his lance-tip for the joint where Kay's breastplate met the shoulder-plate. *(Crash!)* There was a burst of sound as Kay was knocked from his horse and clattered to the ground. The kitchen-boy reined up his steed and drew up his lance to attack again, but Kay did not rise.

KAY: *(groan)* Oh! My baaaack!

(loud cheer from the crowd)

LANCELOT: Congratulations, boy! You have unhorsed a knight of the Round Table!

NARRATOR: The boy removed his helmet and beamed.

GARETH: Now, Arthur, I have proved my worth. Please allow Lancelot to knight me so that I might take up the damsel's quest.

NARRATOR: The damsel folded her arms and scowled. Lancelot approached the boy.

LANCELOT: *(whispering)* You must tell me the truth, boy. Who are you? No lowly commoner could fight as you have.

GARETH: If I tell you my secret, you are bound to keep it, right?

LANCELOT: Of course.

GARETH: I am Gareth of Orkney, the youngest prince of that land.

LANCELOT: That would mean Gawain is your very own brother! But he did not even recognize you!

GARETH: When he left Orkney, I was just a child. I am basically a stranger to him and my other older brothers.

LANCELOT: Marvelous! But why all this secrecy? Why pretend to be poor when you are actually wealthy?

GARETH: What I lost in comfort and privilege, I gained in knowledge. During this year, I have seen who are the most valiant and the most false among the knights. You, Lancelot, are the best of the lot, and that is why I have asked you to knight me.

LANCELOT: I will do so gladly! *(pause)* But I cannot dub you Gareth in front of these gathered here, or you will be discovered.

GARETH: Dub me "Beaumains," for it means "fair hands."

LANCELOT: "Girl-hands" is Kay's cruel nickname for you! Why would you want such a name?

GARETH: To prove that names do not matter. Whatever my name is, I will make it great! Besides, I know my hands are small and womanly, but it does not bother me.

LANCELOT: They are nothing to be ashamed of! They hold a lance as skillfully as I do!

NARRATOR: Once the knighting ceremony was completed and the royal court dispersed, Beaumains rode to where the damsel Lynette was mounting her palfrey.

GARETH: My lady, I am prepared to take up your quest.

LYNETTE: *(rudely)* Are you sure you're not too busy? Aren't there dishes to be done? Or maybe some laundry?

GARETH: You refer to my past position at the castle, but you have seen that I am a valiant knight.

LYNETTE: Armor does not make a knight! I can still smell your true nature. You stink of grease!

GARETH: If your ladyship will lead the way, we will be off on our quest.

LYNETTE: I can't believe this! There's no telling where you got that armor! You probably stole it off a *real* knight.

NARRATOR: Lynette spurred her palfrey into motion.

LYNETTE: (*sarcastically*) Perhaps the Red Knight will die laughing when I show up with Camelot's best kitchen-maid to fight him.

GARETH: My lady, you just saw me defeat a knight of the Round Table.

LYNETTE: Well, that must have been the oldest and weakest knight they had! He probably already had one foot in the grave!

GARETH: I have done nothing to deserve your meanness.

LYNETTE: What have you done *not* to deserve it? Ugh! Please! Don't ride so closely. You smell like rotten vegetables.

GARETH: Yes, my lady.

NARRATOR: Beaumains bit his tongue and dropped back behind the damsel's palfrey.

They had not journeyed the length of a full day when they ran into trouble. There was a bridge across a fast-flowing river, and on the far side stood two armed knights.

LYNETTE: Oh, look. *Real* knights. Maybe one of them would want to take up my quest.

GARETH: (*under his breath*) They wouldn't if they knew what a shrew you were.

KNIGHT ONE: Halt! This is our bridge. Any who wish to pass it must pay a toll!

GARETH: I escort this damsel here. What is your toll to pass?

NARRATOR: The two knights leaned toward one another and conversed in hushed tones.

KNIGHT ONE: We want the woman!

LYNETTE: (*in shock*) Heaven save me! I know that this smelly boy cannot!

KNIGHT TWO: Give the maiden to us, and we will do you no harm.

LYNETTE: Why did Arthur give me such a coward for a knight? Girl-hands, do something—if you can!

GARETH: This damsel is under my protection. I will defend her even unto my own death.

KNIGHT ONE: (*roaring*) Then prepare to meet your death!

NARRATOR: The first knight lowered his lance and rumbled forward across the bridge. Beaumains drew his sword, and Lynette scrambled for the cover of the woods.

LYNETTE: (*cry of fright*) Ah!

NARRATOR: Beaumains dodged the enemy knight's lance, striking him hard against the helm and driving him from his horse. *(crash of armed knight hitting the ground)*

KNIGHT ONE: Oof! *(groan of pain)* Ughn.

KNIGHT TWO: Yah!

NARRATOR: The second knight began his approach. Beaumains galloped forward, too, meeting the knight in the midst of the bridge. Both drew their swords and hacked at each other violently. *(clanging noises)* As the two knights maneuvered their horses for the superior position, the hind-hooves of the evil knight's mount slipped backward off the bridge. *(neighing of a horse)*

KNIGHT TWO: Ah!

NARRATOR: The horse and rider toppled into the river. *(splashing sounds)* Beaumains ran to where the first knight had fallen, ripped loose his helmet, and raised his sword to strike.

GARETH: *(yelling)* Your comrade has fallen! You are defeated! Yield! Yield!

KNIGHT ONE: I yield! I yield! Spare me!

GARETH: I will only spare you if my lady commands it.

NARRATOR: He turned to Lynette, who was creeping forth from the protection of the woods.

GARETH: What do you say, my lady?

LYNETTE: I am not your lady, you foolish pot-licker! But please spare his life! He's suffered enough humiliation just by being defeated by the likes of you!

GARETH: *(gritting his teeth)* Yes, my lady.

NARRATOR: Beaumains slammed the knight's helmet roughly back into place. *(Clang!)*

KNIGHT ONE: *(cry of pain)* Ahh!

LYNETTE: What luck, kitchen-boy! You just happened to be fighting the two clumsiest knights in the world. That second knight practically fell off the bridge all on his own!

KNIGHT ONE: *(wearily)* No! This knight fights with great might. Never before have my companion and I been vanquished. We have slain many knights and taken many damsels, but this knight defeated us. And he is a knight of honor, because he has spared my life even when I tried to take his.

LYNETTE: Ha! This one must have landed on his head. He's delusional! Now, get him out of here, Girl-hands!

GARETH: *(annoyed)* Yes, my lady.

NARRATOR: Beaumains clenched his jaw, pulled the knight up by his breastplate, and shook him until his teeth rattled.

GARETH: Return to Camelot and pledge your sword to King Arthur. He is your master now and your days of evil are done.

KNIGHT ONE: I swear it!

GARETH: Go!

NARRATOR: The recreant knight remounted his steed and rode wearily away.

LYNETTE: Where is my palfrey? It must have run away! Why didn't you catch it? You are the biggest fool I have ever met!

GARETH: *(angrily)* Yes, my lady.

NARRATOR: Beaumains helped his bitter damsel pitch her tent by the river for the night.

LYNETTE: Now, don't get any ideas! Stay away from my tent tonight! Just imagine sending a defenseless maiden like me out in the wild with a dirty-minded little weasel like you!

GARETH: Trust me, your ladyship. You have nothing to worry about.

LYNETTE: I probably would have been better off with those ruffians.

GARETH: *(under his breath)* I wish I had left you to them.

NARRATOR: Beaumains laid his aching body down upon the hard ground and waited for the morning light.

The next few days of travel brought many adventures to the knight and his hateful damsel. Beaumains was challenged by many rogue knights—a silver knight, an indigo knight, a knight the color of midnight—yet he vanquished each one and sent them back to Camelot to join the service of Arthur.

LYNETTE: What is the world coming to? Chivalry must be dead if Sir Scrub-brush can defeat all the knights in the land! Are you cheating somehow?

GARETH: My lady, I have honestly and nobly defeated the silver knight, the indigo knight, and the black knight.

LYNETTE: I don't care if you defeat a knight from every color of the rainbow, you'll always be a disgrace to me!

GARETH: *(between gritted teeth)* Even in the kitchens with Kay, I did not suffer as much as I suffer here!

NARRATOR: One day, they rode into a dismal forest filled with trees that drooped their skeletal arms into the path of the travelers. Soon a mist started to form along the ground, bearing a foul stench with it.

LYNETTE: Ugh. Girl-hands, is it too much to ask for you to bathe every once in a while?

GARETH: That is not me, my lady.

LYNETTE: I've smelled peasant before, and it's definitely you.

GARETH: Shhh! Something stirs ahead.

NARRATOR: In the branches before them hung armored bodies—swaying in the wind. Then Beaumains spied the shadow of a castle looming through the mist.

GARETH: Heaven preserve us! My lady, is this the castle of the Red Knight?

LYNETTE: *(sarcastically)* No, broom-brain. It's someone else who uses dead bodies in his decorating. Of course, it's the castle of the Red Knight! That is where my sister, the damsel Lyonesse, is being held captive. I have brought knight after knight here to rescue her, but they have all failed. Those are their bodies that hang from the trees.

GARETH: *(to himself)* That's encouraging.

NARRATOR: The mists were clearing a bit, and Beaumains saw that even on the castle ramparts there were nailed many rotted corpses of knights.

GARETH: How could this monster have existed for so long without the king's knowledge?

LYNETTE: All who see this place die. It's the same story over and over again. I bring knights here, and they fail. I have brought you here and—*obviously*—you will fail. After all, the Red Knight has the strength of six men—and you barely have the strength of a girl.

NARRATOR: From a low-hanging limb dangled a giant horn fashioned from the tusk of an elephant.

LYNETTE: Blow that horn to summon Sir Ironsides, the Red Knight.

NARRATOR: The damsel Lynette calmly examined her fingernails.

LYNETTE: He will be victorious once again, but at least I will finally be rid of you.

NARRATOR: With this remark Beaumains had finally reached his limit.

GARETH: Enough! I will bear no more of this! I must speak freely, my lady!

LYNETTE: Say whatever you want! They will probably be some of your last words anyway!

GARETH: *(angrily)* You are the worst! You are the most savage damsel I have ever met! Instead of cursing me, you should be praying for my victory! At least thank me for what I've done! I think I deserve something for all I've put up with thus far!

LYNETTE: *(enraged)* Excuse me? How dare you speak to a lady in such a fashion! Especially a lowly peasant like you!

GARETH: Peasant? I am as high-born as you are! Probably higher! My father was King Lot of Orkney, and my mother is the very sister of King Arthur himself.

NARRATOR: At this news the eyes of the damsel practically bugged out of her head.

LYNETTE: What? Is this a joke? Is someone playing a trick on me?

GARETH: Does everything have to be about you? Of course, no one is playing a trick on you! Haven't you been paying attention? I have vanquished every enemy in the land. Obviously, I'm a valiant knight, but you're too thick-headed to see it!

LYNETTE: *(confused)* I don't understand. They said you were a kitchen boy.

GARETH: I was, and it taught me many valuable lessons about people like you! It taught me to value my own worth instead of relying on silly titles! This entire time you have been looking down your nose at me because you *thought* I was a commoner. And you just couldn't bear the thought of your precious quest being taken up by a servant! You're arrogant, selfish, and rude!

LYNETTE: *(growing sad)* You're right. I have been so cruel to you.

GARETH: Well, spare me your pity. The only reason you show regret now is that you know I'm *not* a peasant.

LYNETTE: But I was so rude! I insulted you time and time again!

GARETH: Why do you think I have conquered these knights so easily? Every day you've caused rage to boil up inside of me! I couldn't wait for a chance to hack someone's head off or gash their throats! I just pictured *your* head on *their* body, and death came quickly for them!

NARRATOR: The maiden blinked back tears.

LYNETTE: *(sniffing)* I'm a horrid person.

GARETH: Don't cry. We're here now. We have to rescue your sister.

LYNETTE: *(weeping)* You are truly the most valiant knight I have ever met—to endure such insults from me. I have displayed such unladylike behavior, and you have been so courteous to me!

NARRATOR: Beaumains sighed and turned to pick up the hanging horn.

LYNETTE: *(between tears)* Wait! Oh, gentle knight! If you should die in this battle, I could never forgive myself! I would die of a broken heart.

GARETH: You have a heart? That's nice to know.

LYNETTE: There is something I haven't told you!

GARETH: What?

LYNETTE: I told you that Ironsides had the strength of six men, but that's not entirely true. Throughout the day, the Red Knight's strength grows stronger and stronger—until noon when his strength begins to diminish. So only at noon does he have the strength of six men.

NARRATOR: Beaumains looked heavenward.

GARETH: Then I suppose we must wait, for it is near to noon now. Come. Let us cut some of these noble knights down from the trees and forget our past disagreements.

NARRATOR: When the afternoon had dragged on and the shadows began to lengthen, Beaumains saw that it was time to summon the Red Knight. He snatched up the hunting horn and sounded a mighty note upon it. *(sound of a horn)*

The Red Castle's drawbridge clanked to life and crashed to the ground. Then the dreaded Sir Ironsides rode forward. He was red from head to toe, his armor smeared with the dried blood of his victims. Even his violent steed had been dyed red with blood. His helmet was formed from the skull of an unlucky opponent.

RED KNIGHT: *(evil-sounding voice)* At last! It has been months since I have had a challenge! My battle-lust has been maddening. I need some fresh blood to give my armor a new coating!

LYNETTE: Courage, Sir Gareth! I have faith in you.

NARRATOR: Beaumains leveled his lance and charged toward the blood-stained knight. The Red Knight began his advance as well. The two knights' lances broke upon the other's shield, and both riders flew loose from their saddles. *(Crash!)*

RED KNIGHT: Ah!

NARRATOR: Beaumains was up in a flash, drawing his sword. The Red Knight rose, his own curved sword drawn as well.

RED KNIGHT: I see you have removed my knights from the trees! No matter. It will leave me more room when I hang you there tomorrow.

GARETH: Silence, demon!

NARRATOR: Beaumains's sword flashed through the air, his target the sword arm of the Red Knight. Sir Ironsides's other arm—protected by a stout shield—shot out and deflected the blow. *(Clang!)* Then the Red Knight thrust with his own blade, but the young knight dodged to the side.

RED KNIGHT: If you had the courage to face me at high noon, this skirmish would be over by now!

GARETH: What's the matter? Afraid of a fair fight?

RED KNIGHT: Never! *(roar of rage)* Argh!

NARRATOR: The Red Knight threw down his shield and—gripping his sword with both hands—slashed at Beaumains's helm. The young knight faltered under the attack and fell backward onto the ground. The full force of the Red Knight landed upon him—knocking the breath from his lungs. The cruelly scarred face of the Red Knight hovered over him.

RED KNIGHT: So ends your life!

LYNETTE: Beaumains! Get up! Pleeeease!

NARRATOR: As his enemy struggled to rip his helm from his head, memories begin to flash through the mind of Beaumains—his year at court, the cruel taunts of Kay, the insults of the spiteful maiden. He felt anger boiling up like a storm within him.

RED KNIGHT: Huh? What?

GARETH: *(roar of rage)* Rargh!

NARRATOR: With superhuman strength, Beaumains toppled the large knight from him and retrieved his sword. Beaumains gripped the stained beard of the fallen Red Knight and held the blade a fraction below his pulsing throat.

GARETH: Yield.

RED KNIGHT: *(laugh)* Ha! Yield? I will never yield to you! Long ago, I made a vow to kill you—even if it meant losing my life!

GARETH: A vow to kill me?

NARRATOR: Beaumains looked to Lynette in confusion. She shrugged her shoulders.

GARETH: What do you mean? You have never seen me before in my life. You do not even know my name.

RED KNIGHT: Oh, yes, I do! You are Sir Lancelot. Who else could you be? Only Lancelot is strong enough to defeat me.

GARETH: You are wrong. I am not Lancelot. I am Gareth of Orkney, and I have beaten you.

RED KNIGHT: *(in shock)* What? It can't be!

GARETH: Believe it, villain.

NARRATOR: The scarred face of the knight puckered, and large tears began to fall from his eyes.

RED KNIGHT: (*between sobs*) All these years! All these knights I slaughtered! For nothing! For nothing!

LYNETTE: What are you babbling about, you cur?

RED KNIGHT: (*sniffling*) There was a raven-haired maiden that I once loved. She came here to my castle and enchanted me with her beauty. She told me that Sir Lancelot had killed her brother and begged me to avenge him. What could I do? She was so lovely. I could deny her nothing. Somehow she gave me the strength of six men. I guess she must have been a sorceress. Then she went away and said she would not return until I had the mangled body of Lancelot hanging upon my ramparts.

GARETH: Why did you not challenge Lancelot to a duel?

RED KNIGHT: My power only functions here in my own lands, so I knew I had to lure Lancelot to me. How else could I defeat him unless on my own turf? I began a reign of terror—kidnapping maidens, attacking travelers, killing valiant knights.

GARETH: You became a murderer—just for love?

RED KNIGHT: You did not know this woman. She was captivating. I had to have her back, and the only way to get her back was to kill Lancelot. I knew that for sure my horrible acts would bring the greatest of all King Arthur's knights to my realm.

LYNETTE: It has. Sir Gareth is the greatest of knights.

RED KNIGHT: This brat? Look at his hands! They're like the hands of a girl!

LYNETTE: Well, he has defeated you, hasn't he?

RED KNIGHT: Good point.

NARRATOR: The damsel smiled at Beaumains.

GARETH: Knight, you must forget this oath of vengeance on Sir Lancelot. He is the best and greatest knight ever born. I fear you have been at the mercy of my evil aunt, Morgan le Fay. She has poisoned you with her lies. She told you that Lancelot murdered her brother, but Lancelot is no murderer. Her brother is the very King Arthur, whom she wishes dead.

NARRATOR: The Red Knight looked up in bewilderment.

RED KNIGHT: (*in bewilderment*) All this time—all this carnage—I was tricked?

GARETH: I'm afraid so, but all will be made well. Go to Camelot. Pledge yourself to Arthur. He will forgive all these trespasses if you serve him. He is the noblest king this land has ever seen.

RED KNIGHT: Yes! I will, gracious knight. You are too kind! (*pause*) And sorry about that hand comment.

NARRATOR: As the Red Knight departed for Camelot, Beaumains and the damsel Lynette entered the Red Castle. There were many grisly sights to behold within, for Morgan le Fay had given Sir Ironsides the heart of a butcher. Locked inside the highest chamber of the castle, they found the damsel, Lyonesse.

LYONESSE: Lynette! I knew you would not leave me here to die!

NARRATOR: The two sisters ran forward and embraced, and Beaumains marveled at the beauty of the damsel Lyonesse. While Lynette was fair, Lyonesse put her to shame.

LYNETTE: Sister, you must meet Sir Beaumains, the knight who has saved you.

NARRATOR: Beaumains knelt before her.

GARETH: My lady, you are truly the fairest maiden I have ever seen.

NARRATOR: Lyonesse extended her hand to him, and he kissed it.

LYNETTE: He is the bravest and most valiant knight in all the world.

LYONESSE: You do not need to tell me, Lynette. I see this with my own eyes. How could anyone miss it?

NARRATOR: Since Beaumains's departure, the court of Arthur had seen a steady stream of vanquished, variously-colored knights, arriving in Camelot to pledge their loyalty to the Round Table. The last and most impressive of these knights was Sir Ironsides the Red Knight, who fell at Lancelot's feet and begged his forgiveness.

ARTHUR: Recreant knight, who among my knights has bested you?

RED KNIGHT: The one who calls himself Beaumains.

ARTHUR: All of these knights have been beaten by the boy of the fair hands!

KAY: *(in shock)* It can't be!

LANCELOT: Indeed! This boy is a mighty knight—almost as mighty as myself!

NARRATOR: Soon it was Beaumains himself who arrived in Camelot, returning with the two sisters, Lynette and Lyonesse, in tow. His arrival brought much rejoicing.

ARTHUR: My boy, you must tell us your name—your lineage! Surely you come from a noble family!

GARETH: I do come from a great family, my lord—it is your own.

ARTHUR: What do you mean?

GARETH: I am the son of Margawse, your half-sister. I am the brother of Gawain, Gaheris, and Agravaine.

KAY: *(in shock)* What?

ARTHUR: Heavens above! This is a marvel!

GAWAIN: *(in shock)* Gareth? My little brother? It can't be!

NARRATOR: Gawain embraced the brother he had not seen in many years.

GAWAIN: Why all this secrecy? Why Beaumains? Why did you accept such a dishonorable nickname? Why did you bear Kay's insults for a whole year?

GARETH: I did not want my glory to come just from my title and my line. I wanted to prove my worth.

LANCELOT: You have! What a wise boy! I am proud that it was I who knighted you!

ARTHUR: Beaumains—I mean, Sir Gareth—you may now join the fellowship of the Round Table.

KAY: (angrily) Sire, I object!

ARTHUR: On what grounds?

KAY: We're short-staffed in the kitchen. We need this boy to return to his duty.

(laughter from everyone)

ARTHUR: Find someone else to do the dishes, Kay. This boy's duty is to be a great knight!

KAY: Bah! (grumbling)

GARETH: It's a duty that I accept gladly!

NARRATOR: So Gareth was made a knight of the Round Table. He then asked to wed the damsel Lyonesse, and the king consented. As for Lynette, whose disposition had been much improved by the adventure, she caught the eye of Gareth's older brother, Sir Gaheris. The two knightly brothers married the two damsel sisters in a double ceremony. All the court of Camelot was in attendance—that is, except for Sir Kay, who decided to sulk in the kitchen instead.

DISCUSSION QUESTIONS

1. What makes Beaumains worthy of knighthood?
2. What is admirable about the way Beaumains chooses to earn his knighthood?
3. What point does Beaumains prove about a person's position in society?
4. Does Beaumains's quest have a theme? What is it?
5. How does Beaumains show courtesy to Lynette, even though she is rude to him?
6. What does this story show about Lynette's personal character?
7. What does this story show about Kay's personal character?
8. If someone is rude to you, does that give you the right to be rude back? Explain.
9. What is a real-life situation where you are required to be courteous?
10. Should you still help someone who doesn't deserve your help? Explain.

RETURN OF THE MISBEGOTTEN
TEACHER GUIDE

BACKGROUND

Misbegotten, a term that means "illegitimate," can also mean "contemptible" or "deformed." Here the term is applied to Mordred, the illegitimate son of King Arthur, incestuously conceived by the king with his own half-sister. Mordred is both illegitimate and contemptible.

Medieval thought embraced the idea that the sins of the father would be visited upon his children. It seems that Mordred, born of incest, has virtually no chance of being good. Yet King Arthur, his own father, was born from one man taking advantage of another man's wife, and despite his flaws he strived for good. What determines whether a character will end up being counted among the good or the evil? The story seems to say that it is our choices that lead us down either path—the choice between revenge and forgiveness—the choice between hostility and peace.

Mordred eventually becomes the personification of Arthur's sin—come back to destroy him. But the question remains: Could Mordred's life have gone down a different path? Could he have become a force of good instead of evil? It is an intriguing question—one that may affect our own journeys through life.

SUMMARY

Perceval is a young man who has been raised by his mother in the backwoods of Britain. His mother, fearing that he would become a knight like his father and brothers, moved him into the wilderness and raised him ignorant of the world. One day Perceval sees a knight riding through the forest and thinks that he is an angel because of his shining armor. The knight, who is Sir Gawain, explains that he is a knight from the court of Camelot.

Perceval returns to his mother and tells her that he wishes to become a knight. Since this is what she has always dreaded, Perceval's mother tries to talk him out of this plan—telling him that everyone in Camelot will mock his leather clothes and his silly weapons—long, sharpened sticks. Perceval cannot be swayed, so his mother gives him some parting advice: If he ever sees treasure, take it; if he ever sees a church, go in and pray; if he is ever offered a kiss from a damsel, receive it. As Perceval leaves for Camelot, his mother falls to the ground in a swoon.

On the road to Camelot Perceval sees a tent pitched in a field, and he mistakes this for a church. Going inside to pray, he finds a sleeping maiden with a ring on her finger. Since his mother told him to take any treasure he saw, Perceval removes the ring from the maiden's finger. He also decides to take a kiss. This causes the maiden to wake up—screaming for her knight to protect her. Perceval flees.

Soon after, Perceval crosses paths with Mordred of the SeaCastle, a young man on his way to Camelot as well. When Perceval reaches Camelot, Arthur's court is in a hubbub. A golden-armored knight called the Haughty Knight of the Heath had just thrown Guinevere's drink in her face and stolen her cup. The reason for this was that he was demanding justice from Arthur. Apparently, his damsel had been attacked in her tent by a thief. When Arthur would not give him justice, the knight had reacted by dashing Guinevere's drink in her face.

Arthur asks which knight would be

brave enough to return Guinevere's cup. Mordred and Perceval simultaneously volunteer, and Arthur sends the two potential knights out to quest together.

They soon locate the haughty knight, and Mordred tries to defeat him singlehandedly, but Perceval intervenes before Mordred is slain. A blind, holy hermit has been taken by the haughty knight, and when Perceval speaks to him, the old man tells him that when he left for Camelot, his mother actually died of grief. Perceval leaves at once to see if this is true.

Mordred speaks to the old man, who then tells him his true identity, the illegitimate son of King Arthur. Shocked by this, Mordred slays the holy man before he can say more. Not long after Morgan le Fay appears to Mordred, telling him that he is ready to become her instrument of hate.

ESSENTIAL QUESTIONS

- What is the difference between good and evil?
- Why should we not judge one another based on appearances or social status?

ANTICIPATORY QUESTIONS

- Do people judge others by what they wear and how they talk? Explain.
- Does being born rich make you a better person than someone born poor?

CHARACTER QUEST

Personal Choices We may not realize it, but the choices we make on a daily basis determine our path in life. While Mordred feels that he is destined for evil and cannot escape this curse, he does not realize that it is his own choices that lead him down the path of evil. How could he have made different choices? How would this have caused different results? How do our choices define who we are and what we stand for?

CONNECT

I Am Mordred **by Nancy Springer** This novel retells the Arthurian legends from Mordred's point-of-view. Young Mordred is shocked to learn that this father is actually King Arthur, and Merlin has prophesied that Mordred will one day kill his father. But Mordred doesn't want to kill Arthur—he only wants his love.

TEACHABLE TERMS

- **Onomatopoeia** On pg. 179 Perceval's mother uses the word "Bam!"
- **Buddy story** This type of story involves two male friends, who are opposites in many ways but through the course of an adventure come to understand each other. Examine how this tale might be a buddy story. Think of another example of this type of storyline.
- **Tone** Although the story begins lightheartedly, its tone shifts dramatically toward the end as Perceval learns of his mother's death and Mordred commits murder.

RECALL QUESTIONS

1. What does Perceval mistake for an angel?
2. What does Perceval steal from a damsel?
3. What does the Haughty Knight of the Heath steal from Guinevere?
4. What startling news does a holy man give to Mordred?
5. What does Mordred do after hearing this news?

RETURN OF THE MISBEGOTTEN

CAST

PERCEVAL	*Backwoods Boy*
MOTHER	*Perceval's Mother*
GAWAIN	*Knight of Arthur*
MORDRED	*Knight of the SeaCastle*
HAUGHTY	*Haughty Knight of the Heath*
DAMSEL	*Haughty Knight's Damsel*
ARTHUR	*King of Britain*
GUARD	*Watchman of Camelot*
KAY	*King Arthur's Seneschal*
GIRL	*Servingmaid in Arthur's Court*
HERMIT	*Holy Man*
MORGAN	*Evil Enchantress*

NARRATOR: In the great wilderness of Wales, there existed a simple dwelling. It was barely more than a hut, but it housed a woman, her few servants, and her young son. The life of those who lived there was a rustic one, and the son, Perceval, spent his days hunting the wild things that roamed the forests.

MOTHER: Perceval! What are you doing with those pointed sticks? You could poke your eye out!

PERCEVAL: I'm going hunting, Mama. These are my pig-stickers. I whittled them from tree branches. I can spear any game from far away with these beauties!

MOTHER: You could also poke your eye out! Ugh! *(frustrated sigh)* You know how I feel about hunting! If we didn't need the food, I wouldn't dream of sending you out in the forest alone.

PERCEVAL: I'm not afraid, Mama.

MOTHER: You may not be, but I am! And remember, Perceval, don't stray too far. If you go into the deep forest, there are beasts there that will gobble you up! *(scary voice)* Beasts as tall as trees, with eyes like fire, and fangs that drip blood! Ooooh!

PERCEVAL: Mama, I'm not a child! I've lived in this wood my whole life, and I've never once seen the beasts you're talking about.

MOTHER: They're crafty! They want you to think they don't exist, and then—Bam!—you're dinner. Just stay close to the dwelling, my son, and you will always be safe.

NARRATOR: Perceval had grown accustomed to his mother's dramatic monster stories. What he did not know is that she harbored a deep secret, and her worst fear was that her son would one day discover the truth about his identity.

Once Perceval had gone deep into the

forest to hunt, he heard the sound of a large beast approaching through the underbrush.

PERCEVAL: What is that? A wolf? A wild boar? No! It's a sound I've never heard before.

NARRATOR: A sudden chill overtook him.

PERCEVAL: Maybe Mama was right! Maybe there are monsters in the woods!

NARRATOR: Perceval hid beneath the bushes—one of his javelin darts clutched in his hand. The beast's approach grew louder and louder. *(rustling of bushes)* And then he saw it. But instead of the monstrosity he expected, what appeared was the most amazing creature he had ever seen. Its body had a strange, angular shape, its skin glinted in the sunlight, and as it moved, it clicked like a beetle. *(clinking and clanking)*

PERCEVAL: *(to himself, in awe)* What is this creature? It's not a beast! It must be an angel!

NARRATOR: Perceval walked out of the bushes.

PERCEVAL: Hello, angel! Have you come down from Heaven to give me a message?

NARRATOR: The creature responded in an otherworldly tongue.

GAWAIN: *(muffled speech)* Hmph hmph hmph.

PERCEVAL: What?

NARRATOR: The creature twisted its strange head from its body. Beneath was the head of a human.

GAWAIN: I said—I am lost! Is there a castle near here?

PERCEVAL: A what?

GAWAIN: A castle. You know, where a king lives?

PERCEVAL: A king?

GAWAIN: Are you slow or something? Surely even you backwoods types have heard of a king!

PERCEVAL: Can't say that I have. I never saw a creature like you either.

GAWAIN: A creature? I am a human like you—or similar at least.

PERCEVAL: What? It can't be! How does your skin shine like that?

GAWAIN: How dense are you, boy? This is not my skin. It's armor.

NARRATOR: The creature removed one of his hands and threw it to the boy.

PERCEVAL: *(cry of fright)* Ah! Can you take your whole body apart like that? Piece by piece! You must be an angel!

GAWAIN: An angel? Ha! I'm a knight! Who has never heard of knights? The land is full of them.

PERCEVAL: I never saw one. But I stay close to the home with my mama.

GAWAIN: Then come to Camelot someday, the castle of King Arthur, and you will see many knights. It might improve your education. Now, I must be on my way. I see that you can be very little help to me—

or anyone else for that matter. Farewell, forest boy!

NARRATOR: Once the knight had ridden away, Perceval ran home.

PERCEVAL: Mama! Mama!

MOTHER: Perceval! Did you fall on one of those sticks of yours? I knew it! Help! My son has been wounded!

PERCEVAL: No, Mama! I'm not hurt. I thought I saw an angel—in the woods!

MOTHER: An angel? That is a miracle! What did the angel look like?

PERCEVAL: He was riding on a horse, and he had this shiny material all over his body.

NARRATOR: His mother's face turned pale.

PERCEVAL: I thought he was an angel, but he called himself a knight—from a place called Camelot or something like that. I've decided I want to go this Camelot place and be a knight, too.

MOTHER: Ooooh. *(swooning sound)*

NARRATOR: His mother's eyes rolled back into her head, and she fell to the ground.

PERCEVAL: Mama!

NARRATOR: The servants rushed forward to revive their mistress. When she came to, she glared at Perceval angrily.

MOTHER: *(angrily)* Perceval, how could you! All I have worked for! Ruined! *(crying)* You are the worst boy ever!

PERCEVAL: *(almost in tears)* Mama! What are you talking about? Don't cry! When you cry, it makes me cry!

MOTHER: I gave up everything! I brought you here to the forest—to raise you ignorant of your true identity.

PERCEVAL: I am ignorant, Mama! Just don't cry!

MOTHER: I knew someday one of *those horrible men* would find you somehow. Knighthood is like a disease in this country! Young men should stay home with their mothers instead of riding around with dangerous weapons!

PERCEVAL: You mentioned my true identity. What did you mean?

MOTHER: Oh, I guess I've hidden the truth from you long enough. I've never told you about your father.

PERCEVAL: I have a father?

MOTHER: Of course, you have a father! Where else would have you have come from? Maybe I have raised you ignorant. Anyway, your father was King Pellinore. He was a great man, but he insisted on all this knight business—slaying damsels, and rescuing dragons. Or maybe it was the other way around…

PERCEVAL: Where is my father? Can I meet him?

MOTHER: That's just it! Guess where all this chivalry nonsense got him? Dead! That's where! And your dear brothers, too! They became knights and left me all alone. You were my baby, and I decided I would not have you being a knight. So I brought you here and raised you ignorant of the world. And that's the whole truth. *(pause)* Phew! That's a load off my chest. Now, let's go about our lives and never mention it again, okay?

NARRATOR: Perceval was looking at her intently.

PERCEVAL: I can't.

MOTHER: You can't what?

PERCEVAL: I've loved growing up here in the woods—hunting beasts and being with you—but when I saw that knight today, something changed inside of me. I know now that a knight is what I'm supposed to be.

NARRATOR: Perceval's mother almost swooned again.

MOTHER: No! I forbid it! You'll stay right here with me forever—and that's final!

PERCEVAL: Mama, my mind is made up. I'm going to Camelot.

MOTHER: *(sarcastically)* Oh, I can see it all now. You, the backwoods boy, ride into the great city of Arthur. Everyone there will be *so* impressed with your mighty weapons. I bet those pointed sticks will be the envy of all the knights. And your armor! Well, they have probably never seen the tanned hides of animals worn like you wear them. You'll set a new fashion trend in Arthur's court!

PERCEVAL: *(happily)* Wow! You really think so?

MOTHER: It's sarcasm, boy! I meant to raise you ignorant—not stupid. But mark my words—if you go to Camelot, they will mock you.

PERCEVAL: Well, I am what I am. I just have to be myself. You taught me that.

MOTHER: Well, fine! Go! Leave your mother here all alone with the beasts and the servants—I don't know which is worse. I'll be waiting here when they laugh you out of Camelot.

PERCEVAL: That sounds like a good plan! I'll leave immediately.

MOTHER: If you must go, please let me give you some advice that will make you successful. Be respectful! Keep your mouth shut in the presence of others. Out of courtesy for maidens, bow to them and kiss them when they require it. If you are offered treasure, take it. And whenever you see a church, the most beautiful building man has made, go inside and say your prayers.

NARRATOR: She caught Perceval's hands up in her own.

MOTHER: Please don't go! It will mean your death!

PERCEVAL: If the forest taught me anything, Mama, it's that all things die eventually. But everything has a purpose, and my purpose is to be a knight.

NARRATOR: Perceval's mother began to sob uncontrollably, and her son prepared to leave for Camelot.

PERCEVAL: Well, I planned to pack, but I don't have anything to take with me—except maybe these sharp pig-stickers I use. Goodbye, Mama.

NARRATOR: Perceval headed down the forest path, and his mother began to wail. In fact, she cried so hard that day and the night after that she died of grief.

Perceval traveled through the woods, going further from his home than he had ever dared venture before.

At last he came to a clearing, and his breath caught in his throat. A strange dwelling stood there—its sides were made of fabric, supported by poles and ropes. Bright flags flew from its peak.

PERCEVAL: I know what this is! This is a church! Mama said that when I pass a church, I must always go inside and pray.

NARRATOR: Perceval neared the tent and boldly ducked inside. Within it was shady and cool. Lying across a makeshift bed of pillows, he saw a beautiful maiden.

PERCEVAL: Lord of Mercy! What a beautiful lady. And that's a nice ring on her finger, too. Hmmm. What did Mama say about seeing a treasure? Oh, I remember. Take it when it's available.

NARRATOR: The boy slipped the ring off the maiden's finger. The maiden stirred but did not wake.

PERCEVAL: Now what else did Mama say about seeing a beautiful lady? Something about taking kisses when you get the chance. Hmmm. Okay. I guess I have a chance. Here goes.

NARRATOR: Perceval leaned down and planted his lips upon the lips of the sleeping maiden.

DAMSEL: (*scream of fright*) Ahhhhh!

PERCEVAL: Goodness! I must have done it wrong!

DAMSEL: (*screaming*) What are you doing? Get out! Get out!

NARRATOR: The damsel started to hurl pillows at Perceval, and he beat a hasty retreat.

PERCEVAL: Sorry, miss! I was just doing what my Mama told me!

NARRATOR: Perceval disappeared down the forest road, as the maiden continued to cry out.

DAMSEL: (*yelling*) Help! Help!

NARRATOR: A knight in golden armor appeared from the forest near the tent.

HAUGHTY: (*angrily*) What's all this racket? I just found a stream where I could see a good reflection of myself! A knight has to look good—even in the wilderness.

NARRATOR: The golden knight removed his helmet, very carefully so as not to muss his hair.

DAMSEL: I have been attacked! A boy just barged into my tent.

HAUGHTY: He didn't touch my armor polish, did he?

DAMSEL: No! Your precious armor polish is fine! But he stole my ring, and he kissed me!

NARRATOR: The haughty knight glared at his damsel suspiciously.

HAUGHTY: He barged into your tent—or you invited him in?

DAMSEL: I did no such thing!

HAUGHTY: Ha! This happens every time I get a damsel! At first she's attracted by my dazzling features—and, of course, my hair—but then she starts going behind my back! I'm going to track this boy down and kill him—or my name's not the Haughty Knight of the Heath.

DAMSEL: *(confused)* Who are you talking to?

HAUGHTY: Definitely not you, you tart! From now on, you're my prisoner, and I'm not taking my eyes off you for a second! *(pause)* Unless it's to focus on more important things.

NARRATOR: He held up his shiny gauntlet and tried to fix his mussed hair.
   Meanwhile, Perceval had continued down the forest road. Soon, he heard hoofbeats behind him. *(hoofbeats)* Rounding the bend came a young man with a perplexed look upon his face. Perceval thought about hailing the young man, but he remembered his mother's words.

PERCEVAL: *(to himself)* Mama said, "Keep your mouth shut."

NARRATOR: Perceval stood casually against a tree, and the young man glared down at him.

MORDRED: Hello there, boy! Is this the road to Camelot?

NARRATOR: Perceval stared back at him dumbly.

MORDRED: *(loudly)* Do—you—speak—English?

NARRATOR: Perceval only shrugged.

MORDRED: Well, judging by those ridiculous clothes you're wearing, you're obviously not refined enough to speak French. Anglo-Saxon perhaps? Can you at least grunt and point?

PERCEVAL: I can speak well enough, sir.

MORDRED: Then why didn't you speak when I addressed you, peasant?

PERCEVAL: Oh, I'm not a peasant. I'm headed to Camelot for Arthur to make me a knight.

MORDRED: *(laughing)* You? A knight? Why would anyone make you a knight looking the way you do?

PERCEVAL: Because I'm brave and strong.

MORDRED: Well, you certainly have a strong scent. I am on my way to be made a knight. You're on your way to make a fool out of yourself.

PERCEVAL: Why do you think you'll make such a good knight?

MORDRED: Good breeding—something a backwoods moron like you wouldn't know anything about. I am Sir Mordred of the SeaCastle. My father is King of the SeaCastle. Since a boy, I have been trained in the duties of knighthood and in the manners of courtly grace.

PERCEVAL: Manners, huh? Did you skip a lesson?

MORDRED: Why you—! If I wasn't in such a rush, I would thrash you! Now tell me! Is this the road to Camelot or not?

PERCEVAL: Well, I can't tell you, sir. I've never been to its end.

MORDRED: I cannot waste time conversing with a fool! Yah! Yah!

NARRATOR: Mordred spurred his horse and disappeared down the road.

PERCEVAL: Well, there's one knight I won't be mistaking for an angel.

NARRATOR: Perceval continued his journey, and his high spirits returned. Soon the trees parted, and in the distance stood the white towers of Camelot. The sight of it filled Perceval with a happiness he had never known.

PERCEVAL: If only Mama could see this! Then maybe she wouldn't be so dead set against knights.

NARRATOR: Perceval made his way into the city. A watchman stopped him at the gates.

GUARD: Who are you? You look like a shifty fellow! What is the meaning of those clothes you wear? And those pointed sticks? Are they some kind of weapon?

PERCEVAL: Oh, I'm Perceval. I've come to see King Arthur about becoming a knight.

GUARD: You and everybody else! Contrary to popular opinion, the king doesn't just make anyone a knight. You have to have the breeding! Who was your father?

PERCEVAL: Well, my mama said he was a man named King Pell—Pell-something.

GUARD: King Pellinore? Heavens above! Let's take you before the king at once! Your father was one of Arthur's greatest knights.

PERCEVAL: Was he? Oh great!

NARRATOR: Perceval was brought into the chamber of the Round Table. Much to Perceval's disappointment Mordred was there as well. He sneered in Perceval's direction.

MORDRED: You again, blockhead? I'm surprised you had enough sense to find your way here.

PERCEVAL: You were the one asking me for directions.

MORDRED: Touché. Well, you might as well know that King Arthur is not here right now. There has been quite a hubbub. I was in the middle of being introduced to the king, when we were interrupted. Some arrogant knight wearing a gaudy set of golden armor arrived in court and accused the king of letting outlaws run wild in the countryside. He was quite haughty. Don't you just hate stuck-up people like that?

PERCEVAL: (*sarcastically*) Yeah. I can't stand them.

MORDRED: Apparently, some measly peasant had snuck into his lady's tent and stole her ring. Boo hoo. Big deal.

PERCEVAL: (*nervously*) Oh. You don't say?

MORDRED: Apparently, he also tried to get familiar with her—if you know what I mean.

NARRATOR: Perceval stared back at Mordred blankly.

MORDRED: Or maybe you don't. You are ridiculous. Anyway, the haughty knight demanded that Arthur send out a party of knights to hunt for the outlaw. Arthur, of course, refused. He handled it masterfully. He said it was the job of knights to take care of their own ladies. The haughty knight flew into a rage, seized up Queen Guinevere's cup, and dashed her drink in her face. Everyone was outraged, but in the confusion, the haughty knight escaped with the queen's cup. Arthur is consoling the queen now, but I have already decided that I will pledge to retrieve the cup for the queen. Everyone expects Lancelot to do it, but this is the perfect way to prove that I am ready for knighthood.

NARRATOR: A tall man, who was standing nearby, had been eying Perceval while the two young men chatted. He drew near to them.

KAY: Mordred of the Sea Castle, I believe. I am Kay, King Arthur's seneschal. Who is this…*person* here? Surely not your squire.

MORDRED: No, sir! This is no one—some peasant I happened to meet on my journey. I would never have a squire as dismal as this.

NARRATOR: Perceval's face grew red with shame.

KAY: Yes, he looks more like a good stable-boy. What is he wearing? Is that supposed to be some type of armor? Speak up, boy! Is this the type of clothing one wears when shoveling horse manure?

NARRATOR: A plain-faced girl, a servingmaid, stopped to listen as Kay berated the poor boy.

PERCEVAL: I have come to be a knight.

KAY: A knight? *(laugh)* Ha-ha! We should hire this boy as the court jester!

NARRATOR: The girl stepped forward, a strange, faraway look upon her face.

GIRL: No. You are wrong! This boy will be great—one of the greatest of the Round Table. I see it in his eyes.

KAY: What?

NARRATOR: Kay turned and slapped the girl roughly across the face. *(slapping sound)*

KAY: Get back to work! That's enough from you!

NARRATOR: Perceval lunged toward Kay and drew his javelins, but Mordred barred his way.

MORDRED: What are you doing, you fool?

PERCEVAL: He struck the girl—for no reason.

MORDRED: She is a servant—apparently an insane one.

PERCEVAL: It doesn't matter! He should not have struck her!

KAY: Watch it, boy! You might have made an impression on the kitchen staff, but I say you'll never be a member of the Round Table.

PERCEVAL: I swear, I will meet you in battle one day, and I will defend that damsel's honor.

KAY: Defend the honor of a servingmaid? Against me? *(laugh)* I cannot wait.

MORDRED: Get out of here, you idiot! You can ruin your chances of becoming a knight, but don't ruin mine as well!

NARRATOR: A horn was sounded as Arthur and Guinevere returned to the feast. Everyone in the hall bowed respectfully.

ARTHUR: Today we have witnessed a horrible spectacle. The queen has been shamed by a haughty knight. Who among you will now be brave enough to apprehend this knight and retrieve the queen's golden cup?

NARRATOR: None of the Knights of the Round Table stood. They knew this was Lancelot's territory. The respected champion began to rise.

MORDRED, PERCEVAL: *(in unison)* I will go.

NARRATOR: Sir Lancelot jerked his head toward the pair of voices. Mordred and Perceval stared at one another in surprise.

ARTHUR: I have just met young Mordred of the SeaCastle, but who is this other…knight?

MORDRED: No one! He is some bumpkin from the deep woods, your majesty. But I will be happy to go on your quest for you.

PERCEVAL: I am Perceval, the son of King Pellinore.

(murmuring of the crowd)

ARTHUR: I knew your father well. You dress…differently in the deep woods, I see.

MORDRED: Yes, and they apparently do not bathe either. *(laugh)*

NARRATOR: Arthur furrowed his brow at the young Mordred.

ARTHUR: I myself was raised in the deep woods on a country plantation. There is no shame in it.

MORDRED: Oh, yes, sir! I love the deep woods myself! I go there often when I am not at my castle—training for knighthood and things like that.

ARTHUR: Perhaps you should take the quest.

NARRATOR: Lancelot opened his mouth to object, but Arthur raised his hand.

ARTHUR: Maybe it is time we older knights allowed the new generation to try their hand at questing. Very well. These two young knights shall take up the quest…together.

NARRATOR: Mordred sneered at Perceval.

MORDRED: Together? Why must he go as well?

ARTHUR: Because I am the king. Mordred, I know your pedigree, but there are some things in life that pedigree cannot get you. Some lessons must be learned the hard way. An old friend taught me that once.

NARRATOR: Mordred's face turned red.

MORDRED: Yes, your majesty.

NARRATOR: When the two young men rode out from Camelot, Mordred confronted Perceval angrily.

MORDRED: Why did you volunteer for this quest? I told you it was mine!

PERCEVAL: I had to. This whole business is my fault. I was the one who took the lady's ring and kissed her. I caused the haughty knight to come to Camelot and insult the king and queen. All this trouble started because I was doing what my Mama told me to do.

MORDRED: You and your blasted Mama! You'll get us both killed with your foolishness! Now stay close and don't do anything stupid. Oh wait. Look who I'm telling that to!

NARRATOR: Mordred looked contemptuously at the horse Perceval had chosen as his steed.

MORDRED: Was that the worst-looking nag Camelot had to offer?

PERCEVAL: I like him. He is simple.

MORDRED: Then he suits you perfectly.

NARRATOR: Soon an adventure was presented to the knights. Screams rang throughout the forest.

DAMSEL: *(screaming)* Help! Help me!

NARRATOR: A clearing opened up. In its midst was a damsel tied to a tree.

DAMSEL: Please save me!

MORDRED: Don't interfere! You'll just mess things up! Let me show you how a real knight works. *(loudly)* Never fear, my lady.

NARRATOR: Mordred dismounted, drew his sword, and neared where the damsel was tied.

MORDRED: I will have you freed in just a moment.

NARRATOR: There was a sudden snapping sound as a hidden trap was sprung.

MORDRED: Ah!

NARRATOR: Mordred now dangled upside down from the tree branches, his leg snared by a rope.

MORDRED: This is some kind of trap! Don't just stand there! Help me!

PERCEVAL: I would, but you told me not to interfere. I'd hate to mess up your master plan.

NARRATOR: The haughty knight in golden armor charged out from the underbrush. *(hoofbeats)*

HAUGHTY: Ha! There is the culprit! I will teach you to mess with my damsel!

NARRATOR: He lowered his lance and charged toward the suspended Mordred.

MORDRED: Do something!

PERCEVAL: *(sarcastically)* Are you talking to me, the ignorant backwoods boy?

MORDRED: Yes, you!

PERCEVAL: All right. Fine!

NARRATOR: Perceval drew a javelin and hurled it through the air. *(Clang!)* It caught the haughty knight in the helm, and he fell backward from his steed. *(crashing sound)*

HAUGHTY: Argh!

NARRATOR: The knight rose, leaving his helmet upon the ground, and drew his sword.

HAUGHTY: All right! That's it! Now my hair is mussed!

NARRATOR: For the first time he noticed Perceval standing at the edge of the clearing.

HAUGHTY: Two of you, eh? Well, no matter! No one can defeat me! Or no two—for that matter! I am the Haughty Knight of the Heath!

PERCEVAL: Well, at least you admit it! Maybe this will knock you down a peg or two.

NARRATOR: Perceval hurled a second javelin, pinning the knight's arm to the tree behind him. *(shunk)* The knight struggled to free his hand.

HAUGHTY: What? Javelins!

PERCEVAL: Actually, back home I call them pig-stickers. I use them on wild pigs. But you'll do, too. You seem like a pompous swine. Do you yield? Or shall I give you another demonstration?

NARRATOR: The haughty knight lunged against his pinned arm.

HAUGHTY: Never! Never! The Knight of the Heath will never yield!

NARRATOR: Perceval hurled his third javelin. It split the knight's coiffed hair-do.

HAUGHTY: Ah! My hair! I yield! I yield!

PERCEVAL: Ha! Look, Mordred, I did it! My first victory as a knight. I even worked in some clever banter. I can't believe it!

MORDRED: *(dryly)* Neither can I. Cut me down already.

NARRATOR: Perceval complied, and Mordred collapsed in a heap. Perceval freed the damsel.

DAMSEL: Oh, thank you! This haughty knight has been using me as bait to trap any poor man who tried to help me. He has even taken prisoner an old hermit—a man of God. I tell you this knight is deranged—not to mention incredibly conceited.

NARRATOR: Perceval neared where the knight was pinned to the tree.

PERCEVAL: You yielded, so you must do whatever I tell you.

HAUGHTY: Oh, I will! I will! Just spare my beautiful face!

PERCEVAL: I command you to ride into Camelot and return the cup you have stolen from the queen. You will promise to serve her in any way she sees fit.

HAUGHTY: I will! Do you think Camelot is looking for a new armor model?

PERCEVAL: Lord of Mercy, you are haughty! *(pause)* Here is my second command. I wish you to challenge Sir Kay to a duel championing the honor of the servingmaid. Can you do that?

HAUGHTY: A servingmaid? That's not very good for my image.

NARRATOR: Perceval held the pointed end of a javelin up to the knight's face.

HAUGHTY: On second thought, that sounds lovely!

NARRATOR: Perceval freed the haughty knight, who quickly remounted his steed, and after a little combing and coiffing of his hair, rode off.

DAMSEL: The holy man I spoke of is held right over there in the haughty knight's tent. I, too, will ride to Camelot and tell the king of your bravery. Farewell!

NARRATOR: After the damsel had departed, Mordred glared at Perceval.

MORDRED: I had him right where I wanted him, you know! Then you had to butt in and ruin everything!

PERCEVAL: Just admit it, I saved your life.

MORDRED: That is something I will never admit. Now see to that holy geezer, so we can go back to Camelot and be knighted.

NARRATOR: Inside the haughty knight's tent Perceval found the old holy hermit. His eyes were milky white and looked on nothing.

PERCEVAL: Sir, you are free to go. You have been released.

HERMIT: Thank you, my son. But first, come closer. Let me see the face of the one who rescued me.

NARRATOR: He ran his old hands over Perceval's face.

HERMIT: You have a kind face—not like that knight who imprisoned me. He had a handsome face, but an evil heart. *(pause)* I can see that you will go far. You will become one of Camelot's greatest knights.

PERCEVAL: Really? Do not tell Mordred. He will not be happy.

NARRATOR: The old man's brow clouded as he continued to feel the boy's face.

HERMIT: But I have sad news for you, as well. Someone you love is dead. Your mother has died of grief.

PERCEVAL: *(in shock)* Mama is dead?

HERMIT: Yes. I am afraid so.

PERCEVAL: I must go back home at once!

NARRATOR: Perceval fled from the tent.

MORDRED: What did his holiness tell you?

PERCEVAL: I have to go. He told me of my future, but he also told me that my mother has died. I must go to my home to see if this is true.

NARRATOR: For a brief second a look of compassion passed over Mordred's face.

MORDRED: He's probably just a crazy old man. But he told you of the future, huh?

PERCEVAL: Yes, he said I would be one of Camelot's greatest knights.

MORDRED: See? He is crazy.

PERCEVAL: Farewell, Mordred. I know we have not seen eye to eye, but I wish you the best of luck. Farewell.

MORDRED: Farewell.

NARRATOR: Perceval rode way. Mordred turned back to the tent. The holy man sat just inside.

MORDRED: The future. Hmmmm.

HERMIT: Who is there?

MORDRED: You tell me, old man.

HERMIT: That voice. Come closer. Let me see your face.

NARRATOR: The wrinkled hands passed over Mordred's face.

HERMIT: A young man from the seaside…*(cry of shock)* Ah!

MORDRED: What is the matter?

HERMIT: What is your name, boy?

MORDRED: Mordred of the SeaCastle.

HERMIT: Who was your father?

MORDRED: The King of the SeaCastle. Who else?

HERMIT: No. There is much you do not know. But if I tell you what I see, you will be the saddest knight who ever lived.

NARRATOR: Mordred laughed nervously.

MORDRED: *(laugh)* You're joking. That fool Perceval put you up to this, didn't he?

HERMIT: No. I ask you in all earnestness. Do you wish to know your future? If you do not, ride away and forget you ever saw me this day.

NARRATOR: Mordred hardened his jaw.

MORDRED: I fear nothing.

HERMIT: *(slowly)* You are not the son of the King of the SeaCastle.

NARRATOR: Mordred turned pale.

MORDRED: What?

HERMIT: Your father is King Arthur himself.

MORDRED: No! That can't be true!

HERMIT: Your mother was his half-sister, the Lady Margawse. You were born from their incest.

MORDRED: No! Stop your lies! No!

HERMIT: There was a prophecy, and your father tried to slay you.

MORDRED: Stop! Enough!

HERMIT: Somehow you were spared, and you washed up on the seashore, where the man you call Father found you. You are destined to one day kill…

MORDRED: I said—enough!

NARRATOR: Mordred's sword flashed through the air, and at last the old man's words stopped. His blood covered the grass. Mordred dropped his sword and stared in horror.

MORDRED: What have I done?

NARRATOR: Then he bolted from the tent.

Mordred spent hours in agony—lying in the tall grass, cradling his own head and weeping. Everything he had ever known was a lie. A hole had rotted through his soul. His world was lost forever.

Finally, he raised his bleary eyes. A crow was perched upon a nearby stone, croaking out a greeting. *(crow calls)* In the next instant, the crow vanished, and a dark, imperial woman stood before him. Somehow this did not surprise him.

MORGAN: Rise. You are in the presence of a lady.

NARRATOR: Mordred did as she commanded him, and the cat-like eyes of Morgan le Fay filled with pleasure.

MORGAN: Mordred, you do not know me, but for many years I have watched you. I have called to you in your dreams. I am your aunt, Morgan le Fay.

NARRATOR: Mordred pointed toward the tent.

MORDRED: I killed a holy man there! He is the first man I have ever slain.

MORGAN: I know. And it has opened a door inside of you. You have taken a step that cannot be undone. Finally, you are ready to hear my words.

MORDRED: I have heard of you. You are the enemy of Camelot—the enemy of Arthur.

MORGAN: You shall be, too, when I tell you all the deeds that Arthur has done.

MORDRED: You are an evil sorceress.

MORGAN: Evil? You are the one who just killed a holy man. Good and evil are in the eye of the beholder.

MORDRED: Is Arthur truly my father?

MORGAN: He is.

MORDRED: An hour ago I was the son of a wealthy lord. Now I am an illegitimate—a nobody.

MORGAN: Yes, Arthur has taken away your world. And once he tried to take away your very life. But *I* will give you life.

MORDRED: You can give me nothing.

MORGAN: Nothing is what you will be without me. You want to be a great knight? Look how you have failed today! But I can make you the most powerful knight in Britain. I will give you the strength of ten men. I will give you nerves of steel. I will even make *you* the King of Camelot. But you must trust me and do as I say.

NARRATOR: Visions of grandeur filled Mordred's mind.

MORDRED: But I was raised to idolize Arthur. Even now—knowing all that I know—I do not hate him.

MORGAN: Only hatred can give you power. If you have none of your own, I will give you mine. But it is a gift that cannot be undone. Once it passes from me to you, it will consume you, as it has consumed me.

NARRATOR: Mordred paused, staring up into the high branches of the trees.

MORDRED: I have nothing else—nowhere to go. Fine. Teach me your hate.

NARRATOR: Morgan reached out her pale hand and laid it upon Mordred's chest. She closed her eyes, and a sudden power flowed from her into the young knight. His body recoiled from the shock.

MORDRED: Ah! *(cry of pain)*

NARRATOR: Morgan removed her hand. She seemed spent—much older. Gray streaks stood out in her raven-black hair. Her eyes seemed softer—more human.

MORGAN: I have given you my hatred. I have harbored it for so long, it is a strange feeling to be without it. But now you see what I have seen these many years.

NARRATOR: A new light had come into Mordred's eyes.

MORDRED: Yes! Arthur must die! All that he has worked for must be destroyed!

MORGAN: That's my boy! At last I have found the weapon to bring down Camelot! Now return there. With the skill I have given you, it will be no feat for you to join the ranks of the Round Table. Through deception and deceit, you must find a way to bring Arthur to his knees.

MORDRED: *(happily)* I will! Then it will be *he* who mourns the loss of *his* world.

NARRATOR: Merlin's prophecy of long ago had come true. The child of May Day had survived. Now Mordred's mind was fixed upon a new purpose—the destruction of Camelot and the death of Arthur.

DISCUSSION QUESTIONS

1. What makes Perceval a hero? Explain.
2. Is Perceval's mother right for hiding him away in the forest? Explain.
3. How are some of the other knights judgmental toward Perceval?
4. How does the tone of the story shift toward the end?
5. Did you know that Mordred would turn out to be the long-lost son of King Arthur? Explain.
6. Does Mordred have a right to seek revenge on Arthur? Explain.
7. Consider the title of this play. *Misbegotten* means "illegitimate" or even "deformed." Who is the misbegotten and how is he misbegotten—either literally or figuratively?
8. Will Morgan le Fay change since she has given her hatred to Mordred? Explain.
9. What do you predict will happen in the latter parts of the King Arthur legend?

QUEST OF THE HOLY GRAIL
TEACHER GUIDE

BACKGROUND

The search for the Holy Grail is one of the most famous episodes of King Arthur's story. The idea of a God-given quest for spiritual purity is one that has captured the imagination of many. Yet the irony of the Grail quest is that instead of strengthening Arthur's kingdom, it greatly weakens it. Many knights attempt the Grail quest only to fail and lose their lives. The question remains: If the quest were truly sent by God, what was its purpose? Was Heaven's goal to test the spiritual fortitude of Arthur's knights? Was this God's way of judging Arthur's kingdom and finding it wanting?

Unlike a typical quest, the Quest of the Holy Grail presents mystical challenges and teaches spiritual lessons. For example, Lancelot learns that his infidelity with Guinevere has damaged his purity as a knight and, therefore, he cannot succeed. Others, such as Galahad the Pure, earn the title of Arthur's greatest knight by demonstrating his purity and prowess on the perilous quest.

SUMMARY

Camelot is celebrating the feast of Pentecost when a holy hermit arrives with a young boy named Galahad. Lancelot realizes that Galahad is his long-lost son conceived with Elaine, the daughter of the Maimed King. Galahad sits at the Round Table in the Siege Perilous, revealing that he is the knight to fulfill the special seat. As soon as this happens, a vision of the Holy Grail, covered in a cloth, appears to Arthur's court. Arthur asks which knights will be willing to venture forth to seek the Holy Grail. Galahad is the first to volunteer. Lancelot, and 150 knights follow his lead and pledge to seek the Grail for a year and a day.

Galahad and Lancelot ride out from Camelot and spend the night in an abadoned chapel, where another vision of the Grail appears to Galahad. Lancelot is shocked that he cannot see the Grail as his son does, but a heavenly voice tells him that his sinful affair with the queen prevents him from succeeding on the quest. Galahad continues on his journey, following a mysterious white knight, but Lancelot must turn back.

In a monastary graveyard, Galahad encounters a group of monks who are tormented by an evil spirit. Galahad does battle with this evil spirit and, upon defeating it, receives a special shield from the monks. After this adventure Galahad encounters Perceval, who is fleeing on foot pursued by a demonic knight. Galahad defeats this demon-knight, and Perceval tells him how the enemy knight appeared when Perceval picked up a crown that had been lying alonside the road. It was a spiritual test of his greed. Galahad and Perceval part ways.

Perceval encounters several spiritual traps. A damsel offers him a horse, which turns out to be a winged demonic horse. Before the steed can fly him to his doom, Perceval makes the sign of the cross, and the horse vanishes. Then Perceval finds himself on a strange island where he encounters a lion and a large serpent doing battle. Perceval saves the life of the lion, which appears as tame as a cat. A woman in a barge offers Perceval a ride off the island, which he takes. She offers him wine and works him into a passion until he is begging her for a kiss. She says she will give him one if he swears to serve no one but her. He is about to swear this when he sees the cross-shape of his sword hilt, regains his senses, and denies her. She suddenly transforms into a demonic monster, but Perceval defeats her by making the sign of the cross.

Perceval, Galahad, and the knight Bors are reunited, and the Grail Damsel appears to them, telling them that they have been chosen to see the Holy Grail unveiled. She invites them onto a ship built by King Solomon, and they sail away to the Grail Castle.

Only Bors returns to Camelot and tells what befell the three knights at the Grail Castle. The Holy Grail was taken back into heaven by God. Galahad and Perceval were taken into heaven as well.

ESSENTIAL QUESTIONS

- How can being a good person make you successful in the quests of life?
- Which is most important—developing your body, your mind, or your soul?

ANTICIPATORY QUESTIONS

- How might a spiritual quest be different from a physical one?
- What is the Holy Grail?
- Why would anyone want to find the Holy Grail?

CHARACTER QUEST

Virtue Rather than being a test of physical strength, the Quest of the Holy Grail is one of moral strength. Many knights who typically succeed on quests, like Lancelot, are defeated because they are not virtuous. The Grail raises the question: Is it better to be mighty or good?

CONNECT

Monty Python and the Holy Grail **(1975)** The bizarre wit of Monty Python takes aim at Arthurian legend in this classic spoof. From the Knights Who Say, "Ni!" to the killer rabbit to the black knight (sans limbs) who refuses to concede defeat, the King Arthur story has never been so wacky. (Note: Some portions of this film are not appropriate for middle-school and high-school audiences.)

TEACHABLE TERMS

- **Symbolism** The lion and snake that appear on pg. 206 are symbolic of Christ and Satan respectively.
- **Charactonym** When a character's name suggests his or her personality traits (such as the mystical maidens presented in this story), it is called a charactonym. *Una* means "one" to indicate truth and unity. *Duessa* means "two" to indicate untruth and division. *Lucifera* means "bright one" and is a reference to Lucifer, another name for the Devil. *Fidessa* means "loyalty," but this damsel reveals herself to be a creature named *Sansfoy*, which means "without faith." In the original version of the story, the damsels are nameless, but here they have names borrowed from Edmund Spenser's poem *The Faerie Queene*.

RECALL QUESTIONS

1. Who sits in the Siege Perilous?
2. Why can't Lancelot see the Holy Grail?
3. Every evil damsel tries to get Perceval to swear what?
4. Perceval sees what two types of animals fighting?
5. What happens to Galahad and Perceval?

THE QUEST OF THE HOLY GRAIL

CAST

GALAHAD	*Long-Lost Son of Lancelot*
NASCIEN	*Holy Hermit*
ARTHUR	*King of Britain*
GUINEVERE	*Queen of Britain*
LANCELOT	*Arthur's Greatest Knight*
GAWAIN	*One of Arthur's Best Knights*
PERCEVAL	*One of Arthur's Best Knights*
MORDRED	*Knight of the SeaCastle*
VOICE	*Heavenly Voice*
BORS	*Knight, Nephew to Lancelot*
SPIRIT	*Evil Spirit*
MONK	*Holy Man*
DUESSA	*Mysterious Damsel*
LUCIFERA	*Mysterious Damsel*
UNA	*Mysterious Damsel*
FIDESSA	*Mysterious Damsel*

NARRATOR: Red banners hung from the walls of Camelot to celebrate the Feast of Pentecost. But as the city rejoiced, its monarch, King Arthur, was troubled. His best knight, Sir Lancelot, stood at his side upon the castle ramparts.

ARTHUR: Another Pentecost already. It seems like the years just fly by. It is in these times that I remember that I won't live forever. I have no heir—no one to rule after me.

LANCELOT: There is yet time, sire. The queen is still young.

ARTHUR: I have given up all hope of a child. At least it does not seem to trouble the queen as much as it troubles me. She has something else to distract her from it—some secret joy.

NARRATOR: Lancelot looked quickly away.

LANCELOT: But the Siege Perilous is still empty! Merlin said that the greatest knight ever born would sit there. Perhaps that knight will be the one to rule after you?

ARTHUR: I have given up hope of that, too. *(sigh)* All we have worked for could be wiped out in a single generation. Is Camelot doomed to be as short-lived as this?

LANCELOT: No! Camelot will never fade away!

ARTHUR: That's what I thought once, but I'm beginning to doubt.

LANCELOT: I, for one, will never abandon Camelot—not until my dying breath.

ARTHUR: Thank you, my friend. There is no one as loyal to me as you are.

NARRATOR: Lancelot's face flushed, and he bowed his head. Arthur thought this was out of humility, but it was really from shame.

ARTHUR: Now, look there! On the road. It is an old man clothed in white.

NARRATOR: Lancelot looked to where the king pointed.

LANCELOT: It must be a hermit monk of some sort.

ARTHUR: He has a young man riding with him. It's probably another knightly pledge. *(sigh)* Come. Let us go to the feast.

NARRATOR: The king and his knight made their way down to the celebration. No knight had eaten. In fact, the tables were still bare. Among the knights Mordred, the knight of the SeaCastle, was seated by Perceval the Welsh knight.

MORDRED: *(grumbling)* What's the hold up? Where is the food?

PERCEVAL: It's a tradition in Camelot that King Arthur does not begin a feast until a marvel has presented itself.

MORDRED: Sounds like a stupid tradition to me. We'll probably starve to death before that happens.

PERCEVAL: I think it's a grand tradition!

MORDRED: You would. Old traditions should be done away with. Let the old pass away and the new rule in their place. *(pause)* Speaking of that, who is this old geezer?

NARRATOR: The holy monk and the young man were being led into the hall of the Round Table.

ARTHUR: *(boredly)* Greetings, holy man. What brings you to Camelot? Let me guess. This young man wants to be a knight.

NASCIEN: I am Nascien, a holy hermit. This boy was raised by the nuns of the Maimed Land of King Pelles. Now he is fifteen, and I bring him to you.

ARTHUR: Fifteen? That's hardly older than a squire. What is the boy's lineage?

NASCIEN: He is from the line of Joseph of Arimathea. His grandfather was King Pelles, the guardian of the Holy Grail. His mother was the Lady Elaine of Corbenic.

NARRATOR: At the mention of Elaine, Lancelot bristled. Guinevere noted his discomfort.

ARTHUR: Grandfather, mother…but most importantly, who is his father?

NASCIEN: That is not for me to say.

ARTHUR: What is the boy's name?

NASCIEN: Galahad.

LANCELOT: Galahad? That was my name when I was a boy.

NARRATOR: Lancelot walked forward and looked intently at Galahad. The young man had a pure, intense stare that showed wisdom beyond his years.

GUINEVERE: *(somewhat angrily)* So, Lancelot. This boy has your name, and he looks so much like you it's uncanny. Is there some secret you need to tell us?

LANCELOT: Yes, I am his father.

(*murmuring from the crowd*)

NARRATOR: Galahad bowed reverently before his father.

GALAHAD: Father, I have grown up hearing stories of you and your greatness. Now you do not seem happy to meet me.

LANCELOT: I am! I am! This is all a bit overwhelming. I had no idea I had a son.

GUINEVERE: Neither did the rest of us. What other secrets have you been keeping, Lancelot?

NARRATOR: Lancelot, ignoring the queen's comment, shook Galahad's hand awkwardly.

ARTHUR: (*happily*) This is indeed a marvel! Let's feast! Of course, Galahad shall be knighted! And he is welcome at our table.

NARRATOR: Nascien pointed the boy toward a nearby seat of the Round Table—one draped with a white cloth.

NASCIEN: Sit there, boy.

NARRATOR: Galahad did as the hermit bade him.

LANCELOT: (*in shock*) No, Galahad! Not that seat!

NARRATOR: But it was too late—the boy had already sat down upon the Siege Perilous—the seat reserved for only the greatest of knights. (*collective gasp*) The whole room expected the boy to be engulfed in heavenly fire. But no fire appeared. Galahad only looked around confused. (*murmuring from the crowd*)

GALAHAD: (*innocently*) Did I do something wrong?

LANCELOT: (*in shock*) But—but—you're only a boy! And you have not even been knighted...

NARRATOR: Nascien raised his hand for silence.

NASCIEN: It was for him that this seat was made. The Siege Perilous has been filled. King Arthur, your Round Table is completed! Camelot is whole.

ARTHUR: Heaven be praised!

NARRATOR: Just then a second wonder shook those assembled. All the doors and windows in the hall slammed shut, plunging the hall into darkness. (*murmuring*) A single window opened, and a scent like the smell of heaven wafted into the room. Then a glowing dove carrying a censure of gold in its beak flew in through the casement. (*angelic choir*) The air began to glitter, and in the midst of the enormous table, a golden image appeared—it was the image of a cup–carefully concealed by a jeweled cloth.

LANCELOT: (*in awe*) The Holy Grail!

ARTHUR: Here in Camelot!

NARRATOR: As quickly as it had appeared, the vision vanished. Everyone in the room stood breathless. To their further surprise, they realized that the table before them was now laid with sumptuous dishes.

NASCIEN: Arthur King, this is a mighty portent—a message sent from Heaven. You have been visited today by the Holy Grail. It is the same Grail that once resided with King Pelles, the Maimed King, but now it has left his realm. In it, lies the key to everlasting life.

ARTHUR: *(to himself)* Everlasting life? Perhaps this is the tool that will allow Camelot to endure forever.

NASCIEN: It is waiting to be sought by only the bravest of knights.

NARRATOR: Sir Gawain stood boldly.

GAWAIN: Bravest of knights, huh? Then let me be the first to pledge that I will find this Grail…er…thing and claim it for our king.

NASCIEN: Be warned! This is no ordinary quest requiring strength and knightly skill. It will be the most dangerous quest you have ever faced, for it is a spiritual quest. The invisible world has become visible. The forces of Darkness have been loosed on this land. Great evil is waiting to assail you at every step. Failure on this quest could cost you your life—or even your soul.

GAWAIN: Hmmm. On second thought…

NARRATOR: Gawain quickly reseated himself at the table.

NASCIEN: Let no knight accept this quest if he is unworthy. If any unworthy knight quests for the Grail, he will return a worse man than when he left. Only the purest knights should attempt it—the prayerful and the chaste.

NARRATOR: Young Galahad stood.

GALAHAD: I will go.

LANCELOT: No, son. This is not a quest for you. You are too young and inexperienced.

GALAHAD: I do not mean to disagree, Father, but the quest *is* mine. The Grail once belonged to my grandfather and to my ancestor Joseph of Arimathea before him. It is my destiny to seek the Grail. I can feel it.

NASCIEN: The boy is right! Galahad is young, but he is the purest of knights. Only purity can help you on this quest.

LANCELOT: Then I shall go, too! I will not leave him alone on such a quest!

NARRATOR: Lancelot's gaze strayed to the queen. She did not look pleased.

ARTHUR: Lancelot, I cannot lose my best knight.

LANCELOT: *(quietly)* Did you hear him, sire? The Grail gives eternal life! *(loudly)* I vow to pursue the Grail with my son for a year and a day. Tell us the paths we should take, Nascien.

NARRATOR: Mordred witnessed this all with a sneer and whispered to Perceval.

MORDRED: What kind of idiot would risk his neck for some stupid cup?

NARRATOR: Perceval boldly stood up.

PERCEVAL: I will go, too! This is a holy quest, and my mother always taught me to honor the holy things of life.

BORS: I will go, as well!

MORDRED: *(to himself)* What a bunch of brainless fools!

NARRATOR: In the end one-hundred-and-fifty knights vowed to quest for the Grail for a year and a day.

PERCEVAL: What about you, Mordred? Will you not go on the greatest quest of all time?

MORDRED: Someone must stay and guard Camelot. Are all of you so eager to abandon your king?

ARTHUR: Mordred is right. When you all depart, Camelot will be quite emptied!

MORDRED: Do not worry, sire! I will stay by your side—always.

NARRATOR: Over the next week, as the knights prepared to quest, Lancelot found a time to speak to the queen in secret.

GUINEVERE: So when were you planning to tell me about your son—and the Lady Elaine?

LANCELOT: Never! It was a deed performed through a trick. I thought she was you.

GUINEVERE: Ha! I doubt that.

LANCELOT: This is no time for your jealousy! What is done is done. I am leaving on a dangerous quest. I may never come back alive.

GUINEVERE: Don't try to cheer me up.

LANCELOT: You know my love for you is my deepest devotion.

GUINEVERE: Yet you're leaving me for some silly quest?

LANCELOT: I must do this. I have a son. I have to go with him. Surely you understand!

GUINEVERE: I wish I did. Arthur desires a son. I can see it in his eyes. But I cannot give him one.

LANCELOT: That is why I must seek the Grail. In it is the secret of everlasting life.

GUINEVERE: Then you must go—for Arthur's sake.

NARRATOR: In a week's time the Grail-questers rode out. Arthur sadly watched them depart, his queen at his side.

ARTHUR: I do not like this. So many knights are leaving.

GUINEVERE: I feel that many of them will not return.

NARRATOR: The questers dispersed. Lancelot and Galahad rode far into the wilderness and met with many adventures.
   One day, in the midst of a deep forest, they found an abandoned chapel.

LANCELOT: We should stay here tonight. It would make a nice shelter.

GALAHAD: Yes, it is a chapel. We should pray for success on our quest.

LANCELOT: Oh yes. That, too.

NARRATOR: Galahad knelt down at the front of the church and prayed fervently. Lancelot watched his son in wonder.

LANCELOT: (*to himself*) Can this boy really be my son?

NARRATOR: He went forward and knelt down by his son. Suddenly, Galahad's youthful eyes looked heavenward—filled with light.

GALAHAD: (*in awe*) Father! Look! There it is again! The Cup of Christ! Do you see it?

NARRATOR: Lancelot looked frantically into the empty air.

LANCELOT: No, my son. I do not!

GALAHAD: It is there before us—covered in the same immaculate cloth.

LANCELOT: Why can I not see it?

NARRATOR: Then Lancelot heard a voice speak in his mind.

VOICE: (*heavenly voice*) Lancelot, your love for Guinevere and the deception of King Arthur has tainted you. Your sin with the queen has made you weak. Renounce it. Or it will doom you to failure.

NARRATOR: Lancelot's eyes filled with tears.

LANCELOT: I repent of it all! I renounce my love! Show me the cup!

NARRATOR: Then the Grail appeared to him in all its glory.

LANCELOT: I see it! I see it!

VOICE: Lancelot, this will be your last glimpse of the holy cup. You renounce the queen with your lying lips, but in your heart you cannot give her up. If you continue on this quest, you will fail.

NARRATOR: The vision faded, and Lancelot began to weep.

GALAHAD: What is it, Father?

LANCELOT: Nothing. Nothing.

NARRATOR: The next morning, Lancelot awoke to see Galahad staring out the chapel doorway.

GALAHAD: Look!

NARRATOR: A white knight upon a white horse stood at the edge of the forest. His armor and cape glistened with a strange intensity. He lifted his hand in a gesture of beckoning.

LANCELOT: (*breathlessly*) Who is that?

GALAHAD: I have watched this knight all morning. I feel he is not of this world. He summons me.

LANCELOT: Here we must part ways, son. This is your quest. I have never before failed in a quest, but this one is too much for me.

NARRATOR: Galahad took his father's hand warmly.

GALAHAD: Thank you for coming with me this far, Father.

LANCELOT: I am sorry that I was never there for you—all these years.

GALAHAD: It happened as it was meant to happen. Goodbye, Father.

NARRATOR: The young knight mounted his steed and rode off in pursuit of the white knight.

Galahad found a path that led through the hills, but never again did he catch sight of the white knight. In a valley, he came upon a monastery. The white-clad monks stood within the graveyard.

MONK: Greetings, knight. Have you come to try to claim the sacred shield?

GALAHAD: Holy fathers, what do you mean?

MONK: We monks are the guardians of a holy shield. Many knights have come here and tried to claim it, but their souls were impure. They paid with their lives, and their bodies are laid here in this graveyard.

NARRATOR: A chilling voice suddenly appeared in the air—an evil voice.

SPIRIT: *(evil laughter)* Why try, foolish knight? You will fail like all the rest! No one is holy. No one is pure enough to claim the shield.

NARRATOR: The monks cowered in fright and hurriedly crossed themselves.

GALAHAD: What is that voice?

MONK: It is an evil spirit that torments us. See that large slab of stone there? It is a grave, and an evil voice speaks from it. Any who venture near it lose their wits permanently.

GALAHAD: Who is the voice?

MONK: It is the voice of the Enemy.

GALAHAD: Then let us be rid of it.

NARRATOR: Galahad dismounted and walked boldly toward the gravestone. Disturbing, arcane symbols had been crudely carved into it.

GALAHAD: Come forth, evil one! Go and torment these holy men no longer. I am a pure knight, and I will face you.

SPIRIT: You were a fool to come upon this "holy" quest. Every devil from the Underworld has been unleashed upon the earth. You will fail, and we will feast upon your soul!

NARRATOR: A black shadow rose from the cursed stone—one transparent and solid at the same time.

SPIRIT: *(hissing)* Argh!

NARRATOR: The shadow struck at Galahad, but the knight sliced through it with his sword.

SPIRIT: *(shrieking)* No!

NARRATOR: The shadow shrieked and disappeared. Galahad pushed the slab from the grave. Below lay the twisted remains of a foul knight.

GALAHAD: Remove this evil body from your graveyard, and you will have no more problems.

MONK: Truly, you are the only one worthy enough to claim our sacred shield!

NARRATOR: The monks presented him with a masterfully built shield, white with a blood-red cross in its midst.

GALAHAD: I thank you.

MONK: There is a castle not far from here called the Castle of Maidens. Seven deadly knights protect it, and they abduct all damsels who ride by their castle and kill any knights who try to save them. Perhaps you could help those unfortunate maidens.

GALAHAD: With God's help I will. Thank you, holy fathers.

NARRATOR: As Galahad rode away, the monks saw a white knight riding at his side.

MONK: See? The very angels ride beside this young one.

NARRATOR: Galahad continued through the forest. As he entered a clearing, he saw a strange sight.

PERCEVAL: *(yelling)* Help! Help!

NARRATOR: Sir Perceval was fleeing from a mounted knight clad in spiked armor, who slashed at him with his curved sword.

GALAHAD: *(shouting)* Halt, fiend!

NARRATOR: The enemy knight drew up, and Galahad charged at him. Galahad drove his sword into the side of the knight's helmet. *(evil shriek)* The knight and his horse dissolved into smoke.

PERCEVAL: *(out of breath)* Lord of mercy! I never fought an opponent like that before! Thank you, Sir Galahad! Thank you!

GALAHAD: Don't thank me! Thank Heaven! That was no knight of flesh and blood. Where did he come from?

PERCEVAL: Well, along the road, there was this beautifully carved throne and on its seat a sparkly, jeweled crown. I don't know why, but I saw that crown, and I just had to have it.

GALAHAD: It was a test of your greed.

PERCEVAL: Apparently. When I picked up the crown, a great crack opened in the ground, and this devil-knight rose from it. He slayed my horse beneath me and was about to slay me when you arrived. I have learned my lesson—don't pick up strange treasures just lying around. I just wish I could have learned my lesson without losing my horse!

GALAHAD: I am journeying to the Castle of Maidens to free them from seven deadly knights.

PERCEVAL: Then I wish you well. I must find a steed and continue my quest.

GALAHAD: Watch for the Enemy! His servants are everywhere! They can take any shape they please. Be careful! God speed!

NARRATOR: Galahad rode away, and Perceval continued along the dusky forest road. Walking in full armor soon tired him.

PERCEVAL: *(tiredly)* I can't take much more of this!

DUESSA: I've never seen a knight without a horse before.

PERCEVAL: Huh?

NARRATOR: Perceval had not seen her through the gloom, but a maiden was sitting upon a stump by the side of the road. Perceval eyed her suspiciously. She looked harmless enough.

PERCEVAL: Oh hello.

DUESSA: You need a horse? I have one. He's tied up on the other side of these trees. I could give him to you—if you'd like.

PERCEVAL: That would be wonderful! I am a knight of the Round Table, and we are on a quest for the Holy Grail.

DUESSA: How exciting! Well, I will fetch my horse.

NARRATOR: She disappeared into the trees and returned with a large, coal-black charger.

PERCEVAL: That is your horse? That's a big horse for a damsel, isn't it?

DUESSA: I like a horse with some power.

PERCEVAL: I thank you!

NARRATOR: Perceval reached forward to take the reins from her, but she pulled back.

DUESSA: If I give you this horse, you must promise me something in return.

PERCEVAL: *(tiredly)* Anything! I am just so weary of walking!

DUESSA: You must promise to serve me—you know, as a knight serves a lady.

PERCEVAL: Yes, I will serve you. Yes.

DUESSA: Lovely. Enjoy your steed.

NARRATOR: She placed the reins into his hands. The weary knight pulled himself onto the back of the steed.

DUESSA: *(evilly)* Oh, I should tell you one more thing, you foolish boy. That is no normal steed! It is a steed bred in Hades, and it will carry you there now!

PERCEVAL: What?

NARRATOR: The horse's eyes flamed red, and it reared on its powerful haunches. *(neighing)* Then with a hellish neigh it took off. *(hoofbeats)*

PERCEVAL: *(screaming)* Ah! No!

NARRATOR: Perceval tried to roll from the saddle but could not. He was somehow stuck to it. The horse increased its speed. *(neighing)*

PERCEVAL: *(yelling)* Stupid! That was no maiden! It was a devil temptress! And I promised to serve her!

NARRATOR: A pair of leathery wings sprouted from the horse's side, and it took to the air. *(whoosh)*

PERCEVAL: Ah!

NARRATOR: The horse soared high into the sky, and then to Perceval's horror, it plunged downward. He heard the devil damsel's voice hissing in his ears.

DUESSA: Time to die, foolish knight! I am going to plunge you into the sea! Go to a watery grave!

NARRATOR: Black water rushed up toward Perceval and his hell-horse. In preparation for death, he made the sign of the cross across his chest. *(evil shriek)*

DUESSA: No!

NARRATOR: Flames erupted in all directions, and Perceval fell free from the saddle. Then he knew nothing more.

Perceval's mind swam in a sea of frightful dreams. Out of the darkness two women approached him. Neither one of them had a face. One rode upon the back of a lion and spoke sweetly. The other rode upon the back of a snake and spoke harshly.

LUCIFERA: *(harshly)* Twice you have thwarted my plans, you piece of scum. Only luck has saved you!

UNA: *(sweetly)* Luck has nothing to do with it. This knight had survived because he is a holy knight.

LUCIFERA: *Wholly* stupid. He's fallen for two of my traps. He took the crown. He took the horse. Tomorrow he will be mine!

UNA: Knight, do not listen to her poisonous words. I come here tonight to tell you to beware. Tomorrow you will face the most dreaded warrior of this world—one called Sansfoy. You will meet this champion in battle, and if you fail, you may lose your soul.

LUCIFERA: *(mockingly)* Yes, so be on your guard, sweetcakes. I will still feast upon your flesh!

NARRATOR: Perceval awoke. He was in a strange place—a rocky island, surrounded on all sides by boundless water. Bizarre creatures—tiny winged serpents—covered the ground and filled the air. *(growling)* Perceval jumped when he noticed a white lion on the hillside above him, crouched and ready to spring.

PERCEVAL: Ah!

NARRATOR: Perceval drew his sword, and the lion sprang. *(roar of a lion)* But instead of landing on him, the lion fell upon an enormous serpent that had been lying nearby—only inches from the knight. The lion and the serpent fought fiercely. *(hissing and roaring)* The snake rose into the air and breathed out fire, repelling the lion. Perceval backed away, watching the fight helplessly.

PERCEVAL: I never saw anything like this! I must do something!

NARRATOR: Perceval drew his sword and hacked the serpent in two. As its severed body fell helplessly to the ground, he heard a strange voice escape it.

LUCIFERA: Curse you...

NARRATOR: The lion sniffed at the corpse of its enemy and then came forward and laid its head in Perceval's lap. The knight hesitantly stroked its fur and surveyed the island once again. Land was not visible in any direction.

PERCEVAL: The dream told me that I would face the most dreaded champion in the world, but how? There is sure no way off this island that I see.

NARRATOR: The day passed, and finally Perceval spied a black speck on the horizon. As it drew closer, he saw it was a richly decorated barge. He waved his arms frantically in the air, and the barge pulled in closely.

PERCEVAL: Help! Help!

NARRATOR: A servant aboard the barge pulled out a gangplank and laid it across to the island.

PERCEVAL: Whose ship is this?

NARRATOR: But the servants did not reply.

PERCEVAL: I am Sir Perceval, and this lion here—

NARRATOR: He turned. The lion had vanished. The servants upon the barge beckoned for him to come aboard. Glancing over his shoulder for one last glimpse of the lion, Perceval complied.

PERCEVAL: Where did it go? Farewell, my friend.

NARRATOR: A large silken tent had been pitched in the center of the barge, and he smelled exotic food within it.

PERCEVAL: My, my! That sure smells good. Now that I think about it, I can't remember the last time I ate!

NARRATOR: A beautiful woman's face appeared from within the tent.

FIDESSA: Greetings, good sir knight! I am the mistress of this ship. My servants said you have been stranded on this island.

PERCEVAL: I'm afraid so. Can I get passage back to the mainland?

FIDESSA: Of course! Come aboard. Come aboard! Knights of the Round Table are always welcome here.

PERCEVAL: How did—?

FIDESSA: I can tell you are a Knight of the Round Table because you are so handsome. Tee hee.

PERCEVAL: Why thank you, ma'am.

NARRATOR: The regal lady invited him into her tent, and her servants seated him upon comfortable cushions and poured him wine.

PERCEVAL: No thanks! I am on a quest.

FIDESSA: Please. I insist. I will not take no for an answer! Drink. You will not find a finer wine.

PERCEVAL: Well, maybe just a little.

NARRATOR: Perceval gulped down the tasty wine. Only then did he notice the woman's beauty.

PERCEVAL: What is a beautiful lady like you doing on a sea like this?

FIDESSA: Oh, you are too kind. But please. It is a long journey back to the mainland. At least loosen your armor for the ride. Make yourself comfortable.

PERCEVAL: Well, it does get awfully heavy.

FIDESSA: Servants, pour this brave knight more wine.

PERCEVAL: You know, I was told I would face my greatest adversary today. He's a villain named Sansfoy.

FIDESSA: Oh my! That name means "without faith." He must be a monster indeed! You should rest then. Here. Lie down.

NARRATOR: Something in the wine had muddled Perceval's head, and he felt woozy. The beautiful woman reclined beside him upon the couch.

PERCEVAL: I say, you must be the fairest maiden I have ever seen. You must let me have a kiss! My mother always told me to take a kiss from a maiden when it was available.

FIDESSA: Oh, sir! I could not! That would not be proper.

PERCEVAL: Just one kiss!

FIDESSA: Oh no, no, no!

NARRATOR: The damsel expertly dodged Perceval's advances, teasing him until he was at the point of madness.

FIDESSA: Oh, I can't, Sir Perceval. But I must admit that from the first moment I saw you, I wanted to possess you as my own.

PERCEVAL: Possess me? That's kind of a funny way of saying it.

FIDESSA: *(strangely)* Is it? I will be yours—only if you swear to serve no one but me and to be at my command and no other's. Then we will be together for eternity.

PERCEVAL: Anything! I must have you for my love!

FIDESSA: *(strangely)* Then swear it!

PERCEVAL: I swear…

NARRATOR: Driven into such a passion, Perceval was at the point of swearing this vow, but his eyes happened to catch sight of his sword hilt, sticking up from his gear. Its handle and pommel formed a cross, and suddenly his mind cleared.

PERCEVAL: No! No, I will not!

NARRATOR: A fire sprang up in the damsel's eyes.

FIDESSA: *(monster voice)* What?

NARRATOR: The damsel clamped the knight with her strong arms.

FIDESSA: Fool! Swear it! I lost you twice, and I will not lose you again!

PERCEVAL: Never!

FIDESSA: Then you shall die.

NARRATOR: In an instant the beautiful damsel transformed. Her gown lengthened into an enormous tail, her fingernails grew out to horrible claws, and her sweet lips revealed rows of razor-sharp teeth.

PERCEVAL: Ah! *(cry of fright)*

NARRATOR: Before the knight could react, the demon-damsel encircled him with her serpentine tail. Perceval struggled to free his arms, pinned at his side.

FIDESSA: Struggle all you want. You are mine forever.

NARRATOR: The monster opened its mouth and spewed forth black filth. *(sliming sounds)* The filth was filled with the squirming bodies of toads and snakes.

Perceval felt his soul weakening, succumbing to the hideous power.

PERCEVAL: Heaven help me!

NARRATOR: It was then that he ripped his arm free, and with it he formed the sign of the cross in the monster's face. She shrieked.

FIDESSA: *(shrieking)* No!

NARRATOR: Perceval felt himself falling, and he hit sandy ground. The ship had vanished. He was now lying upon a beach. The damsel's ship was quickly skimming away over the horizon.

PERCEVAL: *(breathlessly)* Thank heaven I am safe! I did face my greatest adversary today.

NARRATOR: When Perceval finally rose, a knight was riding up the sea-shore. It was Sir Bors. He hailed Perceval as he drew closer.

BORS: Perceval, I am glad to see you alive! You would not believe the trials I have endured upon this quest!

PERCEVAL: Oh, I would.

BORS: I tried to save six damsels that I saw imprisoned on a high cliff. But when I made my way up to their perch, they begged me to be their lover. In fact, they threatened to throw themselves from the cliff if I did not.

PERCEVAL: I hope you kept your virtue intact.

BORS: Of course! They cried and wailed, but I would not give into them. Then they jumped to their deaths. Or so it seemed!

Before they hit the ground, they sprouted leathery wings and flew away.

PERCEVAL: Devils! Probably some of the same who attacked me.

BORS: I could tell you many more stories of the same. Have you seen any of the other knights? Gawain rode with me for a time, but then we parted ways.

PERCEVAL: I have seen Galahad, but he was traveling to the Castle of Maidens. *(pause)* Wait. There he is!

NARRATOR: Galahad appeared from the woods. He hailed them.

PERCEVAL: Galahad, did you rescue the damsels from the seven deadly knights? Or is that a stupid question?

GALAHAD: I did—through the power of Heaven. How did you fare?

PERCEVAL: Not as well. I am alive—barely. But I can say that I am wiser.

GALAHAD: The Enemy has laid countless snares. I fear many of Arthur's knights will be destroyed.

NARRATOR: A mist had covered the water that lay before the knights, and just then a barge appeared from the fog. Standing upon its bow was beautiful maiden.

PERCEVAL: Oh, no! Not again! I'm never going to trust a damsel on a boat as long as I live!

UNA: *(musical laugh)* Peace, good sir knight! Do you not recognize us?

NARRATOR: A white lion appeared at her side.

PERCEVAL: The lion! And you are from my dream!

UNA: Yes, I am the Grail damsel. I know the tests that all you knights have endured. You have faced many devils and found yourselves triumphant. You have earned the right to come aboard this blessed vessel and see the Holy Grail face to face. Across these waters lies the Grail Castle.

NARRATOR: A distant castle could be made out through the mists.

PERCEVAL: Wait a minute. That castle was not there before.

UNA: *(laugh)* And it will not be there afterward. It is a spiritual place. There you shall accomplish your quest. The Maimed King will be healed of his wounds, and his realm will be made whole. Will you come aboard?

GALAHAD: Blessed damsel, I will!

UNA: First, I must warn you. Only proceed if you wish to never see this earth again. For many who see the Grail unveiled, wish to never return to this mortal world.

NARRATOR: She looked into each of the knights' faces intently. Bors and Galahad nodded solemnly. But Perceval hung his head.

PERCEVAL: Three times I was tested. And three times I failed. I am not like Galahad here, who is a perfect knight. I am a failure.

UNA: *(musical laugh)* You did not fail, Perceval. You were tempted—to be sure. But you endured through the grace of Heaven. You are all welcome aboard this holy ship! It was carved by King Solomon of old. Now it will bear you to your destiny.

NARRATOR: The three knights boarded the ship.

As the barge was lost within the mist, a lone watcher viewed its departure from a high hill. It was Lancelot—catching one last glimpse of his son.

LANCELOT: Farewell, my son.

NARRATOR: In the end many knights perished upon the Quest of the Holy Grail. Only a few returned to Camelot, and those who did were lesser men. The holy hermit had been right. The Grail had weakened or destroyed those who were unworthy.

Much later a lone knight rode into Camelot. It was Sir Bors. Many pressed him for details about his journey, but he could not describe the many miracles that occurred on the mystical voyage to the Grail Castle. All he could say is that they had seen the blessed cup unveiled.

ARTHUR: Where is the Holy Grail?

BORS: Gone from this world forever.

LANCELOT: Where is Galahad?

BORS: After many adventures a shining hand came from Heaven to take the Holy Grail back to its master. There was a blinding flash of light. And when it cleared, Galahad and Perceval were gone as well. You see, they could not stand to be parted from the Grail—and were taken with it.

ARTHUR: *(breathlessly)* Taken into Heaven?

NARRATOR: Bors nodded.

LANCELOT: Then the holy hermit was right. The Grail did give everlasting life. But what they have gained in Heaven, we have lost here on earth.

BORS: Only I was left behind to bear back the tale of Britain's two holiest knights, Perceval and Galahad.

NARRATOR: They sat in silence for some time—the gravity of their loss pressing upon them.

ARTHUR: I wish this quest had never come to us. Our fellowship of the Round Table is nearly broken. So many knights have perished.

NARRATOR: Mordred, who had been watching with a smirk, stepped forward.

MORDRED: Do not worry, Arthur. Camelot will rise again—stronger than ever before. I am sure of it.

ARTHUR: *(sadly)* I hope you are right, Mordred. I hope you are right.

NARRATOR: As the Quest of the Holy Grail ended so began Camelot's darkest days.

DISCUSSION QUESTIONS

1. What makes the Quest of the Holy Grail more dangerous than a typical quest?
2. What does it take to be successful on the Quest of the Holy Grail?
3. What were the supernatural elements of the Grail quest?
4. Why does Lancelot fail on the quest?
5. What makes Galahad successful?
6. What makes Perceval successful?
7. How did the Quest of the Holy Grail actually weaken Camelot?
8. How are the challenges of a spiritual quest different from those of a physical quest?

THE TRIAL OF GUINEVERE
TEACHER GUIDE

BACKGROUND

Arthur's kingdom seems as strong as Camelot's walls, but his enemies discover a crack in his fortress—the trust he places in those he loves. Although Guinevere and Lancelot believe that their affair will harm no one as long as it stays secret, they fail to see the potential it has for ruining Arthur and his kingdom. When the truth is revealed, Arthur finds himself in a dreadful position—does he uphold the laws of the land, or does he spare those that he loves?

It is in this chapter of his story that Arthur's triumphs turn to tragedy, and his legacy is truly tested. It seems that Mordred, the embodiment of evil, will inherit Camelot and pervert it to his own will. Lancelot, once a loyal knight, becomes an enemy. The civil war among those loyal to Arthur and those loyal to Lancelot fractures the bonds among the Knights of the Round Table. It seems that Britain's only hope is if Arthur can recover from a broken kingdom—and a broken heart—and lead his people once again.

SUMMARY

Following the Quest of the Holy Grail, a cloud of gloom settles over Camelot, and Arthur feels a great spiritual weight has been placed upon him. Sir Mordred, Arthur's illegitimate son, grows in power among the court and replaces many of the knights who died during the Grail quest with knights who share his evil passions.

Although Lancelot's previous failure on the Grail quest caused him to swear off his love for Guinevere, he decides to resume their affair. Mordred and Sir Agravaine hatch a scheme to expose the affair to Arthur. Almost all of Arthur's court knows of Lancelot and Guinevere's affair, but none of them wants to cause grief to the king. Agravaine finally brings these accusations to Arthur, who merely laughs them off. Mordred suggests that Arthur leave Camelot temporarily to see if Lancelot and Guinevere will take the opportunity to meet together. This plan is put into motion, and the knights discover Lancelot and the queen in each other's company. When the knights try to arrest Lancelot, he battles his way out of Camelot, killing Agravaine in the process.

Arthur, devastated and despondent, hands the prosecution of Guinevere over to Mordred, who declares she must be burned at the stake for her treachery. As Guinevere's sentence is about to be carried out, Lancelot returns with a group of allies and rescues the queen. In the confusion Lancelot kills several innocent knights—including Gaheris and Gareth, the brothers of Gawain. Gawain, once Lancelot's friend, becomes his enemy and vows revenge.

Mordred advises Arthur to ride after Lancelot and Guinevere, who have escaped to the knight's castle, Joyous Guard, while he stays behind and protects Camelot. Arthur blindly agrees.

Arthur's army surrounds Lancelot's castle. Lancelot begs for peace, but Arthur will not consent. Their armies fight a bloody battle. Amid the carnage, Lancelot has an opportunity to slay Arthur, but he spares the king. The night following the battle, Guinevere realizes that Camelot will fall unless she returns to Arthur. Lancelot returns Guinevere to her husband, and Arthur swears to spare her life. But Gawain will not forget his grudge against Lancelot and challenges him to a duel. Lancelot reluctantly accepts and wounds Gawain many times—but finally spares his life. Gawain later dies of his wounds, realizing that it was his own lust for revenge that killed him and asks others to bear his forgiveness to Lancelot. Arthur heads back toward Camelot.

ESSENTIAL QUESTIONS

- How can our actions have far-reaching consequences?
- What happens when we betray the trust of a loved one?

ANTICIPATORY QUESTIONS

- How could Mordred attempt to bring down Camelot?
- Who are Gaheris and Gareth?
- What would King Arthur do if he learned about Lancelot and Guinevere's affair?

CHARACTER QUEST

Consequences Lancelot and Guinevere are both unfaithful to Arthur, and they believe their actions will not harm anyone since they are secret. When their betrayal is found out, its impact is far-reaching—harming Arthur, innocent parties such as Gaheris and Gareth, and Camelot itself. Although Lancelot and Guinevere try to repair the damage they have done, they cannot. The fellowship of the Round Table is broken because of their actions. How can secret betrayal still become hurtful? Why is it important for us to consider the consequences of our actions *before* we act? When our actions will harm others, why should we reconsider them?

CONNECT

The Once and Future King **by T.H. White** This novel is the definitive modern adaptation of the King Arthur legends. The latter portion of the book focuses on the relationship between Lancelot and Guinevere and their part in the destruction of Camelot.

TEACHABLE TERMS

- **Dramatic Irony** The readers of this story know that Mordred is King Arthur's illegitimate son, who has secret plans to bring down his kingdom, but the other characters do not. Examine how this creates tension in the story.
- **Metaphor** On pg. 222 the story says, "Arthur's face had become a blank stone."
- **Symbol** On pg. 227 Lancelot tells Guinevere the history of his castle Joyous Guard, which was once Dolorous Guard. Once it was cursed, but he thought he lifted the curse from it. Then he compares it to his relationship with Guinevere, which he feels is also cursed.
- **Ambiguity** The word *trial* in the title of this play can mean a trial where a person is tried for a crime, or it can mean a trial or struggle that a person undergoes.

RECALL QUESTIONS

1. Who fights his way out of Camelot?
2. How will Mordred execute Guinevere?
3. Which innocent victims are killed during Lancelot's rescue of Guinevere?
4. What character duels with Lancelot?
5. What news does Arthur receive from Camelot at the end of the story?

THE TRIAL OF GUINEVERE

CAST

ARTHUR	*King of Britain*
GUINEVERE	*Queen of Britain*
LANCELOT	*Arthur's Best Knight*
GAWAIN	*Knight of Arthur*
AGRAVAINE	*Brother of Gawain*
GARETH	*Brother of Gawain*
MORDRED	*Secret Son of Arthur*
KAY	*Arthur's Foster-Brother*
BORS	*Knight, Nephew of Lancelot*

NARRATOR: A cloud of gloom had settled upon Camelot. Losses on the Quest of the Holy Grail had reduced the fellowship of the Round Table to a ghost of its former glory. Worst of all, the fire seemed to be going out of King Arthur. He was growing visibly older—weaker—as if his life was being slowly sapped by an invisible force.

In the absence of the other knights, Mordred, the snarky, young knight of the SeaCastle, had become Arthur's right arm.

MORDRED: These empty seats at the Round Table are just depressing! I have spoken to many knights who are eager to fill them.

LANCELOT: Do you mean that pack of rogues that you associate with? They have no faith! No allegiance!

MORDRED: Easy, old man. No need to be testy. I was merely thinking of Camelot's safety. But apparently that is not a concern of yours.

ARTHUR: *(in a daze)* Mordred is right. The Round Table must endure. And in order for it to do so, new knights must join our cause.

MORDRED: Well said, your majesty.

NARRATOR: A look of pain crossed the king's face, and he held his forehead with a shaking hand.

ARTHUR: *(weakly)* But I cannot be the one to choose them. A great weight has been placed upon me—upon my soul. Mordred, would you take on this task? You know this next generation of knights better than we do.

MORDRED: I humbly accept this honor, sire.

LANCELOT: *(shocked)* Arthur! Why Mordred? Why not choose a noble young knight like Sir Gareth for this task?

ARTHUR: Mordred is loyal. He stayed by my side during the Quest of the Holy Grail.

LANCELOT: Just because he was too cowardly to come with the rest of us! Should a recreant knight be the one to choose who sits at the Round Table?

MORDRED: Call me a coward if you want to. All you fools risked your life for that ridiculous cup—part of God's dish set apparently. And what good did it do? Half of you died and the other half came back Grail-less! *(chuckle)* It's actually kind of funny when you think about it.

LANCELOT: Watch your tongue!

MORDRED: *(angrily)* Why don't you make me, gramps!

ARTHUR: Enough! Mordred will oversee the addition of new knights to the Round Table, and that is final.

NARRATOR: Lancelot stood, still defiant, and exited the hall. For months, as he watched the king deteriorate, Lancelot had suffered, too. Ever since the Quest of the Holy Grail, he had avoided the presence of Queen Guinevere. His love for her had been the cause of his failure on that quest, and he had made a covenant with his heart that the queen would not weaken him again. But returning to this dark version of Camelot had shaken his resolve.

LANCELOT: *(to himself)* Camelot is a different place. Arthur has changed, too. I have no one left now but…

NARRATOR: Without another word Lancelot made his way up to the queen's chambers.

GUINEVERE: *(shocked)* Lancelot!

LANCELOT: I know you are surprised to see me here. I came to speak to you—and to apologize.

GUINEVERE: *(angrily)* You should! Why have you avoided me these many months?

LANCELOT: Because of my failure. I could not achieve the Grail because of…us.

GUINEVERE: *(sarcastically)* So you gave up our love because it was interfering with *your* work?

LANCELOT: I've lost so much. I lost my only son. And now it seems that I have lost my king.

GUINEVERE: Yes. He is quite a changed person.

LANCELOT: All I have left is you. But you are the wife of a man I made a promise to serve—a man who is my friend.

GUINEVERE: *(sadly)* I made a promise to him as well.

LANCELOT: But didn't we make an oath to each other—one of love? Deep down I know that is the oath I cannot bear to break.

NARRATOR: Guinevere rushed into her champion's arms.

GUINEVERE: *(sadly)* I'm a cruel woman to give you harsh words after all that you have endured.

LANCELOT: Let us ride away together.

GUINEVERE: Where would we go?

LANCELOT: To my castle, Joyous Guard.

GUINEVERE: And all of Britain would pursue us there!

LANCELOT: Then we will go to France—the land of my ancestors.

GUINEVERE: Even France is not far enough. No matter where we go we will never be free! These are only dreams, Lancelot. Besides, you and I both know that we could never abandon Arthur.

LANCELOT: Then we shall stay here. But at least do not deny me your love.

GUINEVERE: We cannot be together. Love like ours would not stay a secret for long.

LANCELOT: I don't care who knows!

GUINEVERE: We aren't just common people, Lancelot. Our love is treason against the king.

LANCELOT: Who will accuse us? If anyone speaks against us, I will challenge him and deal him his death.

GUINEVERE: *(laugh)* What will you do? Kill all of Camelot to keep our love a secret?

LANCELOT: I would do anything to be with you.

GUINEVERE: Oh, Lancelot.

NARRATOR: As the knight and his lady continued their secret conversation, a stealthy eye watched them through a chink in the door. The eye belonged to Sir Agravaine of Orkney, the slightly dimwitted brother of Gawain, Gaheris, and Gareth. When the spying knight had seen enough, he slipped away and reported this news to Mordred.

AGRAVAINE: Sir Mordred, I followed Lancelot just as you said. He went into the queen's chambers. What do you think they're doing in there?

MORDRED: *(sarcastically)* Playing chess. They're handing me Camelot's doom on a platter—that's what they're doing. Ha! It's too good to be true! The queen and Arthur's most trusted knight cozying up to each other! *(evil laugh)*

AGRAVAINE: *(laughing)* That's good for me, too, right?

MORDRED: Of course. King Arthur killed your father, King Lot, remember? And that makes you very mad, right?

AGRAVAINE: Oh yeah! That *does* make me mad!

MORDRED: Your brothers call you a fool, Agravaine—and rightly so—but you are the only one in your family smart enough to see Arthur for what he truly is—a murderer.

AGRAVAINE: I'm confused about one thing.

MORDRED: *(sarcastically)* Just one?

AGRAVAINE: What does all this have to do with Lancelot and the queen?

MORDRED: Well, dung-for-brains, we're going to bring this affair to Arthur's attention, and then he will have to choose. Will he execute his best knight and the woman he loves for treason? Or will he spare them and lose all credibility?

AGRAVAINE: Ooh. That's a tough choice.

MORDRED: Exactly. And either way he chooses, it will bring him to his knees.

AGRAVAINE: What's wrong with his knees?

MORDRED: Nothing, you moron. It's a figure of speech.

AGRAVAINE: Let's go tell the king about Lancelot and Guinevere right now!

MORDRED: Patience, my fatheaded friend. We must let Lancelot think he is safe, and then he will grow careless. Soon all of Camelot will know of Lancelot and the queen's affair, and *then* we will strike.

NARRATOR: Mordred bade his time. Meanwhile, Lancelot and Guinevere renewed their secret affair—much more boldly than before. As Mordred predicted, Lancelot and Guinevere's actions grew so reckless that soon much of the court knew about the affair. Yet out of love for Lancelot and the king, no one dared share this information. Mordred perceived that the time was right.

One day, after Arthur had returned from a hunt, Agravaine was admitted to speak before the king and a group of his closest knights.

AGRAVAINE: (*awkwardly*) Sire, I have an urgent matter to discuss with you!

ARTHUR: Mordred, could you deal with this? I have a splitting headache.

NARRATOR: Agravaine faltered for a moment, but Mordred motioned for him to continue.

AGRAVAINE: This is a matter that concerns you—personally.

ARTHUR: Fine. Speak.

AGRAVAINE: I was just passing by the queen's chamber, and I saw a knight leaving it.

GAWAIN: (*angrily*) Brother! Don't trouble the king with this idle gossip!

ARTHUR: A knight? In Guinevere's chambers? That's odd. Who was it?

AGRAVAINE: It was Sir Lancelot.

MORDRED: Hmmm. Now why would Lancelot be in Guinevere's chambers?

NARRATOR: Arthur waved a feeble hand.

ARTHUR: I'm sure there is some reason for Lancelot being there. Perhaps the queen was frightened by a mouse, and Lancelot heard her screams.

AGRAVAINE: But the situation had the look of in—in—in…

MORDRED: Indecency?

AGRAVAINE: Yeah! That's it.

GAWAIN: How dare you! You are speaking of the queen and one of Camelot's greatest knights!

AGRAVAINE: I saw it! I did!

GAWAIN: Be gone, brother, before I strike you!

AGRAVAINE: I will not! I saw Lancelot with the queen!

ARTHUR: This is preposterous! (*pause*) What do you say, Mordred?

MORDRED: The whole thing is ridiculous! Agravaine is obviously an idiot—and apparently a liar to boot. *(to Agravaine)* You're lying! Admit it!

NARRATOR: Mordred rose and advanced upon Agravaine. For a second, the dimwitted knight feared he had been betrayed.

AGRAVAINE: *(defensively)* It is not a lie! Everybody knows about it!

MORDRED: *(skeptically)* Do they? Ha! Fine. Let's just ask Sir Gawain. Gawain, how long have you served King Arthur?

GAWAIN: Almost all my life. But I...

MORDRED: Gawain, by your oath as a holy knight, have you ever heard a ridiculous rumor of an affair between Lancelot and Guinevere?

NARRATOR: Gawain looked stunned.

GAWAIN: *(slowly)* I cannot answer. I cannot betray my friend. Lancelot once saved my life.

ARTHUR: *(in shock)* Gawain?

MORDRED: *(fake shock)* What? Are you in this plot, too? What about you, Sir Kay? You are always good for a bit of cruel gossip! What have you heard?

NARRATOR: Mordred turned to the king's foster-brother and seneschal.

KAY: *(quietly)* Some words should never be spoken.

ARTHUR: *(numbly)* I can't believe this.

MORDRED: *(gasp)* A secret kept from the king by his closest knights? Please tell us there is not more to this scandal! *(pause)* I said, please tell us there is not more!

NARRATOR: Mordred kicked Agravaine roughly.

AGRAVAINE: Ouch! Oh yeah! Sire, Lancelot and Guinevere always meet when you are gone hunting. I think if you were to leave but then return suddenly, you would find that what I say is true!

ARTHUR: It can't be true! It can't! What do you say, Mordred?

NARRATOR: Mordred bit his lip in false sadness.

MORDRED: Sire, it pains me to think of Lancelot and Guinevere *trampling* on their vows of loyalty to you, but perhaps it would be best to put this rumor to the test. You should ride away and allow *me* to investigate. I'm sure I will find nothing, but at least it will give you some peace.

ARTHUR: You speak wise words, Mordred! The sooner this rumor is put to rest, the better! I return to the hunt!

MORDRED: *(to himself)* And so do I.

NARRATOR: After the king had departed, the loyal knights turned angrily on Mordred.

GAWAIN: What kind of game are you playing, you little weasel?

MORDRED: Me? I'm not the one who has kept such a juicy secret from the king!

GAWAIN: We kept it because we knew it would destroy Camelot!

NARRATOR: Mordred sneered at Gawain.

MORDRED: Why fear the truth? Is it dishonorable to expose a crime? You protect Lancelot because he is your friend, but to me he is just another criminal.

GAWAIN: *You* are the criminal. You may have fooled the king but not the rest of us!

MORDRED: Fine! Then challenge me! Defeat me! Prove that I am evil. But be warned—I have the strength of ten men.

NARRATOR: None of the knights moved to challenge him.

MORDRED: That's what I thought. Now if you'll excuse me, I have a pair of traitors to catch.

NARRATOR: As King Arthur departed Camelot, Lancelot and Guinevere took the opportunity to meet together in the queen's chambers once again.

GUINEVERE: I hate all this sneaking around, but at least we get to be together.

(*knocking on the door*)

MORDRED: (*through the door*) Knock, knock.

GUINEVERE: (*gasp*) Someone knocks. (*loudly*) Who's there?

MORDRED: Justice!

AGRAVAINE: Justice who?

MORDRED: Shut up, you fool!

GUINEVERE: (*in shock*) Lancelot! They've found us out! We'll be convicted of treason!

NARRATOR: Lancelot drew his sword. (*shing*)

LANCELOT: We'll fight our way out!

MORDRED: Open up—in the name of the king!

GUINEVERE: You have no armor! You must leave me behind. If you try to take me with you, you will never make it!

NARRATOR: Lancelot knew that Guinevere spoke the truth.

LANCELOT: I cannot leave you!

GUINEVERE: You must! I will throw myself at Arthur's mercy. He would not have me put to death—even for treason.

LANCELOT: Then we will stand trial together.

GUINEVERE: No! As your lady, I command you to go!

LANCELOT: (*slowly*) I will go—but I will return to you.

MORDRED: Okay. Break down the door! The rest of you, be ready!

NARRATOR: Mordred's knights prepared to batter down the door. But to their surprise it swung inward all on its own. (*creaking of a door*) Agravaine looked hesitantly from the open doorway to Mordred.

MORDRED: After you.

NARRATOR: Agravaine advanced cautiously—his sword drawn. In a flash he was jerked the rest of the way into the room, and the door slammed shut. (*door slamming*)

AGRAVAINE: Argh! (*dying cries*)

MORDRED: (*yelling*) Break down the door! Now!

NARRATOR: The knights slammed themselves against the barred door. (*crashing sounds*) Suddenly, the door swung open again, and to their surprise Agravaine was standing there.

MORDRED: What happened? Where is Lancelot? Speak, Agravaine!

NARRATOR: But it was not Agravaine. It was Lancelot, now wearing the slain Agravaine's armor.

LANCELOT: (*battlecry*) Ah!

NARRATOR: Lancelot flew at his enemies. (*battle sounds*) Mordred turned and fled, leaving the battle to the other knights. (*fanfare*) He sounded the alarm, and soon all of Camelot was in arms. Yet this was not enough to stop Lancelot. He fought his way out of the castle into the stables, where he mounted his steed and rode from Camelot.

When Arthur returned, he found the city in turmoil. Only then did he first believe himself betrayed.

ARTHUR: Tell me all that has happened.

MORDRED: (*dramatically*) Oh, sire! My heart breaks to speak these words—but here goes. You are betrayed! Lancelot *was* with the queen, and he butchered his way out of the city!

ARTHUR: Lancelot dared to raise his hand against his fellow knights?

MORDRED: Yes. It appears that he has been a traitor this entire time! Who knew? Agravaine was slain—which was not much of a loss—but many other valiant knights met the same fate!

GAWAIN: Your henchmen do not count as valiant knights! No *valiant knight* would raise his sword against Lancelot! He fought to save his life! What other choice did he have? He was trapped by your foul trick!

MORDRED: (*angrily*) Are you defending that traitor?

GAWAIN: I am defending a friend—a noble man!

MORDRED: This "friend" of yours just slayed your brother. Doesn't that stir something in you?

GAWAIN: Agravaine got what he deserved for partnering with you.

ARTHUR: Silence! Where is the queen? Where is Guinevere? Bring her to me.

NARRATOR: Soon two knights entered, restraining the struggling queen between them. They released her, and she ran forward and fell at the feet of her husband—sobbing. Arthur refused to look at her.

GUINEVERE: (*weeping*) Arthur, forgive him! Forgive me! Forgive us both!

MORDRED: Oh please.

GUINEVERE: I know I do not deserve mercy, but please spare me!

NARRATOR: Guinevere reached for Arthur's hands, but he pulled them away. He continued to stare upward, and his voice was barely more than a whisper.

ARTHUR: *(quietly)* How could you? Now I have lost everything. *(pause)* You must stand trial. It is the law. By betraying me you have betrayed all of Camelot.

GUINEVERE: Arthur! Please! Have mercy!

GAWAIN: Uncle, she is right. Camelot is built on mercy! Let he who is without sin cast the first stone.

MORDRED: Stoning? Interesting idea. I thought we would just burn her at the stake.

ARTHUR: There will be no mercy. Lancelot is now my enemy. And Guinevere must die for her part in this crime.

MORDRED: I couldn't have said it better myself! Okay, gentlemen, this "lady" needs to be removed. Take her to a cell in the dungeon.

GAWAIN: But this is the queen!

MORDRED: *(grudgingly)* Okay. Okay. A *nice* cell!

KAY: Sire, will you stand for this?

ARTHUR: She is a traitor.

MORDRED: Couldn't have said it better myself! Take her away!

NARRATOR: In the dark hallway Gawain angrily confronted Mordred.

GAWAIN: *(angrily)* Why are you doing this?

MORDRED: For justice! She broke the law. She deserves to die!

GAWAIN: At the expense of Camelot? This will kill the king! He has lost his love and his best friend in the same day!

MORDRED: I don't make the rules. I just enjoy them. If Arthur is so fond of her, he can pardon her. But oh wait. If he does, the laws of Camelot are out the window. Whoops! I guess the harlot will have to burn.

GAWAIN: You are a traitor! I cannot prove it, but I know it in my heart! Cursed is the father who spawned you!

MORDRED: *(laugh)* Ha! You have no idea!

NARRATOR: It stormed the following day—a storm as Camelot had never seen. The howling of the wind filled the damp throne room, where all had gathered for the trial of the queen. Mordred presided over the hearing. It went quickly enough. Everyone present knew Guinevere was guilty. Her flowing tears were enough to convict her.

MORDRED: Guinevere, not surprisingly, you are found guilty of treason against his majesty, King Arthur.

GUINEVERE: *(quietly)* Mercy, Arthur. Please give me mercy.

NARRATOR: Arthur's face had become a blank stone—his eyes, lifeless.

MORDRED: Guinevere, you will receive the full punishment—death. You are to be burned at the stake.

GUINEVERE: *(weeping)* Please…

MORDRED: Ready a stake! This drizzle will clear up soon! Then we will light a fire under our treacherous queen.

NARRATOR: Arthur looked away as Guinevere was taken from the throne room.

In the castle courtyard stood a platform with a single stake in its midst, kindling piled all around. Mordred's knights had been posted about the city. He knew that Lancelot would not leave his love helpless for long.

MORDRED: See, gentlemen. I told you the rain would clear up. I guess I'm just an optimist at heart.

GUINEVERE: You'll never get away with this!

MORDRED: Really? That old line? *(to the guards)* Bind this adulterer. *(to Guinevere)* Or do you prefer the term "nuptially-challenged?"

GUINEVERE: You may tie me if you wish. But my champion will save me!

MORDRED: Funny you should mention that, harlot, because that's exactly what we're hoping for.

NARRATOR: The queen spat into Mordred's face.

GUINEVERE: *(spits)* You are a demon! You will burn for eternity!

NARRATOR: Mordred's eyes glittered with hatred.

MORDRED: You first.

NARRATOR: A solemn assembly of knights had gathered to watch the spectacle. Gawain was among them, shaking his head in despair. His younger brothers, Gaheris and Gareth, stood beside him. While other knights had attended the execution in full armor, these Orkney knights refused—as a sign of protest.

GARETH: Gawain, do something! This is a disgrace—executing the queen! If Lancelot was here…

GAWAIN: Let's hope he stays far away—for his own sake.

NARRATOR: The notable absentee from the proceedings was Arthur himself. Mordred appeared on the platform and raised a flaming torch above his head.

MORDRED: *(shouting)* People of Camelot! Your queen has been found guilty! And so now, she will receive her final judgment.

NARRATOR: Mordred turned to light the kindling when the faraway peal of a trumpet reached their ears. *(fanfare of trumpets)*

GUINEVERE: *(excited)* Lancelot!

NARRATOR: Thundering through the gates of the city came a troop of knights. *(hoofbeats)* At the front rode Lancelot—swinging his sword from side to side.

MORDRED: Perfect! *(laugh)* Knights! Kill them at once!

NARRATOR: Lancelot and his allies battled ferociously against the guards of Camelot. *(battle sounds)* Lancelot hacked his way to the platform where Guinevere was held.

MORDRED: *(in a rage)* Kill him already! Stop him!

NARRATOR: Lancelot jumped from his steed onto the platform and quickly untied the queen's bonds.

GUINEVERE: Lancelot! I knew you'd come back for me!

NARRATOR: Lancelot whisked Guinevere onto his steed.

MORDRED: They're getting away!

NARRATOR: Lancelot slashed left and right, making his way to the palace gate. His knights covered his escape.

MORDRED: *(infuriated)* Get them! What are you pigs good for? Get them!

NARRATOR: As quickly as he had come, Lancelot was gone once again. It was then that the wails of Gawain were heard throughout the courtyard.

GAWAIN: *(in grief)* No! No! He has killed them! My brothers!

NARRATOR: Gawain was kneeling over two forms fallen in the mud. They were the bodies of Gaheris and Gareth. Mordred neared the weeping knight and admired Lancelot's handiwork.

GAWAIN: Young Gareth. Murdered by Lancelot.

MORDRED: *(coldly)* Lancelot even knighted him, did he not? Do you see now? Lancelot deserves death for what he has done this day.

NARRATOR: Gawain looked up with a fire in his eyes.

GAWAIN: Yes. And *I* want to be the one to give it to him!

NARRATOR: As all of Camelot mourned the death of many noble knights, Arthur summoned Gawain, Mordred, and Kay to conference with him.

GAWAIN: *(angrily)* There's no time to lose, Arthur. Lancelot has gone to Joyous Guard! We must ride after him and kill all we find there!

KAY: Please, Gawain. We are not talking about enemies. This is Lancelot and the queen!

GAWAIN: They are my enemies now.

ARTHUR: What does Mordred say?

MORDRED: Sire, after his dramatic rescue of the queen, you have no choice but to pursue Lancelot. *But* someone must stay behind here in Camelot and protect the city.

GAWAIN: I will not stay behind! I want to slaughter Lancelot with my own two hands!

KAY: I will go, too. Someone must be the voice of reason!

ARTHUR: Mordred, I will leave Camelot in your care. You have proved yourself most loyal in this matter.

MORDRED: You can trust Camelot with me, sire.

NARRATOR: So Arthur led a great number of knights out of Camelot toward Joyous Guard, the home of Lancelot.

KAY: Many knights are missing from our numbers. I can only assume they have ridden off to side with Lancelot.

ARTHUR: *(tiredly)* So it has come to this. War has divided us. The fellowship of the Round Table has been split. *(pause)* Camelot cannot survive. I should have done something to prevent all this.

KAY: None of this is your fault.

ARTHUR: I have always tried to be a good king, Kay. But was I a good husband? Maybe if I had—

KAY: It is pointless to speak such things. You are a good man—a good king. I have always been a pompous fool, I know that. But it has been the pride of my life to serve you, Arthur.

NARRATOR: For the first time in many days Arthur smiled.

ARTHUR: Thank you, my brother.

NARRATOR: Finally, Arthur's army reached Joyous Guard. *(horn sound)* A distant horn sounded, and the drawbridge lowered. Lancelot and his nephew, Bors, rode out at the head of their army of knights.

LANCELOT: Arthur, my king! Let there be peace between us!

ARTHUR: There will never be peace between you and me. I trusted you, and you disgraced me. You have stolen my queen and murdered my nephews.

LANCELOT: Your nephews? What do you mean?

GAWAIN: Don't act like you don't know! You butchered Gareth and Gaheris in cold blood.

NARRATOR: Lancelot bowed his head in grief.

GAWAIN: Don't insult their memory with your tears!

LANCELOT: I—I did not know. Gareth was like my own brother. It was an accident! I beg your forgiveness.

GAWAIN: Uncle, I have heard enough of this. Let's cut out his lying tongue!

LANCELOT: Arthur, you are still my king. Will you give me your forgiveness?

NARRATOR: All the knights stared at the king anxiously.

ARTHUR: Never! Not while there is breath in my body!

LANCELOT: Then I have no choice but to fight—to defend my home.

ARTHUR: Ready your army, and prepare for death!

NARRATOR: The two armies prepared to face off. Lancelot and Bors arrayed their knights on the battlefield.

BORS: Don't worry, uncle. Our position is strong. We will win today.

LANCELOT: Bors, how can a man win a battle when he battles against his friends?

NARRATOR: Holding Excalibur high, Arthur led his troops forward.

ARTHUR: (*shouting*) Knights of Camelot who now serve Lancelot, know this—you fight for a traitor! And you will be treated the same as he. There will be no mercy! Charge!

NARRATOR: The two armies charged toward one another, and the battle was thick. (*battling noises*) The fight raged on throughout the day, until at last the sun began to set.

KAY: Sire, we must retire for the evening!

ARTHUR: Not until I have faced him.

NARRATOR: In the midst of the fighting, King Arthur spied Lancelot on foot, and he spurred his horse toward him.

ARTHUR: There you are, traitor! Let's see how you fare against Excalibur!

NARRATOR: Lancelot despaired when he saw the king bearing down on him. He did not even raise his shield to defend himself but offered himself up to Arthur's blow.

ARTHUR: Defend yourself, coward!

NARRATOR: Before Arthur could strike, Bors charged in and knocked Arthur from his horse. (*Clang!*)

ARTHUR: (*cry of pain*) Argh!

NARRATOR: The king fell helplessly to the ground—Excalibur flying loose from his hand.

BORS: There, Lancelot! Your enemy is unhorsed and weaponless! Kill him, and this war will be over.

NARRATOR: Lancelot picked up Excalibur from where it had fallen.

LANCELOT: No. I have no enemy here.

NARRATOR: Lancelot stuck Excalibur into the ground at Arthur's feet. The king stared up at him in shock.

LANCELOT: I will never lift my hand against you, Arthur. You may call yourself my enemy, but I am still your friend—and I ever will be.

NARRATOR: Wounded and weary, the knights of both sides retired for the evening. Arthur, still stunned from his encounter with Lancelot, found his way back to his own camp.

GAWAIN: Argh! Never once did I come across Lancelot!

ARTHUR: (*thoughtfully*) I met him today. I was unhorsed, and he was in a position to kill me—but he did not.

GAWAIN: Trust me! If he had been able to, he would have. The coldblooded killer!

ARTHUR: No. He has conquered me more with his gallantry than he ever could have by force. We were wrong to come here. I wish this war would have never begun.

NARRATOR: From the safety of Joyous Guard, Guinevere had watched the battle that day—as the ground became littered with the bodies of many valiant knights. Their faces haunted her. Although she was relieved that Lancelot had returned from battle safely, Guinevere greeted him with sorrow in her eyes.

GUINEVERE: All this bloodshed—it is all because of me.

LANCELOT: This is the only way we can be together. Isn't that what you want?

GUINEVERE: (*weeping*) Don't you see? I must go back to him. I cannot endure another day of this.

LANCELOT: I, too, thought I would do anything to be with you—betray my king, betray my friend. But I came face to face with him today. If I would have killed him then, we could be together forever. But I could not—and will not. I guess there are things more important than love.

NARRATOR: Lancelot looked down at the sturdy ramparts that he leaned upon.

LANCELOT: You know, this castle was once cursed. They called it Dolorous Guard—a name that means the source of misery. But I came and conquered it. I cleansed it of all evil-doing. Then I renamed it Joyous Guard. I thought I could change its nature. Now I see that I cannot change it. It will be cursed forever.

NARRATOR: Lancelot took Guinevere's hand into his own.

LANCELOT: I have loved you more than a knight has ever loved a lady. But our love is cursed, and a life with me would only bring you dishonor. Arthur is a good king. Perhaps he will take you back and make you his queen once again.

GUINEVERE: Maybe we can make things right again.

NARRATOR: In the morning Guinevere, riding on a white palfrey, and Lancelot, armor-less and wearing his finest doublet, appeared on the field of battle.

GAWAIN: Look! What is that villain doing? Surrendering?

ARTHUR: Let us ride out and meet him.

NARRATOR: Arthur and Gawain met with Lancelot and Guinevere in the midst of the battlefield.

LANCELOT: Here is the one I stole from you, Arthur, and I beg your forgiveness. I will return her to you if you will treat her as a queen again and never punish her for what has transpired.

GAWAIN: (*angrily*) You expect him to forget all that has happened?

LANCELOT: I expect him to do what is right.

ARTHUR: I swear. And I give you my forgiveness.

LANCELOT: It is more than I deserve.

NARRATOR: Lancelot dismounted and put the reins of Guinevere's palfrey into Arthur's hands.

LANCELOT: Take care of her. She is truly the worthiest woman in the world.

ARTHUR: Lancelot, I never should have doubted your noble heart. What plans lie ahead for you?

LANCELOT: I will return to my homeland of France and forget that all of this ever happened.

ARTHUR: I wish you well.

GAWAIN: *(angrily)* Run, coward. But I will still find you wherever you go.

NARRATOR: Lancelot faced the glowering Sir Gawain.

LANCELOT: I mourn the death of Sir Gareth more than even you, for I was the cause of it. I ask your forgiveness, too, Gawain.

GAWAIN: Here is my answer!

NARRATOR: Gawain removed his gauntlet and hurled it to Lancelot's feet.

LANCELOT: I have never refused a challenge in my life, but I have no desire to fight you.

GAWAIN: Why? Are you afraid that you will be beaten?

ARTHUR: Lancelot and I have made peace. Forget your anger.

GAWAIN: I can never forget.

ARTHUR: Kay, take the queen back to Camelot. Let her be spared this spectacle.

NARRATOR: As Kay returned with the queen to Camelot, the king took Gawain aside and tried to persuade him to forget his challenge against Lancelot. Finally, Gawain fell down upon his knee before Arthur.

GAWAIN: Uncle, I have always been faithful and true to you, and I have never asked for anything—until now. I must fight Lancelot, but let me fight with Excalibur.

NARRATOR: Arthur nearly wept at this request because he knew he could not refuse it.

Knights of both factions gathered to watch the duel of Gawain and Lancelot—Camelot's two greatest knights.

LANCELOT: Gawain, I ask you to reconsider. I will gladly be your servant if you will forgive me for your brothers' deaths.

GAWAIN: The only thing that can answer for their blood is yours! *(battlecry)* Argh!

NARRATOR: The duel began, and Gawain attacked Lancelot savagely. *(Clang!)* The two battled for hours, their mighty blows tearing chunks of armor loose from one another, until they were both covered by many wounds. The grass ran red with their blood.

LANCELOT: *(panting)* Gawain, we cannot continue this much longer. Let us call a truce before we both die!

GAWAIN: This duel is to the death!

NARRATOR: Finally, Lancelot struck Gawain a mighty blow upon the helm. *(Clang!)*

GAWAIN: *(cry of pain)* Argh!

NARRATOR: Gawain fell to the ground, and Excalibur flew from his grip. Lancelot could barely stand, but he was victorious.

LANCELOT: You are defeated! Yield!

GAWAIN: Never! You must kill me!

LANCELOT: I would rather drive this sword through myself.

NARRATOR: Lancelot left Gawain lying there, too exhausted and wounded to rise. Lancelot faced his own knights and pointed his sword toward Arthur.

LANCELOT: I will fight no more! Knights, who have served me faithfully, here is your true king! There is none better in all the world. Return to him!

ARTHUR: Thank you, my friend. You are truly the noblest knight in the world.

NARRATOR: Lancelot, wounded to the point of death, was taken back within Joyous Guard and cared for by his physicians. Gawain, also severely wounded, was prepared for the journey back to Camelot. The feeble knight summoned Arthur to him.

GAWAIN: Uncle, I am dying. I can feel it. I have been wounded deeply. But it is a wound of my own making. *(cry of pain)* Argh!

ARTHUR: Save your strength.

GAWAIN: It is nothing compared to the pain I feel when I think of how I have wronged Lancelot. If only I could speak to him once more and tell him so. If you see him again, tell him that I give him my forgiveness. And ask him—*(cough)* ask him to give me his.

ARTHUR: I will.

NARRATOR: Finally, the spirit of Gawain departed his body, and the king wept with great sorrow.

ARTHUR: How much heartbreak can one mortal heart bear? Let us return to Camelot and pick up the pieces. All I desire now is rest.

NARRATOR: Arthur hoped his days of war were over, but, little did he know, the battle for Camelot was only beginning.

DISCUSSION QUESTIONS

1. Why does Mordred seem to have so much power over King Arthur?
2. Does Guinevere deserve to die? Explain.
3. How does the theme of forgiveness play into this portion of the story?
4. Does Gawain deserve to die because of his inability to forgive? Explain.
5. How is Dolorous Guard (renamed Joyous Guard) a metaphor for Lancelot and Guinevere's doomed relationship? (*Dolorous* means "distinguished by grief or causing misery.")
6. Are Lancelot's actions noble? Explain.
7. A *trial* can mean a court trial or also a test of suffering. How do the dual meanings of the word apply to the title, "The Trial of Guinevere"?
8. Should Arthur allow Guinevere to be his queen once again? Explain.
9. Re-read the last line of this script-story. What does this foreshadow? What do you think has happened while Arthur has been fighting with Lancelot?

THE FALL OF CAMELOT
TEACHER GUIDE

BACKGROUND

Although Arthur disappears to Avalon and his kingdom fades away, Camelot's fall is not a defeat. The tales of Arthur and his knights created a powerful legacy—one that has inspired rulers for centuries. It is no coincidence that many kings of England tried to link their ancestry back to King Arthur and modeled their own courts on the ideals of the Knights of the Round Table. The influence of Arthur extends even into modern times where the principles of chivalry, honor, and duty are still highly prized. The legend of Arthur lives on.

Yet, much like his legend, Arthur himself refuses to die. Not only is Arthur a king of the past, but also a king of the future. There is a tale that one day, when the world needs him most, Arthur will awake from his magical sleep and return from Avalon. Merlin, too, will awake in his enchanted cave, and together they will usher in a new era of peace. Then Arthur will truly live up to his title, the Once and Future King.

Even if you do not have confidence in Arthur's Christ-like return, the legacy of Camelot can still help us make the world a better place. Arthur was a man who strived to live for something larger than himself. What is nobler than that? We can literally take a page from his book—learning from his mistakes and emulating his successes. As the preface to *Le Morte D'Arthur* says, "Do after the good and leave the evil." If we can do that, the world *will* be a better place.

SUMMARY

As Kay escorts Guinevere back to Camelot, they are captured by Mordred, who has taken control of the city. Kay sacrifices his life to allow Guinevere to escape, and she warns Arthur of Mordred's betrayal. Arthur tells Guinevere to seek out Lancelot, forget about Camelot, and find some happiness in life.

Arthur meets with Mordred, who reveals his true identity as Arthur's son—declaring that he is the rightful heir to the throne. Arthur rallies his loyal knights to face off against Mordred. On the eve of this final battle, Arthur dreams he is sitting on a revolving wheel and falls into a pit of snakes. After this, he is visited by the ghost of Gawain, who warns him that he must put off the battle against Mordred because Lancelot is coming with reinforcements. If Arthur fights without Lancelot, he will lose.

The next day the two armies meet, and Arthur suggests a truce to Mordred. Meanwhile back in the ranks, a snake bites into the ankle of one of Arthur's knights. As the knight draws his sword to strike the snake, Mordred sees this action and calls for his army to attack. The final battle begins.

Mordred and Arthur meet on the battlefield. Arthur drives a lance into Mordred, but before he dies, Mordred deals Arthur a mortal wound. As he lies dying, Arthur commands a knight named Bedivere to throw Excalibur into the nearby lake. Bedivere keeps the sword, and when Arthur asks him what he saw at the lake, Bedivere says he saw nothing. Arthur knows Bedivere is lying, and he tells him to return the sword to the lake. Bedivere throws Excalibur into the lake, and a hand reaches up to grasp it and pulls it beneath the waves. When Bedivere returns to tell Arthur the news, Bedivere sees Arthur on a barge upon the lake with three ladies—the Lady

232 The Road to Camelot

of the Lake, Nimue, and Morgan le Fay. The ladies tell Bedivere that Arthur is going to the Isle of Avalon, where Arthur will sleep for many years until he is needed again. Then he will return.

Lancelot arrives a day too late and sees that Camelot has fallen. Guinevere, grieving over her role in Camelot's downfall, becomes a nun, and Lancelot becomes a monk. The two do not see each other for years. Soon after learning of Guinevere's death, Lancelot dies as well.

ESSENTIAL QUESTIONS

- If we live our lives for a purpose higher than ourselves, can our legacy live on after us?
- Why should we continue to hope and fight—even in the face of defeat?

ANTICIPATORY QUESTIONS

- Do you think Arthur can regain control of his kingdom?
- If you were one of Arthur's knights, would there be any reason for you to side with Mordred? Explain.

CHARACTER QUEST

Leaving a Legacy Although Arthur's kingdom ends, legends of Arthur and his knights continued to inspire future generations of heroes. It's an important lesson about striving for character. When we live lives filled with character, it can inspire those who come after us to do the same. Who are some of the people in your life who have inspired you with their legacy? Who are some people you might inspire with *your* legacy?

CONNECT

Excalibur (1981) This film is a bloody and brutal re-telling of the Arthurian legends that sticks closely to the events of *Le Morte D'Arthur*. Although much of the film is not appropriate for young viewers, there are a few scenes which faithfully recreate events from the legends. (Note: Viewer discretion is strongly advised.)

TEACHABLE TERMS

- **Wheel of Fortune** The medieval idea of the wheel of fortune is referenced on pg. 241 in King Arthur's dream. In this concept those who experience a rise to power can also suffer a quick fall. This idea warned men not to become too confident in their own earthly power as compared to God's.
- **Symbolism** The serpent is a symbol of the Devil or Satan. The snake's appearance on pg. 242 is meant to insinuate the Devil's involvement in Arthur's downfall.
- **Character Development** Morgan le Fay, once Arthur's enemy, seems to be his ally as he passes on to the Isle of Avalon. Examine what might have caused this change in her behavior toward Arthur.

RECALL QUESTIONS

1. What secret does Mordred reveal to Arthur's lords?
2. Whose ghost appears to Arthur?
3. What causes one of Arthur's knights to draw his sword during a truce?
4. What errand does Arthur command Bedivere to perform?
5. What happens to Arthur at the end of this story?

THE FALL OF CAMELOT

CAST

ARTHUR	*King of Britain*
GUINEVERE	*Queen of Britain*
LANCELOT	*Knight of the Lake*
KAY	*Arthur's Seneschal*
MORDRED	*Secret Son of Arthur*
BEDIVERE	*Knight of Arthur*
GAWAIN	*Nephew of Arthur*
LADY	*Enchantress of the Lake*
NIMUE	*Enchantress*
MORGAN	*Enchantress*
GUARD	*Servant to Mordred*
KNIGHT	*Knight of Arthur*
LORD	*Lord of Britain*

NARRATOR: A group of travelers neared the gates of Camelot. The castle entry, which for many years had stood open welcoming all visitors to enter, was now closed, and a troop of menacing guards stood before it.

KAY: *(angrily)* Why is this gate closed? Open it at once!

NARRATOR: The guards seized the reins of Kay and Guinevere's horses.

KAY: Unhand my horse! I am Sir Kay, and this is the queen!

GUARD: You must come with us. You are under arrest!

KAY: By whose order?

GUARD: By order of the king—Mordred!

NARRATOR: The guards forced Kay from his horse and relieved him of his sword.

GUINEVERE: How dare you! This is Arthur's very own brother!

KAY: They know, my queen. Arthur has been betrayed.

GUARD: Take these prisoners to the king!

NARRATOR: All that had once been bright and beautiful about Camelot was changed. The festive banners that had hung from the walls were gone, and in their place hung the grisly bodies of executed knights—a cloud of crows hovering above. The people passing through the streets moved with furtive, hunted looks. Everywhere ranks of strange knights stood at guard.

GUINEVERE: I do not recognize any of these knights.

KAY: They must be Mordred's new recruits—faithless rogues.

NARRATOR: Guinevere and Kay were led into the great hall, where the throne of Arthur was occupied by Mordred himself—a jagged, black crown upon his head.

MORDRED: My, my. Look who has returned! The prodigal queen. I'm surprised you would show your face around here again—after what you did.

GUINEVERE: *(disgusted)* Mordred, what have you done to Camelot?

MORDRED: Oh, you like it? I added a few personal touches. A definite improvement, wouldn't you say?

KAY: Only a villain like you would think so.

NARRATOR: Mordred smirked at Kay.

MORDRED: I see the queen brought her babysitter with her. So, Kay, did Arthur send you along to keep an eye on her? I don't blame him. She has quite the reputation.

KAY: You traitor! The king shall know of this!

MORDRED: Didn't you hear? I *am* the king.

KAY: Never.

MORDRED: Actually, yes. You see, Arthur left me here with two important items—his royal ring and the key to the treasury—both to use as I saw fit.

GUINEVERE: Arthur trusted you!

MORDRED: That was his last mistake. But where are my manners? It is rude to speak ill of the dead. The old king is dead. Long live the new king!

KAY: Arthur is *not* dead!

MORDRED: *(mock confusion)* Are you sure? Because according to this document I hold in my hand, he has been dead for two weeks—slain by Lancelot. Tsk. Tsk. A fitting end for him, don't you think? Stabbed in the back by the one he trusted the most.

GUINEVERE: Who would believe such a lie?

MORDRED: Quite a few people actually—after your boyfriend murdered his fellow knights just to rescue you. Thanks for that, by the way.

GUINEVERE: Arthur will arrive here soon. Then everyone will see he is alive and well!

MORDRED: A slight technicality—a problem that will easily be solved.

KAY: You would dare declare war on your king?

MORDRED: You're still not getting this, are you? *(screaming)* I—am—the—king! *(calming)* And now that I am the king, I require a queen. You are bit used, but you will do.

GUINEVERE: I would never marry you!

MORDRED: Not even if torture was the alternative? It's very persuasive. Just ask the Archbishop. He refused to crown me king, and the poor fellow lost his head. *(laugh)*

GUINEVERE: You're insane!

MORDRED: No, just troubled. I never had a father. *(pause)* So what is your answer? I warn you—if it's no, I will burn you at the stake. Only this time I will get it right.

GUINEVERE: Then I guess I have no choice. But, please, give me some time to prepare myself.

MORDRED: Fine. But don't take too long. Arthur will be back soon. I can't wait to see the look on his face when I tell him that I have taken his throne *and* his queen.

GUINEVERE: What will be done to Sir Kay?

MORDRED: Mr. nanny-knight? Well, he has been loyal to Arthur for far too long. Therefore, he cannot be trusted. He will meet the same fate as the other loyal knights. Let's just say they're not half the men they used to be. *(evil laugh)*

KAY: Death is preferable to serving a reptile like you!

MORDRED: *(happily)* Death it is then! That was easy, wasn't it? Shall we get on with it? We love a good execution around here.

NARRATOR: Kay gave the queen a pointed look, and a silent message passed between them.

MORDRED: Now what will it be, Sir Kay? Hanging? No. Too quick. Crucifixion? Nah. Too symbolic. Drawing and quartering? Hmmm. Interesting.

GUINEVERE: Wait, Mordred. Please! Let me kiss this noble knight one more time before he meets his death.

MORDRED: Is there anyone in this kingdom you haven't kissed? Fine. Do it quickly.

NARRATOR: As the queen leaned in closely to Kay, she whispered to him.

GUINEVERE: *(whispering)* What shall we do?

KAY: *(whispering)* Flee to the east tower of Camelot. Barricade the door.

MORDRED: Easy, Kay. Leave some for the rest of us.

KAY: *(whispering)* Go!

NARRATOR: Kay swiftly drew a secret dagger from his belt.

KAY: *(shouting)* Die, you traitor!

NARRATOR: He hurled the dagger toward Mordred, who barely had time to duck beneath the blade. *(shunk)*

KAY: *(shouting)* Run, my queen!

MORDRED: *(shouting)* Kill him!

NARRATOR: Mordred's guards descended upon Kay as Guinevere dashed from the throne room. The tall east tower of Camelot appeared before her, and she ran toward it. She flew through its door and began to barricade it behind her. But as she did, she saw the bloodied form of Kay fleeing from Mordred's guards.

GUINEVERE: Kay! Quickly!

NARRATOR: Kay made it inside the tower, slamming shut the door and barricading it against his pursuers.

GUINEVERE: However did you escape?

KAY: *(panting)* I wasn't always a housekeeper, you know. I still have a few tricks left up my sleeve.

NARRATOR: She noticed blood dripping from his side.

GUINEVERE: You are wounded.

KAY: It's nothing. Here. Help me block the door. All this will prove pointless if they break through. This tower was fortified in case of attack, but it cannot hold out forever.

NARRATOR: The knights of Mordred battered against the door for many hours, but it held firm. *(booming of a battering ram)* Finally, the booming died away.

GUINEVERE: They have given up!

KAY: I do not think so. At least we have bought ourselves some time. Maybe Arthur will come soon and save us.

GUINEVERE: Thank you for this, Kay.

KAY: It is nothing.

NARRATOR: Soon an enormous blow shook the tower to its very roots. *(enormous boom)* Dust and debris fell loose from the walls.

GUINEVERE: *(gasp)* What was that?

KAY: *(in shock)* Mordred has turned Camelot's catapults against us! He's going to bring the tower down upon us. Quickly! Into the cellar!

NARRATOR: As they descended into the cellar, the booming continued overhead. *(booming of catapults)* Kay and Guinevere huddled in the darkness of the cellar.

GUINEVERE: I guess this is the end, Kay. I will be forced to become Mordred's queen, and you shall be put to the sword. I don't know which fate is worse.

KAY: Yours by far. *(chuckle)* Wait. How stupid of me! I almost forgot! Ha!

GUINEVERE: What is it?

KAY: Do you feel this trapdoor below us, made into the floor? Beneath it flows an underground river. The tower was constructed so that this could be used for fresh water in times of siege.

GUINEVERE: I don't understand.

KAY: Here. Roll one of these barrels down through the opening and cling to it. It will carry you out into the Great River.

NARRATOR: A tremendous din from above drew their attention. *(tremendous crash)*

KAY: They have breached the tower. Hurry! You must go through the trapdoor and find a way to warn Arthur. I will go and hold them off until you are safely away!

NARRATOR: Kay began to depart, but Guinevere caught his hand.

GUINEVERE: You will die, Kay.

KAY: I am wounded deep, my lady. There is no hope for me. It would be my honor to give my life to protect you.

GUINEVERE: Kay, you have shown me true kindness. I will never forget this.

NARRATOR: Guinevere lifted the trapdoor, and the rushing of the river could be heard in the darkness below. *(rushing water)*

KAY: Hurry!

NARRATOR: Above ground, Mordred surveyed the gaping hole his catapults had made in the side of the tower.

MORDRED: Perfect! Now retrieve the prisoners! Go easy on the harlot. She is to be the new queen!

NARRATOR: The guards hurried to carry out his command. But Kay rose from the debris, brandishing his sword against the guards. *(sounds of fighting)*

MORDRED: So, the old goat still has some fire in his bones!

NARRATOR: Mordred drew his cruel sword. *(shing)*

MORDRED: Leave him! He is mine!

KAY: Ha! Come forward, Mordred! I have never felt as alive as I do today!

MORDRED: How ironic! Because now you die!

NARRATOR: Kay charged toward Mordred.

KAY: Argh! *(battlecry)*

NARRATOR: Mordred shattered the sword of Kay in a shower of sparks and seized the older knight by the throat. To Kay's shock, Mordred raised him up into the air.

KAY: *(coughing)*

MORDRED: Surprised? No one realizes what they're up against with me. I have the strength of ten men. I am the mightiest knight in the world. Now, I will kill you.

NARRATOR: Kay felt Mordred's sword enter his stomach.

KAY: *(dying sounds)* Ughn.

NARRATOR: Mordred threw the limp body of Kay to the ground.

MORDRED: Enough of this foolishness! Bring me my queen!

NARRATOR: His guards, after searching the remains of the tower and returning empty-handed, fell at his feet.

GUARD: She is gone! There is no sign of her! She must have escaped.

MORDRED: What? *(growl of anger)* Raar!

NARRATOR: With a swift stroke, Mordred ended their lives.

MORDRED: *(relieved)* Ah! Now I feel better. *(shouting)* Prepare for war!

NARRATOR: Miles away, King Arthur was having a dream. He was standing on a high cliff, staring out to sea. In the distance lay a castle, shrouded in mist.

ARTHUR: Argh! *(cry of pain)*

NARRATOR: A sudden pain drew his attention. A snake was coiled at his side, biting him with its poisonous fangs. He tried to fling the snake from him, but he couldn't. It was a part of him. He felt himself growing weak. The poison was acting fast. The castle in the mist was fading away. He was dying. Then he woke up.

BEDIVERE: Sire! Are you all right? You were crying out in your sleep.

NARRATOR: Arthur was within his royal tent. Bedivere, his attendant knight, was gazing in at him with a look of concern.

ARTHUR: I am fine, Bedivere.

BEDIVERE: The men are prepared to travel on. We are nearly to Camelot.

NARRATOR: Arthur and his army were camped upon the banks of the Great River. As the camp was being dismantled, sudden cries rang out along the riverside. (*surprised shouting*)

BEDIVERE: Sire! A woman has been found in the river! The guards are bringing her here.

NARRATOR: The woman, carried between two knights, was ragged and nearly drowned. When Arthur beheld her, he recognized her at once.

ARTHUR: Guinevere! This is the queen! Get her near the fire! Fetch my physician.

NARRATOR: Guinevere was nursed back to consciousness. Then she told Arthur of all that had befallen her and Kay at Camelot. As Guinevere spoke of Mordred's treachery, a light seemed to come into Arthur's eyes—a light that none had seen for a long time. He stood, his back straightened, and the years seemed to fall from him.

ARTHUR: So Mordred has betrayed me completely. He is the snake who has bitten me in the side, poisoning me with his words. Now his death is all that I seek.

GUINEVERE: He has tricked your lords into joining with him. You will need help. I will ride on to Joyous Guard and alert Lancelot. Perhaps he can muster an army of French knights to come to your aid.

ARTHUR: Yes, go. But once you reach safety—stay there. Forget about Camelot. Do not return. Find happiness, Guinevere.

NARRATOR: Arthur's knights presented Guinevere with a palfrey for her journey. As the queen bade her husband farewell, her eyes filled with tears.

GUINEVERE: I cannot find the words to tell you how sorry I am, Arthur—for all of this.

ARTHUR: All is forgiven. Go with my blessing. Farewell, Guinevere.

GUINEVERE: Farewell, Arthur.

NARRATOR: Arthur watched his queen ride away, until she was lost around the bend of the road. Then he sighed.

ARTHUR: On to Camelot.

BEDIVERE: Sire, if all the lords of Britain have turned against you, what hope do we have?

ARTHUR: Many of them believe I am dead. Let's show them the truth.

NARRATOR: The great city appeared in the distance. Arthur sent messengers ahead to request a parley with Mordred. Many of the lords in Camelot were shocked to hear that Arthur still lived.

LORD: You swore that Arthur was dead!

MORDRED: He will be soon enough.

LORD: We will hear what he has to say.

(murmuring, agreement of the other lords)

NARRATOR: Arthur's messenger returned with a summons to meet with Mordred, King of Britain.

BEDIVERE: You cannot go, your majesty! It's a trap. You will be killed.

ARTHUR: Then I will be killed. I have never feared death. The only hope against faithless rogues in this world is to act honorably—and expect them to do the same.

BEDIVERE: Then I must come with you!

NARRATOR: Arthur and Bedivere boldly rode into the shadowy city of Camelot. It was strange to see the castle's king approaching it like a stranger. The lords and knights of Britain were gathered in the chamber of the Round Table. Mordred glared at Arthur with thinly-veiled hatred.

MORDRED: So, Arthur, former-king, you dare return here to Camelot.

ARTHUR: I return to reclaim my throne.

MORDRED: I have a claim upon it myself.

ARTHUR: What claim could a villain like you have?

MORDRED: I'm so glad you asked. (loudly) Fellow knights! Lords of Britain! There's something that you don't know about me and dear Arthur here. A secret—a dark secret. A secret, we shall say, that has come back to haunt him.

NARRATOR: Arthur looked at Mordred blankly.

ARTHUR: There are no secrets in Camelot.

MORDRED: Really? I believe you have overlooked one…Father.

(collective gasp)

NARRATOR: Arthur's face paled.

MORDRED: Yes. Gasp. That's right. Arthur of Camelot is my father.

ARTHUR: (infuriated) Another lie! You have no proof!

MORDRED: (rabidly) Don't I? Years ago you laid by the lady Margawse, your half-sister. You certainly tried to cover that one up, didn't you? Incest does not look good in the public eye!

ARTHUR: (in shock) It can't be!

MORDRED: Killing a shipload of babies didn't do the trick, did it? I survived. And I came back! The child of May Day came back! And now I am the heir to your throne!

NARRATOR: Arthur stood in stunned silence.

MORDRED: Now, speak the words, Father. Tell them the truth. It is the truth that shall set me free!

ARTHUR: I will never admit being the father of a creature like you.

NARRATOR: Mordred slammed his fist down upon the Round Table.

MORDRED: *(yelling)* This kingdom was not built on lies! It was built on truth! *(quietly)* So tell them, Father—tell them the truth. Or destroy everything you have worked for these many years.

NARRATOR: Arthur looked down into his hands. They looked so wrinkled and helpless. Far away, he heard his own voice crawling its way forth from his numb lips.

ARTHUR: *(numbly)* He is my son.

MORDRED: *(sing-song voice)* Music to my ears! Music to my ears! *(fake happiness)* Oh, my tender heart! Our handsome hero is reunited with his long-lost father! Where is a minstrel? This would make a wonderful ballad. Wouldn't it, Father?

ARTHUR: Don't call me that.

MORDRED: *(yelling)* Father! Father! Father!

ARTHUR: Why have you done all this?

MORDRED: My hatred compels me to.

ARTHUR: You have been close to me for many months. Why not end my life then?

MORDRED: Oh, I want to do more than end your life. I want to destroy your world—piece by piece. I made a vow that before you die, you will see your knights turned upon one another—your wife stolen away—your precious virtues forsaken. Then when everything you have worked for is destroyed—and only then—I will allow you to die.

ARTHUR: Only one person has ever hated me with so fiery a hatred—my half-sister, Morgan le Fay.

MORDRED: Very good, Father. Aren't you clever? It was she who showed me your true nature, but she has grown soft! Now her hatred lives on in me!

NARRATOR: Mordred jauntily seated himself upon the Round Table.

MORDRED: I know you were trying to make something beautiful here. Something grand—something that would last forever. But *I* am Camelot's future now.

ARTHUR: *(forcefully)* Mordred, I command you to leave my kingdom.

MORDRED: *(fake shock)* What? But, Father, I thought maybe we could have a snowball fight or maybe a piggy-back ride. I missed so much of my childhood, you know!

ARTHUR: Leave.

MORDRED: You have no authority here! I am your heir, and you can do nothing about it!

ARTHUR: Yes, I can. I can meet you on the field of battle. Then with these hands, the hands of a father, I will end your life.

MORDRED: *(laughter)* You're serious, aren't you? Look! You've been beaten! Admit it!

ARTHUR: *(to the lords)* Lords of Britain, for many years I have served as your king. Will you throw me away for some incestuous brat? I will be upon the Plain of Camlann. Join my army if you value everything the Round Table stands for.

NARRATOR: Mordred stared wildly at his father.

MORDRED: *(cry of rage)* Ahhhh!

NARRATOR: Mordred struck the Round Table with his sword. *(cracking sound)* Under the force of his blow, the table cracked and splintered in half.

MORDRED: *(screaming)* Relics! Useless traditions! Follow me! I am the future! I am Camelot now!

NARRATOR: Arthur stared impassively at the split Round Table.

ARTHUR: Until tomorrow, Mordred—farewell.

NARRATOR: Without another word, Arthur rode out from under the shadow of Camelot.

BEDIVERE: Sire, our numbers are too few to face Mordred. What if we fail? What if Camelot falls?

ARTHUR: Camelot is not in these walls of stone. It is in us. Not even death can take it away. Merlin taught me that long ago.

NARRATOR: Arthur arrayed his army on the Plain of Camlann. Mordred's army gathered there as well, amassing like a swarm of locusts. While some of the lords returned to Arthur, many chose to remain with Mordred. In him they saw the strength and the might that Arthur had lost.

BEDIVERE: There has been no word from Lancelot or the queen.

ARTHUR: I only hope they have found safety.

NARRATOR: The two armies faced off and pitched their tents to rest on the eve of the final battle. Although King Arthur was not expecting it, sleep came to him in his tent, and once again he dreamt.

Arthur was seated upon a giant wooden wheel. As the wheel turned, he rose higher and higher until he was at the height of its rotation. He looked out, and he could see all the world. But then the wheel began to turn again. Below him there was a pit filled with a brood of vipers—writhing and striking. His seat continued to descend, and then he fell down, down into the awaiting pit.

ARTHUR: Argh! *(cries of pain)*

NARRATOR: Arthur awoke in his tent. The flap was open, and he could see the battle-plain beyond bathed in the moonlight.

ARTHUR: More visions?

NARRATOR: A ghostly train of figures was floating across the plain toward him. As they grew closer, he saw it was a knight accompanied by many noble ladies.

ARTHUR: *(in fear)* Who—who are you?

GAWAIN: *(ghost-like)* Have you forgotten me so soon, uncle?

ARTHUR: Gawain? I must still be dreaming! You are dead!

GAWAIN: Yes, but I have been sent back. These are all the damsels I rescued in my long career. We bring you a message, my lord.

ARTHUR: What is it, Gawain?

GAWAIN: Mordred has you hopelessly outnumbered. If you fight tomorrow, there is no chance that you will succeed. You will be killed.

ARTHUR: Is this all you have to give me? No hope?

GAWAIN: There is hope. Lancelot is on his way with two-hundred French knights to reinforce you. If you two fight together, you will be victorious. But he will not arrive until the day after next. You must truce with Mordred for a day and wait for Lancelot's return.

ARTHUR: Thank you for this news, Gawain. Is there more?

GAWAIN: It was a pleasure to serve you, my king. And one more thing—when you face Mordred on the field of battle, will you do me a favor?

ARTHUR: Anything.

GAWAIN: Cut his smirking face open for me.

NARRATOR: The dawn was breaking, and it brushed the ghostly figures from Arthur's vision. Soon Bedivere was there to armor the king for battle.

BEDIVERE: What is our plan, sire?

ARTHUR: We are going to truce.

BEDIVERE: (shocked) With that villain?

ARTHUR: Yes.

NARRATOR: The ranks of knights on either side were lined up—weapons at the ready. The sign of truce was sent ahead, and Arthur rode his steed into the middle of the battlefield. Mordred rode forward as well—glowering at his father.

MORDRED: A truce? What is this?

ARTHUR: Perhaps I acted too hastily. Maybe there is some way to end this conflict peacefully.

MORDRED: Who are you trying to kid, old man? I know you're up to something! But what does it matter to me? One day. Two days. Either way, you will die. I can wait. (laugh)

NARRATOR: This truce would have held if it had not been for an accident. Back in the ranks of Arthur, as the knights stood stiffly watching their king negotiate, an adder came crawling from the grass and sank its teeth into the heel of one of the men.

KNIGHT: (cry of pain) Gah!

NARRATOR: The knight drew his sword and raised it to cut the serpent in half.

From the center of the battlefield, Mordred saw this action. A flicker of joy came into his black heart.

MORDRED: That knight draws his sword! Arthur has tricked us! Attack! Attack!

NARRATOR: The knights of Mordred rushed forward—the ground shaking underneath as they charged. The army of Arthur quickly moved to meet them, and they clashed together. *(sounds of battle)*

The king rode between his men urging them on—Excalibur singing as it swung through the air. Mordred barreled through the mass—cutting men down left and right as he advanced.

So the field was bathed in blood for many hours—and as the sun began to set it spread the same red about the sky. Finally, amid the battle, Arthur and his son found themselves face to face.

MORDRED: *(hatefully)* Father! Your army is beaten!

ARTHUR: Perhaps. But I am not.

NARRATOR: Mordred laughed and wiped splattered blood from his face.

MORDRED: I will make this a slow death for you.

ARTHUR: *(angrily)* Come forth! I am responsible for your cursed life, and I will deal you your death.

NARRATOR: Mordred sprang forward—his sword cutting through the air like a wasp. Arthur countered this blow with the mighty Excalibur. *(Clang!)*

MORDRED: *(sarcastically)* Oh, how I've dreamt of this day! Father and I are finally spending time together.

NARRATOR: Mordred lashed out toward Arthur—the black blade beating the king back. As Arthur staggered backward, he grabbed a long-spear from one of the bodies that littered the field.

MORDRED: Now, Father. Let me show you the sting of my hatred!

ARTHUR: You are my sin come to life. And with Heaven's help, I will slay you this day.

MORDRED: Heaven has left you, Arthur—helpless and alone.

NARRATOR: Mordred charged forward, swinging wildly. Arthur knelt to the ground and drew up the long-spear. Not seeing Arthur's weapon until it was too late, Mordred ran upon the spear, driving the end deep into his stomach. *(shunk)*

MORDRED: Argh! *(coughing sounds)* No!

NARRATOR: Arthur stared at his skewered son without emotion—holding tightly to the undriven end of the spear. A weepy look washed over Mordred's face.

MORDRED: *(helplessly)* Father?

NARRATOR: Then Mordred's face suddenly became a demonic mask of hatred.

MORDRED: *(hatefully)* Father! No! No! *(hacking, coughing)* This is *not* how it shall end!

NARRATOR: With superhuman strength, fueled by his malice, Mordred took the spear into his hand and began to pull himself up its length. Arthur watched in shock as his bleeding son made his sickening advance.

MORDRED: *(between gasps)* King and Father—taste my hatred!

NARRATOR: Now within reach, Mordred brought his sword up and smote the king across the head—cleaving his helmet in two. *(Clang!)*

MORDRED: Die, Father, die! We shall die together!

NARRATOR: Mordred pitched to the side—his features going slack. He was dead before he hit the ground.

ARTHUR: (cry of pain) Argh!

NARRATOR: Arthur had felt the blow come through his helm and gash his head. He, too, fell to the ground and lay there breathing shallow breaths beside the corpse of his son.

ARTHUR: (weakly) It is done.

NARRATOR: A thin rain began to fall onto the field. Most of the fighting had ceased. Now, only motionless bodies dotted the landscape. It was Sir Bedivere who found Arthur where he lay.

BEDIVERE: (breathless) Sire, here you are! Mordred's army is defeated! Almost all of our knights have fallen, but Camelot has prevailed.

NARRATOR: Bedivere then noticed the slash across the king's head.

BEDIVERE: (terrified) My king, you are wounded!

ARTHUR: (through gasps of pain) Find me a litter at once—you must take me to the lake. I am dying, and I have something to return to the lady who dwells there.

NARRATOR: Bedivere ran through the field, stooping among the wounded, trying to find one who would help bear their king. He soon returned with another knight, who walked strangely holding his arms about his stomach.

BEDIVERE: I have found this knight. He is wounded, but he will help me to bear you.

NARRATOR: Bedivere produced a litter, and the king was carefully rolled upon it. Arthur groaned, and the two men lifted him into the air.

BEDIVERE: Careful. He is badly wounded.

NARRATOR: They did not take three steps before the knight stumbled—and with a sickening sound, his guts fell about his feet. The litter of the king crashed to the ground.

BEDIVERE: (shocked) Heaven preserve us! He was more wounded than I thought! Not to worry, sire. I shall find another.

NARRATOR: In his agony, Arthur waved a feeble hand.

ARTHUR: I am fading fast. You must go for me. Here! Take Excalibur.

NARRATOR: Arthur held up the majestic sword, and Bedivere took it reverently.

ARTHUR: Take it to the lake and throw it in. Return quickly and tell me what you saw when you cast the sword into the water.

BEDIVERE: I will, my lord.

NARRATOR: The knight mounted his horse and rode toward the nearby lake. But as he rode, he began to think about his actions.

BEDIVERE: (to himself) Throw away a sword like this? That would be madness. Arthur is not in his right mind. I will hide the sword under a rock and tell him that I have thrown it in. That way it will be preserved for future generations.

NARRATOR: Bedivere decided this was a good plan. He deposited the sword behind a rock and returned to the dying king.

BEDIVERE: I have done as you have asked, your majesty.

NARRATOR: Arthur opened his cloudy eyes.

ARTHUR: *(whispering)* What did you see when you threw it in?

BEDIVERE: *(nervously)* Only the waves, my liege.

ARTHUR: *(angrily)* Do you lie to your king—even now? You did not do as I commanded! Return at once and do not disobey me again!

NARRATOR: As Arthur lay waiting for Bedivere to fulfill his request, he felt his mind leaving him. A mist rose from the battlefield, and in it Arthur saw scenes from his life pass by his eyes. Familiar faces appeared there—noble Lancelot, beautiful Guinevere, wise Merlin.

ARTHUR: *(softly)* Oh, Merlin, my old teacher. You tried to warn me of this day. Camelot has fallen. And so have I.

NARRATOR: Among the misty visions appeared the face of Morgan le Fay. At first Arthur thought it was another vision, but she seemed so real—and there were tears in her eyes.

MORGAN: *(kindly)* Arthur. Dear brother. I have come back to you.

ARTHUR: My sister, you've had your revenge at last. If I had my scabbard this day, I would not be dying here now. *(cough)* But you look different. Better.

MORGAN: Dear brother, why have you tarried from me so long? Alas. This wound on your head has given you a deathly chill. Come. Let us bear you away.

ARTHUR: Where?

MORGAN: A different place. A better place.

ARTHUR: Very well.

NARRATOR: Arthur felt himself lifted by invisible hands and lightly borne along. He smiled and closed his eyes in peace.

Meanwhile, Bedivere stood upon the bank of the lake. Once again he stared at the glittering hilt of Excalibur, and doubt stirred in his breast.

BEDIVERE: *(forcefully)* No! I must obey my king.

NARRATOR: With a determined look, he drew back and lobbed the great blade out over the water. Just as it was about to hit upon the surface, a silver-clad hand slid silently out of the deep and caught the handle neatly in its grasp.

BEDIVERE: *(in shock)* Heaven be praised!

NARRATOR: Without a sound, the hand and sword descended back below the waves for the final time. Excalibur had returned home. Bedivere rode swiftly back to where the king had fallen, but he was no longer there.

BEDIVERE: *(in shock)* He has been stolen!

NARRATOR: Then Bedivere caught sight of a ship rocking in the misty shallows of the lake. Upon the deck stood three otherworldly ladies, singing softly, the wind catching their flowing hair. Below them lay a form. It was Arthur. The ladies, each in turn, spoke to Bedivere.

LADY: *(musically)* Do not fear, good sir knight. We are bearing your king through the mists to the isle of Avalon.

NIMUE: There he will be healed of his wounds, and he will sleep for many years.

MORGAN: But someday, when good people are in need of a holy king once more, he shall awaken and return in all his glory.

BEDIVERE: What shall I do?

LADY: Keep the good deeds of Arthur alive. Men years from now will scarcely believe that a man such as he ever existed. The stories of his great realm will be passed down from generation to generation. All the knights yet to come will eagerly await the day of King Arthur's glorious return.

NARRATOR: As Bedivere watched the mystical barge disappear out over the foggy lake, he felt tears upon his cheeks. The mists shrouded the vessel, and it was lost from Bedivere's sight. Arthur, the Once and Future King, had passed on.

When Lancelot arrived a day later with his troop of two-hundred-and-fifty knights, he grieved at all that Bedivere reported.

LANCELOT: Camelot is gone forever. What will I tell the queen?

NARRATOR: For the first time in their long relationship, Lancelot and Guinevere were free to be together. But love seemed like such an impossibility now. Downtrodden, Lancelot returned to Joyous Guard and broke the news to Guinevere.

GUINEVERE: *(weeping)* Arthur has departed this world, and it is all our fault. What do we do now? We cannot continue on as if none of this ever happened!

LANCELOT: We must! Arthur gave us his forgiveness. Now we are finally free to love.

GUINEVERE: I am not. I can never forgive myself. My husband may be gone, but my heart has gone with him. *(pause)* There is only one thing left to do. I must give myself to God and ask for His forgiveness.

LANCELOT: I cannot let you go again.

GUINEVERE: God is the one opponent that you can never beat, Lancelot. His will is mightier than yours.

LANCELOT: Then what shall I do?

GUINEVERE: Return to France and forget about me.

LANCELOT: I will be lost without you.

GUINEVERE: We are all lost, Lancelot. I go to be found.

NARRATOR: And so Guinevere embraced her champion for the final time and departed Joyous Guard. She submitted herself to the Order of Holy Sisters. The woman who had once been queen took a simple life in an abbey, and the years passed her by. From time to time she thought of Lancelot and what had become of him, but that part of her heart had died.

One day, a group of traveling monks stopped for the night at the abbey.

Guinevere was busy tending the garden when one of the monks drew near to her.

LANCELOT: If I am not mistaken, you were once the queen of Camelot—the greatest beauty the earth has ever seen.

NARRATOR: Guinevere recognized the monk's voice. How could she not? It was a voice as familiar to her as her own.

GUINEVERE: Do not tell me that you believe such stories. Do you also believe in Lancelot, the Knight of the Lake?

LANCELOT: I do. He was a man doomed by his love. *(pause)* Sister, will you give me the kiss of peace? A holy kiss?

GUINEVERE: I cannot. *(pause)* You would do well to forget the old stories. They are nothing but dreams.

NARRATOR: The monk smiled sadly.

LANCELOT: You are right. Nothing but beautiful dreams. Farewell.

NARRATOR: The monk bowed and rejoined his brethren.

Not long after this encounter Guinevere passed away. A trio of monks arrived to collect her body. They had once been Sir Lancelot, Sir Bedivere, and Sir Bors, but now they were humble servants of God. They bore her body to the holy abbey of Glastonbury and buried her beside the empty tomb of her husband—as she had wished.

LANCELOT: So my life is done as well.

NARRATOR: Six weeks afterward Lancelot himself passed away. Only a few were there to hear his last words.

LANCELOT: God, do not judge me by my sins.

NARRATOR: As he took his final breath, the last bit of Camelot slipped away, leaving the world behind forever.

DISCUSSION QUESTIONS

1. Who is *most* responsible for the downfall of Camelot? Explain.
2. How does Kay's character change in this story?
3. How did the early events of Arthur's life affect the end of his life? What can we learn from this?
4. What are the various meanings of Arthur's dreams and visions? Why are they included in this last portion of his story?
5. Does Mordred deserve to die? Explain.
6. At Glastonbury Abbey there is a tomb that is marked as the grave of King Arthur and Queen Guinevere. Do you think this is their actual resting place? Explain.
7. Is it strange that Arthur and Morgan le Fay make peace in the end? Explain.
8. According to legend, King Arthur and Merlin will return someday when Britain needs them most. What do you think about this legend? Why do you think it gave the British people hope?
9. Do you like the manner in which the lives of Lancelot and Guinevere end? Explain.
10. Can our legacy live after us if we live in a virtuous manner? Explain.
11. Is the story of King Arthur a tragedy or a triumph? Explain.

SO YOU WANT TO BE A KNIGHT

Everyone is familiar with the image of a knight in shining armor—fighting for honor and the love of a fair damsel. These heavily-armored, mounted warriors from the Middle Ages were named *knights* from the French word *chevalier*, which means "horseman." They were the most powerful force in their time. They allowed kings to win battles and maintain control of vast kingdoms. Ultimately, they went on to become the symbol of their age. But how did one come to be a knight? There wasn't a Future Knight Club that you joined at school. In fact, there wasn't even school. So how were knights made?

Prospective knights needed to begin the process early in life. Young, wealthy boys with their hearts set on knighthood would be sent away from their homes around the age of 8 to become a page (or serving boy) in an established knight's household. A page's job was to run errands in the household. Later, probably around the age of 14 or 15, the boy would become the knight's squire or personal attendant. Through this service a squire learned the trade of knighthood. He cared for his master-knight's weapons and horses. He waited on his master's table, carved his meat, and helped him dress. In his spare time the squire worked on his own training with a lance and sword. Finally, if the squire proved himself capable, he would be knighted around the age of eighteen.

But training wasn't all that went into knighthood. If you wanted to be a knight, you had to have the right equipment. For protection early knights wore chain mail—a mesh-like armor made from iron rings. This protected their skin from being cut by sword blows or pierced by arrows. Beneath their knee-length, chain-mail shirt (or *hauberk*), they wore a cloth coat to cushion their skin against battle bruises. The next piece of equipment every knight needed was a horse. This is what separated him from the peasant infantry soldiers. Knights also needed the right kind of saddle—one which had stirrups—so they could stand up and lean into their thrusts as their horses charged. Knights also needed weapons such as long lances, swords, and maces to do battle with. All of this equipment added up to a hefty price tag. This meant that in order to be a knight in the first place, you either had to come from a family with enough money to afford this expensive equipment or inherit it from a rich relative. Since armor was basically indestructible, it could be passed down from one generation to another.

Most young men bound for knighthood entered the service of a rich lord. There wasn't really a way to "get rich" in the Middle Ages. You were either born with money or without it. Owning land was the only way to obtain wealth. During this time Feudalism was the predominant system of government. Feudalism was a pyramid of power, and power was determined by land. On top was the king, and he owned all the land in his kingdom. But he needed faithful lords to help him protect it. So he divided most of his land among these lords and allowed them to manage it. In return these lords would fight for him when he called them. Then these land-holding lords further divided the land, giving small patches to their knights. From this land the knights could earn enough money to afford their costly equipment. In return the knights vowed to fight for the lords when called upon. The lowest level on the feudal pyramid of power was reserved for the peasants—workers who toiled in the fields of the knights and lords. They lived in poverty, had few rights, and had no hope of rising any higher than their lowly position. Some estimate that nearly 90 percent of the people living in European feudal societies were peasants.

Not all knights were able to enter the service of a rich lord. After all, there was only so much land to go around. So instead some knights earned their living by participating in tournaments. These tournaments were spectator-sport battles between knights that offered prize money to the winners. Wealthy lords came to watch these events, and ladies came to flirt with their favorite knights. Early tournaments were just big brawls between knights, but later they incorporated sport-like events like jousting. Some tournaments were so involved that they lasted an entire week! Even though these battles were staged, they still used actual weapons and could be deadly.

Knights were expected to follow the rules of chivalry (or the code of conduct for the ideal knight). The medieval church charged knights to be God's warriors, protecting the weak, upholding a godly life, and battling the enemies of goodness. Becoming a knight was also an official act of the church. Every knight had to undergo a "dubbing" ceremony—complete with symbolic rituals. The night before a young man was knighted, he took a ceremonial bath to symbolize his purification. Afterward, he was clothed all in white. Then he spent the rest of the night in the local church praying, asking for God's guidance. In the morning he would be dubbed an official knight. He was girded with a belt to remind him to avoid sins of the flesh and human lust. He was presented with gilded spurs to give him the courage to serve God. And finally, he was given a sword, with which to defend the poor against the rich. His sponsor—who must also be a knight—would strike him to help him remember the momentous day. The tapping of a sword on either shoulder later replaced this blow.

It was not only the church that promoted the ideals of chivalry, but also the popular literature of the day. Troubadours, traveling singers who traveled from one castle to another, told tales about valiant knights. Many of these tales featured the legendary British king Arthur and his noble Knights of the Round Table, who were the exemplification of chivalric ideals—courteous, well-spoken, brave, loyal, and honorable.

Although knights remained a power to be reckoned with for centuries, as technology advanced, they were forced to adapt. The invention of the crossbow, which could fire arrows through chain mail, caused knights to use armor made from interconnected sheets of solid metal called plate armor (the type of "shining armor" typically associated with knights). While plate armor was more effective at combating the crossbow, it made knights much bulkier. Suits of plate armor often weighed from 55-90 pounds. If a knight fell to the ground in battle, he would require help in order to stand again. When gunpowder was introduced into battle and bullets were able to penetrate even plate armor, armored knights were no longer effective. They were merely bulky moving targets. Knights, as we know them, began to fade away. They became the stuff of legends, yet their spirit lives on through tales like King Arthur and his Knights of the Round Table.

DISCUSSION QUESTIONS

1. What information about knights do you find most surprising or interesting? Explain.
2. Why do you think people still enjoy hearing stories about knights today?
3. Are the rules of chivalry still good rules to live by today? Explain.

THE QUEST FOR CHARACTER

In the old legends a questing knight is often presented with a choice. The road forks and offers two different paths, two different adventures, two different fates. The path that the knight chooses may determine the outcome of his quest or even his life. But he must act. He must choose, or the quest will be lost.

Nothing in life is more important than making good choices. Choices today affect tomorrow. Wrong turns and perilous pitfalls can divert your life away from the path that leads to success and contentment. Many of these decisions are difficult. Some must be made in a split second. They may affect your fate or the fate of others. So how do you know which path to take? How do you make sound decisions? The stories of knights give us an answer: Decisions based upon character are more rewarding than decisions made out of personal emotion or selfishness.

Character is also defined as "moral excellence"—or, in other words, having high-minded ideals and sticking to them. When a famous book of knights was published in 1485, it included this preface: "Herein may be seen noble chivalry, courtesy, humanity, friendliness, hardiness, love, friendship, cowardice, murder, hate, virtue, and sin. Do after the good and leave the evil." Hearing stories of knights was all about learning how to behave in tough decisions. In other words, many of these stories were lessons about character.

Take, for example, the following tale of two young brothers, Sir Bors and Sir Lionel. One day Sir Bors was riding through the forest looking for a quest when he saw an enemy knight carrying away a maiden against her will. Bors was about to act when yet another knight crossed his path. This second knight had taken prisoner Bors's brother, Lionel. Bors had to choose between two courses of action. On one hand, Bors had taken an oath to aid all maidens in distress, but on the other, he naturally wished to help his brother. This dilemma affected not only *his* future, but also the future of the two in need.

Bors made his decision: He decided to save the maiden. Bors chose the path of character by laying aside his personal feelings. His oath to serve and protect was put ahead of family obligations. What a noble knight! As he rode to the aid of the maiden, he prayed that somehow Lionel would be rescued. Lionel did manage to escape his captor, but he was enraged at Bors for not helping him. In fact, when he found Bors, he threatened to kill him. As you can see, Lionel was not as honorable as Bors. Instead of basing his decisions on character, he was selfish and harsh.

Lionel drew his sword, but Bors said he will not fight his own brother. Even in the face of death, Bors was sticking to his ideals. Lionel tried to strike Bors down, but a passing priest who saw the battle intervened. Lionel's anger was so great that he murdered the holy man for interfering. Bors still refused to fight, so Lionel raised his sword for the kill. Just then a column

252 The Road to Camelot

of fire fell from heaven, blasting Lionel to the ground. Heaven had intervened to keep him from committing a horrible crime. What's the message of this story? Bors made his decision based on character, and it was the right decision. Lionel's decision was not based on character, and it was the wrong decision.

All medieval knights were expected to abide by a code of honor called chivalry. One knight, called the best and greatest knight of his day, said this, "It is not good just to live, but to live in a good way." In order to show just what they believed in, King Arthur's Knights of the Round Table swore something called the Pentecostal Oath, a vow renewed each year at the feast of Pentecost. The Oath charged them to never murder and never be cruel. They must always give mercy to anyone who asks for mercy—even if it is the most evil villain in the world. They must always be of service to damsels in distress and anyone besieged by evil. They must never give battle for wrongful reasons or worldly gain. That was quite a list of expectations!

When a young man was knighted, he set out on a quest to prove that he could live by his code of honor. It's one thing to swear the Pentecostal Oath. It's another to live by it in the real world. In the legends the most successful knights are the ones who lived and died by their character. The less successful were those who gave into the temptation of thinking only of themselves, taking the easy road out of situations, or trading character for personal gain. The Knights of the Round Table had a special term for evil knights: They referred to them as *recreant* knights. *Recreant* is an old word meaning both cowardly and unfaithful. In other words these were knights who did not keep the faith and broke with their values.

Like the Knights of the Round Table every young person's goal should be to become a champion of character—not in words only, but in action. It is a lifelong quest but one well worth the reward.

Below is a list of virtues that knights were expected to uphold as part of their character:

Charity	Forgiveness/Mercy	Justice	Responsibility
Cheerfulness	Fortitude	Kindness	Self-control
Compassion	Gratitude	Love	Selflessness
Cooperation	Helpfulness	Patience	Self-Reliance
Courage	Hopefulness	Perseverance	Sportsmanship
Courtesy/Manners	Humility	Prudence	Wisdom
Faithfulness/Loyalty	Integrity/Truthfulness	Respect	Work ethic

DISCUSSION QUESTIONS AND ACTIVITIES

1. Did Sir Bors make the right decision in his dilemma? Explain.
2. Did Sir Lionel have a right to seek revenge upon his brother for not saving him? Explain.
3. Why is good character still important today?
4. How could good character make the world a different place?
5. Who are some of the people in the world today who still embody the virtues listed above?
6. **Connect:** Pick five of the listed virtues that you think are important. How could you exemplify them in your life?
7. **Activity:** In a group make a pledge similar to the Pentecostal Oath that outlines a set of virtues that you think are important. If you want, perform this oath for the other students.

MERLIN THE BOY MAGICIAN

Read this story about Merlin the magician's boyhood before you read "The Begetting of Arthur."

After seizing control of Britain through deceit and bloodshed, the cruel King Vortigern summoned his court magicians to ask them what he should do next. They all gave him the same advice: He should build an immensely strong tower-fortress upon Mount Erith. So Vortigern summoned many stonemasons, and they began to lay the foundations of a mighty tower. But however much they built, the earth swallowed it up each night, in such a way that they had no idea where their work had vanished to. Vortigern angrily consulted his magicians a second time to give them a chance of explaining the reason for this. The magicians were completely baffled, and when Vortigern threatened to slay them, they told him this: "You should look for a boy that has no father, and when the boy is found, his lifeblood should be sprinkled into the mortar. Then, and only then, the foundations of the tower will stand firm." The magicians gave this answer because they thought it was impossible to find a boy with no father. Little did they know that one really did exist.

Vortigern's knights were immediately sent out through Britain to search for a fatherless boy although they had no idea how to locate such a strange person. After days of searching the knights wandered into a muddy village and sat down by the town gate. Two boys, whose names were Merlin and Dinabutius, were playing in the street. Dinabutius was taunting Merlin, "Merlin, you fathead! I am of royal blood on both sides of my family. As for you, nobody even knows what blood you came from! You never even had a father!" Hearing this, the knights caught Merlin by the arm and ordered him to take them to his mother. Merlin nodded and calmly led them to the nearby nunnery, where his mother resided. When the knights had both Merlin and his mother in their custody, they took them back to Mount Erith.

The knights told King Vortigern all that they had heard. Then the king asked Merlin's mother if the boy truly had no father. "By my living soul, lord king," she said, "I know only this: When I was in my private apartment, someone or something used to come to me in the form of a most handsome young man. He would often hold me tightly in his arms and kiss me. When he had been some time with me, he would disappear, so that I could no longer see him. And in that way he made me with child. So it is up to you to decide in your wisdom who was the father of my son." Vortigern was very puzzled by this.

It was then that Merlin spoke, "King, you ask a question of my mother for which she knows no answer. But I do. It is true I have no earthly father, yet I have an unearthly father—an incubus, an evil spirit with the power to mate with mortal women. The powers of darkness intended me to be their instrument—a doer of evil. But when I was born, my pious mother had me baptized at once before darkness could seize me. So was I saved from a wicked fate. I retained the powers of my evil father, but the Lord took pity on me and blessed me with sight of the future. So here I am—born for evil, but preserved by goodness. Your magicians told you to search for me in order to slay me. They were given that message from my evil father and the forces that now seek for my death. Yet I came here today because I knew no harm would befall me." King Vortigern was amazed by all this and also by how eloquently the lad spoke.

Merlin continued, "Now I will prove your magicians to be liars. They told you my blood would cause the foundations of your tower to hold, but they did not know the true cause of your troubles. No structure may be built upon Mount Erith, and I will show you why. Summon your workmen. Order them to dig in the earth below your foundation, and, underneath, you will find a pool of water. That is what is preventing the tower from standing."

The king commanded that this be done, and the magicians scoffed that Merlin's words were preposterous. Workers toiled at removing the soil with large buckets and horses. At last a subterranean pool was discovered. All those present were equally amazed at Merlin's knowledge, and they realized that there was something supernatural about him.

The boy turned to the magicians. "Do any of you lying flatterers know what lies at the bottom of the pool?" They stared at him blankly. "No? Then I will tell you. King, order the pool to be drained, and at the bottom you will observe two hollow stones. Inside the stones are two great dragons which are sleeping. Each night they roll over in their sleep and shake the earth so that it swallows your foundations. Drain the pool by digging ditches and channels to remove the water. Then you will see if I speak the truth. If I am lying, you can drag me to death behind your horses, but if I am right, put these faithless magicians to the same fate."

The king agreed, and the terrified magicians watched as the pool was drained to reveal two enormous boulders. When the boulders began to smoke and hiss, Merlin cried, "Behold! The dragons sense each other. They are enemies—one is red, and one is white. They will soon break free." Everyone looked to the boy in terror. "You have nothing to fear. Draw away from this place, and the dragons will battle fiercely, but the white will slay the red." They did as Merlin said. Soon after, they saw flames sprouting from the two boulders, and the dragons broke free and fought fiercely. The two beasts battled for three days, but at last the red dragon was consumed by the flames of the white. When the red dragon was dead, the white dragon lay upon the ground, breathing slowly.

"Now that its enemy is defeated, the white dragon will slowly die," said Merlin. "King Vortigern you may now build your tower wherever you wish. But know this: The dragons are symbolic. The red dragon symbolizes you, who have taken this land forcefully and deceitfully, and the white dragon represents your enemies, who will return to reclaim their rightful lands. Now let my mother and I depart peacefully. You must prepare for war."

King Vortigern grew angry at these words, but he did nothing to stop Merlin and his mother from departing. He saw that the boy had great powers, and he feared him above all others. Instead he directed his wrath toward his magicians, whom he put to death. Because of this event, all of Britain began to whisper of Merlin, the boy with magical powers.

DISCUSSION QUESTIONS

1. What does this story show about Merlin? Explain.
2. What details make King Vortigern seem like a cruel and ruthless leader? Explain.
3. How might Merlin use his magical powers to make Britain a better place?

THE KNIGHTS OF THE ROUND TABLE

Read this information about the Knights of the Round Table before reading "The White Hart."

The Middle Ages was a tumultuous and dangerous time. Ruthless kings and lords won power by brute force and then viciously defended it. It was not uncommon for lords to murder their neighbors in order to steal their land. Anyone who did not have power—the poor, the weak, the ill-defended—were at the mercy of those who did. It was a time when "might made right," meaning that the powerful made the rules and ground everyone else under their heel.

Yet amid all this corruption, bloodshed, and chaos, King Arthur emerges and becomes a monarch who valued the poor, weak, and oppressed. Merlin the wizard tells Arthur that his destiny is to create a new kind of kingdom. Arthur's Britain becomes an experiment to answer this question: Can a kingdom be founded on the ideals of justice, mercy, and equality? To defend his new realm, Arthur creates the order of the Knights of the Round Table. The mission of these knights is to see that justice is upheld by taking up the cause of the oppressed and defenseless. Women, who were often at the mercy of their male overlords, were offered special protection by Arthur's knights. The Knights of the Round Table were to defend women at all times and accept any quest that was offered to them by a woman. Arthur's knights also abandoned the kill-or-be-killed mentality of the Middle Ages. Arthur commanded his knights to spare enemies who asked for mercy—no matter how deserving of death they might be. It becomes the first society to even approach the idea that "all men are created equal."

In the brutal Middle Ages it might seem that building a kingdom based on these principles would be suicide. Yet, instead of being easily overrun by its enemies, Arthur's kingdom flourishes. Knights from all over Britain are drawn to Camelot's call for justice and pledge themselves to its grand cause. Because of their dedication to these ideals, Arthur's knights become the first example of a band of heroes fighting for abstract principles such as justice, honor, and purity. For once it is not the external qualities of the knights—wealth, position, physical strength, and size—that measure their success, but rather their private integrity and devotion to their cause.

The Round Table itself symbolizes the kind of humility and sense of duty Arthur expects from his knights. Because of its shape, none of its sieges (or seats) is better than any other. All places are equal—even that of the king himself. In *Le Morte D'Arthur* Malory describes the formation of Arthur's knightly order in this manner: "The king stablished all his knights and gave them that were of lands not rich, he gave them lands and charged them never to do outrageousity nor murder and always to flee treason. Also, by no means to be cruel but to give mercy unto him that asketh mercy…and always to do ladies, damosels, and gentlewomen succor upon pain of death. Also, that no man take no battles in a wrongful quarrel for no law, [nor] for no world's goods. Unto this were all the knights sworn of the Table Round, both old and young. And every year were they sworn at the high feast of Pentecost." This yearly oath taken by the Knights of the Round Table became known as the Pentecostal Oath.

In the long run Arthur becomes a great king not because of the power he holds, but by his skill in inspiring, uniting, and leading others. Many of Arthur's knights hail from different backgrounds—Perceval is Welsh, Tristan is Cornish, Lancelot is French, Gawain and his brothers come from Orkney (or Scotland), and Palamedes is from the lands of the Saracens (Muslims). These are all lands that were in constant conflict with one another. Yet, inspired by Arthur's leadership, these knights lay aside their differences to band together for a common purpose: peace. Because of their diligence and willingness to work together, Arthur's reign becomes a golden age.

Arthur's leadership is key to the knights' success. In the Middle Ages different types of leaders were represented by the lion, fox, and pelican—three allegorical animals that appeared in the medieval bestiary (a collection of pictures and stories about the symbolic properties of animals). The lion represented bold and fearsome kings, who used their strength to overpower weaker opponents. The fox, a smaller and weaker animal, represented crafty kings, who used treachery and politics to outwit their opponents. The pelican, that was rumored to pierce its own breast so its young could feed on its blood, represented compassionate, humble, self-sacrificing kings. Arthur is neither a roaring lion nor a treacherous fox. In fact, it is the lions and foxes of Britain who threaten to get the best of him. Instead he is the pelican, who lives for something higher than himself and sacrifices himself for the good of his people.

Arthur's kingdom becomes so strong that it seems that no external force could ever destroy it. Yet a powerful danger lurks inside the heart of those who defend it. Only the Knights of the Round Table themselves and their human shortcomings have the power to destroy the kingdom they have helped create. Arthur and his knights are not perfect—as the stories about them prove. They are frail human beings with all the same faults that we have. If Arthur's knights choose to abandon the ideals that made them great, choosing selfishness and division over unity and brotherhood, they sow the seeds of their own destruction. It is a lesson that is still relevant today.

Ultimately, King Arthur and the Knights of the Round Table teach us two things: First, lofty ideas and goals can make the world a better place. And, secondly, these ideas can only survive through the commitment and integrity of those who diligently defend them.

DISCUSSION QUESTIONS

1. Why is King Arthur's reign ground-breaking?
2. What leadership lessons can be learned from King Arthur? Explain.
3. Is King Arthur's Britain a democracy or a monarchy? Explain.
4. What part did Merlin play in shaping King Arthur's outlook on kingship?
5. Should a great leader be a lion, a fox, a pelican, or some sort of combination of the three? Explain.
6. Do people today still believe in protecting the oppressed? Explain.
7. Read the Pentecostal Oath again. Is this a good charge for Arthur's knights? Should something be added to it?
8. Do those who serve and protect in your own society have a similar oath that they swear? Why is this oath important? Explain.

THE HOLY GRAIL

Read this information about the Holy Grail before reading "The Loves of Lancelot."

The Holy Grail, the golden vessel commonly alluded to as the Cup of Christ, is an object of legend that derives from a variety of ancient sources. Tales of supernatural Grail-like objects existed in Britain long before the arrival of Christianity. The Celts, the pagan inhabitants of the British Isles, had many tales about a mysterious cauldron imbued with the ability to provide eternal food and drink to its owner. In some stories this magical item could also bring the dead back to life. A quest to obtain this object (or one similar to it) was a frequent storyline in the tales of the Celts and their Welsh descendants.

When the Romans invaded Britain and subdued the peoples there, these stories of the Celts were driven underground. Centuries later these pagan tales found a new revival through an unexpected means—Christianity. The Roman Church, the continuation of the Roman Empire, started to supplant the pagan beliefs and holidays found in conquered lands with Christian ones. The pagan fertility symbols—evergreen trees, rabbits, and eggs—were adopted into the celebrations of Christ's birth and resurrection. The celebration of Mithras, December 25th, became the birthday of the Son of God. Legends of Arthur and other otherworldly heroes were modified. Arthur became a Christian king. The Grail, too, originally a magical object, became the holy cup of Christ. It still possessed awe-inspiring powers, but its powers now came from God.

FORMATION OF A HOLY LEGEND

Most of the stories and legends that concern the Grail as an object connected to Christ were written between the years of 1190–1240 A.D., over 1,000 years after the death of Christ. It was a time of high chivalry and Christian duty—a time when the glories of Heaven could be found upon the earth and good men could be taken directly into Heaven for their piety.

In many of these early stories the Grail is referenced as the *Graal* or the *Sangreal*. The word *graal* in Old French means merely *dish*, and the Grail, though often referenced as such, is not always a cup per se. Some of its more interesting appearances were: a platter from which Christ supped at the Last Supper, a carved head depicting the face of Jesus, a jewel from the crown of the fallen angel Satan or Lucifer knocked loose when he plummeted from Heaven, and, the most bizarre account of the Grail, a salver (a serving tray) containing a severed head swimming in blood. (This tale is probably a distortion of the biblical story of John the Baptist.) In every case, it was a relic that held otherworldly power—the object of many a knight's holy quest.

When these accounts became more unified and the image of the Grail as Christ's cup used at the Last Supper solidified, the Grail became associated with Joseph of Arimathea. Joseph of Arimathea is briefly mentioned in the gospels as the man who lent his tomb to be the final resting place of Christ. Later legends added another leg to the tale. The risen Christ appears to Joseph and entrusts to him a holy relic, the cup from the Last Supper, which the man uses to catch some of Christ's divine blood. Joseph's sacred duty is to now guard this prize and use it to convert the far reaches of the world to Christianity. Following the orders of his Lord, Joseph of Arimathea journeys from the Middle East to the British Isles where he establishes a line of Fisher Kings, men devoted to keeping and protecting the sacred relic of Christ. In later editions of this tale, the Last Supper platter and the spear that pierced Christ's side were added to this list of supernatural artifacts guarded by the legendary kings. Some even claimed those who kept these items received eternal youth.

THE QUEST FOR PURITY

Thanks to these various legends, the Holy Grail became the symbol of heavenly purity. Chivalry dictated that the goal of every knight was to achieve Christian perfection and to resist the temptations of the devil. Therefore, it should come as no shock that the pursuit of the Grail became a symbolic journey for the Knights of the Round Table. Only the knight who was purest of heart could find the Grail. Only the knight especially blessed by God could see its wonders.

The journey for the Holy Grail is a perilous one, filled with physical dangers and spiritual ones as well. If a knight's soul is not spotless, he will fail in his quest. Therefore, evil temptresses attempt to lure knights into lust, supernatural enemies assail them, and mortal opponents try to defeat them in battle and ruin their favor with God. In early versions of the grail quest story, it was a young knight named Perceval who finally found the holy resting place of the sacred cup. In later versions such as Thomas Malory's *Le Morte D'Arthur*, Bors, Lancelot, and Galahad are involved in the search as well. In all versions of the Grail quest, it is a goal that endangers the lives and souls of those who pursue it.

THE SYMBOLISM OF THE GRAIL

Many historians have given up the hope that there was an actual Holy Grail. If there was a special jeweled cup sought after by knights, it could not have been the cup of Jesus Christ—the son of a carpenter from Nazareth. The Grail is, therefore, left only its symbolism. It is the prize that many strive for in life, that perfection of heart and soul that allows one to sense the power of heaven on earth.

DISCUSSION QUESTIONS

1. What details about the Holy Grail do you find most surprising or interesting? Explain.
2. Why do you think people still enjoy hearing stories about the Holy Grail?
3. What are some stories or legends that you have heard that feature the Holy Grail?
4. How could the Holy Grail continue to be an inspiration in our own time?
5. Watch *Indiana Jones and the Last Crusade* (1989). How is the Holy Grail presented in this film? How does it match up with what you have learned about the Grail?

CASTLES AND CATAPULTS: RULES OF THE GAME

OBJECT OF THE GAME: Defeat your opponent by destroying all the battle pieces in his or her realm.

SETUP: This game is for 2 players. Sit across from your opponent so that neither of you can see each other's game-sheet. Secretly fill out your game-sheet by marking the location of your battle pieces with X's on the "Your Realm" bottom grid. These pieces can be laid out horizontally or vertically, but not diagonally. (See Figure 1.) Try to place pieces strategically in locations and arrangements that your opponent would least suspect. No piece may overlap another piece or go over the edge of the grid.

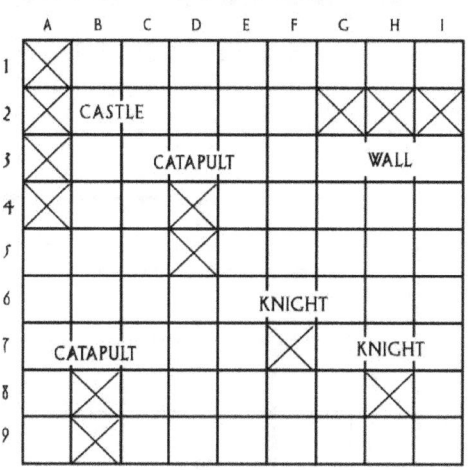

Figure 1: Sample Grid

HOW TO PLAY: You and your opponent will alternate turns, calling out 1-3 shots per round. The number of shots you take each round is determined by how many catapults you still have in operation. You are always guaranteed 1 shot, but you also receive 1 additional shot for each operational catapult. (Example: 1 of your catapults has been completely destroyed during the game. The next round you will get only 2 shots—1 guaranteed shot and 1 for your 1 intact catapult.)

YOUR 6 BATTLE PIECES

- Castle — 4 squares
- Wall — 3 squares
- Catapult — 2 squares
- Catapult — 2 squares
- Knight — 1 square
- Knight — 1 square

CALL YOUR SHOTS: To call a shot look at the "Your Opponent's Realm" top grid on your game-sheet and select a square to fire upon. Each square has a number-letter coordinate. (For example, on Figure 1, a knight is located at 7F with another at 8H.) Call out the square coordinate that you want to attack. You will do this 1-3 times per round. Your opponent must tell you after each shot whether it was a hit or a miss.

IT'S A HIT: If you call out a square that is occupied by a battle piece on your opponent's game-sheet, your shot is a hit! Your opponent then tells you which battle piece you have hit (castle, wall, catapult, etc.) Record your hit by drawing an "X" on that square of the opponent grid. If one of *your* battle pieces is hit during a round, black out that square on your grid.

IT'S A MISS: If you call out a square that is not occupied by a battle piece on your opponent's game-sheet, your shot is a miss. Record your miss by drawing an "O" on that square of your opponent grid.

DESTROYING BATTLE PIECES: Once all the squares of a particular battle piece have been hit, that piece is destroyed. The owner of that battle piece must announce which type of piece has been destroyed. **Note:** Catapults still give players an extra shot until they have been *completely* destroyed (hit twice).

WINNING THE GAME: If you destroy all your opponent's battle pieces, you win the game!

CASTLES AND CATAPULTS

USE THE TOP GRID TO MARK YOUR HITS AND MISSES ON YOUR OPPONENT'S REALM.
USE THE BOTTOM GRID TO LAYOUT YOUR REALM.

YOUR OPPONENT'S REALM

O = MISS
X = HIT

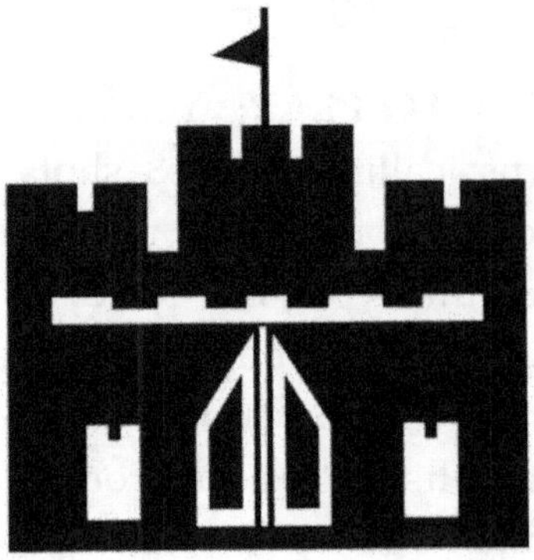

YOUR REALM

CASTLE
WALL
CATAPULT
CATAPULT
KNIGHT   KNIGHT

Introduction: Times are dark in Camelot. Mordred, the evil son of King Arthur, and his spies have infiltrated Arthur's court—poisoning it to the point where Arthur no longer knows who is a Loyalist and who is a Traitor among his Knights of the Round Table. To make matters worse, the Traitors are plotting to murder the Loyalists of Camelot one by one. It is up to the citizens of Camelot to determine who is a Loyalist and who should be executed as a Traitor.

Gameplay: This is a game of conspiracy and paranoia. The Loyalists are trying to determine who among the group is a Traitor. The Traitors are trying to murder the Loyalists before they can discover their identities. Gameplay is based on *Mafia* (also known as *Werewolf*), where a group of murderous conspirators have infiltrated an unsuspecting group of innocents.

Needed Supplies: A copy of *Conspiracy in Camelot* cards (enough for all players)

Number of Players: 8+

- A minimum of 8 players is needed (2 Traitors, 6 Loyalists)
- There is no maximum number of players, but groups of 20-25 work best. Larger groups can be broken down into smaller groups, but note that each group will need its own Gamemaster.
- An odd number of players leads to smoother gameplay, but this is not necessary.
- The teacher acts as Gamemaster (moderator).

Cards: 10 Loyalist cards, 1 Rogue card, 4 Traitor cards, and 3 special cards pgs. 275-276. (Note: To accommodate groups larger than 15 players, make a copy of the generic "Loyal Knight" and "Traitor Knight" cards on pg. 277 to fill out the needed amount.)

<u>How the Game Works</u>

1. The Gamemaster distributes the correct number of Loyalist and Traitor cards to all players.
    a. Players view their identities but keep them a secret from other players.
2. Rounds: Each round is made up of two parts (Night and Day).
    a. <u>Night</u>: All players go to sleep (put their heads down) while the Traitors wake up and try to murder a Loyalist. Once the Traitors have selected a Loyalist to murder, they go back to sleep, and the Day portion of the round begins.

b. <u>Day</u>: All players wake up (open their eyes), see who was murdered during the Night, and debate the identity of the Traitors. When the players have decided on the identity of a Traitor, they vote to execute that player. If a majority of players vote to execute the player as a Traitor, the player dies.
   i. This is where the roleplaying aspect of the game comes in. Players must somehow prove (or fake) their innocence to avoid execution as a Traitor.
3. <u>Winning the Game:</u> The Loyalists win if they execute all of the Traitors successfully. The Traitors win if the number of Traitors is equal to the number of Loyalists. (Or in other words, they have murdered enough Loyalists to gain control of the Round Table.)
4. A typical game lasts 15-45 minutes based on group size. Smaller groups can play through the game more quickly.
5. Bluffing and roleplaying are a large part of this game. Players take on the personality of the character they are dealt. If they are a Traitor, they will do best if they seem innocent to the Loyalists and protest when they are accused of crimes. If players are uncomfortable with the bluffing aspect of the game, the Gamemaster could secretly make sure that they are dealt a "good guy" card that would prevent the need for them to take on the role of a deceptive character.

Beginning the Game

1. The Gamemaster calculates how many players will be Traitors and how many will be Loyalists.
   a. 1/4 of the group should be Traitors.
   b. 3/4 of the group should be Loyalists.
   c. To determine the correct number of Traitors, divide the number of players by 4 and round to the nearest whole number.
   d. The Green Knight counts as a Loyalist although he is technically a rogue.
2. The Gamemaster determines if the game will be played using Simple or Advanced Gameplay.
   a. Simple gameplay works best for smaller groups (fewer than 10 players) and has no special roles other than Loyalist and Traitor. (See "Simple Gameplay" section for more details.)
   b. Advanced gameplay works best for larger groups (more than 10 players) and has special roles added to the Loyalist and Traitor teams. (See "Advanced Gameplay" for more details.)
3. The Gamemaster copies and cuts out the correct number of cards for the group, so that each player has a card—keeping the correct ratio of Loyalists to Traitors.
   a. To accommodate larger groups, make extra copies of the generic "Loyalist" and "Traitor" cards on pg. 277.
   b. The brick wall pattern on pg. 278 can be copied onto the back of the cards to make them less transparent.
   c. Laminating the cards keeps them from wear and tear.
4. The Gamemaster sets up the room for gameplay. The game works best if all the players sit in a circle. This gives players a clear view of all the other players (not to mention a Round Table feel).

5. The Gamemaster randomly distributes a Loyalist or Traitor card to every player.
    a. It is *imperative* that players do not show what cards they have been dealt.
    b. Any players who try to cheat in any way should be removed from the game immediately.

<u>Simple Gameplay: Instructions for the Gamemaster</u> This method of gameplay works best for small groups (fewer than 10 players). These instructions are intended for the Gamemaster. Actions performed by the Gamemaster are indicated by bold type.

1. <u>Distributing the Cards:</u> **Pass out the appropriate number of Traitor and Loyalist cards.**
    a. In this version of the game there are no optional player roles; therefore, the character names and pictures on the cards will have no meaning other than indicating whether the player is a Traitor or a Loyalist.
    b. The Green Knight, Excalibur, Siege Perilous, and Holy Grail cards are *not* used in Simple Gameplay and should be excluded from the deck.
2. <u>Players view their cards:</u> **Say, "You may look at your card, but keep your card a secret. Keeping your identity a secret is very important in this game. Some of you are Traitors, and some of you are Loyalists."**
3. <u>Revealing the Traitors to One Another:</u> **Say, "All players, sleep or close your eyes. If you received a Traitor card, wake up or open your eyes."**
    a. All the Traitors have a chance to see one another.
4. <u>Traitors Murder a Loyalist:</u> **Say, "Now, Traitors, choose one player whom you would like to kill."**
    a. The Traitors collaborate through silent gesturing to indicate which Loyalist character they would like to kill.
5. <u>The Traitors Choose a Victim:</u> **Once the Traitors' victim has been chosen, say, "All players, sleep. All players, open your eyes. [Player name] was murdered during the night."**
    a. It is very important that no players speak or gesture once they are dead.
6. <u>Players Accuse Other Players of Treason:</u> **Say, "Now the court of Camelot must decide who is a Traitor among you."**
    a. Players debate who is a Traitor by using evidence (such as "I heard Billy moving" or "Jill seems to be acting suspicious").
    b. Players can also ask other players questions like, "Did you kill Roger?" to see their reaction.
    c. Accused players also have a chance to defend themselves.
    d. Any player can suggest that the accusation be brought to a vote.
    e. The vote is always visible and conducted during the Day portion of the game. How players vote is a clue in determining who is a Traitor and who is a Loyalist.
7. <u>The Loyalists Choose a Player to Execute:</u> **When the group has decided they would like to execute a certain player as a Traitor, say, "[Player name] has been accused of treason. Who votes [Player name] is guilty? Who votes that [Player name] is not guilty?"**

a. All living players vote on whether or not the accused is guilty by a show of hands. A tie in number of votes cannot condemn a player to execution, so the debate continues.
8. <u>The Majority of Players Votes *Not Guilty*:</u> If the majority of players vote *not guilty*, the debate continues until another vote is called for. **Say, "Continue the debate to locate the Traitors."**
9. <u>The Majority of Players Votes *Guilty*:</u> **If the majority of players vote *guilty*, say, "[Player name] has been hanged for treason. Now [Player name] tell us your true identity."**
    a. The player reveals whether he or she was a Traitor or Loyalist.
10. <u>Day Turns to Night:</u> **Say, "All players sleep."**
    a. Night falls, and the Traitors choose their next victim.
11. This cycle of murders and accusations continues until either the Traitors or Loyalists win.
    a. <u>Traitors win:</u> The number of Traitors equals the number of Loyalists. The Traitors have control of the voting and the court of Arthur.
    b. <u>Loyalists win:</u> All the Traitors have been found and executed.

Advanced Gameplay: This form of gameplay is best for larger groups (more than 10 players).

- Advanced Gameplay makes use of many different character roles (for both Loyalists and Traitors) as well as three power cards (the Excalibur, Siege Perilous, and Holy Grail cards).
- Adding in these optional roles will make the playing of the game much more complex by adding quite a bit of diversity and strategy.
- While it is recommended that *all* these extra roles be added into Advanced Gameplay, the Gamemaster *can* pick and choose which extra roles to add. But it should be noted that many of them skew the odds of winning toward one particular side.
- Players should have a copy of the sheets (pgs. 272-274) that tell about the different character roles.

Advanced Gameplay Instructions for the Gamemaster: These instructions are intended for the Gamemaster. Actions performed by the Gamemaster are indicated by bold type.

Distributing Character and Power Cards

1. <u>Distributing the Cards:</u> **Pass out one character card to each player.**
2. <u>Players View Their Cards:</u> **Say, "You may look at your card, but keep it a secret. Keeping your identity a secret is very important in this game. Some of you are Traitors, and some of you are Loyalists. Some of you are secretly characters who have special knowledge or special powers. These cannot do you any good unless you keep them hidden."**
    a. Each card will indicate two things: a character role for the player and whether the player is a Traitor or a Loyalist. (The Green Knight is a rogue but appears as a Loyalist.)
3. <u>Defining Character Roles:</u> **Read the character role profiles aloud to the players.**

a. For example, tell them that the Lady of the Lake has the power to protect one player each Night.
b. Giving the players a list of the special character roles is recommended.
4. <u>Explaining the Power Cards:</u> **Read aloud the descriptions of the Excalibur, Siege Perilous, and Holy Grail cards.**
    a. Say, "If you receive one of these cards, you can choose to keep it hidden, or you can reveal it."
5. <u>Distributing Power Cards:</u> Say, "All characters, sleep." This means that all players must close their eyes.
    a. Say, "If I place a power card in your hand, you may open your eyes to view it. Once you have seen the card, close your eyes once again."
    b. Randomly distribute the Excalibur card to any player (Loyalist or Traitor). Allow the player a chance to open his or her eyes and examine the card and then go back to sleep before distributing the next card.
    c. Randomly distribute the Holy Grail card to any player (Loyalist or Traitor). Allow the player a chance to open his or her eyes and examine the card and then go back to sleep before distributing the next card.
    d. Randomly distribute the Siege Perilous card to any player (Loyalist or Traitor). Allow the player a chance to open his or her eyes and examine the card and then go back to sleep before distributing the next card.
6. <u>Revealing Character Roles to Select Players:</u> Say, "All players, keeping your eyes closed, put your fists out in front of you."
    a. Gawain Sees King Arthur: Say, "The player who is Gawain, open your eyes. Whichever player is King Arthur, keep your eyes closed but lift your thumb. Gawain, this is your uncle, King Arthur. You have sworn to protect him at any cost. King Arthur, put down your thumb. Gawain, go back to sleep."
    b. Traitors See One Another: Say, "If you were given a Traitor card, lift your thumb. Now, Traitors, open your eyes and see your comrades. Traitors, put down your thumbs and go back to sleep."
    c. Lancelot and Guinevere See One Another: Say, "If you are Lancelot or Guinevere, lift your thumb. Now, Lancelot and Guinevere, open your eyes to see your one true love. Lancelot and Guinevere, lower your thumbs and go back to sleep."
    d. After this is done, the first Night of the game can begin.

Night: Committing the Murders When characters die or cards have been eliminated, the steps associated with them can be skipped.

1. <u>Merlin Learns a Player's Identity:</u> Say, "Night has fallen on Camelot. Merlin, awake. Whose identity would you like to know?"
    a. Merlin points to a player.
    b. **Motion *thumbs up* for Loyalist and *thumbs down* for Traitor.**
    c. Say, "Merlin, sleep."
    d. If Merlin has been killed and Nimue is still living, she inherits Merlin's powers. Substitute Nimue's name for Merlin's in this step.

2. <u>Mordred Attempts to Identify Lancelot:</u> **Say, "Mordred, awake. Who do you think is Lancelot?"**
    a. Mordred points to a player.
    b. Motion *thumbs up* if the player is Lancelot and *thumbs down* if it is not.
        i. **If Mordred successfully identifies Lancelot, say, "Mordred has revealed the affair between Lancelot and Queen Guinevere. Lancelot is now called a Traitor. Lancelot, when other Traitors are asked to open their eyes, you must open yours as well."**
        ii. If Mordred does not identify Lancelot, he can try again the next Night.
    c. Say, **"Mordred, sleep."**
3. <u>Morgan le Fay Attempts to Identify Merlin:</u> **Say, "Morgan le Fay, awake. Who do you think is Merlin?"**
    a. Morgan le Fay points to a player.
    b. Motion *thumbs up* if it is Merlin and *thumbs down* if it is not.
    c. Say, **"Morgan le Fay, sleep."**
    d. If Morgan le Fay has been killed and the Evil Dwarf is still living, Morgan's abilities pass to him. Substitute Evil Dwarf's name for Morgan le Fay's in this step.
4. <u>Gawain Speaks from Beyond the Grave:</u> **If Gawain has been killed, say, "Ghost of Gawain, you may write one letter—and one letter only—of a message to your fellow Loyalists. You will be able to write another letter tomorrow night."** Make sure Gawain writes only *one* letter of a message and makes no other indications to the other players.
5. <u>The Lady of the Lake Protects One Player:</u> **Say, "Lady of the Lake, awake. Whom would you like to protect this night with your magic?"**
    a. The Lady of the Lake indicates a player. This player cannot be killed by the Traitors for the Night portion of the round.
    b. Say, **"Lady of the Lake, sleep."**
6. <u>Traitors Attempt to Murder a Loyalist:</u> **Say, "All Traitors, awake. Whom would you like to kill this night?"**
    a. Give the Traitors time to indicate by silent gestures which player they would like to murder.
    b. Say, **"Traitors, sleep."** The round moves on to the Day portion of the round.

Day: Announcing the Murder, Making Accusations, and Executing a Traitor

1. <u>A Failed Murder Attempt:</u> If the Traitors attempt to kill a character, but their attempt is thwarted for some reason (Excalibur card, Lady of the Lake's protection, etc.), the character survives.
    a. Say, **"All characters, wake up. No murder was committed last night."**
2. <u>A Successful Murder Attempt:</u> If the Traitors chose to kill a character not protected by magic or the Excalibur card, the player is murdered.
    a. Announcing the Murder: Say, **"All characters, wake up. During the night the Traitors have murdered one of the Loyalists. [Player name] has been murdered."**

b. Add creative details to the murder. See "Tips for Modifying the Game" section on pg. 270.
   c. It is very important that no players speak or gesture to anyone else once they are dead.
3. Objections: At this point it is possible for the murder to be reversed.
   a. **Say, "Are there any objections to this murder?"**
   b. Perceval can volunteer to die in the character's place.
   c. The murdered player can reveal that he or she has the Excalibur card.
   d. Another player can play the Holy Grail card to spare the murdered player's life.
4. No Objections: The murder stands.
   a. **Say, "If there are no objections, [Player name] is murdered. [Player name], please tell us your identity and your character's name."**
   b. The player does so.
5. Consequences of a Character's Death: At this point any consequences of the character's death are performed.
   a. Arthur: The death of Arthur allows the Traitors to murder two victims the following Night.
      i. **Say, "King Arthur, Camelot's leader, has fallen, but the Knights of the Round Table will carry on. Tonight the Traitors, emboldened by their victory, will be able to kill two victims."**
   b. Galahad: Galahad gets to kill one other player of his choosing.
      i. **Say, "Galahad, Camelot's holiest knight, has been murdered. Because of this, he will call down heavenly fire on a person he believes to be a traitor." Galahad selects a player to execute. The player dies automatically unless the player is holding the Excalibur card. Say, "[Player name], you have been incinerated by heavenly fire. Now tell us your true identity."**
   c. Guinevere: Guinevere's death causes the death of Lancelot.
      i. **Say, "Guinevere, Queen of Camelot, has been murdered. Because of this, her lover, Lancelot, will die of a broken heart. Lancelot, reveal yourself."**
      ii. Lancelot dies automatically.
   d. Lancelot: Lancelot's death causes the death of Guinevere.
      i. **Say, "Lancelot has been murdered. Because of this, his lover, Queen Guinevere, will die of a broken heart. Queen Guinevere, reveal yourself."**
      ii. Guinevere dies automatically.
   e. Green Knight: The Green Knight's death prevents the Loyalists from executing anyone the following Day.
      i. **Say, "The Green Knight, a magical opponent, has been murdered. He has put a curse on his murderers. Tonight the Traitors may not murder anyone."**
   f. Merlin: Merlin's powers pass to Nimue if she is still living.
      i. **Say, "Merlin the Good Enchanter has been murdered. His magical powers now pass on to Nimue, his assistant."**

6. <u>Accusations:</u> Say, "Now Knights of the Round Table, you know that there is a Traitor among you. You must decide who it is."
    a. The players are given a chance to interrogate and accuse one another. They also have the chance to defend themselves as well.
    a. Players can give evidence to accuse one another such as "I hear her moving. He looks guilty. She's lying because last round she said this…"
    b. Players have a chance to defend themselves against accusations. They can give evidence of their innocence (without revealing their character-identity). They can even make up fake alibis about their whereabouts during the Night such as "I couldn't have done that. I was out on a quest last night slaying a dragon!"
7. <u>Exchanging Power Cards:</u> This is also the time that players can trade the Excalibur, Holy Grail, or Siege Perilous card. The Excalibur card *must* change hands every round. The Holy Grail and Siege Perilous cards do *not* have to change hands.
    a. Card-trading can be done by players saying, "Who would like to have the Excalibur card next?"
    b. Players *can* give the card to another player silently.
    c. The Gamemaster must see that the Excalibur card has changed hands each round.
8. <u>Playing the Siege Perilous card:</u> Any time during the Day portion of the round, players can use the Siege Perilous card to test another player.
    a. Players do this by saying, "I would like to test [Player name] using the Siege Perilous."
    b. Say, "[Player name] you sit in the Siege Perilous. If you are a Loyalist, you will survive. If you are a Traitor, you will be destroyed by heavenly fire. Now tell us whether you are a Traitor or a Loyalist."
        i. If the character is a Traitor, say, "[Player name], you have been destroyed by heavenly fire. Now reveal your character name to everyone."
        ii. If the character is a Loyalist, say, "[Player name], you have survived the test. Thank you for being loyal to your king!"
9. <u>Voting on Traitors:</u> Any player can call for a vote at any time.
    a. **When the group has decided they would like to execute a certain player as a Traitor, say, "[Player name] has been accused of treason. Who votes [Player name] is guilty? Who votes that [Player name] is not guilty?"**
    b. All living players vote on whether or not the accused is guilty by a show of hands. A tie in number of votes cannot condemn a player to execution.
    c. **If the majority of players vote *not guilty*, the debate continues until another vote is called for.**
    d. **If the majority of players vote *guilty*, say, "[Player name] will be hanged for treason unless someone has the power to intervene."**
        i. Perceval can volunteer to die in the character's place.
        ii. The player can reveal that he or she has the Excalibur card.
        iii. Another player can play the Holy Grail card to spare the murdered player's life.
        iv. If the player is Arthur, he or she can reveal this to escape execution.

10. <u>Execution:</u> **If no one intervenes, say "[Player name] has been hanged for treason. Now [Player name] tell us your true identity."**
    a. The player reveals whether he or she was a Traitor or Loyalist and reveals his or her character name. At this point any consequences of the character's death are performed.
11. <u>Consequences of an Executed Character's Death:</u>
    a. <u>Galahad:</u> Galahad gets to kill one other player of his choosing.
        i. **Say, "You have executed Galahad, Camelot's holiest knight. Because of this, he will call down heavenly fire on a person he believes to be a Traitor."**
        ii. Galahad selects a player to execute.
        iii. The player dies automatically unless the player is holding the Excalibur card.
        iv. **Say, "[Player name], you have been incinerated by heavenly fire. Now tell us your true identity."**
    b. <u>Guinevere:</u> Guinevere's death causes the death of Lancelot.
        i. **Say, "You have executed Guinevere, Queen of Camelot. Because of this, her lover, Lancelot, will die of a broken heart. Lancelot, reveal yourself."**
        ii. Lancelot dies automatically.
    c. <u>Lancelot:</u> Lancelot's death causes the death of Guinevere.
        i. **Say, "You have executed Lancelot. Because of this, his lover, Queen Guinevere, will die of a broken heart. Queen Guinevere, reveal yourself."**
        ii. Guinevere dies automatically.
    d. <u>Green Knight:</u> The Green Knight's death prevents the Loyalists from executing anyone the following Day.
        i. **Say, "You have executed the Green Knight, a magical opponent. He has put a curse on you. Tomorrow you may not execute anyone as a Traitor."**
    e. <u>Merlin:</u> Merlin's powers pass to Nimue if she is still living.
        i. **Say, "You have executed Merlin the Good Enchanter. His magical powers now pass on to Nimue, his assistant."**
    f. <u>Mordred:</u> Mordred's death allows the Traitors to kill twice the next Night.
        i. **Say, "You have executed Mordred, the illegitimate son of King Arthur. Because of this, the Traitors will have a chance to kill two victims tonight."**
    g. <u>Morgan le Fay:</u> Morgan le Fay's powers pass to the Evil Dwarf if he is still living.
        i. **Say, "You have executed Morgan le Fay, the evil sorceress. Her magical powers now pass on to the Evil Dwarf."**
12. <u>End of Day:</u> **Say, "Night is coming again. All players, sleep."**
    a. Night falls, and the Traitors choose their next victim.
    a. Return to the instructions for the Night portion of the round.
13. <u>Winning the Game:</u> This cycle of murders and accusations continues until either the Traitors or Loyalists win.
    a. <u>Traitors win:</u> The number of Traitors equals the number of Loyalists. The Traitors have control of the voting and the court of Arthur.

b. <u>Loyalists win:</u> All the Traitors have been found and executed.
c. <u>Green Knight wins:</u> Since he is a rogue, the Green Knight wins only if he is still alive at the end of the game.

<u>Tips for Modifying the Game</u>

1. Having all players hum or tap their hands on the desk during the Night portion of the round eliminates the risk of the Loyalists hearing the Traitors moving as they gesture to one another.
2. The rules of Advanced Gameplay can be confusing for some players. Playing the game once in Simple Gameplay may be a good idea before progressing to Advanced Gameplay.
3. In Simple Gameplay having executed players *not* reveal whether or not they are Traitors or Loyalists makes the game more challenging. Using this rule, players do not learn the identities of any players until the end of the game.
4. If you would like gameplay to be a bit more complicated than Simple Gameplay, but don't think you are ready for Advanced Gameplay, simply add the three Power cards to Simple Gameplay to make it a bit more complex.
5. Designating 1/3 of the players as Traitors and 2/3 as Loyalists (rounding to the closest whole number) makes the game more challenging for the Loyalists.
6. Setting a time limit on how long the Day debates can last helps speed up gameplay. If the group has not decided on a player to accuse of being a Traitor by the time limit, they lose the opportunity to execute someone that Day.
7. The Gamemaster can come up with fun and creative ways to describe the deaths of the murdered characters such as "[Player name] was murdered last night. He went on a quest with his fellow knights to rescue a long-haired maiden from a high tower. When no one was looking, one of the other knights cut his rope as he was scaling the tower—dropping him to his death."
8. Adding special effects such as dimming the lights or playing spooky music for the Night makes the game more fun.

SPECIAL CHARACTER ROLES

These special character roles intensify the roleplaying aspect of the game. Certain character roles are given special knowledge, such as Guinevere and Lancelot who know each other's identity. Others are given special powers, such as the Lady of the Lake, who can protect one player from murder each Night portion of the game.

LOYALISTS: ALLIES OF CAMELOT

Arthur (Loyalist) King Arthur is the ruler of Camelot. If King Arthur is murdered, the Traitors get to commit two murders during the next Night. If King Arthur is slated for execution, he can reveal his identity and be spared—but this will make him a prime target for the Traitors.

Gawain (Loyalist) Gawain gets to see the identity of King Arthur at the beginning of the game. In this way he can help protect Arthur from harm. Once Gawain is killed (either through murder or execution), his ghost can send messages back from the grave. He can stay awake at Night, see who the Traitors are, and deliver a message to the other Loyalists. The only catch is this: The message can be written only one letter at a time—with one letter of the message written each Night. (No names or initials can be used in this message.)

Perceval (Loyalist) Kindhearted Perceval has the power to give his life for another character. When the death of a character is announced (either by murder or execution), Perceval can voluntarily substitute his life. Perceval dies, and the character returns to regular play. This must be done *before* the identity or loyalty of the character is revealed. If Perceval is fooled, he *can* forfeit his life for the life of a Traitor, whom he believes to be innocent.

Merlin (Loyalist) Each Night Merlin gets to wake up and use his magic to determine the allegiance of one player. Merlin will point at the player, and the Gamemaster will motion *thumbs up* for Loyalist and *thumbs down* for Traitor. In the event that Merlin is murdered or executed, his magic abilities pass on to Nimue, his apprentice.

Guinevere (Loyalist) Guinevere remains a Loyalist throughout the game. At the beginning of the game, Guinevere and Lancelot are shown each other's identity. If Lancelot dies (either by murder or execution), Guinevere will automatically die of a broken heart. If Lancelot becomes a Traitor, it is still in Guinevere's best interest to keep him from being executed. After all—if he dies, she dies.

Lady of the Lake (Loyalist) The Lady of the Lake can use her powers to protect one player each Night. During the Night, she will point at one player whom she would like to protect. That player cannot be murdered by the Traitors. She cannot choose the same person two Nights in a row, and she cannot choose to protect herself.

Nimue (Loyalist) Nimue plays the game as a regular Loyalist. In the event that Merlin is killed, she inherits his powers. Merlin's Powers: Each Night Merlin gets to wake up and determine the allegiance of one player. Merlin will point at the player, and the Gamemaster will motion *thumbs up* for Loyalist and *thumbs down* for Traitor.

Galahad (Loyalist) Galahad is Camelot's holiest knight, and Heaven will have revenge for his death. If Galahad is murdered or executed, with his dying breath he can call down heavenly fire upon someone he suspects of being a Traitor, and that player will die automatically.

Lancelot (Loyalist/Traitor) Lancelot plays the game as a regular Loyalist—unless his identity is discovered by Mordred. If this happens, Lancelot's affair with Guinevere is exposed, and he is forced onto the side of the Traitors. He will play as a Traitor the rest of the game. Also Lancelot and Guinevere know each other's identity. If Guinevere dies at any point during the game (either by murder or execution), Lancelot dies as well.

Loyal Knight (Loyalist) As a loyal member of the Round Table, it is this character's duty to detect the identity of the Traitors in Camelot and execute them.

The Green Knight (Rogue) The Green Knight is a mysterious rogue knight who appears as a Loyalist but is only out for himself. When either side kills the Green Knight by murder or execution, their team is cursed and cannot kill for one round. Since he is a rogue, the Green Knight only wins if he is alive at the end of the game.

TRAITORS: ENEMIES OF CAMELOT

Mordred (Traitor) Mordred is the leader of the Traitors. Each Night he gets to wake up and try to identify Lancelot. If Mordred is executed by the Loyalists, the Traitors get to commit two murders the next Night.

Morgan le Fay (Traitor) Morgan le Fay uses her magic to wake once per Night and attempt to identify Merlin. She does this by pointing at one player she thinks might be Merlin. The Gamemaster will indicate *thumbs up* if the player is Merlin or *thumbs down* if the player is not. If Merlin has died,

Morgan then tries to identify Nimue, who has inherited Merlin's powers.

The Evil Dwarf (Traitor) The Evil Dwarf plays the game as a regular Traitor. In the event that Morgan le Fay is killed, he inherits her magical powers—waking up once each Night to try to detect Merlin or Nimue.

Traitor Knight (Traitor) The Traitor knight has infiltrated the Round Table and is secretly murdering the loyal knights of King Arthur. His allegiance must remain a secret, or he will be executed by the Loyalists.

POWER CARDS

Power cards must be played during the Day portion of each round. They do not need to be kept secret. In fact, they should be used as tools to win friends by proving or faking innocence. They can be traded from player to player during the Day portion of each round.

Excalibur Card Whoever wields the Excalibur card (whether Traitor or Loyalist) is invincible. If a character is announced as murdered or executed, the character may reveal the card to escape death. A player *cannot* keep the Excalibur card more than one round, so it must change hands during each Day. A player can choose to "throw Excalibur into the lake" by returning it to the Gamemaster and removing it from play.

The Holy Grail Card This card can be used only once per game to save another character (Loyalist or Traitor) from death. The card must be played during the Day *after* the death of a player is announced but *before* the player's character name and allegiance are announced. A player *cannot* use the Holy Grail card to save his or her own life. The Holy Grail card is distributed randomly by the Gamemaster to either a Traitor or a Loyalist at the beginning of the game. Once the card has been used, it is returned to the Gamemaster. Until it is used, the card can be transferred from player to player multiple times during the Day, but it does not have to change hands until it is used.

The Siege Perilous Card This card, which tests the loyalty of a player, can be played *once* during the entire game. This card should be played during the Day portion of the game. The cardholder selects a player to "test" using the card. If the tested player is a Traitor, the player will die because of the test—consumed by heavenly fire. If the tested player is a Loyalist, the player will survive. After it is used once, the Siege Perilous card is removed from play.

Camelot Find-It Puzzle 279

CAMELOT FIND·IT PUZZLE

CAN YOU FIND ALL OF THESE ITEMS HIDDEN IN THE PICTURE?

- Adder
- Apple
- Arrows (5)
- Bird's Nest
- Blind Worm
- Cart
- Catapult
- Caterpillar
- Copy of *Le Morte D'Arthur*
- Crowns (8)
- Dollar Sign
- Dove with a Censure of Gold in Its Beak
- Evil Dwarf
- Excalibur
- Eye of Newt
- Fork
- Foxes (2)
- Galahad
- Ghost of Sir Gawain
- Holly
- Holy Grail
- Jesters (2)
- Killer Rabbit
- King Arthur
- Ladder
- Lady Elaine
- Lancelot
- Lion
- Merlin
- Miniature Camelot Castle
- Miniature Round Table
- Miniature Stonehenge
- Morgan le Fay
- Musical Note
- Name: Malory
- Queen Guinevere
- Red Herring
- Rings (2)
- Shields (3)
- Skulls (6)
- Spider
- Spiked Helmet
- Spurs
- Stars (6)
- Swallow Carrying a Coconut
- Swan
- The Green Knight
- The Green Knight's Head
- The Road to Camelot
- The Siege Perilous
- The Sword in the Stone
- The Sword in the Stump
- The Sword in the Swiss
- Toe of Frog
- Tongue of Dog
- Turtle
- Unholy Grail
- Unicorn
- White Donkey
- White Stag
- Wool of Bat

Camelot Find-It Puzzle Key

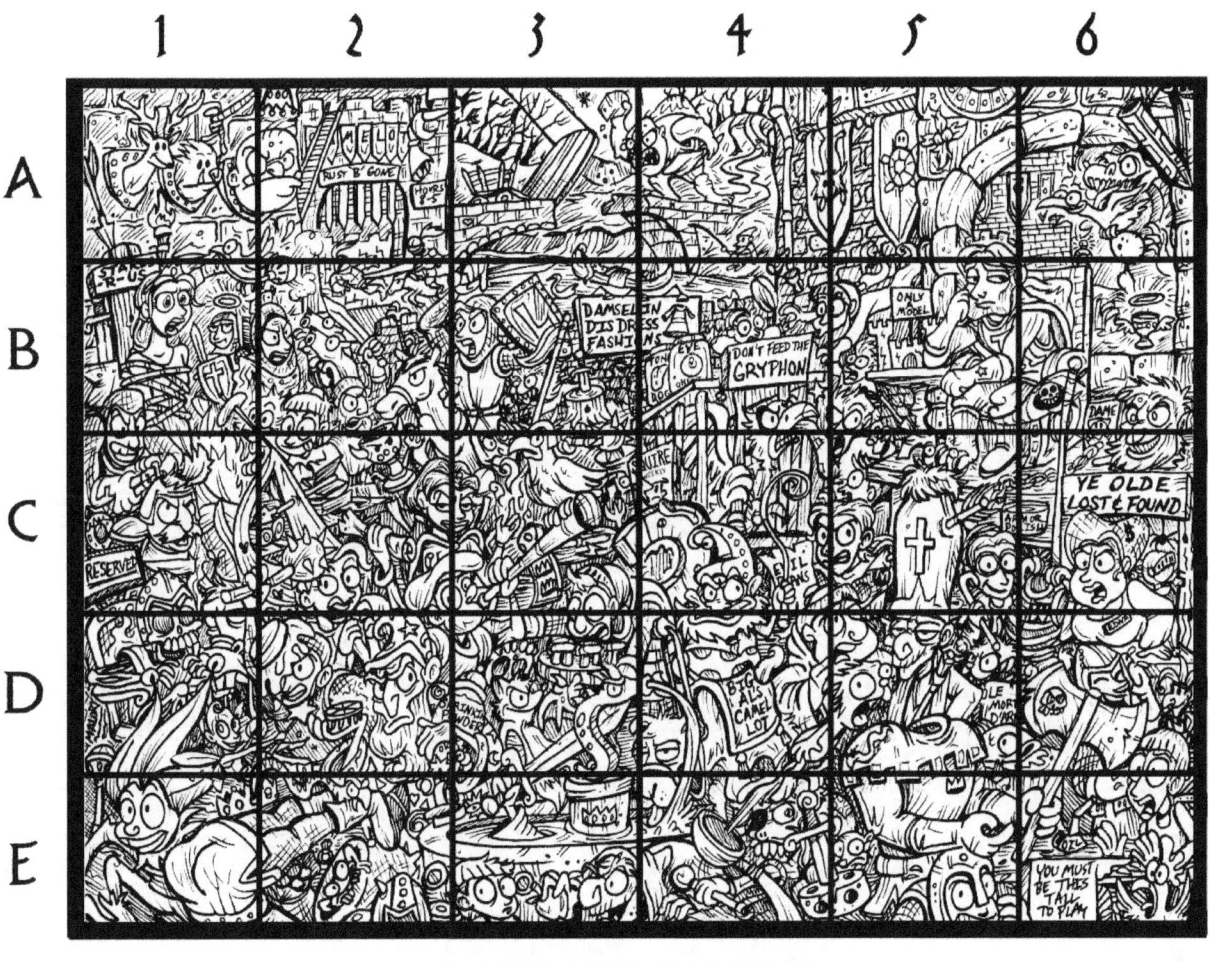

CAMELOT FIND·IT PUZZLE KEY

Adder, **E2**
Apple, **E3**
Arrows (5), **A1, A2-3, B5, C2, C5**
Bird's Nest, **C5**
Blind Worm, **D5**
Cart, **A3**
Catapult, **E4**
Caterpillar, **D3**
Copy of *Le Morte…*, **D5**
Crowns (8), **A2, A5, B1, C3, C3, E1, E3, E5**
Dollar Sign, **C6**
Dove with a Censure of Gold…, **B1-2**
Evil Dwarf, **C4-D4**
Excalibur, **D3-E3**
Eye of Newt, **B4**
Fork, **C3**

Foxes (2), **A4-5, D3**
Galahad, **B1**
Ghost of Sir Gawain, **B5**
Holly, **A5**
Holy Grail, **B6**
Jesters (2), **D6, E1**
Killer Rabbit, **D5-6**
King Arthur, **B5-6**
Ladder, **A2**
Lady Elaine, **B3-4**
Lancelot, **B3**
Lion, **B3**
Merlin, **D2**
Mini. Camelot Castle, **B5**
Mini. Round Table, **D2**
Mini. Stonehenge, **D3**
Morgan le Fay, **C2-3**
Musical Note, **C3**

Name: Malory, **D1**
Queen Guinevere, **B1**
Red Herring, **D5**
Rings (2), **A6-D6, E2**
Shields (3), **A5, B1, B3**
Skulls (6), **A6, B4, B6, D1, D3, D6**
Spider, **C6**
Spiked Helmet, **E2**
Spurs, **E2**
Stars (6), **A4, B4, B5, C4, D2, D2**
Swallow…Coconut, **A6**
Swan, **B3**
The Green Knight, **D5-E5**
The Green Knight's Head, **B6-C6**

The Road to Camelot, **A4**
The Siege Perilous, **D1**
The Sword in the Stone, **B1**
The Sword in the Stump, **B3**
The Sword in the Swiss, **E4**
Toe of Frog, **E2**
Tongue of Dog, **B4**
Turtle, **A5**
Unholy Grail, **C2**
Unicorn, **A4**
White Donkey, **D1**
White Stag, **A1**
Wool of Bat, **B3**

GLOSSARY OF IMPORTANT NAMES

ACCOLON knight, secret lover of Morgan le Fay

AGRAVAINE son of King Lot of Orkney, brother of Gawain, nephew of Arthur

ARTHUR King of Britain, son of Uther Pendragon, husband of Guinevere, father of Mordred

AVALON mysterious island shrouded in mist, home to the Lady of the Lake

BAGDEMAGUS Ruler of Gore after Uriens, father of Meleagant

BAN French king who aids Arthur against his rebellious lords, father of Lancelot

BEDIVERE one of Arthur's knights

BERTILAK green knight, servant of Morgan le Fay, tests Gawain

BLAISE magician, master of Merlin

BORS knight, nephew of Lancelot

BRISEN sorceress who worked magic for King Pelles and Lady Elaine

CAMELOT Arthur's capital city

CAMLANN plain where Arthur's final battle is fought

DUKE OF TINTAGEL ruler who rebelled against Uther, husband of Igraine, father of Arthur's half-sisters

ECTOR Arthur's foster-father, father of Sir Kay

ELAINE daughter of King Pelles, lover of Lancelot, mother of Galahad

EXCALIBUR Arthur's enchanted sword, whose scabbard prevents the loss of blood, not the Sword in the Stone

FISHER KINGS legendary line of kings who kept the Holy Grail

GAHERIS son of King Lot of Orkney, brother of Gawain, nephew of Arthur

GALAHAD greatest knight, illegitimate son of Lancelot and Lady Elaine

GARETH also known as "Beaumains," son of King Lot of Orkney, brother of Gawain, nephew of Arthur

GAWAIN son of King Lot and Queen Margawse, nephew of Arthur, one of Camelot's best knights

GORE magical realm, enchanted by Morgan le Fay

GUINEVERE wife of Arthur, secret lover of Lancelot

HOLY GRAIL sacred object, cup of Christ at the Last Supper, also caught his blood at the cross, brought to Britain by Joseph of Arimathea

IGRAINE wife of the Duke of Tintagel, later wife of Uther Pendragon, mother of Arthur and his half-sisters

JOSEPH OF ARIMATHEA original keeper of the Holy Grail, brought his treasure to Britain, established the line of Fisher Kings

JOYOUS GUARD castle of Lancelot, once known as "Dolorous Guard"

KAY Arthur's haughty foster-brother, son of Sir Ector, seneschal or overseer of all his lands

LADY OF THE LAKE mysterious enchantress who resides on the isle of Avalon, giver of Excalibur

LANCELOT son of King Ban of Benwick, raised by the Lady of the Lake, Arthur's greatest knight and close friend, secret lover of Guinevere

LEODEGRANCE father of Guinevere

LIONEL knight, nephew of Lancelot

LOT King of Orkney, father of Gawain, Gaheris, and Gareth, husband of Margawse, leads a rebellion against Arthur

LYNETTE damsel aided by Beaumains

LYONESSE damsel, love of Beaumains

MARGAWSE daughter of Igraine and the Duke of Tintagel, half-sister to Arthur, wife of King Lot of Orkney, mother of Gawain, Agravaine, Gaheris, Gareth, and Mordred

MELEAGANT evil knight, abductor of Guinevere

MERLIN the Good Enchanter, arranged for Arthur's raising by Sir Ector, counselor to the king

MORDRED illegitimate son of Arthur, lost son of Margawse, raised by the King of the SeaCastle

MORGAN LE FAY half-sister to King Arthur, necromancer and enchantress, sworn enemy of her half-brother

NASCIEN holy hermit

NIMUE damsel of the lake, enchantress

PELLES Fisher King, keeper of the Holy Grail, father of Lady Elaine

PELLINORE one of Arthur's knights

PENTECOST celebration occurring fifty days after Easter, commemorates the descending of the Holy Spirit on the apostles

PERCEVAL knight of Arthur, son of King Pellinore, succeeded on the Quest of the Holy Grail

ULFIUS one of Uther's best knights, one of Arthur's knights as well

URIENS King of Gore, husband of Morgan le Fay

UTHER PENDRAGON King of Britain, father of Arthur

VORTIGERN King of Britain, preceded Uther Pendragon

PRONUNCIATION GUIDE

Accolon	(AK-UH-LAWN)	Lancelot	(LANS-UH-LAWT)
Agravaine	(AG-RUH-VĀN)	Leodegrance	(LEE-Ō-DĒ-GRANS)
Arimathea	(AR-IH-MUH-THĒ-UH)	Lionel	(LĪ-O-NEL)
Astolat	(AS-TŌ-LAT)	Longinus	(LAWN-JĪ-NUS)
Avalon	(AV-UH-LAWN)	Lucifera	(LOO-SIH-FER-UH)
Bagdemagus	(BAG-DĒ-MAG-US)	Lynette	(LIH-NET)
Ban	(BAN)	Lyonesse	(LĪ-Ō-NESS)
Beaumains	(BŌ-MĀNZ)	Magog	(MĀ-GOG)
Bedivere	(BED-UH-VĒR)	Margawse	(MAR-GOWZ)
Benwick	(BEN-WIK)	Meleagant	(MEL-Ē-UH-GANT)
Bertilak	(BUR-TĒ-LAK)	Michaelmas	(MĪK-UL-MUS)
Blaise	(BLĀZ)	Millicene	(MIL-UH-SĒN)
Bors	(BŌRZ)	Mordred	(MŌR-DRED)
Brisen	(BRĪ-SIN)	Nascien	(NĀ-SĒ-UN)
Cameliard	(KAM-EL-YARD)	Nimue	(NIM-OO-WĀ)
Camlann	(KAM-LAN)	Orkney	(ŌRK-NĒ)
Chevalier	(SHĒ-VAL-YĀ)	Pelles	(PEL-LĒZ)
Corbenic	(KOR-BEN-EK)	Pellinore	(PEL-IH-NŌR)
Dinabutius	(DIN-UH-BOO-TĒ-US)	Perceval	(PER-SIH-VAL)
Duessa	(DOO-EH-SUH)	Rience	(RĒ-ENTS)
Ector	(EK-TŌR)	Samite	(SĀ-MĪTE)
Erith	(EH-RITH)	Sangreal	(SAN-GRĀL)
Excalibur	(EX-KAL-IH-BER)	Sansfoy	(SANZ-FOY)
Fidessa	(FIH-DES-UH)	Seneschal	(SIN-UH-SHAL)
Gaheris	(GUH-HEH-RIS)	Shalott	(SHUH-LAWT)
Galahad	(GAL-UH-HAD)	Terrabil	(TER-UH-BIL)
Gareth	(GAR-ETH)	Tintagel	(TIN-TAH-JEL)
Gawain	(GUH-WĀN)	Troubadour	(TROO-BUH-DOOR)
Glastonbury	(GLAS-TUN-BUR-Ē)	Ulfius	(UL-FĒ-US)
Gringolet	(GRIN-GŌ-LET)	Una	(OO-NUH)
Guinevere	(GWEN-UH-VĒR)	Uriens	(YOOR-Ē-UNS)
Hauberk	(HAW-BERK)	Uther	(OO-THER)
Igraine	(Ē-GRĀN)	Vortigern	(VORT-IH-GERN)

ABOUT THE AUTHOR

Zachary "Zak" Hamby is a teacher of English in rural Missouri, where he has taught mythology for many years. In mythology he has seen the ability of ancient stories to capture the imagination of young people today. For this reason he has created a variety of teaching materials (including textbooks, posters, and websites) that focus specifically on the teaching of mythology to young people. He is the author of two book series, the *Reaching Olympus* series and the *Mythology for Teens* series. He is also a professional illustrator. He resides in the Ozarks with his wife and children.

For more information and mythology products including textbooks, posters, and electronic content visit his website **www.mythologyteacher.com.**

Contact him by email at **hambypublishing@gmail.com**

www.ingramcontent.com/pod-product-compliance
Lightning Source LLC
Chambersburg PA
CBHW080727230426
43665CB00020B/2644